A Fate
Worse
Than
Debt

SUSAN GEORGE

A FATE WORSE THAN DEBT

GROVE WEIDENFELD
NEW YORK

For Bob Borosage and my IPS/TNI Family

and

For Robin Sharp and my World Food Assembly Colleagues

Published by Grove Weidenfeld
a division of Wheatland Corporation
841 Broadway
New York, N.Y. 10003-4793

First published in Great Britain in 1988 by Penguin Books,
Ltd., London

Library of Congress Cataloging-in-Publication Data

George, Susan.
    A fate worse than debt.

    Bibliography: p.
    Includes index.
    1. Debts, External—Developing countries.   I. Title.
HJ8899.G46   1988   336.3′435′091724   878-35733
ISBN 0-8021-1015-0
ISBN 0-8021-3121-2 (pbk)

First American Edition 1988
First Grove Weidenfeld Evergreen Edition 1990
Manufactured in the United States of America
Printed on acid-free paper

10 9 8 7 6 5 4 3 2

CONTENTS

ACKNOWLEDGEMENTS

Of the many people who contributed to this book, none has read the entire manuscript. Thus the usual disclaimer about everything being my fault and not theirs is especially applicable in this case.

My acknowledgements are sometimes to be found in the body of the text among the names I cite, and actually began with the dedication page. The Institute for Policy Studies in Washington and its sister, the Transnational Institute in Amsterdam, have been my intellectual home for over a decade now, giving me time, freedom – and grants – to pursue my work wherever it might take me. I would have to cite the names of all the IPS/TNI Fellows, past and present, to do justice to the riches their own reflections have brought me over the years. This being impossible, let me thank Bob Borosage, Director of IPS, as a kind of surrogate for all of them; then John Cavanagh and Jorge Sol of our World Economy Working Group, who particularly helped me to penetrate the debt question and commented with great pertinence on parts of the manuscript.

As I mention in the Introduction, the World Food Assembly identified debt as a key question bearing on people's livelihoods. What I do not explain there is the crucial role of Robin Sharp, without whose vision and hard work the WFA would never have existed. Robin, and his assistant Julie Hill, undertook some material tasks like mailings or finding documents on my behalf; more important, perhaps, Robin believed in the project and inquired regularly after its progress with exactly the right mix of discretion and solicitude.

Joe Collins, Kevin Danaher and Ann Kelly at the Institute for Food and Development Policy contributed documents and comments. Sylvie Léveillé helped me sort out my materials in Spanish. Claudio Schuftan provided a kind of one-man clipping service; my father, Bob Akers, also kept an eye on the financial press for me. Michael Latham showed me how to take the Afterword further than I would have done alone. The last time I thanked the person who provided my word-processor, I had to do it anonymously – now I know her name. Without her gift, I would doubtless have collapsed in mid-project: a thousand thanks to Gen Vaughan.

I've been blessed on both sides of the Atlantic with splendid editors. In Britain Andrew Franklin at Penguin first gave me confidence by saying, 'Yes, we want the book,' long before it was in any sort of shape. He then gentled it along with comments consistently on target. Walt Bode at Grove in the US deserves enormous credit for improving my prose without ever being heavy-handed about it. I've incorporated about 90 per cent of both Andrew's and Walt's suggestions; the book would probably be better if I'd taken their advice 100 per cent. Both deserve a whole alphabet soup of adjectives, starting with able, bright, competent, diligent – but I'll stop there.

In Latin America, let me single out for special praise and thanks Jorge Dandler and his team at CERES in Bolivia (whose members included Jorge Muñoz, Carmen Medeiros, Freddy Peña, Pablo Cuba, Cesar Soto, Virginia Claros); Gustavo Esteva (COPIDER, Mexico), Enrique Fernandez (Solidarios, Dominican Republic); Dra. Josefina Padilla (CIAC, Dominican Republic), Miguel Teubal (Argentina), researchers at IBASE (Brazil). For reasons of balance, I wasn't always able to use everything they took the trouble to assemble, but I am no less grateful for their solidarity.

Here comes the part where one *knows* that as soon as the copy is in press, more names will occur. May those I've left out forgive me. Let me thank here (in alphabetical order) at least some of the kind people who supplied materials, comments, encouragement:

Najib Akesbi, Jim Barnes, Jocelyn Boyden, JGB, Zdenek Cervenka, Stephen Commins, Belinda Coote, Jules Devos and his colleagues at NCOS, Brussels, Cameron Duncan, Leith Dunn, Richard Gerster, Teddy Goldsmith, RG, André Gunder Frank, Gerald Helleiner, Judith

Hurley and Project Abraço, Tony Jackson, Richard Jolly, Claude Julien, André de Lattre, Richard Lombardi, Kathy MacAfee, Anne-Marie Masse-Raimbault, Harold Miller (and other Mennonites around the world), Vincent Minier, Rogathe Mshana, JTM, Michael Nieta, Luisa Paré, GP, Nick Powell, Bill Rau, Kumar Rupesinghe, Jamil Salmi, Ralph Sell, Pierre de Senarclens, Paul Streeten, Alfredo Suarez, Patricia Vandaele.

Special and very personal thanks to CHG for putting up with even more than usual; to JW for help at a critical moment; to KN, SS and Camille and her parents for the gift of friendship; to JAV for arriving exactly on time at the end.

A NOTE ON VOCABULARY

I am fully aware that 'Third World' is no longer a valid concept, if indeed it ever was. The countries lumped together under this heading are far too diverse for that. The expression is used here as a kind of verbal shorthand. I employ the distinction North/South in the same spirit, regardless of actual geographical position. Like the United Nations, I occasionally call the 'less developed countries' LDCs. This is a euphemism. A more accurate description of the two major country groups (roughly equivalent to the debtors and the creditors) would require such adjectives as 'dominated' and 'dominating'; I fear such usage would soon grow tedious.

The use of 'America' when one means the United States of America is often offensive to Latin Americans, who correctly point out that they have just as much right to the word as their northern neighbour. At the risk of repetition, I try to use 'US' or 'United States' exclusively.

'Adjustment' (or 'structural adjustment') is the formal, International Monetary Fund (IMF) term to describe the programmes it designs for Third World debtors. Practically everybody else calls them 'austerity' programmes, but you'll get into trouble and receive a long lecture if you use that qualifier at the IMF. I use the two words interchangeably.

The French rule for citing proper names that come with a *particule* (*de*) is that you leave the *particule* out unless the name begins with a vowel or has only one syllable. Thus, Jacques de Larosière is 'Larosière' when his forename is not used, but André de Lattre is 'de Lattre' (like 'de Gaulle').

A billion is one thousand million; a trillion is one thousand billion.

For reasons pertaining to the physical production of this book, data included stop at 30 June 1987. Only a few figures could be altered on proof in October.

INTRODUCTION

This book is the result of several converging factors. First came the concern of members of the World Food Assembly (WFA) network that debt was becoming the great, unsung cause of increased hunger and lack of food security. The final Assembly resolution in November 1984 and its 1985 Manifesto made this clear. Since I've been active in the WFA since it was first planned, and have more freedom to define my agenda than most of its other members, duty obviously called!

Second, my own home base – the Institute for Policy Studies (IPS) in Washington and its sister Transnational Institute (TNI) in Amsterdam, where I've been a Fellow since 1974 – was already involved in research and action on debt issues. IPS/TNI was instrumental in founding and leading the Debt Crisis Network in the US and has since published the best short study extant on the topic.[1] Colleagues there encouraged me to join them in working on the problem, which our World Economy Group was discussing all the time anyway at Institute meetings.

Finally, my longtime friends at the Institute for Food and Development Policy (also known as Food First) in San Francisco believed that work on the human side of debt could contribute to the political debate in the US and elsewhere on relationships with the Third World. They asked me if I would write on the subject for their list.

Though these may sound like quasi-irresistible forces, I wasn't simply buffeted into doing the job. Before the external motivations came into play, I was already tired of seeing the debt 'crisis' described exclusively as a problem for the private banks, the rich-country governments, the International Monetary Fund (IMF) and *tutti quanti*. Mainstream reporting was concerned almost entirely with the dangers of financial collapse (and more generally with the survival of capitalism-as-we-know-it).

The 'crisis' periodically disappeared when countries seemed to be paying back in an orderly way. *Fortune*, for instance, announced in February 1985: 'The debt crisis is over.' But for whom? Reams of reports, shoals of studies appeared on the problems of the rich, none (or nearly none) on the plight of those who were actually being called upon to shoulder the burden of other people's stupidity, cupidity or lack of foresight. The pursuit of short-term gain was paramount, without a thought for long-term consequences.

So I said O K. Since then, I've regretted it more than once. There are only two ways to undertake a book like this. One is to travel to every indebted country to take the measure of events oneself. Aside from the unrealistic amount of time and money such an approach would require, it would display a self-confidence bordering on arrogance that, once one was there, the proper nuggets of information would miraculously appear in the sieve.

The other way is to press into service one's friends, and the friends of those friends, to turn towards relationships of trust built up over a good many years of efforts to speak on behalf of the victims of hunger and under-development. This approach assumes that local people have far more useful knowledge of their own situations – not to mention the requisite linguistic and cultural skills.

For obvious reasons, I chose the second avenue, in particular with WFA members. What I've learned, and duly pass on to other researchers, is: don't launch such a project without a budget. People want to help; they also have to survive. Most people in the Third World already shoulder heavier burdens than they can manage. They can't drop their urgent work to take on yours. Many are already donating time, in addition to their jobs, to a variety of independent development organizations, writing for local conferences and publications without remuneration, etc. I got several letters from friends and colleagues asking if I could find x dollars for Mr or Ms Blank, a good unemployed researcher who could put a month or two into the project. I did not have x or even y dollars; they would have made a big difference. Funders approached were not forthcoming. I'm being frank, perhaps brutally so, about this situation, because readers have a right to know what to expect. The price I paid for not having a budget is a certain unevenness. My intention from the outset was to use mostly local material, drawn from the grass-roots perspective. About half the writing I did on this project was letters. For some debtor countries, including some quite small ones like Jamaica, I found myself with an abundance of information: for others, including some quite large ones, with very little.

My thanks to all those who *did* help will be found at the front of the book, in the 'Acknowledgements'. This is the standard word, but a poor, weak and neutral one, considering their contributions and the gratitude I feel towards them. Read their names. They are those of generous, overworked and courageous people for whom 'solidarity' evokes something besides a Polish trade union. One of the most beautiful words in the English language has become almost unprintable due to selective use and tainted users. That word is 'comrade'. I am proud to count these people as my comrades; I hope they will find I've kept faith with them.

The absence of full geographical coverage worried me mightily at the beginning, but it doesn't any more. Indeed, if I've learned a major lesson, it's that the impact of debt shows a depressing sameness throughout the world, for the simple reason that the measures demanded by creditors, especially IMF adjustment programmes, are carbon copies of each other. Same causes, same effects. Local variants exist, naturally – but the suffering borne by ordinary people as a result of these programmes is largely a question of degree measurable on a scale from A to Z. It's bad in Argentina, unbearable in Zaïre. The absence of examples from *every* debtor country no longer strikes me as a serious drawback: they would, alas, be much the same.

Most of the examples that figure here are drawn from Africa and Latin America. At least until mid-1987, indebted Asian countries – with the notable exception of the Philippines – were paying back without apparent trauma. The IMF and the bankers invariably point to them as sterling examples and, like other good news, they take up little space in the literature. I fear that even these goody-goody countries will soon have repayment problems and that their people will suffer as well. Probably they already do, but we hear little about them.

So in geographical terms, and in others, this book in no way claims to be exhaustive. In particular, it treats the basic facts of debt – what it is, how it got there, etc. – in rather cursory fashion. This attitude is justified by the thousands of pages extant elsewhere on these matters. I wanted to keep the book long enough to be useful but, perhaps more important, short enough not to be daunting. I hope it encourages others to take a similar line of inquiry, to worry about what's happening to the real victims, not to Citicorp and the IMF.

I wish I could have included more instances showing how people are actually organizing to cope with the disastrous policies that are imposed upon them. Unfortunately for us, those who are involved in these struggles haven't time to write about them, and unless one can go to the scene oneself, details are lacking. One Mexican colleague went so far as to tell me that he sees the debt crisis as a great opportunity in a perverse sort of way. It helps to keep an overburdened government off the people's backs, and it prompts innovative solutions, born of despair though they may be.

Although I don't fully share his view, I do believe that most authentic development is what people manage to do against official 'developers' like the World Bank. Third World social and political creativity is the big unwritten story of this decade. New kinds of organization are, of necessity, springing up in all sorts of unlikely spots. Many are unclassifiable and do not even have recognizable leaders. Thus we in the North tend to ignore them because they don't behave like our own political parties, trade unions, civic associations and so on. Allow me to suggest that, compared with the inventiveness now being displayed in the Third World, our own organizations appear paralysed, congealed and very old hat.

Is this book 'scientific'? Not if that means full of measurements and authoritative statistics. Most Third World governments are not, in any event, anxious to compile accurate statistics on increases in malnutrition and disease, school drop-outs, unemployment and the like. It *is*, I think, scientific in a qualitative sense. Nothing is made up or exaggerated. It doesn't need to be. The misery and destruction out there, described herein, are real.

Just as war is too important to be left to generals, so the debt crisis is too serious to be left to financiers and economists. Practitioners of the dismal science have, for the most part, mystified the debt issue and frightened away that famous though possibly mythical creature, the general reader, by convincing him/her that anything to do with finance is (1) incomprehensible and (2) boring. I am not an economist. This is a statement of fact, not an apology. Though some may see this as a fatal flaw, I tend, most days, to think of it as my secret weapon.

Jargon and soporific language are useful for certain purposes because they convey an impression of impenetrability, provide an excuse for apathy and thus prevent change. 'Here is a problem,' they implicitly say, 'you must leave to the specialists.' If I've succeeded here in sharing my own learning experience and in making it as interesting for you as it was for me, we shall both have proved that everyday language is adequate to the task of understanding a crucial issue, that its use can be a political virtue as well.

An introduction is perhaps the best place to put some of one's conclusions, especially when these are tentative and bear further watching. When I started out, I thought the IMF was financial public enemy number one. I don't now. It may be the most visible, but its role is largely to take the heat off other actors in the international system. Tips of icebergs can absorb quite a lot of heat.

Before going any further, let me state in italic caps: *I DON'T BELIEVE IN THE CONSPIRACY THEORY OF HISTORY.* I take special pains to state this, because I've been accused of just such beliefs the moment I pointed out that a great many forces were converging in a single direction. They don't have to conspire if they have the same world view, aspire to similar goals and take concerted steps to attain them.

In the present case it seems to me that the Third World debt crisis has brought about greater internal consistency and cohesion of purpose among major actors in the international financial system. There are still some contradictions, but basically these actors are all working together, more or less harmoniously, *to keep the Third World in line.* These upstart nations made entirely too much noise in the 1960s and 1970s, with their demands for equal status with the rich countries, Codes of Conduct for this and that, a New International Economic Order (NIEO) and whatnot. The debt has become, at least partially, an opportunity for turning the clock back.

It is perhaps useful to recall that the debt and default crisis of the 1870s led directly to foreign (colonial) occupation of several debtor countries. Today's debt crisis is leading to something similar, though outward appearances are in tune with changing times. We already have an accelerated transfer of wealth from the poor countries to the rich, exactly as in the 'good old days'. Over $130 billion net – repayments minus new loans – has left Latin America and landed in Northern banks in the past five years alone. Banks are also beginning to take over national industries and other assets in the Third World in lieu of interest payments.

Most debtor-country governments and elites are co-operating fully with what I call the Consortium – the informal financial–political club of big banks, creditor-country governments and their central banks, the World Bank and, of course, the IMF. Indebted governments have so far avoided collective action and have not used the debt as an instrument to further democratic development in their countries. I never fully supported calls for an NIEO during the go-go Second Development Decade, when the NIEO was the centrepiece of United Nations rhetoric. Demands formulated by the likes of the Brandt Commission – a conglomeration of First and Third World elites – for massive transfers of wealth from the First World to the Third have, in fact, been satisfied. Just as would have been the case with a more formal, negotiated NIEO, elites of the First World *did* transfer huge sums to elites of the Third. The cumulative effect of these transfers is called the debt crisis.

Why don't the debtor governments act? As one perceptive economist argues, 'The orthodox [adjustment or austerity] programs being followed in Latin America do in fact serve the interests of the ruling groups . . . Rich Latin Americans have not totally disconnected themselves from the fortunes of their enterprises in their own countries but they have succeeded in insulating themselves – and may even have gained – from the adjustment process.'[2] There are some hopeful signs – the stance of Peruvian President Alan García, for one, who refuses to pay debt service amounting to more than 10 per cent of Peru's export revenues. Unless and until Third World governments adopt a coherent and unified strategy of their own, they must be regarded as junior partners in the Consortium, counting on their people to pay.

Economic policies are not neutral. Contrary to received opinion, they can even kill. To be sure, those who make them would be outraged at the suggestion that their intent is to deprive people of their livelihoods or to murder, yet the outcome is often the same. The managers of the quiet institutions whose decisions shape millions of destinies are not trained to entertain the notion that their activities might have anything to do with such embarrassing categories as life and death. They are competent, well-paid technicians and go about their work at a comfortable remove from those whose lives they will ultimately touch. Their world is an insulated one, somewhat like that of the encapsulated bomber pilot. He too is simply doing his job.

Our era is the first in history to place in direct contact the most powerful, hierarchical, elitist institutions in rich countries like the IMF and the poorest, most obscure, hungriest peasants or slum-dwellers in poor countries like Brazil or Zaïre. Intermediaries are no longer required between the most centralized bodies of the centre and the most marginal people on the periphery; no buffer zones cushion the impact of the former on the latter. Our centrifugal world spins off its decrees like projectiles from the hub to the rim; these missiles fall where they may, on whom they will. Those who live and work in the centre, those who make the decrees that have an explosive impact on other people's lives are again like the bomber pilot, for whom the shattered bodies 50,000 feet below are simply not there.

The pilot does not feel responsible for the international tensions and diplomatic failures that have led to his mission. He is an instrument. Nor does the national or international civil servant feel responsible for the years of misbegotten policies in North and South, the risky loans, the slump in commodity prices, the general economic morass. His job is to administer the correct medicine, according to received dogma. If, as a result of this medicine, the poor lose their jobs and their children and their hope, if they riot and are shot down for protesting against sudden and unendurable increases in the cost of survival, this is not the international civil servant's concern.

We must try to make it *someone*'s concern. I'm not certain whether we can dislodge received dogma and make bureaucrats and bankers accountable for their actions. In the 'Philosophical Afterword' that concludes this book I try to explain some of the theoretical reasons for my uncertainty. But, as William of Orange is famous for having said, 'One need not hope in order to undertake, nor succeed to persevere.' Or, less elegantly, wobbly theory is no excuse for inaction. With regard to any given policy, we can lean on a simple ethical principle: *those who reap the benefits should also pay the costs.*

This is not, to put it gently, the view of the Consortium – those who enjoy the advantages of power. The Consortium's view could be more accurately stated: those who reap the benefits should reap more benefits; those who pay the costs should damn well go on doing so. People who have realized that only a tiny minority in both the Third World and the First reaps, while vast numbers pay, can aim for several goals and undertake several tasks. Later on in these pages I am more specific. For now, a few general pointers will do.

First, they can explain and denounce the activities of the Consortium and encourage remedial action on the part of the creditors and unity on the part of the debtors. But, above all, they can promote greater welfare for ordinary people. If the debtor countries continue to reimburse, the poor must not bear the burden. If the debt is written down or off, governments thus let off the hook must not simply continue to apply the mal-development models that got them into debt in the first place. Ideally, the debt crisis can be turned inside out and can serve the cause of true development and of democracy.

I hope this book may trace a path towards some of these goals.

PART I: THE PLAYERS AND THE PROBLEM

Understanding why Third World debt concerns all the inhabitants of the planet, no matter where they live, means first understanding the actions and the motives of the major actors in the crisis. Part I tries to convey this knowledge as succinctly as possible.

Chapter 1, 'How Much is $1 Trillion?', looks at what debt is, how it has accumulated, what the money was spent on and for whose benefit. These elements, taken together, add up to a model of mal-development.

Chapter 2, 'The Money-Mongers', deals with Western banks and bankers, how they prospered, their fears that they may no longer prosper and their plans for wriggling out of a crisis of their own making.

Chapter 3, 'The IMF: Let Them Eat Special Drawing Rights', examines the International Monetary Fund, its role as enforcer of the *status quo* and inventor of 'adjustment' programmes now devastating the lives of countless Third World people.

Chapter 4, 'Condemned to Debt?: The Trade Trap and the Dangers of Default', asks if, and how, the Third World can reimburse and discusses the risks of default.

This part of the book deals with the power structures that hold sway over a world where debt is a symptom (one among many) of a crazed economy that operates on behalf of a select few. Those who embody, maintain and reinforce these structures I call the Consortium.

Power structures are – pardon the tautology – powerful. Otherwise they wouldn't be worth writing or reading about – or acting against. As you read about them, remember that 'powerful' does not mean 'invulnerable'.

1.
HOW MUCH IS $1 TRILLION?

What is debt? What a stupid question. Everybody knows the answer, at least in personal terms. People borrow to buy land or houses or automobiles or to educate their children; they pay back the loan over time with interest, which is the cost of using someone else's money. Although debt was regarded by the more Puritan among our ancestors as shameful, it's actually a great invention. Some political systems (in both East and West) supply such basic necessities as health care, schooling and low-cost housing for all citizens, regardless of their income level. In many Western societies, however, especially in the United States, buying on credit is the only way for most people to afford home ownership or an education that they could never pay for in a lump sum. Without credit modern capitalism would grind to a halt. Most people eventually pay back their loans without mishap and find themselves better off. American farmers in the 1980s are a notable and tragic exception, but that is another story. In many cases debt democratizes.*

Beyond the personal and household level, debt is different. Unlike

* Some North American colleagues object that while debt may once have played an equalizing role, it no longer does. U S consumer debt, they say, has got completely out of hand and is now crushing people who borrow just to pay off old loans.

most families, large corporations are permanently in hock. They don't want to be out of debt – and their bankers don't want them to be either. The French company Aérospatiale even went so far as to take out a full page ad in *Le Monde* in late 1986 to brag, '695 Million Dollars' Worth of Credit! The Banks of the Whole World Trust Us.' As soon as a company pays off one loan it takes out another, for periods approaching eternity. It can do so as long as borrowed money finances expansion and, consequently, greater returns.

Sovereign nations issue their own bonds or treasury bills, but they too may often rely on banks for financing and have done so since the Renaissance. There's nothing infamous or irresponsible about corporate or national debt – the modern world couldn't function without it, nor without the banks that oil the global economic machinery. *Not* holding any debt would be real cause for concern – it would mean that a nation or a firm had no valuable assets, that its signature was worthless. In the rarefied spheres of corporate or state power, lack of creditworthiness, not borrowing, is the cardinal sin.

Why, then, is there such a hue and cry about Third World debt? The figures sound enormous – in early 1986 this debt topped the trillion-dollar mark. But is this really much money? There are several ways to measure it. For example, Third World debt acquired over the past *fifteen* years represents only one-eighth of the combined Gross National Product (GNP) generated *annually* by the OECD countries (the twenty-four rich nations that belong to the Organization for Economic Co-operation and Development) – now an astronomical $8 trillion.[1] The amounts owed by developing countries also pale when compared with the public debt of the United States, which in 1986 reached $2 trillion, twice that of all Third World countries put together.

Take another yardstick: the world's top 200 transnational corporations. They now have a staggering annual turnover of more than $3 trillion – equivalent to almost 30 per cent of gross *world* product.[2] Total Third World debt thus amounts to a mere third of the yearly sales of these top 200 firms, or about 10 per cent of the world's yearly economic activity (now estimated at about $10 trillion). So, again, why the fuss? $1 trillion may not be much money after all.

Latin America's debt provokes countless columns of doom-laden journalism, but you won't find hand-wringing articles about France's debt on the financial pages every other day, even though French public debt at the end of 1985 was over $62 billion – much more than Argentina's and about the same as that of Chile, Peru and the Philippines combined. Some nominally 'Third World' countries, particularly in Asia, also carry heavy debt loads, yet rarely appear in the headlines because, for the time being at least, they are servicing their loans without a hitch. Perhaps, then, the newspapers have been exaggerating matters and we can simply ignore reports of impending crisis. Yes and no.

The *absolute* Third World debt figure – say, $1 trillion, give or take a few billion – is not the problem, however astronomical it may sound. Debt produces jitters in high places and becomes a menace to the world financial system and to the general public only when it cannot be *serviced* – that is, when interest payments fall into deep arrears or stop altogether.

Contrary to widespread belief, and notwithstanding your relationship with your bank manager and with your mortgage, creditors don't really care if national ('sovereign') borrowers ever pay off the loans themselves. So long as bankers maintain confidence in a country's ability to pay interest on its debt, they can afford to be magnanimous where principal is concerned. Banks, like other commercial enterprises, care about profits. They care about receiving regular payments for the use of their money, and the longer this money is outstanding, the higher the profit. Loans that are regularly serviced in this way are called 'performing'. Non-performing loans give bankers nightmares.

Most bankers once adopted the ostrich position with regard to the possibility that sovereign loans might one day not be serviced. Some went so far as to justify their own imprudent lending by announcing that such debts *cannot* go bad, since 'countries do not fail to exist.' Thus spake Walter Wriston, former president of Citibank, causing Lord Lever to comment, 'I call Walter Wriston the Peter Pan of bankers, because he still believes in fairies.'[3] Wriston did indeed appear to confuse Citibank's ability to repossess some poor deadbeat's automobile and the likelihood of its taking a controlling interest in Peru should the latter stop making interest payments.

Many Third World countries are now so deeply in hock that all their new loans are devoted *entirely* to servicing old ones. The roster of countries unable to pay interest otherwise is growing ominously long. The world financial arena is coming to resemble the scene in Joseph Heller's celebrated *Catch 22*, in which Milo explains one of his more intricate business deals – an enormously complicated scheme involving eggs – and finally says, look, it's very simple: 'I'm the people I buy from.'

Today's banker might as well say, 'I'm the people I lend to,' because many of his present loans, having transited through the books of Ecuador or Brazil, come straight back to his coffers as interest on previous loans. Such financial sleight of hand serves to mollify bank inspectors and gives everyone an excuse to maintain the vital fiction that loans are still 'performing'. As an eminent banker's banker explained to me, 'It's not the debtor who decides when a default will occur – it's the lender!'[4]

Now we may ask our initial question again: what is debt? It's not quite such a stupid question this time round. If countries aren't paying back their creditors, it means, among other things, that the money they borrowed has not been used productively. Debt for solvent corporations or countries is no problem because they have invested their loans in income-generating activities. This creation of new wealth ought normally to provide for servicing the debt and then some. Faulty choices of activities by businesses must either be corrected fast or end in bankruptcy. Countries making faulty choices can hang on longer but not for ever.

To understand what really constitutes debt, and how it originates, we need to examine the development models, the economic and social choices of countries now under financial siege, since it was largely those choices that got them, and their creditors, into the present mess. Although other factors (to be examined in due course) contributed, the question for the moment is: how could a normal economic phenomenon like national debt turn into such an intractable problem? More bluntly, what actually happened to the money?

THE MAL-DEVELOPMENT MODEL: A DOWNPAYMENT ON DISASTER

The honest answer to the question 'What happened to the money?' is deeply embedded in post-Second World War history. Beginning in the 1950s, a new breed of economists invented the notion of development – a word that has now become well-nigh meaningless. It would take a book in itself to do justice to this all-things-to-all-people concept, and since I do not choose to write that book, I shall evade definitions and simply call the problem at hand 'the model'.

For many years, in many quarters (and still today), it was assumed that 'emerging nations' had a single goal and must follow a single path to reach it. Never mind the appalling poverty of imagination displayed: people in authority both in the North and in the newly decolonized countries wanted the South to become 'like' the rich, industrialized (often ex-colonial) powers.

The model is consequently imitative. It mimics without understanding and copies without controlling. Lacking roots in the local culture or environment, it quickly droops and withers if not sustained by transfusions – of foreign capital, technology and ideas. It goes for growth, usually without asking, 'Growth of what? For whom?' Industrialization is frequently its centrepiece, sometimes export agriculture relying on industrial inputs. The rich countries of the North nearly always built up their own industries on a strong agricultural base; the model conveniently forgets this and favours instant industrialization over food security. Those who designed it were particularly scornful of small-scale peasant agriculture, the source of livelihood for most of the people in the countries concerned.

The model is costly. It neglects resources that the local environment could provide and the skills that local people could supply, counting rather on imports, at escalating prices. It neglects not only peasants but anyone who does not belong to a thin layer at the top of society, identified as the 'modernizing' elements. They will be the targets of development, and their wealth and consequent investments are expected to provide the motor for further growth. Eventually – it is not clear when – everyone in the society will benefit through the 'trickle-down' process. 'Modernization', like 'development' itself, is a myth-word in whose name any destruction, and any expenditure, may be undertaken with impunity.

The model is outward-looking. It never seeks to enhance the specific, generic, original features of 'undeveloped' countries and their peoples, treating them rather as if they were a kind of undifferentiated clay to be moulded to the standard requirements of the world market and of world capital, to the uniform tastes of international bureaucrats and national ones trained in their image. Hunger is one result. People who will not, or cannot, become consumers in the global food system will not get enough to eat. Militarization is another. Masses of miserable people with little to lose are prone to revolt. Armed forces (including the police) in Third World countries are used as often internally as against outsiders.

Debt is a further outcome of the mal-development model. Elites borrowed to put it into practice and now expect their poorer compatriots to bail them out. All of Part II of this book is devoted to showing just how dearly the people must pay. For now, we shall look at various features of the model that together cost $1 trillion.

FINANCING CONSUMPTION: THERE'S NO TOMORROW

In California a bumper-sticker proclaims, 'The guy with the most toys when he dies wins.' This spirit of unabashed consumerism is part of the model, and the purchase of Western consumer goods is part of the image of modernization. Sometimes, as in Chile, loans have been spent almost entirely on current consumption. For an individual or a family this is known as living beyond one's means. A country that borrows to finance imported gadgets for the upper and middle classes, without investing anything in the future, will sooner or later come to grief.

Chile positively encouraged bloated imports, from 1979 until the day of reckoning came in 1982, by allowing people to exchange their pesos freely against dollars and by keeping the peso unrealistically over-valued. In other words, people could buy dollars, and thus goods billed in dollars, with very little sacrifice. The government then proceeded to compound the problem. Inflation in Chile was rampant, much higher than in the US, and Chilean salaries were pegged to the rate of Chilean inflation. Because the exchange rate stayed the same, those lucky enough to hold salaried employment automatically found their purchasing power *in dollars* increasing apace.

Small wonder that the Chilean middle classes went on a durable-goods buying spree.[5] People bought imported rather than nationally made goods. Consequently, Chilean firms couldn't sell their products and bit the dust by the hundreds. Chile was importing far more than it could dream of exporting, while the trade deficit and unemployment both soared. How to finance the deficit? Eureka! By borrowing. Chile now has one of the highest *per capita* debts in all Latin America ($1,540 per head). At least $11 billion of its $19 billion debt is owed to banks and can be ascribed to this spending spree.

INDUSTRIALIZATION: WHY PAY LESS WHEN YOU CAN PAY MORE?

The mal-development model calls for industrialization at all costs. A major cause of debt accumulation was investment in ill-considered, ill-conceived projects, many involving bloated capital costs and healthy doses of graft. A friend at a development bank told me of events that he had observed, though his institution had not been involved in the financing. Background: the 1974 sugar boom encouraged many countries to build additional sugar-milling and -refining capacity, although any serious analysis of world market conditions would have counselled prudence. (Lumbering oneself with all those mills was a poor idea to begin with, but let that pass.)

During this period of unwarranted enthusiasm for sugar in the mid-1970s, a large Asian country called for bids for the construction of a new mill. Like many other products, sugar refineries come in two varieties – plain and fancy. You can buy quality technology or quality plus flash. Flash costs more. In this instance the lowest bid, at about $50 million, came from a US firm. With this the country could buy itself the requisite sturdy, serviceable, workaday sugar mill, no more, no less. A British company bid $55 million. The difference meant that the Brits thought they could furnish the technology for about the same price as their North American counterparts, but from long experience they costed in 10 per cent worth of graft and pay-offs to the locals. A French firm's bid was $75 million. This might seem a bit on the high side. *Au contraire*.

The Asian country's officials, not wishing to offend a major American firm by a flat refusal of its low bid, visited the executives of the US company and gave them to understand that a higher figure could help enormously to create the proper atmosphere for a favourable decision. They were not well received, perhaps because of recent Congressional interest in bribery scandals involving US corporations abroad. The British refused to sweeten their sugar-mill offer as well. The French, however, by asking at the outset 50 per cent more than the lowest bidder, won the contract: it included between $5 million and $10 million for flash and between $15 million and $20 million for the boys.

Even when corruption is absent (which is not terribly often) the gilding of technological lilies systematically adds millions to the bill. Third World purchasers are often content only with the latest, shiniest, glitziest machinery whose additional value, compared with that of more down-to-earth, already amortized models, is marginal or nil, though it costs much more.

Such choices by developing-country decision-makers present delicate problems for technology suppliers: just how profitable for them are these additional items in the bids? True, the seller can charge a mark-up on flash but none on graft. If only to run the business efficiently and profitably, the supplier has to know as accurately as possible what the corruption factor will be. His classification will be based not so much on whether or not one bribes, nor even on the relative greediness of the bribees; for the company the really important point is whether the bribe does any good. In some countries palms must be liberally greased, yes, but papers will be stamped without delay and materials ordered will arrive on time. In the more depressing cases (Nigeria is cited as a particularly nerve-racking example) you pay handsomely, but you still can't be sure of getting the co-operation you need to complete the job.

Inflated capital costs necessarily inflate the sums that countries must

pay back to suppliers, to private banks and, often, to the bilateral and
multilateral agencies that help finance projects. Having an official
development agency on board as co-sponsor can, however, be an
advantage, since its codified procurement procedures normally result in
reduced waste.[6]

With enough bloated projects like the sugar mill, financed entirely by
private firms and banks, one ends up with a kind of industrial Gresham's
Law. Just as bad money drives out good, so do wasteful suppliers
gradually drive out economical ones when the former are consistently
given contracts at the expense of the latter. As high-cost suppliers come
to dominate the market (or as everyone starts aligning bids at the
topmost level in order to survive), national debt levels escalate.

Some outright thefts, like those of Somoza in Nicaragua, will never be
punished, and their victims will never be compensated. On the contrary,
the victims will be expected to continue reimbursing the ill-gotten gains
of their predecessors, and this under increasingly difficult economic
conditions imposed upon them by powerful and hostile neighbours.
Somoza pocketed most of the international loans meant for the reconstruction of Managua after the 1972 earthquake and continued to steal
from his country right up to the moment he was finally forced out in
1979. When he fled the country, he left all of $3 million in the treasury.
Nicaragua's outstanding debt is $4 billion, three-quarters of which was
contracted under the Somoza regime.

In early 1986 the newspapers regaled us daily with the exploits of
Ferdinand and Imelda. One remark said it all: 'Imelda Marcos makes
Marie Antoinette look like a bag lady.' At a conservative estimate, this
couple's Filipino translation of *après moi le déluge* cost their people *at
least* 15 per cent of the country's $26 billion debt. Some of it may return
to the national coffers, thanks to international co-operation with the
Aquino government.

This debt was not, however, accumulated entirely to pay for Ms
Marcos's astounding collection of shoes. One expensive debt-financed
project is the Morong (Bataan) nuclear power plant ordered in 1976
from Westinghouse with a price tag of $2.1 billion. The debt incurred for
this plant alone cost the Philippines at least $350,000 *a day* in interest
payments – a figure that jumped to $500,000 in 1987 when debt to the
US Ex-Im Bank fell due. The reactor is ready to go; that it is not yet
operating is perhaps just as well. The building site chosen is in the
middle of the Pacific 'fire-rim' earthquake zone at the foot of a volcano.
The International Atomic Energy Authority noted in a 1978 report that
the choice of the Morong site in a zone of such high seismic activity was

'unique in the atomic industry' and deemed the risk of a future volcanic eruption 'credible'.[7]

According to a report in the *New York Times*, Marcos received $80 million in commissions from Westinghouse through one of his cronies, who mysteriously snatched the nuclear-plant contract from the jaws of General Electric and got it awarded to its arch-rival Westinghouse. General Electric's much lower bid had already been approved by a panel appointed by Marcos himself and by the then head of the Philippine National Power Corp. Marcos overruled the panel's choice in favour of Westinghouse before the latter had even submitted a detailed bid. The Filipino Secretary of Industry wrote angrily to Mr Marcos that he was buying 'one reactor for the price of two'. The crony who arranged the deal, a Mr Herminio Disini, 'now lives in a castle near Vienna', according to the *New York Times* report. Westinghouse acknowledges paying a commission to a Marcos associate but says, 'Allegations of illicitly inflated costs at its nuclear power plant in the Philippines are "completely without merit".'[8]

Mrs Aquino's government has announced that in the wake of Chernobyl the plant will not go into operation anyway, which is welcome news, except that the interest is still piling up. Other countries fell into the same sort of trap – a substantial proportion of Brazil's debt (some sources claim up to $40 billion) is due to purchases of nuclear reactors, also non-operational as of this writing.

CAPITAL FLIGHT: TAKE THE MONEY AND RUN

Were there other good ways of falling deep into debt besides financing current consumption and wasteful projects? Certainly. One of the best and quickest was capital flight. Money spirited out of the South in huge quantities has allowed Northern commercial banks to defy the adage about cake. It turns out the banks *can* both have and eat it because they control both ends of the financial system. First, they make the loan. Almost instantaneously, a large proportion of it returns to their coffers as deposits because corrupt government officials may transfer it there directly. National companies, heavy borrowers whose governments have guaranteed their debt, may also feel that the money they were supposed to invest at home will be happier abroad. This capital, which in fact left the debtor country long ago, will still, unfortunately, appear on the banks' books as loans on which interest is due. The banks are thus paid back twice for a single commitment – first in deposits from foreigners, then in interest. As one economist remarks, 'The most aggressive banks, such as Citibank, have probably accumulated almost as much in assets from poor countries as they have loaned to them. Their real role has been to take funds that Third World elites have stolen from their governments and to loan them back, earning a nice spread each way.'[9]

The Bank for International Settlements (BIS) – the central banks' central bank in Basle – is not given to inflammatory statements. It none the less announced in its 1983 annual report that capital flight had been taking place on a 'massive scale'. The BIS estimates that $55 billion was wafted northwards from Latin America between 1977 and 1983. A BIS official conceded that this is a 'conservative estimate'.[10] In 1986 Morgan Guaranty appraised capital flight from the big ten Latin American debtors* at fully 70 per cent of all their new loans from 1983 to 1985. Mexico takes the dubious first prize in this category, with new net borrowing of $9 billion during the two-year period and an estimated $16 billion worth of capital flight.[11]

For sheer magnitude Mexico is indeed unequalled. The president of the Inter-American Development Bank, himself a Mexican, is far less conservative than the BIS. He places capital flight from Mexico between 1979 and 1983 alone at $90 billion – an amount greater than the entire Mexican debt at that time. In March 1985 a Mexico City newspaper published the names of 575 Mexicans who were all supposed to have at least $1 million deposited in foreign banks. One of the more affluent among these so-called *sacadolares* may well have been the ex-President of Mexico himself, Lopez-Portillo, who, according to James Henry, writing in the *New Republic*, is 'widely rumoured to have absconded with over one billion dollars' when he left office and moved to Rome.[12]

Karen Lissakers, a former US State Department official who now writes on international banking, points out, 'Bringing back even a fraction of the $130 billion or so in Latin flight capital would take care of the region's debt-servicing problems for years to come.' A lot of these billions have arrived, literally, in suitcases. Many of them are carried by bankers. One banker 'mentioned casually that even now in 1986, with Mexico again on the ropes and capital controls in effect, his bank regularly "sends a guy with two empty suitcases" to Mexico City'.[13]

Bankers are not just porters. They are also adept at designing complex schemes to help their wealthy private clients ferry money out of

---

* The big ten Latin American debtors are Brazil, Mexico, Venezuela, Peru, Colombia, Ecuador, Bolivia, Uruguay, Argentina and Chile.

their countries – offshore trusts, fake investment companies, parallel foreign-exchange swaps that avoid national banks, 'back-to-back' loans in which the bank 'loans' the client his own money. Their inventiveness is admirable. Citibank 'appears to have over 1,500 people dedicated to this activity world-wide'. Thanks to these private deposits, 'Citibank probably comes very close to owing more money to Latin Americans than it is owed' (by their governments), according to James Henry.

What are the chances, if any, that flight capital might go into reverse and head 'home'? Karen Lissakers recommends that banks stop making it so easy, that they stop sending 'guys with suitcases'. She also believes that banks can 'directly press private clients to cough up some of this cash stashed abroad for debt-servicing, instead of forcing already debt-ridden governments to assume the foreign debts of the private sector'.

Fat chance! This naive recommendation ignores the basic rules of the game. Lissakers herself quotes a representative of a major New York bank who explains, 'There is no debate in [my] bank over the dual role of lending money to a country and accommodating flight capital. It is done by different departments. There is no moral issue. If we don't do it, the Swiss will.' A banker who went out of his way to refuse deposits from private clients so that their governments might more easily reimburse their debts, a banker who thus refused to profit only once when twice is the norm, would be considered certifiably insane by his colleagues and would not remain a banker for long.

No, the day the Suitcase Department and its clients fly to Mexico with *full* bags will be the day the Mexican government offers higher interest rates – *much* higher interest rates in order to compensate for inflation and general instability – than the United States is prepared to give. This would bring money back and prevent money from leaving. It would have other, harmful, side-effects too, since funds would become too expensive for most Mexicans, individuals or businesses, to borrow. The local economy would be back to no growth. The moral may be that you can't win unless your name is Citibank, Manufacturers Hanover or Morgan. However, if the debtor-country governments united to demand their flight capital back, that would be a different story entirely – one we shall explore more fully in the final chapter.

THE MILITARY MODEL: GUNS, *SI*; BUTTER, NO

Several countries ran up staggering debts buying toys for their generals. Debt-financed militarization has reached proportions such that the

universally respected Stockholm International Peace Research Institute
(SIPRI) devotes a chapter of its 1985 *Yearbook* to the phenomenon.
SIPRI seeks to elucidate the connections between arsenals and high
finance. Its basic question is: 'How much lower would external debt
have been without arms purchases?

Military spending for the National Security State undergirds and
protects the mal-development model. SIPRI concludes that 20 per
cent of Third World debt – Organization of Petroleum Exporting
Countries (OPEC) excluded – can be attributed directly to arms
purchases. The more affluent Middle Eastern oil producers went all out
for AWACS and other costly military hardware. The economic austerity brought about by debt rescheduling has forced some cutbacks,
especially since 1982, but even when military expenditures have fallen in
real terms, the *proportion* devoted to armaments in Third World
budgets has almost always remained the same or increased.[14]

One might think that in heavily indebted societies austerity programmes would require that flab be first trimmed from defence spending, especially when a sizeable part of the population is living in hunger
and misery. One might further imagine that Western agencies in a
position to do so would insist on such cuts. This, unfortunately, is not the
case. The IMF consistently demands that its pupils make drastic
reductions in civil spending, but arms budgets remain untouched. When
asked about this anomaly, Fund personnel recoil and explain in pained
tones that such measures would be 'interfering in the internal affairs of
sovereign nations' (which is exactly what the Fund does every working
day . . .).[15]

It is precisely the poorest countries, especially those in Africa with
large debts to service, that tend to spend most heavily on national
security. Ethiopia, which has been waging protracted war against liberation struggles in its northern provinces (Eritrea and Tigré), is at the
bottom of the African poverty barrel. Its GNP is $4.3 billion, which
works out to about $110 per Ethiopian, the lowest per capita GNP
anywhere in the world, according to World Bank figures. This does not
prevent Ethiopia from spending $13 per head and per year on its mili-
tary but only $7 on health and education combined. Sudan spends $15
for each Sudanese on arms, Tanzania $16, Kenya $17, Somalia $20,
Zimbabwe a whopping $55 (related to the threat from South Africa).
These countries carry debt loads ranging from $1.5 billion to $4 billion
dollars; Sudan's is close to $11 billion.[16]

Ten billion dollars of the total $54 billion owed by Argentina can be
traced directly to military spending under the generals' regime. Before

Alan García was elected President, Peru was spending a minimum of $300–$400 million yearly on arms, not counting a paltry $700 million for twenty-six French Mirage jets. Debt service and military expenditure between them accounted for over 50 per cent of the Peruvian budget. It is not coincidental that those countries that today find themselves in the deepest debt trouble were those that yesterday bought the most weapons.

Ironically, some mega-debtors like Brazil and Egypt, whose arms budgets helped push them into the debt trap to begin with, are now paying back part of their interest thanks to arms *exports*. Brazil's earnings from its 'no questions asked' weapons-export policy were estimated at $3.5 billion in 1984.[17] Egypt now ranks among the top ten arms vendors, specializing in Middle East markets like Iraq, to whom it provides ammunition for the endless Gulf War. For the moment, Third World arms exporters make only 3 per cent of global sales (and 4 per cent of those to other Third Worlders), but they can only seek to improve their commercial position on these deadly markets as pressure to reimburse debts grows stronger.

Super-powers sometimes give away arms to their Third World client states, but their policies aren't necessarily consistent, and in reality the clients never get something for nothing. In 1972, for example, while the Vietnam war was raging, Uncle Sam behaved like a rich uncle, indeed, by giving Third World countries (the non-oil exporters) 40 per cent of all the arms those countries received that year. The Soviet Union gave away a further 8 per cent of total arms transferred to these countries. Poor countries thus paid nothing for nearly half of the $6 billion worth of weapons they received in 1972.

Ten years later, however, US weapons donations had dropped to a mere 2 per cent of total arms imports of these same countries. The Soviets, on the other hand, increased their gifts to Third World arsenals, giving 12 per cent of total imports in 1982. Thanks to the two super-powers, the non-oil countries were thus still getting 14 per cent of their arms for free. The catch was that they were expected to pay for the rest, and the rest, in 1982, came to $12 billion.*[18]

The end result for the 1972–82 decade, as SIPRI explains, is that 'The value of arms transferred to the non-oil developing countries more

---

* The similarities in US behaviour with regard to food aid and to weapons aid are striking: first come the giveaways or the cut-rate purchases in local currencies. When the customer is hooked, and his generals can make sure their demands are satisfied, the switch is made to cash sales, in dollars.

than doubled in real terms between 1972 and 1982 and their share of total world arms transfers increased from 31 per cent to 41 per cent in the same period.'[19] Not surprisingly, this was precisely the period during which the debt burden was accumulating. SIPRI argues that Third World countries could have borrowed 20 per cent less every year during the decade had they made no foreign arms purchases. An obvious but often conveniently forgotten point is that arms purchases are *never* productive. They produce no wealth and, when not manufactured locally, they don't even create jobs or inject money into the local economy. They are nothing but pure consumption. Those who purchased them on credit must now contend with both principal and interest, with no revenues coming in as a result of these purchases.

Unless they are helping with the crops or building bridges, armies themselves are unproductive, yet cost the state dearly in both peacetime and war. In the US, for example, salaries represent $90 billion or close to 35 per cent of 1985 defence outlays.[20] Military salaries may eat up a smaller proportion in poor countries, but still an immutable law plays havoc with Third World budgets: the more defence establishments can obtain, the more powerful they become; the more powerful they become, the more they can blackmail civilian governments into higher arms purchases – and on up the vicious spiral until the generals take over completely and can do as they please.

This law doubtless accounts as well for *rates* of growth in arms imports, which were particularly alarming in the decade 1972–82. During these ten years Latin America's imports increased by 13 per cent a year, while Africa bought 18.5 per cent more weapons annually (admittedly starting from a lower level). Sixty per cent of Black African countries now live under military rule. The increasing militarization of the continent has been sustained by outside financing: the huge strides in weapons procurement coincide exactly with the 'easy-money' era of 1973–82 (from the first OPEC price increase to the Mexican debt crisis). These unproductive expenditures also helped to set the stage for the African food disaster.

Latin America's evolution towards democracy is fragile. In some cases military regimes simply proved incapable of administering austerity and handed over bankrupt states to civilians. Recent democratic gains could disappear under the pressure of debt – it takes a strong-armed regime to bleed its people dry.

THE PENTAGON CONNECTION: US MILITARIZATION AND THIRD WORLD DEBT

It is not just their own purchases of military hardware that have helped to pile up debt in Third World countries. In a contorted sort of way, the military budget of the United States aggravates debt elsewhere. The links between the North American military monster and the southern-hemisphere crisis need explaining.

US defence spending is forcing the world into a deadly game in which everyone is going to lose (except for the sworn enemies of the United States). The state of play in the early 1980s was as follows. The US had more money than any other player ($140 billion in foreign assets in 1981). The country then proceeded to squander vastly more money than it earned, mostly on armaments, to which nearly a third of the federal budget was devoted. A predictable hole in the national accounts ensued.

By 1986 the US had not only frittered away its initial $140 billion stake abroad but had also borrowed over $250 billion from foreigners, thus racking up an external debt that makes Latin Americans look like dwarfs. This $250 billion is only the *foreign* debt: as of 1986, the US government owed an additional $1,750 billion to American purchasers of government securities, so its total public debt was actually $2 trillion. Most experts concede that the US will have to go on borrowing and that its *foreign* debt will hit a cool $1 trillion in the early 1990s. At that point the government should be forking over $215 billion yearly to its creditors abroad, thanks to what Lord Keynes called 'the magic of compound interest'. If all goes well.

Senator Daniel Patrick Moynihan of the US Senate Finance and Budget Committee tells what happens when all does not go well:

Forty years ago, on the West Side piers of New York, if you were broke on a Monday morning, there was no problem. You could borrow $20, with $30 to be paid back on payday, which was Friday. If you didn't have $30 on Friday, that was no problem. You could pay $40 on Wednesday. The extra $10, then $20, was called 'vigorish'. It kept mounting. Sooner or later your family bailed you out in a big scene or you ended up in St Clare's hospital. This is what the US federal deficit is about. Not spending: interest.[21]

In Washington, as on the West Side, the more you borrow, the more your interest explodes until the deficit is self-propelling. For the other players (the rest of the world) the game consists in giving the United

States the largest financial blood transfusion in history – yet its economy is still anaemic. For a normal country, a country not privileged to print the world's currency, there would be penalties. The player would be forced to admit, 'I'm going to go completely broke. Either I cut spending, or I raise taxes, or I sell a lot more goods abroad – preferably all three – or I lose my shirt and I'm out of the game.'

The US, instead, does none of these things. It *increases* spending (mostly, again, on military hardware). It *cuts* taxes. And it sells *fewer* goods abroad, while importing more. Even its once triumphant agricultural trade slips into the red. So it had both a huge *budget* deficit ($220 billion) and a huge *trade* deficit ($140 billion) in 1986. To finance both, borrowing must continue and interest payments must rise – causing the federal budget (as Moynihan explains) to escape all real legislative control. Messrs Gramm, Rudman and Hollings may as well go fishing, for their Bill cannot slash the deficit when it is *interest payments themselves* that are driving future budget deficits up, up and away.

It would be smart to raise taxes, especially on energy consumption and luxuries, but tax cuts have become an article of faith among US neo-conservatives. It would be smarter still to start earning more dollars abroad, but most economists see no way in which the US can quickly reverse its disastrous trade balance, no matter how far the dollar falls. So the only remaining sane way to deal with the problem is to cut spending, fast. In a context in which interest payments are growing geometrically and cannot be reduced, the logical place to cut is deep into the fat of the Pentagon – that is, unless international bankruptcy for the US, collapse of the world financial system and wipe-out of everyone's savings is your idea of a lark.

The alternative to this scenario is for the US to print money. Since the dollar is the world currency, when the US owes too many dollars and can't or won't earn them by exporting goods and services, it can always decide to pay back creditors in what the French call *monnaie de singe* (monkey money), devalued beyond hope or recognition. The United States is the only country in the world that could eliminate its debt by such an expedient, at the cost, of course, of triggering renewed global inflation.

Because the US is the only country thus privileged, because it could decide unilaterally to wipe out its debt by this simple, if brutal, method, its case ought to cause fear and trembling at the IMF and throw its flying squadrons of economists into high gear. The Fund is supposed to 'aid countries with balance-of-payments problems' – just another way of saying that it loans to countries with terrible trade deficits but only when they agree to 'adjust' and run their economies the Fund's way.

Nobody has a worse balance-of-payments problem than the United States. So I assume the Fund has prepared a custom-tailored austerity programme for the US, with the defence budget as prime target. Sorry, I was dreaming there for a moment – the IMF is an instrument of the G-5, the Western government group led by the United States. No adjustment will be forced upon the world's largest debtor, the international financial system's most destabilizing influence of all.

The US arms build-up, none the less, has a direct influence on the interest rates that other nations must pay. Its defence budget in effect imposes a huge and totally unjustified tax on poor countries and poor people. How? The US government must pay in order to attract the capital that finances its deficit. This deficit, as we've just seen, is created by arms spending. If the foreigners from whom the US borrows savings suddenly get cold feet and decide to cut back or withdraw, they could cause a haemorrhage of capital and possible panic. To keep them happy and their money at hand, the US has to offer an attractive reward in the form of high interest. Because the US rate is, for most practical purposes, the world rate, Third World countries must pay on their own debt a price that they never bargained for.

INTEREST AND OIL: DUE TO CIRCUMSTANCES BEYOND ...

Indeed, interest rates are the bane of Third World debtors' existence. Debt is not attributable entirely to arms purchases, useless, dangerous or cost-inflated projects, conspicuous consumption, graft and capital flight. There were some completely unavoidable reasons for incurring debt, which had nothing to do with the choices of the borrowers themselves. Third World countries could have been run by people of towering moral stature and god-like intelligence – they would *still* have found themselves deep in the red. Two of these uncontrollable factors were interest rates and oil prices.

Third World debtors were subject to OPEC decisions about oil prices and to creditor countries and their bankers where interest rates were concerned. In the 1970s countries contracted much of their debt (especially from banks) at *variable*, or 'market' rates, meaning that the cost of using borrowed money could well change over time. When they borrowed the debtors were, in a sense, betting that they could pay back at x per cent; if they lost their bet, as they later did, they would have to pay back at a far higher *y* per cent (as happened in the context of soaring US deficits).

Interest rates are, furthermore, of two sorts, called 'nominal' and 'real'. Nominal is what it says on the contract; real is what it says minus inflation. For example, if the nominal interest rate is 10 per cent but inflation is 12 per cent, the real interest rate is −2 per cent. Normally, interest rates are directly influenced by inflation. They tend to rise and fall together.[22] But not always. In the mid- to late 1970s interest rates didn't rise as much as inflation, so real rates were negative. Not only did it cost nothing to borrow − people actually paid you to do so. The average real rate over the decade of the 1970s was −0.8 per cent and in some years sank as low as −3 or −4 per cent. In those days every time a Third World country borrowed to pay obligations instead of dipping into reserves, inflation meant it got the goods or services for less in the end.

The rub was that in the 1980s interest rates didn't *fall* as much as inflation, leaving the debtors holding the bag. Every additional point of real interest meant untold extra billions due in debt service (from $2 billion to $6 billion per point, depending on which source you believe). New loans were sought to pay off old ones. Indebtedness snowballed. Even though nominal rates began to subside in 1985 (in mid-1987 they were about 8–9 per cent), *real* rates were still crippling and helping to fuel the crisis.

The other unpleasant surprise for the debtors was the energy crisis, particularly the second oil-price shock in 1979. William Cline of the Institute of International Economics in Washington argues, 'The single most important [external] cause of the debt burden of non-oil developing countries is the sharp rise in the price of oil in 1973–74 and again in 1979–80.' Cline's figures show that over the 1974–82 period these countries imported nearly $345 billion worth of oil.

Assuming the price of oil had merely kept pace with inflation and gone up at the same rate as other commodities, as measured by the US wholesale price index, the non-oil debtor countries would have paid only $85 billion. Simple subtraction shows that importers paid $260 billion more for oil than they would have done without the OPEC effect. Cline notes that his own figure of $260 billion is low because it doesn't take account of the cumulative interest charges on each year's debt for imported oil. The true contribution of higher oil prices to Third World debt is thus even greater.[23]

If we accept Cline's estimates (and there seems no reason not to), then we have to recognize that oil-price increases alone accounted for over a quarter of debt accumulated by the totality of Third World countries.

These prices had an even greater proportional impact on non-oil nations. Those outside the charmed circle of oil producers had no choice in the matter: either they increased borrowing or they allowed their energy-starved economies to come to a screeching halt. The option of paying for oil by dramatically increasing their own exports was not open to them.

But what about oil exporters like Mexico, Venezuela or Nigeria, which rank among the biggest debtors? Didn't they profit by the same token from the oil-price rise and thus enjoy *lower* debts than they would otherwise have contracted? Didn't higher resources from oil for these countries at least help to prevent the $260 billion debt increase from growing even more?

Probably not. First, countries like Mexico borrowed heavily just to develop the oil industry. PEMEX, the Mexican state oil corporation, borrowed $20 billion all by itself – a quarter of the total Mexican debt in 1982.[24] Second, the more oil a country had, the more banks were anxious to push their money at it, confident in the belief that oil revenues would ensure repayment. Without black gold in the ground Nigeria, for one, wouldn't have looked like much of a credit risk.

Were I a Third World leader in the dock, accused of getting my country hopelessly ensnared in debt, my defence would be that money was too cheap in the 1970s not to take advantage of the windfall. Polonius, the fussy old man in *Hamlet* who told his son, 'Neither a borrower nor a lender be,' didn't know what he was talking about (at least not beyond the level of 'Can you let me have twenty until payday?'). If Laertes followed his advice, he probably died a pauper. It would have been less poetic but more practical for Polonius to explain to his boy that in times of high inflation it's smart to borrow, just as in deflationary periods it's better to be on the lending end.

How was I, a debtor government, to foresee – much less control – the unprecedented upward swing of interest rates, due largely to demented military spending by the capitalist world super-power? I would further-more tell the jury: 'Every single Western expert who ever came to our country, especially those from the development banks, told us that to develop we had to industrialize. Was our country to remain for ever in peonage, exporting raw materials north so that others could transform them into finished goods and make all the money? Where were we supposed to get the capital for energy and for industrialization if not by borrowing?'

Given all this, it was easy to run up a $1 trillion tab.

2.
THE MONEY-MONGERS

'It is an odd business, selling money door to door at the edge of the civilized world,' says a reformed banker of his former *métier*, glad to be well out of it.[1] The description of his adventures in the loan trade is by far the funniest – and most chilling – account one is likely to find of a business that in recent years has been odd indeed.

This young man of twenty-five summers and fully eighteen months' banking experience travelled for his bank, a Midwestern one with $5 billion in assets, to twenty-eight countries in six months. He was not some sort of financial prodigy but quite typical of 'the world of international banking [which] is now full of aggressive, bright but hopelessly inexperienced lenders in their mid-twenties. They travel the world like itinerant brushmen, filling loan quotas, peddling financial wares and living high on the hog.' The bosses of these striplings, also hopelessly inexperienced, are about 29; *their* bosses may be somewhat older and may know US domestic banking inside-out but often have not the slightest notion of conditions overseas.

Although the bulk of Third World lending came from the mega-banks, literally hundreds of second-rank US banks got into overseas markets in the 1970s because everyone else was doing it. In less euphoric times they would have stuck with lending to local business. Total US bank exposure in the Third World grew from $110 billion in

1978 to $450 billion at the end of 1982 – over 300 per cent in four years.

Wasn't anyone worried about this runaway growth, particularly those promoting it? As the young ex-banker quoted above explains, reasonably enough, 'As a loan officer, you are principally in the business of making loans. It is not your job to worry about large and unwieldy abstractions, such as whether what you're doing is threatening the stability of the world economy. In that sense, a young banker is like a soldier on the front lines: he is obedient, aggressive and amoral.' In another sense, he is decidedly unlike a soldier on the front lines unless you mean a soldier whose mess regularly serves champagne and lobster and whose quartermasters provide expensive hotel rooms, limousines for transport and, upon occasion, female companionship. An international banker is isolated from, and takes no interest in, the local people to whose country he is peddling money. Even if he were able to escape the attentions of his clients, who carefully insulate him from any such unpleasant contacts, he would not take the poverty of the majority into account. Since 'your job performance is rated according to how many loans you make', you never say to your superiors that country x or y is about to collapse because it's in your interest to keep your mouth shut.

Our young hero was at one point placing a loan with the Construction and Development Corporation of the Philippines (CDCP). There was considerable pressure on him from home to sell this money, since one of his bank's best *domestic* clients was an earthmoving-equipment corporation anxious to sell its machines to the CDCP. A lot of international bank exposure has come simply from trying to follow clients as they themselves go transnational. That's how it all began in the late 1960s: banks followed companies as they expanded overseas.

There was a lot wrong with the CDCP, as even an inexperienced 25-year-old banker could see. The corporation's shaky financial structure was not, however, grounds for refusing a loan. Whereas, he notes, you are trained in domestic banking to make sure a company has enough assets to cover its debts, in international banking you are told to forget about that. The trick, when you know full well the company is not creditworthy but you are under pressure and determined to place the loan anyway, is to 'shift responsibility to a third party' through a 'guarantee' or a 'stand-by letter of credit', preferably from a central bank or from the government itself. This was no problem in the Philippines, since the head of the CDCP and that of the country's biggest commercial bank were both part of the 'crony-capitalism' network fostered by Marcos.

The money that the young man thrust upon a more than eager CDCP came not from some shadowy Eurodollar market, as would normally have been the case had he represented one of the major banks, but from 'the savings accounts of Americans from Ohio'. In this instance, as in dozens of others, 'by the time the borrower suspended its debt payments, *all* the loan officers who worked on it had moved on to other banks . . . the people who make the big international loans are not around to collect them when they go bad.'[2]

Another young banker to spill the beans is Richard W. Lombardi, ex-vice president of the First National Bank of Chicago in charge of loans in Sub-Saharan Africa. Though he published a book on debt in 1985,[3] he was sounding alarms well beforehand and predicting early in 1981 'an unacceptable number of otherwise well-endowed developing countries facing insoluble debt problems . . . We can likewise anticipate quite tragic repercussions of a social and economic nature.'[4]

DEVELOPMENT? NONE OF THEIR BUSINESS

Banks can't possibly contribute to anything called 'development', says Lombardi, when their lending methodology consists in setting 'country limits' in New York or Chicago and then assigning 'marketing officers' in the field to loan up to this limit. He would like the banks to adapt their lending to the real needs and capacities of each country and to refuse deals that are obviously beyond its means or its population's ability to pay. Banks should look at money from the borrower's viewpoint – as a limited resource. 'The offshore financing of . . . luxury items does not represent the optimal use of this limited resource.'

Some of the 'offshore-financed' projects that Lombardi witnessed are tragicomical in the extreme. Take Togo.

West Germany finances an important steel complex near Lomé, Togo's capital. On completion, the Togolese government realizes that no iron ore nor scrap metals are available for start-up. The credibility of Togo's head of state is in jeopardy. German technicians quickly dismantle an iron pier located at the port. Ironically, the pier had been constructed by Germany prior to World War I and was still functional and functioning. The steel mill closed down its operations when pig iron from the pier was exhausted.[5]

Zaïre attracted bankers because of its rich mineral deposits – copper, cobalt, diamonds and rare strategic metals. Zaïre was so spendthrift that it managed to have a fully fledged debt crisis well before the term became current. By 1975 Zaïre was already a frequent visitor to the IMF. Whatever the bankers may have thought they were financing, what they got was a sharp 25 per cent decline in copper and cobalt production between 1975 and 1978, plus a 'world trade center in downtown Kinshasa, an underground parking lot, a fleet of jet aircraft, an elaborate airport next to the head of state's native village', plus hugely swollen imports of food, automobiles and, of course, arms.[6]

Lombardi thinks the banks should have taken a hard look at the kinds of project they were financing and recognized the inevitable and painful dislocations they were bound to engender. Asking banks, on ethical grounds, not to make loans when loans can be made is perhaps a shade naive, especially coming from a banker. Lombardi's stance also poses the classic Competitor's Dilemma: if I don't do it, Jones (or Citibank) will. His 1981 answer to the dilemma was that such 'beggar-thy-neighbour' justifications for unrestrained lending seem reasonable today but could easily sour 'in a Third World where sovereign [government] borrowers often do not enjoy the institutional stability of the banks themselves'.[7]

Even the 'institutional stability' of the banks appears questionable when one considers their (over)exposure in the Third World. If you compare their loans with their capital, you find that in 1984 *all* of the nine largest US banks had placed over 100 per cent of their shareholders' equity in loans to Mexico, Brazil, Argentina and Venezuela alone. Only one of the Americans majors, however, tops the exposure of Lloyds in Britain, which had engaged 165 per cent of its capital in loans to these four debtors in 1984, while the Midland beat them all with a dizzying 205 per cent. By contrast, the most exposed US bank, Manufacturers Hanover (known to intimates as Manny Hanny) had 'only' 173 per cent of its capital outstanding to the biggest debtors in 1984.[8]

Partly because of this dangerous exposure, other members of the banking culture are coming to share Lombardi's prudent views. One of them, writing anonymously, claims to have been involved personally in totting up more than $50 billion of developing-country debt. He even-handedly blames both the governments and the banks: the governments because they used the money in foolish, corrupt and profligate ways, himself and his colleagues because 'We rushed blindly along chasing a rainbow we thought would lead to easy profits.'[9] Governments that squandered past loans now expect the banks to believe they will use new money to 'invest to grow and repay'. The unnamed author thinks this is nonsense. These countries are black holes that will swallow new money as they swallowed the old; as for the banks, 'Our painful experience has demonstrated that private banks are incapable of making reliable judgements about the risks involved in financing economic development. Nor do we have even the slightest chance of influencing how or to what use the proceeds of the loans we make are put.'

Painful experience? Certainly not for the vast majority of banks, as a man who claims he helped to place 5 per cent of total Third World debt should know better than anyone. Their profits have been huge. His prescription for the future? Only public, multilateral financial institutions should get into the sovereign-loan trade, since they alone 'can hope to impose the controls on use of funds and management of economies necessary to ensure that good loans are made on conditions that maximize the chances of repayment and hence of productive use for the borrowers . . . *The disastrous record of private financing for economic development shows that this is no place for banks*' (my emphasis).[10]

Personally, I would not trust this farsighted individual to manage a pizza stand, much less the savings of thousands of depositors. His perception of Third World loans, though it comes rather late in the day, has, however, become a common one among his tribe. Bankers have not undergone virtuous conversion, but a few have been burned and many others are terrified they will be. They have been obliged, by the IMF and its allies in government, to accept 'forced lending' (as we shall shortly see in the story of the Mexican debt rescue). Now they would much prefer to hand over to public, multilateral financial institutions whatever bits of their own portfolios prove dangerous or terminally unprofitable. This attitude displays the banker's version of privatization, which holds that profits should accrue to the private sector. Losses, on the other hand, ought to be off-loaded on to governments or international bodies (i.e. taxpayers).

THE MONEY CENTRES: LEADERS OR LEMMINGS?

Are bankers more like lemmings than the rest of us? They do, in any event, tend to move in packs. The lead lemmings in debt build-up were the money-centre banks (MCBs). These MCBs are a relatively new breed and make up one of the world's more exclusive clubs, generally estimated at nine American members.* A more generous definition might include some fifty banks qualifying as MCBs world-wide.

The notion of a money-centre bank was invented by Citicorp, the biggest of the big nine, just over fifteen years ago. Unlike the traditional bank, an MCB does not loan money on the basis of its own clients' deposits or its shareholders' equity. Rather, it *buys* money, either on the Eurodollar market or from other banks, and becomes less a banker in the classic sense than a financial broker. It no longer relies on *depositors* to supply its funds.

David Rockefeller refers to Chase Manhattan as a 'multinational financial services corporation'. He does not mention anything so banal as 'banking'. Richard Lombardi regrets that 'In the Third World, bankers have not been lending money, they have been brokering money. The very service of recycling for which so many bankers flatter themselves . . . speaks of money changing, not of investment.' Walter Wriston, then chairman of Citicorp, put it even more pithily in a brochure entitled 'The Citicorp Concept': 'Our strategy is not one of making loans; our strategy is one of making money.'[12]

With a view to making money, the nine US MCBs had by the end of 1985 placed close to $50 billion in loans to the six largest Latin American debtors alone (Argentina, Brazil, Chile, Columbia, Mexico, Venezuela). The British big four had loaned about £16 billion to Latin America at the end of 1984.[13] For all the Americans, and for the Midland and Lloyds, this was vastly more money than they actually had. Naturally, banks' loans are *supposed* to exceed the amounts they have stashed in their vaults (or at least on their books), but the difference is that in the US the bank regulators say by *how much* loans should exceed deposits. State and federal regulatory agencies also limit the proportion of funds that may be loaned to a single client. In the case of Third World loans there are no watchdogs and no rules.

Indeed, one reason why banks were so eager to make these loans was that they could behave exactly as they pleased. Financial inventiveness

---

* The big nine in the US are Bankers Trust, Bank of America, Chase Manhattan, Chemical, Citicorp, Continental Illinois, First Chicago, Manufacturers Hanover, Morgan Guaranty. In 1985 their collective net income was $3.4 billion (which takes account of a *loss* of $337 million by Bank of America). This figure represents an improvement of 56 per cent over 1984 profits. British banks in this select group include Lloyds, Barclays, the National Westminster and the Midland. In 1985 their combined pre-tax profits were over £2.6 billion, an increase of 35 per cent over 1984 profits.[11]

is always light years ahead of regulation – the phenomenal growth of 'stateless money' and of offshore banking havens also helps banks to avoid government interference (until, of course, they need to be saved from the consequences of their own heedlessness). The Eurodollar markets themselves, where the MCBs buy so much of their money, now represent about $2 trillion (nobody knows for sure how much) of what Howard Wachtel has called 'the first truly supranational form of money'. This money escapes the ken, much less the control, of any governmental authorities.*

SECOND STRINGERS ON THE LOAN TEAMS

Hundreds of regional and local banks throughout the United States, most of them with little or no previous history of foreign lending, are also deeply involved in the Third World and therefore in the debt crisis. What people do not always realize is that one large, syndicated loan to a major Third World customer like the government of Mexico or Brazil can involve over a thousand participating banks.

Some of the regional banks that are most anxious to disengage today behaved like foolish virgins during the go-go years before the Mexican crisis – at BancOhio, for example, foreign lending went from zero in 1979 to over $1 billion in 1983. The man in charge now concedes that there are 'fewer and fewer safe places to lend'. He is disengaging but calls this a 'flight to quality' – in safer locations like Europe. An Indianapolis bank multiplied its foreign loans by a factor of 15 between 1979 and 1983; one in Baltimore increased its foreign portfolio by 25 per cent per year during the same period.

As in the case of our 25-year-old's employer, many of these banks were drawn into Third World lending because they were financing the activities of their US clients abroad. The rude awakening came when they saw that even 'simple . . . packages cannot be divorced from the overall economic climate in the borrower's country. Suddenly . . . you realize that the bottom line is no longer the financial health of the *individual* customer but how its *country* is getting the dollars,' as a Milwaukee banker put it.

* Wachtel's book, *The Money Mandarins: The Making of a Supranational Economic Order*, Pantheon Books, New York, 1986, is a highly recommended, clear and entertaining account of how the world economy, spearheaded by the banks, today works 'supranationally'. Readers should refer to it for a fuller explanation, which cannot be attempted here.

The MCBs cannot afford to be left holding the bag, nor can they do so without the contribution of the regional banks. This contribution is difficult to assess, but the financial magazine *Euromoney* cites government statistics indicating that regional banks have been a vital factor in Third World lending. Their share of Argentina's loans is estimated at 36 per cent, 39 per cent for Brazil, 44 per cent for Mexico, 32 per cent for the Philippines. The MCBs don't want to wake up and find themselves solely responsible for refinancing these loans. 'I wouldn't say that the money-centre banks are desperate about this, but it is always undesirable to have very many people leave the party,' says a New York banker quoted by *Euromoney*.[14]

One way of persuading the smaller banks to stay at the party was to make sure they didn't panic on the basis of rumours, faulty information or plain lack of confidence in their larger colleagues. The MCBs were not blameless. As a bank president from Indianapolis complained, 'Some [big] banks put these [syndicated] loans together in what we truly think are very sloppy ways.'

With a view to improving the knowledge and calming the nerves of the regionals, thirty-one of the world's most influential bankers met in October 1982 in New York. This meeting came only two months after the Mexican default bomb nearly exploded, an indication that banks needed to move fast to keep the junior partners in line. At this meeting the majors decided to establish 'an international institute to improve the availability and quality of financial and economic information of major country borrowers' (more accurately, *about* major country borrowers).[15]

Thus was the International Institute of Finance (IIF) conceived.* By January 1984 it was ready to function and a year later had 187 members from thirty-seven countries. A few were from the larger borrowing countries like Brazil, Argentina, Mexico and Venezuela; forty-nine of them (over a quarter) were US banks; Japan had fifteen members, France and the UK fourteen each.

The IIF assesses its members' dues on the basis of their Third World exposure: $85,000 annual dues for those with over $10 billion outstanding; $27,000 for those with between $2 billion and $10 billion outstanding; only $5,000 for banks with exposure below $2 billion. The MCBs and other large banks are all members – for them $85,000 is lunch

---

* It is interesting to note that the debt crisis of the 1920s provoked a similar response. In 1928 the Institute for International Finance – as opposed to the 1984 International Institute of Finance – was founded, with headquarters at New York University.[16]

money. The largest banks actually need the IIF's information services the least. They all have their own platoons of economic and political analysts, plus branches in the concerned Third World countries, that keep them up to date. The low membership fee for the smaller fry illustrates a remark of one of the bankers who attended the meeting where the IIF was conceived: 'It's really for the regionals. But we do not want it to appear . . . that we are constructing this for the regionals to help them be good boys.'[17]

Under the leadership of André de Lattre, a Frenchman who has alternated between high positions in public service and private banking, the IIF has become far more than a source of on-line computerized data or in-depth country reports on borrowers. The IIF also plays the role of consensus-maker and policy co-ordinator among the banks. When they have something to say to the IMF, the World Bank or the World Trade Conference, de Lattre says it.*[18]

WALKING ON TWO LEGS? PROFIT AND RISK

Some people still entertain the quaint notion that capitalism – free enterprise, if you will – involves risk-taking. This in turn ought to mean that entrepreneurs, including banks, will assume responsibility for their mistakes, just as they will reap the profits when they get it right. Assuming responsibility, according to this old-fashioned doctrine, means accepting losses and, upon occasion, failure.

Dozens of dismissive remarks that grace the language were doubtless invented for those who misjudge markets: 'Those are the breaks,' 'That's the way the cookie crumbles' or, more succinctly, 'Tough.' If the banks are incapable of making reliable judgements about the risks involved in economic development, yet invest billions of other people's money in just such risky activities, then perhaps their managers should get into another line of business, like selling brushes. People who take this antiquated, Adam Smithian view of how a normal capitalist system should operate are unlikely to be edified by current developments.

Reaganites' *laissez-faire* philosophy stops short of allowing any discomforts to afflict large banks. In 1986 the US Congressional Joint Economic Committee commissioned a Staff Study that concluded:

* De Lattre retired from the IIF in 1987 and was replaced by Horst Schulman.

Instead of trusting the invisible hand to solve the debt crisis, the Reagan Administration marshalled the power of the Federal Government and the resources of the US Treasury to preserve the solvency of the US banking system and shelter individual banks from the consequences of their ill-advised lending decisions . . . Indeed, it is now becoming clear that Administration policies have gone above and beyond what was needed for protecting the [largest] banks from insolvency. Besides preserving their safety and soundness, the Administration ensured, and in fact promoted, their profitability . . . [Its] management of the debt crisis has, in effect, rewarded the institutions that played a major role in precipitating the crisis . . .[19]

The White House might be quick to object that this just represents Congressional grousing, but the numbers are on the Joint Committee's side. Although there were plenty of ominous signs beforehand, the beginning of the debt 'crisis' is generally reckoned from the summer of 1982, when Mexico came within a hair of default. Between 1982 and the end of 1985 profits at Banker's Trust went up by 66 per cent, at Chase Manhattan by 84 per cent, at Chemical by 61 per cent, at Citicorp and Manny Hanny by 38 per cent and at Morgan Guaranty by 79 per cent.

In spite of over-exposure to Latin America, dividends declared by the big nine banks increased by more than a third during the same period. Stockholders not only received higher dividends but also benefited greatly from rising share values. From the end of 1982 to April 1986 the value of Chase's stock rose by 86 per cent, of Chemical's by 97 per cent, of Citicorp's by 83 per cent, while Morgan's and Banker's Trust's shares shot up by 142 and 154 per cent respectively. This is a crisis?[20]

Smaller banks, however, do not receive red-carpet treatment from the federal government. They are, in fact, going under with dismal regularity. There were 428 small-bank failures in the United States between 1982 and 1986 (over a third involved so-called agricultural banks). Furthermore, US regional bank failures are increasing ominously: over three times as many went bankrupt in 1986 as in 1982.[21] If the largest banks, on the other hand, were to show signs of toppling because of foreign insolvency, there would be an all-out national and international *Blitzkrieg* of protective and corrective measures. This is what the Mexican scare of August 1982 proved. The potential crisis was defused, but in a haphazard, *ad hoc* and just plain lucky fashion, after weeks of marathon meetings. The banks came out in excellent shape.

DOWN MEXICO WAY

The tale of the Great Mexican Rescue, admirably told by the late Joseph Kraft,[22] convinced me, for one, that there *is* something new under the international financial sun. This something was born of a necessity made painfully clear by the Mexican red alert. I call it the Consortium. The dictionary definition of 'consortium' is 'an association of several states, companies, etc.', whereas mine is 'an association of states *and* companies (in the present case banks) plus international bodies and *ad hoc* institutions'. Consortium members – lender-nation governments, banks, international agencies – share (mostly) common interests and therefore pursue similar goals. They don't conspire but they do consult, and at the top to upper-middle levels the members all know each other. As a result, they generally act in concert as well, though this may sometimes occur because they have no choice.

Kraft interviewed dozens of participants in the Mexican rescue and pieced their stories together with skill and flair. Unlike most documents about debt, his is fun to read, if retrospectively scary. Here is crisis management in high places, warts and all. The boys pulled it off, but it was a close call. In the process they laid the groundwork for the Consortium.

The Mexican affair began inauspiciously on a Friday, 13 August 1982. The players who worked non-stop to resolve it eventually included a U S home team made up of the Federal Reserve, Treasury, State, the Office of Management and Budget, assorted other Departments and Agencies, the White House, plus the top brass of the commercial banks and their lawyers. The Mexican team was led by the then finance minister, Jesus Silva Herzog (called Chucho by practically everybody, for, as a friend once observed, 'You can't address even him as Jesus'). The IMF alternately acted as umpire and rode herd. The Fed, or rather its chairman, Paul Volcker, oversaw contacts with other rich-nation central banks; these were also co-ordinated by the Bank for International Settlements (BIS) in Basle.

The principal actors later called their achievement 'unprecedented' and 'historic' and themselves 'pioneers'. Silva Herzog observed, 'The world was different after that . . . The blueprints for dealing with this situation quite simply did not exist; we had to draw them up.' What was 'this situation'? As a member of the Mexican team put it:

We didn't crawl to the international financial community as debtors seeking relief through some minor adjustment that could be made back-

*stage . . . We said we had a major problem with a capital P. We didn't say
the problem was a particular debt [but] the whole international financial
structure. We said it was everybody's problem.*[23]

Indeed it was. Mexico at that time held $80 billion of debt, and the
exposure of US banks was huge. The nine largest had fully 44 per cent of
their capital tied up in loans there; should Mexico stop paying interest,
they would be legally forced to classify these enormous loans as 'non-
performing' and take the consequences on their earnings statements.
Their stocks would plummet as shareholders fought to reach the exit; a
crisis of confidence could well ensue and trigger world-wide financial panic. This dire prospect made the Mexican bomb an issue for
governments and the IMF as well.

When the US players went on to the field, they were far from a
well-knit team. Donald Regan, then Treasury Secretary, had always
fought Paul Volcker on monetary policy and had opposed him as
chairman of the Fed. Walter Wriston, then chairman of the most
powerful mega-bank, Citicorp, didn't care much for Volcker either,
resented his penchant for managing everything and called him 'the big
Nanny'.

The White House opposed new resources for the IMF and sought to
use the crisis to its own advantage. 'The perception [was] that since
structures are shaky, the US can exercise maximum influence by not
going along, by hanging tough, and making others plead for the support
of Washington.' In other words, let the Mexicans, and the IMF, grovel.
The big banks didn't trust the smaller ones to co-operate; the smaller
ones were indignant at being pushed around by the majors.

From this motley crew, hitherto characterized chiefly by internecine
squabbling, the Mexican threat produced a unified, well-oiled financial
machine. Committees were formed; communications functioned; team-
work flourished. At one point internal Mexican politics – characterized,
if anything, by even worse squabbling – nearly spoiled the emerging deal
that was to bring Mexico $8 billion in fresh money.

On the night of 31 August, counselled by the more radical elements in
Mexico's ruling PRI party, President Lopez Portillo nationalized the
banks and imposed exchange controls – both anathema to the IMF,
whose austerity programme was to be the linchpin of the planned
rescue. On 1 September the Mexican President made a fiery 'State of the
Nation' address whose centrepiece was this thinly veiled denunciation
of the IMF, which must have especially enjoyed the part about
rats:

The financial plague is wreaking greater and greater havoc throughout the world. As in medieval times, it is scourging country after country. It is transmitted by rats and its consequences are unemployment and poverty, industrial bankruptcy and speculative enrichment. The remedy of the witch doctors is to deprive the patient of food and subject him to compulsory rest. Those who protest must be purged, and those who survive bear witness to their virtue before the doctors of obsolete and prepotent dogma and of blind hegemonical egoism.[24]

The next day half a million peasants and workers bussed in by the P R I were cheering the President in the Zocalo, the vast central square of Mexico City. Hard upon this speech, which rejected every single measure the IMF insisted upon, came the annual IMF/World Bank meeting in Toronto. Here were, in Walter Wriston's words, '150-odd finance ministers, 50-odd central bankers, 1,000 journalists, 1,000 commercial bankers, a large supply of whisky and a reasonably small city that produced an enormous head of steam driving an engine called "the end of the world is coming"'.[25]

But the sky did not fall. An initial salvaging operation was mounted. First, a haemorrhage of money out of Mexican branch banks in New York had to be stemmed. Just as in the 1930s, when individual US depositors started a 'run on the banks', here fearful fellow bankers were starting a run on Mexico by demanding that Mexican branch banks pay back loans and deposits instantly. Although these Mexican banks held a total of about $6 billion in obligations to their depositors, they did not have on hand enough cash to pay and could not honour the cheques they wrote under duress.

The Fed had to cover their losses at the New York Clearing House, where banks cancel out their debts to each other at the end of each day. Had this outflow continued, the whole laboriously arranged package promised Mexico by the US, the BIS in Basle and the IMF could have been totally drained by these repayments. At this point 'Volcker, with the support of other central bankers, put the heat on the Mexican authorities, and the Mexican officials put the heat on the branch banks. They were, in effect, told not to honor demands for repayment of deposits . . .'

Meanwhile, Lopez Portillo was scheduled to hand over the presidency to Miguel de la Madrid, and Mexico was running out of money. The Mexicans tried to use the threat of default to get the best possible terms from the IMF, but Jacques de Larosière, the Fund's managing director, stood firm. Within a couple of weeks the Mexicans had to sign on for a

programme nearly identical to the one that had been negotiated before
Lopez Portillo made his 'rat' speech and took anti-I M F measures.

But Larosière had something more than a single-country agreement
in mind. His idea was 'to engage the major countries, the central banks
and the private banks in a continuing effort to keep Mexico and the
other major debtor nations alive. In so doing, he would save the
international financial system,' explains Kraft.

Larosière had prepared his ground carefully: he had the support of the
Fed, the Bank of England and the U S Treasury, which promised to
work with other governments. On 16 November he called representatives of the major banks to a meeting. He announced that Mexico's total
needs were $8.3 billion. The I M F would contribute $1.3 billion; governments were good for another $2 billion; he expected the banks to kick in
$5 billion. What's more, he expected it within a month.

The bankers were stunned. One of them told Kraft that Larosière's
talk 'caused a kind of frenzy. You could practically hear those bankers
thinking, "Jesus, who does this guy think he is?"' But in retrospect, as a
top man from Morgan put it, the managing director's move was 'a major
action in the history of banking'.

The I M F provided the stick. A quite delectable carrot appeared on
the table on that very night in Boston when Paul Volcker spoke. He
asserted, 'there exists the strongest kind of community of interest among
borrowers and lenders, among governments and private businesses, and
among the developing and the industrialized countries in working
together' to meet a threat to financial stability 'essentially without
precedent in the post-war world'. For banks that co-operated, providing
loans that would 'facilitate the adjustment process and enable a country
to strengthen its economy and service its international debt in an orderly
manner, new credits *should not be subject to supervisory criticism*'
(my emphasis).[26] In other words, the Fed would turn a blind eye to
what it might have considered dangerous over-exposure in other
circumstances.

After that it was simply a matter of ironing out the details. The
bankers' advisory committee, which represented them in the Mexican
negotiations, decided that every bank that had participated in previous
Mexican loans should be assessed on 7 per cent of its original exposure.
Those who resisted – mostly smaller banks – suddenly found punctilious
Federal Reserve regulators making pointed inquiries about every aspect
of their business, refusing mergers and the like. Nearly all knuckled
under.

The banks also made piles of money out of the restructuring by

charging higher interest rates and various fees – a member of the
Mexican team says 70–90 per cent on their capital, though he may be a
spoilsport. They also saved the loans already on their books from the
dread non-performing label. Abroad 'all kinds of official and unofficial
pressures were mounted. The US Treasury quietly prevailed upon the
governments of Japan, France and Switzerland to make their banks see
reason . . . Sir Jeremy Morse of Lloyds raised contributions from British
banks at a session compared by one of those present to a church charity
drive.' Larosière intervened personally where necessary. Willingly or
not, the banks coughed up; the deadline was met.

The Mexican rescue became a model for dealing with other Latin
American debtors, and the Mexicans themselves tout it as such a model,
particularly with Venezuela, Brazil and Argentina. In fact, Kraft believes, 'The Mexican role in the Argentine rescue implies that the
"debtor's club" is going to play by the rules and with the system – not
against them.'[27] The Consortium is working smoothly in both the
northern and the southern hemisphere.

WHY THE BANKS? WHY NOT OPEC?

You may search the literature in vain for any sign of compassion on the
part of the bankers for the ordinary people who will wind up paying the
debt. Bankers deal with governments and are concerned with their
balance sheets, not with the millions whose bad luck it is to be subject to
such governments. The banks' mistakes will be forgiven, if necessary
redeemed, by their home governments; far from being punished,
bankers themselves will suffer no adverse consequences and will
continue to make six-figure salaries.

Meanwhile the victims of reckless lenders and improvident borrowers
will take the consequences. When governments must devote every last
centavo to servicing debt, they cut expenditures at home, drive down
salaries, sack public workers, stop paying for health, education and
welfare and generally neglect their own populations. It's simply not
good enough to say, as does the anonymous banker quoted above, that
banks have no business financing economic development. They freely
chose this course for over a decade. Lives are now being ruined – even
lost – because of these choices. Never before have so few been so wrong
with such a devastating effect on so many, but it is unlikely that the
banks will ever admit it.

At some time in the past their behaviour must have seemed justified.

Banks were certainly needed to grease the wheels of international commerce. Throughout the entire post-war period the price of goods manufactured in the North consistently outran the price of raw materials exported by the South. Because the 'terms of trade' were thus against the South, something had to take up the slack if the Third World was to continue importing these manufactures from the industrialized countries. That something was bank debt.

In many cases banks were simply financing US and European corporations that wanted to sell their products in the Third World.[28] Banks thus had no reason to care about what was happening *inside* the borrowing country: they were financing not the Philippines and Brazil but Boeing and Westinghouse, usually in partnership with the Export–Import Bank (and other national equivalents). In exchange the Western governments gave the bankers iron-clad insurance against losses. As the chairman of Boeing explained to a Congressional committee, 'Without the involvement of Ex–Im, commercial banks will not participate in loans to emerging nations.'[29] Little did these countries realize what they were 'emerging' into!

The surge in lending began, however, with the first oil-price rise in 1973 and accelerated spectacularly after the second one in 1979. When banks assumed the job of recycling oil money, this seemed to be in the natural order of things. The OPEC countries *had* money, while the non-oil Third World countries *needed* it – partly to buy oil. Banks were the obvious intermediaries. One could argue (and I do) that OPEC should have managed its own recycling and loaned directly to the Third World without giving this unprecedented opportunity and extremely powerful tool to the banks. The oil producers would have found themselves better off today as a result.

Indeed, had OPEC countries been both suppliers of energy and purveyors of finance to much of the rest of the world, they could have strengthened immeasurably the collective hand of the South and their own political influence. Islamic law is hard on usury, and the borrowers might have obtained lower interest rates. Even more important, there would have been no excuse to call in the IMF unless OPEC blew the whistle. Today, however, OPEC itself has become a net borrower – of the significant sum of $10 billion in 1984.[30]

Probably it never even occurred to the oil producers to take on the recycling job by themselves. They simply behaved as good capitalists do, expecting a higher rate of return on their money by handing it over to the professionals in New York and London. By so doing they missed a historic opportunity and set the scene for an unprecedented *coup* for the already rich countries. Debt, as managed by Western governments, banks and their helpers such as the IMF, has further weakened the South (including the OPEC countries), left it far worse off than before the borrowing binge and laid it open to virtual recolonization.

Be that as it may, the banks had a pile of money on their hands in the mid- to late 1970s. Bankers argue today that their huge loans to Third World countries were encouraged by states; they claim there was a tacit agreement with Western governments to foster orderly placement of petro-dollars as a matter of public interest. A representative of the American Bankers Association testified before the US House Banking Committee in the spring of 1983: 'There was no government directive that banks act to recycle the funds, but clearly it was expected.'[31]

Such statements also show, of course, that banks want to implicate governments and to make sure they will get them off any future hooks. It is doubtful that the vital interests of these same governments were uppermost in bankers' minds during the palmy days of expanding loans and rising profits. As a professor of international economic affairs remarks:

Are we really to believe that these proud institutions were so meekly submissive to the will of public officials? Would they really have gotten in so deep had they not thought that there was also something in it for them? . . . If they were so ready to recycle petro-dollars, it must have been because they believed that there was money – perhaps lots of money – to be made from it . . . Profit, not public interest, was their driving force.[32]

And profit it remains. The debt crisis is a true windfall. A country like Brazil, for example, paid back $69 billion in interest between 1979 and 1985, and its only reward at the end of this period was to be deeper than ever in debt, owing even greater interest payments. The creditors have pulled themselves together. Thanks to the practice acquired through the Mexican exercise and subsequent rescues, and the new spirit of co-operation (forced or genuine) between banks, governments and the IMF, stretching out Third World debt has been made as trouble-free as possible. The banks, at least the largest ones, are sure of saving their skins. The Consortium is adamant that the debt must continue to be handled on a case-by-case basis. We will now look at one of the principal instruments it uses to keep the debtors in line.

3.

THE INTERNATIONAL MONETARY FUND: LET THEM EAT SPECIAL DRAWING RIGHTS

When I started doing research on the debt crisis I was prepared to assign the role of global ogre to the IMF. Today, better versed in the doings of the Fund, I believe such name-calling would be mistaken or at least misleading. The role of the Fund is important, even peripherally ogrish, but it cannot be understood without reference to the crisis as a whole and to the other actors.

The Fund is highly visible because it is the architect of the 'adjustment' programmes that create serious hardships for low-income groups. But it cannot be held responsible for the circumstances that brought heavily indebted countries to its doorstep in the first place. Nor can the IMF even be credited with an inordinate amount of power in the world financial system – it simply does not have that kind of money at its disposal, and ultimately it takes its orders from outside. One might more accurately describe the Fund's role as that of messenger, watchdog, international alibi and *gendarme* for those who do hold financial power. As we saw in the preceding chapter, the bedrock of the world monetary system is the private banks, with states (including their central banks and treasuries) acting as guarantors. The Fund works on their behalf.

As watchdog and messenger, the IMF helps to ensure that over-exposed banks will be repaid, that even major borrowers like Mexico will be prevented from destabilizing the system as a whole. As alibi, it allows the major industrialized countries and their banks to off-load the consequences of their own shortsighted policies and financial reckless-ness on to the Fund's shoulders. The IMF helps them to consolidate their power over poor nations. At the same time, and in exchange for co-operation, it generally allows the elites of these same nations to maintain their affluence and perks at the expense of the majority of their fellow citizens. The IMF is a sort of Godfather figure – it makes countries offers they can't refuse.

Although the Fund has been an important factor in some nations for a decade or more – the Philippines, Jamaica, Kenya and Zaïre among them – its rise to stardom on the international scene is a recent phenomenon. The 1970s, as we've seen, were the heady days of bank euphoria, with borrower governments succumbing to the charms of apparently endless easy money. In those days nobody wanted the IMF around – the lenders because they were self-congratulatory about their efficient recycling of petro-dollars, the borrowers because they had no desire to submit to the Fund's stringent conditions. Thus little was heard about the IMF in the Third World until the early 1980s, since the banks were playing the lending game to everyone's satisfaction.

Between 1974 and 1979 the IMF supplied less than 5 per cent of the financing needs of the developing countries. Consequently it had little leverage over them. For example, in 1978 non-oil-producing LDCs actually repaid $900 million more to the Fund than they borrowed. In 1979 IMF advances to such countries ($1.8 billion) exceeded repay-ments by only $200 million.[1] The second oil-price shock helped to double LDC trade deficits from $45 billion in 1979 to $90 billion in 1981. The IMF did try to step in at this point but was stymied by the Reagan administration's refusal to grant it more lending resources. As a result, the private banks once more increased their loans to the most heavily indebted countries. By the early 1980s 55–60 per cent of all LDC debt was owed to banks.

BANKS AND THE IMF: A MARRIAGE OF CONVENIENCE

Suddenly, in the wake of global recession, the heedless nature of the banks' lending policies became evident to all. The borrowers woke up to the nasty reality that a lot of their debt was short-term and at 'variable' (market-determined) interest rates that were climbing dangerously. Each increase in interest automatically added billions to their debt-service bill. Borrowers also found interest payments devouring a larger and more unpredictable share of their export earnings just as these earnings were doing a nosedive.

Although their Third World loans remained enormously profitable, the bankers also began to shed their former insouciance and to recognize that even if countries did not 'fail to exist', they could still very well have serious repayment problems. The banks were already over-exposed, yet knew they would have to loan even more just to make sure that they got their interest back, that loans continued to 'perform'. The neo-conservatives' hope for bank 'self-regulation' turned out to be a fantasy.

As the Third World's capacity to pay diminished, jittery bankers realized that, alone or even together, they were unable singlehandedly to force the debtors to make loan servicing their highest priority. Faced with the grim prospect of cascading defaults, they had to have a nominally neutral institution with both the clout to force repayment and the capacity to mobilize enough financial resources to make repayment possible.

The banks, naturally, did not want to contribute all, or even most, of these resources themselves. An international agency like the IMF could use its own money (states' quotas and other contributions). It could also make its member governments see reason and urge them to put funds into the common pot. The Mexican rescue fund was typical: the IMF's share was $1.3 billion; governments paid in $2 billion; the banks put up $5 billion in 'involuntary loans'.

Note, however, that in the Mexican case public money (yours and mine) made up 40 per cent of the total package, compared with the banks' contribution of 60 per cent. Between 75 and 80 per cent of Mexico's debt is, however, owed to banks, which collect a proportionate amount of the interest. The IMF thus works as a *channel for funnelling public money to private banks* – it matters little that these funds transit through the national accounts of Mexico. In this sense the Fund enforces taxation without representation on the citizens of the industrialized countries.

The banks get another bonus by working with the Fund – an IMF adjustment programme is the best available guarantee that countries will continue to have the means to pay. Adjustment puts export earnings above every other goal, and export earnings head straight for the banks. The Mexican rescue story again shows that none of the banks would have budged without the centrepiece of an IMF plan for Mexico. The banks hate involuntary lending, and it may have been a rocky courtship, but the Fund and the banks were made for each other.

THEORY AND PRACTICE: FROM COMPARATIVE ADVANTAGE TO AUSTERITY

Here we will detail neither the origins and structure of the Fund as it was devised at Bretton Woods by Lord Keynes and Harry Dexter White in July 1944 (at the same time as the World Bank) nor its subsequent evolution. We will simply note that the US, the world's strongest economy at the end of the Second World War, was badly in need of an institution that would help to re-establish and promote trade.[2] This is indeed the Fund's *raison d'être*.

The IMF is commonly regarded as a purely financial institution, a kind of super-bank, lender of last resort or bailer-out (of countries or of banks), according to one's viewpoint. All this is so. But to understand the philosophy and practice of the Fund, one must first ask *why* it lends, *to what end* it provides 'balance-of-payments support' to heavily indebted countries.

The answer lies in the IMF's charter, whose first Article prescribes six objectives. Among these are 'To facilitate balanced *growth of international trade* and, through this, contribute to high levels of employment and real income and the development of productive capacity . . . [To] seek the elimination of exchange restrictions that hinder the *growth of world trade*' (my emphasis).

Even those objectives described in the first Article that may appear strictly financial are, in fact, geared to a single, overriding objective: the growth and development of world trade. Countries that consistently import more than they export need financial help so as not to withdraw from trade. No loans, no purchases. IMF intervention not only maintains them as participants in world markets but also, through adjustment programmes, forces them to *increase* that participation, even if this is demonstrably against the best interests of the people concerned.

The IMF has repeatedly stated that it is not, and was never intended to be, a *development* institution. Development is the concern of its sister agency, the World Bank. The Fund exists to impose its own orthodoxy on the world economy, and the foundations of that orthodoxy are the doctrines of free trade and comparative (or natural) advantage. To see the Fund's doctrine in a nutshell, one need not alter a line in economist David Ricardo's original nineteenth-century formulation:

It is quite important to the happiness of mankind that our own enjoyment should be increased by the better distribution of labour, by each country producing those commodities for which by its situation, its climate and its natural or artificial advantages it is adapted, and by their exchanging them for the commodities of other countries . . .[3]

These principles are religiously observed and dictate IMF behaviour. The principle of free trade means that membership of the Fund carries with it a tacit pledge to abolish trade restrictions – and particularly to dismantle controls over foreign-currency exchange. Restricted *money* can be a far more effective barrier to trade than tariffs. Other obstacles to trade, such as quotas, barriers to foreign investment, etc., are also heartily discouraged by the Fund.

What are the IMF's opportunities to put its doctrines into practice? These occur when a country comes to be seen by the international banking community as a poor credit risk, when its debts have reached alarming levels in relation to its ability to export and to earn foreign exchange. It is then that a country comes to the Fund to borrow amounts theoretically determined by the 'quota' it paid in when it became a member. Loans are granted in successive *tranches* (French for 'slices'). Each *tranche* obtained carries with it stricter and stricter conditions.

The number and severity of the obligations the Fund requires even for comparatively small loans causes complaints – but borrowing countries know that they will obtain no further loans from *other* sources without the IMF seal of approval. This seal helps to provide a guarantee that the country will henceforward behave itself in accordance with 'healthy' economic doctrine. It is supposed to be in everyone's interest that Fund clients swallow whatever bitter economic medicine is prescribed. As a long-time official of the IMF has written, 'If the Fund's standards of conditionality were lowered, the change would become known and probably the Fund would have less influence on other potential lenders.'[4]

Nowadays most countries that are obliged to go to the Fund rapidly exceed the allotted *tranches* based on their own quotas. They then appeal to a variety of special 'facilities' that the IMF has added to its members' quota funds over the years. The Fund usually makes loans in its own composite currency, called Special Drawing Rights. Because of much larger recent demands on Fund resources, quotas for many countries have become a polite fiction and have, in fact, been replaced by the 'enlarged access policy' – a way of allowing some members to break all previous rules, provided they undertake 'strong policy measures aimed at redressing payments imbalances'.[5]

The IMF's statutes require that the Fund 'shall adopt policies . . . that will assist members to solve their balance of payments problems . . . . and that will establish adequate safeguards for the temporary use of its resources'. These clauses confer on the IMF a blanket authorization to organize its borrowers' economies according to its own lights. Taken together, the 'strong policy measures' it insists on add up to an 'adjustment programme'. The Fund deplores that so many of its members wait until they are in really hot financial water before coming to it for help. These delays, it says, are the main reason for draconian 'austerity', as 'adjustment' is more popularly and more accurately known (except inside the IMF).

The basic goal of adjustment, and indeed that of many families, is simple enough: increase revenues, reduce expenditures. Third World countries in debt often do not have enough foreign currency to finance even their most basic necessities, and soon suppliers refuse further credit. To remedy this foreign-exchange shortage, the debtor must, in practice, reduce domestic consumption and increase exports.[6]

The most frequently imposed elements of an adjustment programme include devaluation of the currency (to discourage imports and encourage exports); drastic reduction of government expenditure, particularly social spending and elimination of food and other consumption subsidies; privatization of government enterprises and/or increases in prices charged by them (electricity, water, transportation, etc.) and the abolition of price controls; 'demand management' (meaning reduction of consumption) through caps on wages, along with restriction of credit, and higher taxes and interest rates in an effort to reduce inflation.[7]

All this may sound eminently reasonable. Countries cannot live for ever beyond their means, any more than families can. The question remains, however: who is living beyond whose means? As we already know, it was LDC elites, often the military, who were responsible for incurring the heavy debts to begin with. Their development schemes benefited themselves; the majority of their people were left out. We shall shortly see how the indiscriminate application of Fund doctrine intensifies the sufferings of ordinary people.

The IMF knows that it is being singled out as chief culprit for all kinds of social horrors in the Third World. Its defence is to affirm its 'non-political character', indeed its political impotence.[8] The Fund's former managing director, Jacques de Larosière, thus exonerates his institution from any responsibility for social injustice:

It is often said that Fund programs attack the most disadvantaged segments of the population, but people forget that how the required effort is distributed among the various social groups and among the various public expenditure categories (arms spending or social outlays, productive investment or current operations, direct or indirect taxes) is a question decided by governments. Generally, people refrain from drawing attention to the choices made in this respect, and instead allow the Fund to

come under attack and describe its activities as inimical to the least favored
segments of the population.

A question that may be raised in this connection is whether the Fund
should exert pressure in the determination of government priorities and
even make the granting of its assistance contingent on measures that
would better protect the most disadvantaged population groups. An
international institution such as the Fund cannot take upon itself the role
of dictating social and political objectives to sovereign governments . . .
[my emphasis].[9]

This, politely put, is rubbish. As I have argued elsewhere with regard
to the World Bank, which makes exactly the same sort of claim,[10] the
IMF *could* have an enormous influence on the economic (which is to
say, political) choices of its heavily indebted clients if it chose to do so,
for the simple reason that money talks. If the Fund believed, which it
patently does not, that economic growth can also result from greater
social equality, access to education, health care and other basic services,
fairer income distribution, etc., it could perfectly well make such
objectives part of its programmes. On the contrary, exactly those
countries that have most insisted on maintaining social objectives (for
example, Tanzania and Jamaica under the People's National Party)
have had the greatest difficulties in coming to terms with the IMF.

While it's quite true that the Fund is not the only guilty party in this
respect – there are too many truly awful, undemocratic governments
around for that – it is also true that it has *chosen*, as a matter of policy, to
disregard social equality as a criterion for its programmes, much less as
an objective that could be imposed upon governments. Such governments thus may get away with non-metaphorical murder and then place
the blame on the IMF, which is a convenient, but also willing,
scapegoat.

Another former managing director of the Fund, Johannes Witteveen,
stated quite baldly in 1978, 'The Fund avoids taking a view on the
appropriate distribution of the burden of adjustment as between various
sectors of society.'[11] Larosière, cited above, follows in his timorous
footsteps. One study of IMF loan conditions counted 196 objectives of
Fund programmes between 1964 and 1979, among which the aim to
'protect poor against possible adverse effects of programme' occurs
exactly once.[12]

This hypocritical, hands-off attitude is attracting flak, even from
moderate critics like Tony Killick, author of the just mentioned study.
In another context Killick inquires, in tones of sweet reason:

Is it not unwise for the Fund management to refuse as a matter of policy to consider such repercussions [on income distribution] when designing and calculating their programmes? . . . No doubt this is primarily a matter for governments but that is true of all aspects of national policy. Fund missions provide policy advice on the balance-of-payments price stabilization, and growth aspects of its programmes; on what principle can it decline to do so for the distribution results?[13]

There are signs that the Fund may at last have recognized that it cannot entirely skirt such questions – but then again, perhaps it can. A paper prepared for the internal use of the IMF's Executive Board and department heads notes, 'The official Fund view that distributional policies are entirely a sovereign issue . . . has the practical advantage of circumventing a potentially contentious issue.'[14] The (anonymous) author, however, suggests an alternative:

If the Fund were to attempt to specify the specific functional expenditures with a view to improving internal income distributions, the following might be considered:

a. *Focusing educational outlays on basic skills and vocational training;*
b. *Focusing health outlays on the provision of basic health services and away from the doctor–hospital environment;*
c. *Limiting defense expenditure;*
d. *Limiting grandiose public works and 'prestige' projects;*
e. *Advocating much stricter budgetary controls by the Ministry of Finance over spending ministries.*[15]

This would be a great programme for starters. The key word, of course, is at the beginning: 'If'. There are no outward signs that the Fund *wants* to 'improve internal income distributions', or that it has attempted any practical measures in such a direction. An internal memo is not a policy.

THE POLITICS OF THE IMF – INTERNATIONAL MINISTRY OF FINANCE

Those who believe that the Fund is, or ought to be, 'non-political' should also scrutinize its curious and unfailing identity of views with those of its most powerful members, particularly the United States. Some of the countries whose governments contracted the highest debts were/are also the most repressive: Brazil and Argentina under military rule, the Philippines under Marcos, Indonesia, Chile, etc. They are also countries in which the United States takes a keen strategic interest. Was the Fund acting frivolously when it made a sizeable loan to the Somoza regime only weeks before the Sandinista victory in 1979? Or was it gently but firmly encouraged to do so? As the then Treasury Secretary Donald Regan put it, 'The IMF is essentially a non-political institution . . . But this does not mean that United States' political and security interests are not served by the IMF.'[16]

On the principle of paying pipers and calling tunes, it is legitimate to assume that an international institution like the IMF will tend to serve the interests of its richer members first. Voting power in the Fund is proportional to country quotas (the amount each country is assessed when it becomes a member, which is relative to its wealth), but at the Fund a special rule (the '85 per cent rule') grants the US *de facto* veto power on all the most important policy issues.[17]

As a highly experienced Central American economist, formerly with the Inter-American Development Bank, remarks, 'It is hypocritical to assert that the IMF devises austerity programmes *by itself*, even though it is the executing agent. In fact, it is governed by the Group of Ten, the top OECD countries whose central bank governors and/or finance ministers meet regularly in Basle at the Bank for International Settlements. It's the G-10's thinking that determines policy at the IMF.'[18]

The G-10 is careful that the IMF remain an instrument helping it to manage the world system. Although the Fund did at one time come to the aid of both the UK and Italy, in recent history it has been concerned exclusively with debtors in the Third World. These debtors are not, by a long shot, the only possible sources of financial destabilization. Potentially the US debt, including corporate and private (household) debt of $2.6 and $1.8 trillion respectively, is far more alarming.

If the IMF were consistent, it would listen to people like Felix Rohatyn, the highly respected financier who saved New York City from bankruptcy. He notes:

The continuing deficit requires the [US] government to borrow between $180 and $240 billion each year . . . The situation of the US too closely resembles that of . . . Argentina, Brazil and Mexico between 1975–82.

Rohatyn also warns:

The [US] government's borrowing requirements, a major factor in maintaining interest rates at very high levels, increase the risk to our banking system of large-scale failure by Third World countries to pay their debts. We are purchasing short-term prosperity by starving the rest of the world of badly needed capital and destabilizing the international monetary system. Since we live in a world market whether we like it or not, we cannot continue much longer.[19]

Although the IMF is unlikely ever to say so, it is clear that the *United States*, not the LDCs, is the greatest present threat to international financial stability. The net amount that Latin America remitted to its Northern creditors between 1982 and 1986 ($130 billion) exceeded all the net financing these countries received during the preceding eight years.[20] The Fund does not seem to appreciate that this kind of financing of the rich by the poor also poses a grave threat to the system of which it pretends to be a pillar.

Nor does the Fund appear to recognize that poor countries (and even more the poor people who end up paying the debts) have no power whatever over several important factors affecting their balance of payments. Among these factors are *international inflation*, which boosts the prices of imported manufactures, services, oil and food, *high interest rates* and *weak export prices*. When one asks, as I did at Fund headquarters in Washington, how it is possible to encourage *all* countries at once to pursue policies favouring exports, the reply is that the Fund was created 'to increase world trade', so 'the more goods on the market the better'.[21]

But who will pay for these goods? The Fund seems mindless in its pushing of the *same* policies on everyone but finds justification in its claim that countries are 'free' to change the composition of their exports. IMF officials cited to me the so-called NICs (newly industrializing countries of Southeast Asia) as good examples of countries 'adapting'. This is wishful thinking on a par with the song in *My Fair Lady*, 'Why can't a woman be more like a man?' IMF economists seem to believe that Latin America and Africa could be more like Taiwan and South Korea if they would just put their minds to it. But where are Latin America and Africa to find enough capital to diversify, especially now that they have to pay back such a huge proportion of their earnings in debt service? And even if they could scrape together the capital, to whom would they then export?

The Fund lives in a never-never-land of perfect competition and perfect trading opportunities, where dwell no monopolies, no transnational corporations with captive markets, no protectionism, no powerful nations getting their own first. (I was even told by Fund officials that there is 'no evidence of a secular decline in commodities' prices' – a statement belied by the IMF's own statistics.) Even the second Brandt Report, although it advocates an expanded role for the IMF, asks that the Fund 'avoid advocating policies for a number of countries which, when carried out by all of them together, will reduce world income and employment at a time when expansion is needed'.[22]

One must recognize that, *on its own terms*, the IMF is, temporarily, 'successful'. The trade deficit of non-oil-exporting countries was, for example, reduced from $110 billion in 1981 to $56 million in 1984. But the patient has gone into a deep coma as a result of the cure. Economies are everywhere contracting, employment opportunities shrinking; investment is next to nil, growth a dim hope.

The rich are also feeling the backlash of massive deflation in the poor countries. US exports to Latin America fell by 42 per cent between 1982 and 1984. Hundreds of thousands of US workers have lost their jobs because an indebted South America has curbed imports.[23] Faced, however, with a choice between banks and workers, we know that the Reagan administration will take the banks any day. The Northern establishment has proven itself immune to moral suasion and human suffering; it will act to change present Fund policy only if it feels its own interests are at stake.

The ultimate threat to those interests may be the political one as discontent rises and people feel they have nothing left to lose. In the South too many governments are using IMF programmes as a convenient excuse for more severe repression, for breaking the backs of trade unions, driving down wages and bringing their own people under greater control.

Because the pivotal role of the Fund in managing the debt crisis is part of the global power struggle, real change will come about only through altering the present balance of forces. If the IMF is to reflect the needs of *all* its members for an equitable world financial system as well as a concern for the basic needs of *all* citizens, including the poorest, it will be because of political action. Until this happens, IMF will also stand for 'International Ministry of Finance'.

4.

CONDEMNED TO DEBT?: THE TRADE TRAP AND THE DANGERS OF DEFAULT

Just as a debtor country, in order to make a foreign debt payment, must sell to foreigners more goods and services than it buys from foreigners, so a creditor nation, in order to receive a completed debt payment, must be prepared to buy from foreigners more goods and services than it sells to them . . . The degree to which such a creditor country accepts an import surplus measures its willingness to receive debt payments . . . One thing is certain – a country which is unwilling to receive payments cannot be paid.

Harold G. Moulton and Leo Pasvolsky, War Debts and World Prosperity, *The Brookings Institution, Washington, D C, 1932, pp. 16 and 402*

These [indebted] countries must be able to sell their goods abroad to service their debts. If their access to industrialized countries' markets is impaired through protectionism, the developed world will be condemning the indebted nations to perpetual financial crisis.

William E. Brock, U S Trade Representative, Chairman of the Cabinet-level Trade Policy Committee, 'Trade and Debt: the Vital Linkage', Foreign Affairs, *Vol. 62, No. 5, Summer 1984*

The creditor countries, the IMF and the banks pretend to want their money back, with interest, from the Third World – but do they really? If so, it is strange and contradictory that together they should practically ensure the debtors' inability to pay. Unless there is a secret document, stashed somewhere in the vaults of subterranean Washington, ordaining that the debtors must be bled dry, recolonized, reduced to bondage and virtual penal servitude, we need to explain the contradictions exhibited by the major actors in the North.

As need hardly be pointed out, it is hard to pay back money when one hasn't any. Chapter 1 explained why many debt-financed projects aren't bringing in revenues – the money has been squandered on current consumption or spent on sterile pursuits or has ended up in Northern banks. The money must none the less be repaid. This leaves trade. As Moulton and Pasvolsky knew in 1932, if creditors want their loans paid off, debtor nations must be allowed to earn their international keep. Now, as then, countries must not be prevented from exporting and from earning a fair price for their goods.

Without earnings from trade, one can continue to borrow new money only in order to service old loans. 'Rescheduling' is the polite name for this process. It is widespread in spite of the banks' reluctance to keep on lending: there were 144 reschedulings of official debt alone between 1975 and 1985. A strategy that serves only to push debt further and further into the future is unlikely to succeed for ever.

Debtor nations are *not* earning a fair price for their goods, and they *are* being prevented from exporting. The world economy is enfeebled as a result: the debtors' only recourse is to cut imports drastically in a desperate attempt to create a trade surplus that will allow them to pay back the banks. Once they've cut the fat, they start depleting muscle and bone. Agriculture and industry must forgo vital needs like fertilizer, spare parts and machinery. Debtor nations must also deprive their people: they can no longer afford basic drugs or foodstuffs, much less books. The policy – for it does seem to be a policy – of *preventing* countries from repaying their debts or purchasing basic necessities has pernicious consequences for the North as well as for the South.

OF GLUTS AND GLUTTONS

Whenever the hit squads of the IMF arrive to bring an erring member back into line, they scarcely disembark from the plane before insisting that the country increase its exports. As we saw in the preceding chapter, this policy is an article of faith at the Fund. Such prescriptions might theoretically be good medicine for country x or y, taken separately, if they alone could supply cocoa or cotton or computer circuits. The IMF now, however, has over forty countries under surveillance (those that have accepted adjustment packages), and there are other large debtor countries, like Brazil and Nigeria, practising Fund doctrine while refusing formal Fund guidance. For some forty indebted countries, then, the word from Washington is export or perish.

This is all very well except for a few minor points. One is that plenty of other countries, indebted or not, First World or Third, are also trying to get rid of their merchandise on world markets. As the debtors boost exports and slash imports they can't help becoming poor customers, necessarily depressing Northern export industries. As the entire indebted South virtually drops off the map as far as imports go, the concept of 'world' markets begins to translate as 'solvent, Northern-hemisphere, capitalist-economy-country markets'. The Soviet bloc is of little help, accounting for less than 10 per cent of world trade outside its own borders. Northern markets may be rich, but there are limits.

Compounding the problem is the limited range of goods that the debtors can offer, which pits one against another. African coffee producers compete not only against other Africans but against Latin Americans as well. The least developed economies are dependent on one, two or three agricultural or mineral raw materials, and it is folly to tell them to diversify in their present capital-starved condition. Slightly more sophisticated debtor economies compete in textiles, garments, small electronics and the like, but they too are increasing in number. Some agricultural exports from heavily indebted countries face cut-throat, usually subsidized, competition from well-organized OECD nations – for example, Brazilian soybeans compete with American ones; Argentine wheat faces the US, Canada, Australia and the EEC.

Third World commodities are further undermined by substitution. Every time the industrial countries think that the price of some raw material is out of line, they introduce a substitute that they can produce without recourse to outside suppliers. Sugar is a flagrant case: ever since the one-off boom in sugar prices in 1974, the heavy-user industries (such as soft drinks) have been diversifying into high-fructose corn syrup or sweeteners engineered with bio-technology. Many other agricultural products are threatened by substitutes as well – rubber, jute, cotton, timber, even coffee or cocoa.[1] As for non-agricultural raw materials, more efficient Western industries are using fewer mined metals, employing more synthetics and wasting less of the metals that they do use. Glass fibre as a substitute for copper wire in the telecommunications industry is one example.

When Third World countries struggle to sell a limited range of goods in the face of shrinking demand, over-supply and plunging prices are the predictable results. 'Glut' is possibly the ugliest word in the English language. If you look it up, you'll find its root means 'to swallow', but when applied to markets it means just the opposite. Markets, unlike gluttons, simply cannot swallow unlimited quantities of foods or textiles or transistors.

Is the IMF's insistence on the same export-led strategy for all as mindless as it appears? The Fund defends itself by proclaiming its opposition to protectionism as well. If trade were really free, says the IMF, all would be well. No doubt. If we had some ham, we could have some ham and eggs if we had some eggs. Being 'against' trade restrictions is certainly a principled moral and intellectual stance. However, the Fund does not apply the kind of pressure on the restricters that it routinely applies to its indebted pupils.

The relevant issue is not what the Fund is for or against but who benefits and who loses from present Fund doctrine *as applied*, not as it appears in sacred neo-classical economic writ. IMF policy is not mind-less when one considers that (1) the banks *are*, on the whole, being paid back (although it is not clear how much longer this repayment can con-tinue), and (2) the countries that run the IMF and the rest of the inter-national financial system have, so far, reaped a bonanza from the glut.

The size of the bonanza is estimated by the *Economist* at \$65 billion for the year 1985. Sixty-five billion dollars is the size of the 'poor man's gift' to the rich as measured in disastrously low commodity prices – an estimate arrived at *before* the precipitous drop in oil prices. Corpora-tions that process Third World raw materials benefited from a 10 per cent drop in the cost of agricultural raw materials and a 15 per cent drop in metals prices between 1984 and 1985.*[2] Thailand, for instance, followed the IMF's advice and increased its rubber exports by 31 per cent in the first half of 1985 as compared with the same period in 1984. What did it receive for its pains? An 8 per cent *drop* in rubber revenues (from \$262 to \$242 million).

International commodity agreements, the great white hope of the 1970s, are dead as dinosaurs. Intended to stabilize the prices of raw materials, the few that were actually signed fell victim to the pressures of market forces to which IMF policies have prodigiously contributed. The

---

* These percentages are calculated in Special Drawing Rights, the IMF five-currency basket that avoids the built-in mistakes of valuing commodities in sharply fluctuating dollars alone.

United Nations Conference on Trade and Development (UNCTAD) vainly hoped that the Integrated Programme for Commodities (IPC) would stabilize prices for eighteen key raw materials from which roughly 60 per cent of Third World export income derives.

After the IPC launch at the UNCTAD Nairobi meeting in 1976 there ensued dozens of international meetings and thousands of hours of negotiations. The very fact that the rich consumer countries even participated initially in what has been called 'the sorry history of the IPC' partly 'reflected fears about the possible economic and political consequences of not doing so . . . two years after the OPEC oil shock . . . [when] other raw-material producers might consider launching their own cartels, perhaps with OPEC's assistance', explains Alan Spence, writing in the *Banker*. Such fears are now outdated. The West has thus *'not needed to accommodate Third World demands* for commodity agreements,' concludes Spence (my emphasis).[3]

Instead of giving their all to the fruitless IPC process, Third World countries would have been better off banking what they spent on it with, say, Citicorp at 10 or 12 per cent. They could have saved the money committed to travel, hotels, vehicles and sundries, devoted the people-hours put into preparing position papers and haggling in negotiations to less spurious projects; and simply waited until the North put some serious proposals on the table. Had the South shown this kind of healthy scepticism, it would certainly have smaller debts and, arguably, higher commodity prices today. In a convoluted way, its own borrowings, followed by its own desperate attempts to export and the resulting gluts, have given the West such a strong hand that it need no longer 'accommodate Third World demands'. The IMF strategy contributed to the windfall showered on Western industries in the form of rock-bottom prices for basic supplies and to the consequent weakening of the South's hand. This is not a conspiracy (it may not even have been wilful), but it has been mightily beneficial to some.

Today commodity prices are going, going, gone. The IMF, which does keep good track of these matters, measures the purchasing power of a basket of thirty primary commodities, excluding gold and oil, in terms of the manufactured goods that they can buy. Starting from 100 in 1957, the IMF index has risen above that index only twice, in 1973 and 1974. Ever since, though there have been peaks and valleys, the trend has been downwards. By 1985 the index had plummeted to the lowest level ever recorded – a dismal 66.[4]

In spite of the Fund's best efforts to make everybody trade, the General Agreement on Tariffs and Trade (GATT) headquarters reported that after a small surge in 1984 world trade in 1985 slowed dramatically. GATT says that the decline 'signals that the world economy is in danger of slipping back into the anaemic performance of the post-1973 period'.[5]

Experts have a ready answer for the LDCs' commodity problems – for example: 'The implication for producers and exporters is that they will have to rely on cost-cutting and better management to widen their thin profit margins, rather than on more lucrative prices or sustained increases in Western demand.'[6] That may sound like good advice, but what exactly does 'cost-cutting and better management' imply in the context of poor exporting countries, if not *reducing the cost of labour*? Work itself – which is to say workers – is virtually the only element the exporters control, precisely because it is mostly *raw* materials that are at stake. If countries are to try to pay debts through commodity sales at present prices, the only option is that human labour be pushed harder and paid less.

BETTING ON BLOODLETTING: THE PROTECTIONIST TEMPTATION

It's clear that the Third World can't pay – and yet it does! For Latin America alone, new capital inflow (both aid and investment) came to under $38 billion between 1982 and 1985, while it paid back $144 billion in debt service. Net transfer from poor to rich: $106 billion.[7] In 1985 Latin America's per capita product was 9 per cent lower than in 1980 and no better than in 1977. Unemployment and poverty spread inexorably, overtaking large segments of the middle class. Huge cuts in imports mean that productive capacity is eroded, impairing tomorrow's exports. Commodity prices show no signs of improvement.

The pertinent questions are, then, how can this remittance process possibly continue, and why doesn't it stop? The trade surpluses that allow countries to keep on paying have been achieved at tremendous cost. Imports have been slashed and government spending has been severely curtailed. Pounds of flesh have been exacted and blood shed. My own suggestions for 'creative reimbursement' will be found in the final chapter. They are very different in spirit from present practice, and I hope that future political pressure may promote their adoption. Realistically, however, we must examine carefully the system that obtains today and that will dominate tomorrow unless a shift in the present balance of forces takes place. This is why the issue of *protectionism* is so important.

Never would I have expected to come down on the side of Reagan Republicans* or of Jacques de Larosière, former managing director of the IMF. None the less, on the trade question I believe they're right – *always assuming* that political alternatives to trade earnings cannot be pushed through as a means of solving the debt crisis. Without even using the justice argument – massive transfers from South to North are simply *wrong* – the North has to recognize that trade surpluses eked out by the South under present conditions cannot go on for ever.

Every recession in this century has provoked a ritual demand: 'Save us from foreign competition.' It finds supporters among broad segments of the population in industrialized countries, especially those dependent on weak and declining industries. Politicians in democratic societies have to be sensitive to such special pleading. The situation today is beginning to approach that of the 1930s, when 'beggar-thy-neighbour' policies reigned and each country tried to undercut every other one. These desperate trade wars eventually led to disaster, including real war and Fascism; the lessons of history have not, however, prevented the adoption today of a great many *ad hoc* protectionist measures by a great many countries.

What with quotas, 'voluntary' restraints, tougher non-tariff barriers and subsidies to ailing industries, Larosière estimated that 'in 1983, products subject to restriction accounted for about 30 per cent of total consumption of manufactured goods in the United States and the European Community – up from 20 per cent in 1980.'[8] If industrialized countries do not act to dismantle barriers, the debtors cannot possibly earn a big enough surplus to pay back the banks, much less buy anything from the North.

Refusing protectionism is in the interest of the creditors as well, whatever the short-term effects on some industries may be. As William Brock points out, developed-country exports to the Third World were 23 per cent of their total exports in 1973, rising to 28 per cent in 1980. By 1983 the US depended on developing countries to buy fully 40 per cent of its exports – more than Europe or Japan. Export industries in the US are growing fastest and account for four out of every five *new* jobs created in manufacturing.

When the debt crisis hit Mexico in 1982, Brock explains, the effect *on the United States* was immediate and devastating: between the end of

* Reagan administration behaviour, however, speaks louder than its anti-protectionist rhetoric. See its actions with regard to Brazilian computers and to the Generalized System of Preferences below.

1981 and the end of 1982 US exports to Mexico dropped by $10 billion. Every billion dollars in exports sustains 24,000 jobs, so the Mexican crisis alone cost the US 240,000 jobs in just one year.[9] In 1980 the United States had a manufacturing trade *surplus* of $12 billion, by 1984 a *deficit* of $88 billion. Applying Brock's figures to this $100 billion gap, it represents a loss of close to 2.5 million jobs.

Spectacular growth in US farm exports resulted from opening up Third World markets. But compression of agricultural exports, down from a peak of nearly $44 billion in 1980–81 to $28 billion in 1985–6, has hit US farmers hard and has contributed to the epidemic of farm foreclosures. True, lower prices were responsible for part of the drop, but export *volume* also fell by 25 per cent in the first five years of the 1980s.[10] Even if prices for US food exports had remained at the relatively high levels of 1980–81, the volume sold in 1985–6 would still have brought in $10 billion less than in the peak year. As it was, farmers lost nearly $16 billion compared with 1980. That's a lot of missed farm revenue. What proportion of this can we attribute to the Third World's debt burden?

Latin America as a whole was buying $6 billion worth of US farm products in 1980 and 1981. The best customers were Mexico, Brazil and Venezuela, with Peru and Chile as important runners-up. The year of reckoning came in 1982, when US agricultural sales to South America declined by 31 per cent. Mexico's purchases fell by fully 52 per cent, Brazil's and Venezuela's by 25 per cent, Peru's by 40 per cent, all in a single year.

Was this just a fluke, explained by exceptionally good harvests in the region? Unfortunately for US farmers, no. Although farm sales to Latin America did improve slightly in 1983 and 1984, the downward slide continued. The decline one can measure between 1981 (the bonanza year before the debt crisis) and 1985 looks just as grim as the one between 1981 and 1982. In 1985 Latin American imports of US farm products as a whole were still 31 per cent below the record levels of 1981. Using 1981 as a base, Mexico's were down 38 per cent, Brazil's were down 26 per cent, while Chile's and Peru's dropped by fully 77 per cent and 79 per cent in a five-year period![11] Without growth in Latin American economies – impossible so long as they must cope with debt service – slashes in farm imports from the US must be seen as a permanent feature.

If asked which were more important to American farmers, sales to the Soviet Union or to Latin America, most people would reply, offhand, those to the USSR. They would be dead wrong. In 1981 South America imported over three and a half times as many farm products as the USSR ($6.2 billion *v.* $1.7 billion). Even in 1985, when belt-tightening had already reduced southern-hemisphere imports and the Soviets had a poor harvest, the USSR bought 'only' $2.5 billion worth of food compared to Latin America's $4.2 billion.

Indebted countries besides those in Latin America have felt the pinch and had an impact on American farmers too. Since 1981 US farm exports to the Philippines have dropped 12 per cent, those to North Africa by a quarter and to Nigeria by a third. Debt-enforced cutbacks by all these customers is bad news in the corn and wheat belts.

As a study for the Joint Economic Committee of the US Congress shows, American farmers are made to suffer from the foreign-debt crisis in still another way. Debtors like Argentina and Brazil – large agricultural producers in their own right – must export or perish. Consequently, they increase their plantings, and 'this additional production and competition cuts into US sales to non-debtor nations and places downward pressure on virtually all major commodity prices. Falling commodity prices, in turn, make it more difficult for US farmers to continue servicing their debt and push many of them into bankruptcy.'[12]

In spite of all the evidence that protectionism is deeply harmful to *creditor* nations, some 400 trade Bills were introduced in the US Congress in 1985 alone. All were aimed at preventing imports from specific countries and at protecting specific industries. Congress seems to believe that other people's export subsidies and barriers to US goods are the main reason for the soaring US trade deficit. It's more complex than that.

A too strong dollar makes US goods more expensive abroad and contributes heavily to trade deficits. But so does Third World debt itself. 'The Latin American debt crisis has all but shut down a market for US exports that was once almost as large as Europe's,' says Silvia Nasar, writing in *Fortune*. The US is also addicted to imports. In 1980 fewer than 15 per cent of manufactured goods sold in the US were imported; in 1985 more than 20 per cent were. When people have grown accustomed to foreign products, Nasar says, tariffs levied against specific countries don't eliminate imports – they just shuffle them around.[13]

What happens when the US tries to shut other countries out of its market by abruptly slapping tariffs on their exports? Since the foreign exporters can't compensate for the new barrier with, say, a 25 per cent cut in their margins, they raise prices. If US consumers still need or want these foreign goods, they have to pay that much extra. Protectionism also gives domestic industries a *licence to raise prices* – the normal response when competition is eliminated. *Protectionism is therefore inflationary* because people must pay more for protected goods produced in their own countries as well as for imported ones. The *Fortune* article, citing a study by the Federal Reserve Bank of Cleveland, claims that that 90 per cent of any revenues raised by the US through protectionist policies would come straight out of US pockets.

GO TO BLAZES? WHY NOT DEFAULT?

Given all the obstacles set in their paths, why don't Third World countries simply refuse to pay – tell the banks and the creditor governments where to get off, so to speak? Such behaviour has been a constant of international relations for about five hundred years, so why not today? Some leaders, like Peru's President Alan García, have announced they will limit their payments to a specific proportion of export revenues – 10 per cent in the case of Peru. But this is not the same thing as refusing to pay altogether. In the 1840s the United States itself defaulted on loans owed to European creditors, and the world did not come to an end. *All* the indebted Latin American countries defaulted in the 1920s and 1930s. As one scholar has noted, 'Borrowing and default follow each other with almost perfect regularity. When payment is resumed, the past is easily forgotten and a new borrowing orgy ensues. This process started at the beginning of the past century and has continued down to the present day. It has taught us nothing.'[14] This was written in . . . 1933. Today, however, the screws are being tightened on the Third World, and some officials do not hesitate to paint a picture of the grim consequences a default would have for countries that repudiate their debts. Consider the words of R. T. MacNamar, then Deputy Secretary of the Treasury, in a speech before the International Forum of the US Chamber of Commerce:

A repudiation takes place when a borrower unilaterally renounces responsibility for some or all of his debt obligations. Under such circumstances, the foreign assets of a country that repudiated its debt would be attached by creditors throughout the world; its exports seized by creditors at each dock where they landed; its national airlines unable to operate; and its sources of desperately needed capital goods and spare parts virtually eliminated. In many countries, even food imports would be curtailed. Hardly a pleasant scenario.[15]

Indeed not, as Paul Fabra, chief economic columnist of *Le Monde*, confirms. He reports on a conversation with an American banker, described as a 'sensitive and intelligent man', who told him, 'If any Latin American country repudiates its debts with us, we have the legal machinery all ready to go. It would be lightning-fast: we would seize all the country's assets on land, on sea and in the air. We would block all the bank accounts of its citizens; not a single one of its ships could dock or a single plane land anywhere outside that country's borders without being immediately sequestered.'[16]

Argentina was a test case for the bankers, the one they most feared after Mexico. Here was a nation owing $50 billion, more likely than others to default because it is self-sufficient in food and energy. Argentina nearly refused to swallow the IMF's medicine in 1984 until, as *Fortune* puts it, '[The bankers] showed how much pressure can be brought to keep a country from becoming an outcast of the international financial community.' When Argentina tried to stop paying interest, 'it found itself virtually isolated.' It was not only the US bankers who applied coercion: 'Latin American finance ministers, economists from the IMF and commercial banks, and officials from major industrialized countries dropped by to remind the government of the consequences of defying the lenders.'[17]

Mr McNamar again assumed the role of US ogre-in-chief. *Fortune* reports that the US Treasury was 'persuasive': it compiled a list of items that would become 'scarce' in the debtor countries should they default. McNamar 'emphasizes that the list did not single out Argentina. But he says it raised such interesting questions as: "Have you ever contemplated what would happen to the president of a country if the government couldn't get insulin for its diabetics?"'

How, then, could these same Latin American countries repudiate debt with such apparent nonchalance in the 1920s and 1930s? In those days most of their debts were in the form of government bonds, held by private individual investors. In the Thirties the debtor governments defaulted (i.e. declared their bonds worthless), then haggled with a committee representing the bondholders. The latter never came out on top. Today, as a Citibank vice-president explains, 'They don't have a weak committee of individuals across the table, but a powerful group made up of the biggest banks in the world. Any default and the whole banking system would be against them. They would get no credit at all, not even short-term.'[18] A sobering prospect. Mr McNamar, on the other hand, told his US Chamber of Commerce audience that a moratorium, as opposed to a repudiation, is OK in so far as the borrower announces his willingness to repay as soon as he can. Such standstills harm the credit rating of borrowers but do not bring down on their heads the dire consequences described above.

Anatole Kaletsky has undertaken the most thorough examination to date of the costs of default in his booklet of that title.[19] Kaletsky, a correspondent for the *Financial Times*, looks at the problem from the legal, economic and political standpoints: he is worried. He labels today's apparent orderly repayment of debts as a 'deceptive calm', encouraged by the (temporary) boom of the US economy and 'the willingness of debtor governments to cut their nations' living standards farther and faster than even the most sanguine creditor had dared to hope'.

At least this makes clear what is hoped! But can such cuts continue? Countries have been reimbursing only by dint of enormous sacrifices and cannot maintain trade surpluses for ever without renouncing growth in their economies for the next century or two. Kaletsky thinks a solution to the debt crisis is neither black nor white – repayment in full or repudiation. Either would place unacceptable strains on the world economy. He opts for a conciliatory shade of grey and hopes that both debtors and creditors can be lured towards an in-between terrain where realism will prevail and some losses be accepted in order to safeguard the financial system as a whole.

His analysis is perceptive and persuasive: if creditors have the sense to listen – and there are signs that they may – they at least will be making a good bargain. Kaletsky does not dwell on basic injustices in the present system, nor is he interested in encouraging the alternative development models and greater popular control that an imaginative handling of the debt crisis might bring about. In fact, he recommends a *higher* degree of management of debtors' economies by the IMF and the World Bank as the price to pay for relief on the debt front. But because the Kaletsky scenario may be the best we can hope for in the present political context, it is worth looking at carefully. He has a strategist's grasp of the issues involved.

Outright, defiant, confrontational defaults are in no one's interest, he contends. A creditor whose policies provoked them would be cutting off his nose to spite his face. None the less, something will soon have to give or the debtors' temptation to default, singly or collectively, may become irresistible. He sees a place for what he calls 'conciliatory defaults' and, since he believes this is the way the world is moving, begs the creditor community to prepare contingency plans for them.

Whatever happens, the illusion that all is going smoothly must be preserved. Banks of all sizes, and especially governments, must be prepared to orchestrate the necessary transitions that conciliatory (that is, masked) default will necessarily entail. The US government, through its Comptroller of the Currency, has already declared that it will not allow the top eleven US banks to fail, and the federal rescue of Continental Illinois bears this out.[20]

However, even if the mega-banks did collapse in the unlikely event of collective Third World default, Kaletsky says, the rest of the banking system could survive if everyone co-operated. The top eleven, contrary to popular belief, represent only 18 per cent of the whole US banking system (comprising nearly 15,000 commercial banks) in terms of deposits and even less in terms of capital. Everything would hang on the way that a possible crisis was handled. If ordinary American depositors got the idea that banks over-exposed in the Third World were teetering on the brink of insolvency because of a major default, and feared that their demise would endanger the other 14,989 banks (with far less Third World exposure), we would have a 1930s-style panic.

So long as depositors remain confident, not to worry. We live in a world of public relations, and their confidence will depend entirely on the way in which default is *presented*:

The banks are no worse off, in terms of cash flow, if a debtor stops paying interest altogether than if the debtor pays his interest with one hand, only to borrow it back with the other. This is precisely what happened in the five years between 1978 and 1983. The banks received about $125 billion in interest from developing countries and then advanced the very same countries $140 billion in 'new money'.[21]

Outright default by one or several major borrowers could trigger hysteria. 'By contrast, conciliatory default might appear far less disastrous.' Conciliatory default means that you don't pay, but you declare that you have every intention of doing so as soon as you can manage it, or you pay only certain selected creditors, or you make a unilateral decision about lowering your interest rates – all with a pleasant smile and courteous manners.

[A] conciliatory default would be like a slow leak in the banks' balance sheets . . . A repudiation, by contrast, would be like an explosion below decks; it would blow a hole right through the center of the banks' capital structure, which could sink some of the banks before there was even a chance to begin emergency measures.[22]

The creditors' club, particularly the US government and the money-centre banks, would have no interest in unleashing fierce retaliatory measures against defaulters if they too agree to play the conciliation game – this would be small-boy petulance. Kaletsky, however, fears such petulance:

It is at least arguable that the behaviour of the Reagan administration over the first two years of the debt crisis provides evidence that an amicable response to default cannot be taken for granted. At each stage of the debt crisis, the administration's instinctive reaction has been hostility towards the debtors, tempered by pragmatism only after the dangers of adhering to the ideological hard line became overwhelmingly plain.

These lines were written before the Baker Plan, more fully described in Chapter 12, was revealed at the end of 1985. While it means little or nothing in terms of real relief and is now largely dead, it signalled a less emotional, more realistic attitude on the part of the US government. The government has probably realized that provoking default or applying heavy sanctions against a debtor would be a signal to the public that something was horribly amiss and could set off a run on the banks. Retaliation would also further impair the capacity of the errant debtor ever to pay. Creditors must tread a fine line between keeping the debtors at the bargaining table and pushing them out into the cold.

If it were done gradually, the banks – even the most exposed ones – could easily afford to write down or write off a good deal of Third World debt. There are innumerable ways to do this, which we will not detail here except to say that the more farsighted bankers are the ones suggesting them (e.g. Anthony Solomon, former president of the New York Federal Reserve Bank). The Bank of England has reportedly prepared, for internal use, a list of about a hundred schemes for overcoming the debt crisis that have been proposed over the past few years.[23]

The US government does not necessarily have the political backing for a tough stance against a potential defaulter either. Sanctions would not be favoured by transnational corporations with equity investments in a defaulting country – they would be liable to have their property seized by the defaulter as a counter-counter-measure. Trade unions would recognize that no more American products could be sold to a defaulting debtor, causing further erosion of jobs.

If the debtor were smart enough to announce that money saved on interest would be used to import American products, there would be scant likelihood of solidarity between the transnational corporations or their workers with the banks. And who knows if the American public at large could even be counted on, in a crunch, to side with the mega-banks against an impoverished debtor country in economic shambles? There could be a big political constituency for speaking loudly perhaps but carrying a very small stick.

Kaletsky rests his case there. Unfortunately for the creditors, their own protectionist actions can only force the debtors closer and closer to a radical stance. The successful Brazilian computer industry is a case in point. It has grown at 30 per cent a year and managed to outsell the transnational competition for the first time in 1985. The United States claims that it has lost $1.5 billion dollars in sales since 1980, and American Secretary of State George Shultz took the trouble to warn his Brazilian counterpart that this could have 'serious consequences' for US–Brazilian relations. As a follow-up to Shultz's message, the US sent an Under-Secretary of State to Brazil in May 1986 to explain that President Reagan was studying 'trade reprisals' if Brazil insisted on supplying a large segment of its own internal demand for computers instead of letting IBM do it. (IBM used to have half the market.) Brazilian steel, shoes and agricultural products are reportedly on the Americans' hit list.[24] Brazil is therefore expected to find enough dollars both to pay its debt and to buy IBM computers. Heads I win, tails you lose. What should Brazil do? Use its foreign exchange to buy computers that it could perfectly well supply itself? Or make its own computers and lose foreign exchange because it can't sell its steel, shoes and orange juice to the US? This is no choice at all.

Latin American countries have recently made a quite spectacular swing towards democracy even though Chile and Paraguay still blight the southern-hemisphere map. Democratic governments have one great disadvantage: they must try to satisfy their people. If they can't, they are likely to crack down and revert to authoritarian rule. Meanwhile, the United States makes the demented claim that tiny Nicaragua, with 3 million people and an economy in shreds because of the protracted Contra war and other hostile US actions, is a threat to national security. How would the US like it if Mexico, under intolerable pressure from its citizens, became a far more left-wing, or right-wing, anti-American country? Eighty million angry people and a common frontier from California to Texas sounds like a rather more credible threat.

Is this inconceivable? Mexico itself must feel that its northern neighbour has little concern for its problems. It has recently been put on the 'graduates' list of countries to which the US will not extend the General

System of Preferences (GSP) for part of its export production. The GSP, established in 1976, was supposed to help Third World countries export as an aid to their development process. In spite of Reagan's rhetorical attacks on protectionism and his promise to veto Bills that promote it, he has adopted his own brand of protectionism by throttling the GSP. Certain items from certain countries, previously admitted duty-free, will now have to pay tariffs to get into US markets. Copper from Chile, Peru and Zambia – all heavily indebted – is on the list of products no longer eligible for GSP treatment.

US trade representative Clayton K. Yeutter explains, 'As the advanced beneficiary countries become competitive enough in particular products to compete in the US market without GSP benefits, we are graduating their products from the program. These changes reflect the dynamic nature of the US GSP program.'[25] One doubts that these 'advanced beneficiaries' will feel honoured at being thus graduated. Mr Yeutter, and his boss, might do well to remember that other countries, and other peoples, have their own tolerance thresholds and that they can be 'dynamic' too.

POST SCRIPTUM

In April 1987 GATT released provisional figures showing how much the Third World has lost out during these debt-crisis years. While less developed countries held 28 per cent of world trade in 1980, by 1986 their share had dropped to 19 per cent. The developed countries increased their trade share from 63 to 70 per cent during the same period. In 1980 the rich countries bought 29 per cent of their imports from poor ones and 66 per cent from each other. In 1986 they bought only 19 per cent of their imports from Third World countries and 77 per cent from each other. (The Eastern bloc represented 9 per cent of world trade in 1980, 11 per cent in 1986.) World trade volume increased by 18 per cent between 1980 and 1986 but only by 6 per cent in dollar terms. Volume of trade in manufactured goods increased the most: agricultural trade is flat and mining exports well below their 1980 volume. It's still a rich man's world.

PART II: THE PEOPLE AND THE PLANET

The IMF is a relatively recent big-time player on the world scene. Its impact in the 1960s and 1970s in most countries was minimal because they were delighted to do without it and to use money supplied by others without conditions. During those decades the World Bank was the most important single influence on Third World economies, recommending policies that the IMF now enforces in tandem with the Bank.

The debris of these development strategies is strewn across the southern-hemisphere landscape. The strategies have frequently dislocated entire societies, but today the IMF (often with the help of Bank Structural Adjustment Loans) requires their pursuit. Apparently, Keynes's twins are not to be deterred from enforcing their model, and damn the torpedoes.

Part II explores the consequences of the dominant development model and of the resulting debt for people and their environment. I first give pride of place to Africa, partly because so few standard debt sources bother with this poorest of all continents. From the Consortium's viewpoint, this is understandable – Africa's debt is collectively too small to destabilize the world financial system, however intolerable it may be for those who must pay. Then comes Latin America, where societies once relatively prosperous witness the return of massive joblessness, hunger and premature death. More and more people are pushed towards the margins of existence, and the environment fares as poorly as its inhabitants.

Chapter 5, 'Morocco: a Meddlesome Model and a Bitter Harvest', explores the case of a North, as opposed to Black, African country, where the Bank/IMF model was religiously applied. It has led to disastrous consequences, including scores of deaths in what have come to be known as IMF riots.

Chapter 6, 'Debt in Africa: the Black Man's Burden', looks at some East African cases: Zambia,

Kenya and Tanzania, where economic activity is contracting and the human toll increasing daily.

Chapter 7, 'Zaïre: Absolute Zero', lands us at rock-bottom on the debt front. Here are the worst kind of official corruption and theft leading to outright starvation – combined with an apparently unending tolerance for the regime on the part of the Consortium.

Chapter 8, 'Latin America: Debt and Decline', shows that few are left unscathed by the financial crisis. Whatever the nature of the society, a dictatorship like Chile or recently returned to democracy like Brazil and Argentina, the people are the first casualties as jobs and food disappear.

Chapter 9, 'Latin America: Going to Extremes', shows some of the ways in which the debt crisis further polarizes societies: a tiny minority of wealthy people, a huge mass of poor ones and a disappearing middle. Whole countries, like Bolivia, also go to extremes with economies almost entirely beyond the legal pale, while others, like the Dominican Republic, simply gun down their citizens when they dare to protest.

Chapter 10, 'Debt and the Environment: Financing Ecocide', shows how some debt-financed projects have been ecological disasters – now being paid for as natural resources are sold off at bargain-basement prices.

5.
MOROCCO: A MEDDLESOME MODEL AND A BITTER HARVEST

Will the IMF succeed where Marx failed? Riots – which might well one day become revolutions – are more frequently set off in our time by the Fund's austerity programmes, prescribed as a means to pay off debts, than by the 'communist subversion' the West claims to fear. It is both ironic and tragic that crushing debts, with their cortège of destructive social consequences, were inevitable once countries embarked on the very development model enthusiastically promoted by the Fund, the World Bank and the Third World elites with which they deal. It is now clear that debt is a built-in feature of this model.

The standard World Bank/IMF development prescription is outward-looking and therefore cannot satisfy the needs of the local population. Indeed, it is not intended to do so, except indirectly through the prosperity that is supposed to come with trade. It concentrates, rather, on the needs of volatile international markets. Since dozens of countries are practising what the Bank preaches, a good number of them inevitably find themselves in competition. Because the products they can supply fall within a limited range, in order to keep their prices low and attractive to international buyers countries *must also compete to keep workers' salaries severely in check*. For the same reason most peasants, though not necessarily large farmers, will be paid as little as possible for their produce.

As this model takes hold, investment favours the export sector. The part of the economy producing for national needs is simultaneously starved of capital, even though most of the population depends on the local economy for its livelihood. However heavy the burdens laid on workers and peasants to keep the country's prices down, international competition remains cut-throat. Supposedly rich and insatiable international markets, which the Bank/IMF promised would absorb the Third World country's exports, dry up or find shelter behind protectionist barriers. Suddenly nobody wants those T-shirts and trousers, those bales of cotton and crates of oranges or tomatoes. Sometimes decisions made in the North, with absolutely no input from the Third World, may change the latter's situation drastically. For example, when Spain and Portugal – big growers of citrus fruits and off-season vegetables – joined the Common Market, much of North Africa's farm produce for export could no longer jump the hurdles into the E E C.[1]

But while these home truths sink in, a great deal of costly infrastructure has already been purchased with borrowed money, on which interest must be paid. All this machinery and equipment for transportation, electricity, irrigation and what-have-you were supposed to help developing countries produce more, to give them access to outside markets and thus to the foreign-currency earnings that would take care of the debts. But as external markets for the country's goods shrink, the expensive infrastructure gradually becomes redundant and starts to function at a fraction of its real capacity. Meanwhile, thanks to long neglect, the internal market is in no shape to take up the slack – salaries are low and millions of people lack jobs, so there is scant purchasing power to buoy up the economy.

The case of Morocco, a reasonably well-off developing country of North Africa, illustrates how the model works and how it comes to grief. Moroccan economist Najib Akesbi points to the chief consequence: 'The country ends up producing too much of what it doesn't consume, and consuming too much of what it doesn't produce.'[2] The Moroccan example is a sad but graphic illustration of the way in which this style of 'development' generates under-development for the majority. It shows how a country, by following I M F and World Bank instructions, can, in less than twenty years, take a direct route from the export-oriented model to increased unemployment, malnutrition and absolute poverty for a substantial slice of the population – with bloody I M F riots as milestones along the road.

In Morocco, the first of these riots – a clear signal that its outward-looking development model was already bankrupt – occurred in mid-

1981. A sudden jump in the price of basic food staples triggered the popular uprisings, but these increases, though brutal, were the proverbial straw breaking the camel's back: the Moroccan people, like Moroccan camels, had borne more than their share. In an article entitled 'The explosive situation in Casablanca', which appeared just after these riots, Zakya Daoud describes the underlying conditions that led to the rioting.[3]

The population figures tell a good part of the story. Of about 21 million Moroccans altogether, 56 per cent are under 20 and 46 per cent under 15 years old. At least a quarter of the under-15s are in the streets because they have dropped out, or been thrown out, of school. In a city like Casablanca, where the rioting was most severe, there are 300,000 kids between 15 and 20. Two hundred thousand of them have nothing whatever to do, since they lack either a place in school or a job. Even the ones who are at school are mostly destined for disappointment, since only 15 per cent of the annual 100,000-odd candidates for the Baccalauréat (the secondary-school diploma inherited from the French) can expect to leave school with the coveted 'Bac'.

In addition to the unbelievable waste of an educational system that takes its toll on the under-20s, nearly half the 20- to 24-year-olds are also idle. During the 1970s the overflow of unemployed young people was less noticeable because about 400,000 emigrated to work in Europe. Since 1979, however, those gates have been largely barred. According to *official* figures, cited by Daoud, only about a third of the 'active' urban population – defined as able-bodied men between 15 and 64 – is actually employed. In this Moslem country female employment is a small factor; perhaps 80,000 women have salaried work. Two out of every three unemployed men are under 35 – just the age when they are trying, more and more desperately, to raise their own families.

This is the social tinderbox into which the government, mandated by the IMF, dropped the food-price match. Chronically unemployed people, already living hand to mouth, were suddenly asked to pay 40 per cent more for flour and sugar and 50 per cent more for cooking oil. These jumps followed others that had occurred only eight months before: between April 1979 and May 1981 Moroccans suffered price increases of 86 per cent for flour, 97 per cent for sugar, 75 per cent for oil and no less than 100 per cent for milk.

During the same two-year period salaries for those lucky enough to have work rose by 20 per cent (rural workers' daily wage) to a maximum of 29 per cent (urban hourly wage).[4] One should remember that in countries with rampant unemployment, like Morocco, so-called 'minimum' salaries are in fact maxima, which hundreds of thousands do not earn. To hold a job of any kind is already to be part of a privileged class. Devout Moslems, as King Hassan of Morocco would surely claim to be, should not have been surprised at the outbreak of violence: as a companion of the Prophet Mohammed said, 'I am amazed to hear of a hungry man who does not commit a crime.'[5]

The lessons of 1981 were, however, lost on the government. In January 1984 serious riots broke out anew in much of the country when the authorities announced that, following the recommendations of the IMF, food prices were to go up once again. For the disaffected urban population, students and the unemployed, enough was enough. Since 1979 the average cost of the four basic market-basket items (flour, sugar, cooking oil, milk) had gone up by 133 per cent, while wages had improved, at best, by 53 per cent – again only for the favoured few. Massively, they took to the streets.

The government blamed 'outside agitators' for the demonstrations and called out the Army to put them down. It did so, brutally, and when they were over the official body count was twenty-nine dead and 114 wounded. Press reports suggested, however, that at least 100 people had been killed, and some accounts placed the toll as high as 400. King Hassan appeared on television to say that basic food prices would not, after all, be increased. This announcement, plus the repression, brought the country back to 'law and order'.[6]

Law and order cannot, however, solve the country's deeper problems. Morocco, once a North African granary and a major supplier for France, is today reduced to importing over 3 million tons of wheat annually – while its unwanted oranges and tomatoes rot in the fields or on the docks. External debt, contracted to finance the export model, stands at some $16 billion. If the debt had not been rescheduled, the government would have had to devote 47 per cent of all current expenditure just to service it. The IMF austerity programme, in place since 1983, decrees that financial charges are to be paid first. This is what an adjustment programme means for the recipient – all other expenditures must be adjusted with regard to the imperative of reimbursement.

The export-platform model turns out to have been made of rotten planks. How could a country with relatively bountiful resources and adequate land – far from a Third World basket case – get itself into such a mess? Najib Akesbi provides answers to this question.[7]

The story starts in the mid-1960s. Just a few years after its independence from France (1956) Morocco experienced financial difficulties and asked World Bank and IMF experts to help solve them. The experts' recommendations became national development policy. Their basic idea was that Morocco had a comparative advantage in agriculture and should maximize it by modernizing its farming system and orienting it towards export crops like citrus fruit and fresh vegetables. The costs of modernizing would be paid for with export revenues. In practice, modernization mostly meant irrigation (i.e., building dams).

They called it the 'dam policy' – *la politique des barrages* – and it was supposed to lead to 1 million irrigated hectares, or 2.5 million acres, by the year 2000. The modernization schemes drained between a quarter and a third of *all* public investment and two-thirds of all investment in agriculture. Since this costly strategy concentrated improvements on less than 10 per cent of the land, resources left over for the remaining 90 per cent were paltry, even though the livelihood of four-fifths of the rural population depended on the land left undeveloped. The fortunate few with access to irrigation – mostly large landholders – were also able to buy subsidized tractors, fertilizers and Green Revolution seeds at 20 to 35 per cent below real cost. Water itself was sold at such a low price that it was virtually free, while farm credit was reserved almost exclusively for large producers.

The state thus took on the financial burdens of modernization, while large private interests made the profits. What's more, taxes on agriculture, even in the prosperous export sector, were low to non-existent and never brought in more than 1 per cent of state revenues. King Hassan even went so far as to announce, in 1984, that because of the drought there would be *no* taxes on agriculture up to the year 2000.

Since policy explicitly favoured export crops, Morocco voluntarily became a food importer. This seemed a good idea in the 1960s, when world prices were low and stable, and plentiful imports helped to keep down consumer prices for basic staple foods. The country's own hard wheat, the kind that makes good couscous, a delicious national dish, gave way to soft-wheat imports, while native olive oil was largely replaced by soybean oil bought from the U S.

In the early days of the export-oriented model, in the mid-1960s, Morocco was able to finance most of its own agricultural modernization, but soon external financing was called upon to pay for greater and greater chunks of this policy. In the early 1970s the country depended on external credit sources for 23 per cent of the cost of its *politique des barrages* (all projects, not just the dams themselves). By the mid-1970s, as dependency on outsiders for food and for farm inputs grew and the prices of both skyrocketed, the proportion of outside funds needed amounted to *half* the modernization bill. A huge leap between 1980 and 1984 brought the external financial share to 76 per cent – which meant an equally huge increase in the national debt. Debt, which in 1970 was a bearable 18 per cent of GNP, hit 110 per cent of GNP in 1984. Part of the debt explosion was also due to the drastic drop in world market prices for phosphate, one of Morocco's major exports.

The chickens (so to speak) of this policy came home to roost with a vengeance in the 1980s. Although cereals and legumes were still planted on 80 per cent of the land, farmed mostly by smallholders, they had received little or no investment and technical support over the years. Because of stagnant or declining yields on one hand and population growth on the other, per capita production of wheat in 1984 was less than half what it had been in 1955 and even lower than in 1930. Olive oil and legumes suffered similar, though slightly less steep, declines.

The local food situation is hardly encouraging. Morocco, a cereals exporter in the 1950s, today satisfies only a fifth of its own wheat needs. Food imports rose by an average 17 per cent a year between 1970 and 1983 – a stunning 220 per cent. This was not accident but policy. Exports, the object of the government's constant attention, increased also, but at the much slower rate of 8 per cent annually. As a result, neither its markets nor the sources of its food supply are today to be found inside Morocco but are located in the North. Another classic consequence of giving priority to the largest and wealthiest farmers was the impoverishment of small ones and their consequent migration to the cities, where most of them had to get along in the 'informal' economy, a euphemism for no real jobs at all. Of such people, and their children, are food rioters made . . .

How is such a country to pay off $16 billion worth of debt? Since Morocco has no say in the price that its export crops will fetch, nor in the cost of its imported foodstuffs, the only factor that it really controls today is the cost of labour. Debts can be paid only by earning currency on international markets, and the most obvious way to remain competitive when one has a wholly extraverted economy is to keep wages low. Workers, unfortunately, still insist on eating, so one must allow them to acquire at least the basic foodstuffs at prices commensurate with their earnings. If you want to have a stiff wage policy, you have to have a price policy as well, at least for those indispensable items on which the average Moroccan household spends three-quarters of its income.

As a growing population consumes more and more wheat billed in hard-to-earn dollars, more difficult choices have to be made. If the authorities try to pass on to the consumer the real cost of wheat in the form of high-priced flour or bread – the major item in any poor Moroccan's diet – workers will immediately demand higher wages.

Higher wages, in turn, will automatically mean even less ability to compete in already dwindling international markets and a less attractive atmosphere for the transnational manufacturing corporations that Morocco, encouraged by the Bank and the IMF, has done so much to attract. These companies count on low wages and are not amused by strikes and riots.

The only solution is subsidies for staple foods – the state basically taking the heat off foreign and local employers to pay higher wages. In a neat twist, a Third World government choosing such a course is subsidizing not only local and transnational companies but *far richer foreign consumers as well* – those who will buy the Third World country's exports. Subsidized food in lieu of better wages keeps the price of exported goods down, thus providing another example of the law 'Them as has, gets', but on an international scale.

Food subsidies thus keep business costs down and allow the elite, employers, to pursue their affluent lifestyle and the poor to keep their heads above water – barely. The IMF demands that food subsidies be removed in order to reduce public spending but, in doing so, contradicts itself. The Fund is a true believer in the export-oriented model, exactly the one that eventually drives its victims to institute such subsidies. If it really wants a free-market economy, then it should forbid subsidies but at the same time allow higher wages in compensation. Instead it puts a cap on wages (for those lucky enough to have employment) and expects the poor to cut consumption from already painfully low levels. This seems a rather peculiar idea of market truth.

There are plenty of other contradictions in prescribing the 'truth-in-pricing' policy or, as it is called in Morocco, *la vérité des prix*. First of all, food subsidies don't really cost the state that much when one considers the number of people who need them. During the five-year period 1980–85, the government spent an annual average of only 5.3 per cent of its total budget on these subsidies (or, measured another way, an average of just 1.5 per cent of Morocco's GDP). The real scandal is that market truth seems to apply *only to final consumers*. A price, after all, represents the cumulative impact of a whole series of actors – producers, importers, processors, distributors, the state – upon whom the burden of 'truthfulness' should rest just as heavily as on the person who purchases the food in the end.

This is not, to say the least, the case in Morocco. Here Najib Akesbi makes his most devastating points against the way in which the Moroccan state has managed the economy for a minority, against the IMF medicine that is shoved down the throats of consumers, and

consumers alone. Contrary to appearances, 'subsidies' on the final price
of food actually reflect subsidies, and unwarranted premiums, to large
producers and to large, non-competitive private enterprises.

What does the cost or the 'truthful price' of flour mean when one
learns that flour mills sell bran to a handful of large-scale animal raisers
at a government-fixed price 60 per cent *below* the free-market cost? If
you under-value part of the wheat (bran), you have to over-value the
flour the consumer pays for (and consequently to subsidize it, for
reasons already explained). The same thing happens with sugar – a part
of it (pulp residues) is sold well under the true (that is, market) price to
privileged customers.

Many of us have been calling for higher prices to producers in
the Third World for simple reasons of social justice. Akesbi thinks we
must take another, harder, look at this position. In Morocco at least,
producer prices *have* been raised – to the point that they are now way
above world market prices and have in effect made food self-sufficiency
too expensive for the country to contemplate.

Assuming that all farmers have the same costs and that every bushel
receives the same price no matter how many are delivered, the largest
producers will obviously benefit most from a guaranteed price. A small
peasant with little land and low yields can't make a decent living even
with a guaranteed price, but the farmer with 200 hectares (500 acres) will
do supremely well. When landholdings are grossly unequal, when there
are no quotas, when the government's purchase price is the same for all
regardless of quantities, a guaranteed price to producers can only
increase social inequalities.

An aggravating factor is that official cereals agencies generally don't
reach the small farmer. This is as true in Morocco as it is in most of the
rest of Africa. The poor peasant is indebted and cash-starved, so he will
sell to a trader immediately after harvest at whatever price the trader
offers – inevitably well below the 'guaranteed' one. Unless the government can also guarantee efficient and timely collection, the price it
theoretically proposes to the producer has little to do with reality in the
countryside. Not only does the guaranteed producer price reinforce
social inequities but in Morocco at least it hasn't even encouraged higher
cereals production. The large producer who benefits behaves like a
rentier, Akesbi explains. 'The better the price, the less effort he needs to
make to improve yields . . . the pricing policy becomes an incentive for
inefficiency and mediocrity.'

Private agribusiness processors are perhaps getting the biggest share
of the government-baked cake. Much as in the US, food processors in

Morocco are few in number and highly concentrated. As is customary with oligopolies, there is little or no free-market competition. In Morocco food-processing oligopolies have the additional advantage of being wholly isolated from market forces by the state, which *sets their profit margins*. Since these margins are set across the board for each industry, lame ducks and inefficient processors are not weeded out – as the market would have it – but, rather, are encouraged to go on being lame and inefficient, since their profits are guaranteed. Like producers, processors adopt a *rentier* mentality.

Finally, the state takes from consumers with the left hand more than it gives with the right. The other side of the subsidy coin is taxes – and three-quarters of Morocco's tax revenues come from *taxes on consumption*. Practically all of these taxes are paid by ordinary people for ordinary goods and services (only flour is exempt). A mere 5 per cent of the sales-tax revenue is levied on luxury goods. Between 1975 and 1984 taxes on consumers (for all items) came to over seven times the value of subsidies on the five staple foods that receive them (flour, oil, sugar, butter and milk – though milk has now been taken off the subsidized list altogether). The startling conclusion, when all the subsidies and taxes are mixed together in the same pot, is that *consumers are subsidizing the state, not vice versa*!

The IMF claims to act in the name of economic efficiency but travesties its own principles by devising strategies that are not only socially harmful but economically irrational. Targeting consumers to make sacrifices on food in the name of *la vérité des prix* is simply a swindle when there is no *vérité* anywhere else in the food system. Why does the IMF consider only consumer prices distorted when every other component of that price has been determined by non-market forces? If neither the government nor the Fund is willing to take on the real profiteers, it's clear that consumers can only be squeezed further – all in the name of the free market.

And how else, aside from demand reduction (a polite term for less food and greater suffering), does the Fund recommend that Morocco pay off its debts? The IMF wants more of the same: further investment in export production, further integration into world markets – that is, exactly the strategy that has plunged this potentially rich country into its present economic morass. Meanwhile, according to the best-case scenario, the number of the absolute poor has already increased from 7 to 8.7 million since 1980. Over 3 million of them live in cities and many are disaffected young people. One thing is clear: if further riots occur, they cannot be pinned on outside agitators and communist subversion.

6.
DEBT IN AFRICA: THE BLACK MAN'S BURDEN

Africa is on its own. This is the message that came through loud and clear after the United Nations Special Session on Africa in May 1986, which turned out to be little more than a requiem for the continent. Except for those immediately concerned, everyone, having gone through the appropriate motions and mouthed the requisite prayers, can now get back to worrying about more serious matters – like squeezing the continent dry.

Pronounce the words 'hunger' or 'starvation' and 'Africa' in the same breath: you will get a reaction, though perhaps a weary one. Say 'African debt' and you are likely to get a blank stare. Yet debt is now one of the main factors contributing to food insecurity. So long as debt relief is withheld, hunger in Africa can only be compounded. If the continent survives its current crisis, it will be a tribute to the resourcefulness of Africans and to nothing else. They are getting precious little help from outside. Already Africa is transferring more capital abroad in debt-service and other payments than it is receiving in aid and new loans.

African governments, elites and managers have displayed failings without number, but before taking them to task (which some richly deserve) we might also recall that at the time of its independence, less than twenty-five years ago, a country of 5 million people like Zambia boasted all of 100 university graduates. A friend of mine who worked in

Mozambique in the 1970s, just after it had gained independence from Portugal, marvelled that the Ministry of Education could accomplish anything whatsoever, given a grand total of five employees who could read and write. The minister was 23 years old.

The sad truth is that if Africa dropped off the map, international business would scarcely notice. Africa represents a mere 4 per cent of annual world trade,[1] and though it remains a potentially rich continent, those who exploit it can usually find the same resources elsewhere, often with less hassle (e.g. uranium in Australia) and lower political risk (e.g. as caused by apartheid). Naturally, the North sees bits and pieces of Africa as worth safeguarding for future needs, but if Africans count on the tender-heartedness of Northern elites to solve their countries' plight, they risk being not merely disappointed but dead.

Modern Africa has remained dependent on many of the same riches – diamonds, copper, gold, food, beverages, fibres and the like – that drew the colonial powers there in the first place. But drastic changes have occurred since the days when African minerals and agricultural raw materials could command high prices on international markets. Technology has run on apace, while African economies have continued to produce for a world that no longer exists. Telephone and communications equipment has entered the fibre-optic era and is junking its copper-wire installations. Miniaturization of practically everything and more efficient processing reduces demand for metals.[2]

Plastics are more durable than sisal or hemp. Cotton can be purchased from Peru, Egypt, or China – or replaced with man-made fibres. Tropical oils, like peanut oil, may be more expensive and thus less desirable than soya oil from the US or palm oil from Malaysia. Consumers have proven themselves entirely capable of switching from one tropical drink to another – or of abandoning them entirely – if prices go too high. Heightened concern for health has brought sugar into disrepute. And so it goes. Africa is not well placed to adapt to rapidly changing markets.

Objective observers ought to agree by now: tropical agricultural commodities and metal ores are not the ticket to the future. And yet the IMF has never been so dogmatic as it is today in Africa: export or else. Export or you will get no fresh credit. Export what? The same old goods, since nothing else is on hand. Credit for diversification is not forthcoming. This doctrine is now creating perverse effects beyond anything imaginable a few years ago. IMF rigidity may bring ruin to an entire continent, and for years to come.

The largest debtors in Black Africa are Nigeria, the Sudan and the

Ivory Coast. For one reason or another, all are atypical, so here we'll look at three East African countries with differing government philosophies but similar problems, aggravated by their debts. In these former British colonies the IMF, in partnership with the World Bank, places a heavy hand on economic management.

PITY POOR ZAMBIA[3]

Zambia is an extreme case, in one sense at least, because of its subordination to a single export, copper. Such dependency is unwise in any circumstances, and downright catastrophic when copper is less in demand, as is the case today. Fully 90–95 per cent of the country's foreign exchange has traditionally been derived from this single metal. As one observer puts it, 'The bad news is that the price of copper is down. The good news is that Zambia is running out of copper anyway.'[4] This is a sick-joke way of noting that the bottom dropped out of the copper market in 1975. The country's leadership continued, however, to hope for the best and went on importing food and capital goods, while subsidizing social services through borrowing. Everyone, including the Bank and the IMF, not to mention Zambia's own authorities, miscalled copper trends. 'I was in the mining division in 1975,' a former World Bank employee told a reporter, 'and nobody got it right. A lot of decisions were based on [copper] price expectations which turned out not to be true.'[5]

Although responsibility for misjudgement was shared, its costs were not. Zambia alone must pay for everyone's mistakes and can no longer service its debts of over $4 billion when copper sells for a third of what it brought in 1966. This debt may not sound like much money in today's world, but for a small country $4 billion represents $600 owed by each Zambian, with no prospect of ever working its way out of the hole. Zambian GNP per capita, by contrast, is $470. If the country were servicing its debt fully, which it isn't, it would have to devote 195 per cent of export earnings to this purpose alone – one of the highest debt-service ratios of any developing country.[6]

Zambia has obtained several reschedulings of its debts from Western government creditors and from the IMF. Each time it has failed to meet the new agreement's repayment terms. The IMF has now suspended credit, thus turning off the tap on all foreign loans. It has also imposed its usual package of reforms, making life appreciably worse for Zambians, whose incomes had already declined, on average, by 44 per cent since

1974. In late 1985 the price of the staple food, 'mealie meal' (corn meal), suddenly went up 50 per cent, while bread increased by 100 per cent. Zambia is landlocked. When gasoline prices doubled, anything dependent on transport (virtually everything) was also hit, including bus fares (up by 70 per cent). It's no longer even possible to die affordably in Zambia, since the price of a coffin has escalated by 90 per cent.

A *Washington Post* reporter tells the bizarre tale of the elevator. The tallest office building in Lusaka, the capital, is twenty-three storeys high. It has one elevator in working order. Office employees patiently wait their turn to stuff themselves into it. No one bothers to push buttons; they simply shout out their floor numbers. 'As if by magic, the elevator stops at their floors. What they are shouting at . . . is not the elevator, but the elevator operator. They shout because he is standing on top of the elevator car, manipulating a jerry-rigged control device that, with frequent breakdowns, keeps the elevator moving and prevents Zambia's most prestigious building from losing its tenants.'[7] Amusing, perhaps, and surely a sign of resourcefulness. But the makeshift elevator rig is symbolic of how an economy can contract until virtually no economic activity remains possible. For want of horseshoe nails, whole wars are being lost. Zambian industry,

hamstrung by shortages of spare parts and imported raw materials, is currently running at less than 50 per cent capacity. As of [November 1985], only 2,000 of 6,500 tractors in the country were operational; 320 of the national bus company's 555 buses were out of service; the airport [serving Zambia's major tourist attraction, Victoria Falls] was closed because the airport fire-truck had broken down; two and a half million bags of harvested corn had not yet been hauled from the countryside to dry storage, despite the imminent arrival of the rainy season, because of the shortage of trucks, tires, fuel and tarpaulins. At the nation's largest copper mine, only 57 of 190 ore-hauling vehicles were serviceable . . .[8]

A country that *has* no foreign exchange *cannot earn* foreign exchange. Nor can it feed and care for its people for very long or very well. Farmers can't get credit to invest in seeds or fertilizer, and they can't count on sales either. 'Maize sales, after an impressive year in 1980–81 when there were no [IMF] adjustments specifically in place, fell by one-third in the 1981–82 season. The decline was widely ascribed to inadequate rainfall, but was undoubtedly exacerbated by IMF restrictions,' states Bill Rau, an American now working with the development organization Bread for the World who has lived for long periods in Zambia. In late

1981 he saw small farmers journeying great distances in the hope of finding fertilizer at rural depots, only to be turned away for lack of supplies.

A downturn in the rural economy naturally hits the majority of the population. Rau reports that small shops run by local people used to be found throughout the countryside:

Although stocks might have appeared narrow, basic consumer products such as cloth, candles, soap, etc., were readily available . . . Between 1976 and 1981, at least half of all rural shops closed as the distribution system broke down. The squeeze on imports . . . enforced by IMF pressures and devaluation after 1978, effectively cut off many rural areas from consumer supplies. Beyond district towns it is now unusual to find any shops able to meet rural needs. In turn, that means that many rural people must travel to towns for purchases (an expensive and time-consuming process) or pay greatly inflated prices to traders who charge two to five times more than prevailing urban prices for basic commodities. [This] is just one indicator of increasing rural impoverishment.

Again according to Rau:

agricultural extension staff sit by idly during the planting season for they lack vehicles or fuel to visit farmers . . . the rural poor have become poorer during the past decade, a trend accelerated by IMF conditionality.

Rural health centres dependent on imported drugs and equipment 'now turn away the seriously ill for lack of the means to provide treatment'. Urban people are not much better off in this regard:

An American doctor working in Zambia's leading hospital told a reporter it was chronically short of surgical gloves and scalpel blades: most surgery patients bring their own, and non-emergency operations are postponed until they do.[9]

It comes as no surprise that chronic malnutrition is also on the rise, especially among children and pregnant and nursing mothers. The cost of food is a major factor. Even in 1980 (when the cost of maize meal had already gone up by 70 per cent compared with the previous year) a government study noted that low-income urban people would have to spend 80 per cent of their total incomes on food just to ensure a bare minimum diet. Conditions have considerably worsened since then. Two studies indicate that a decade ago children were both taller and heavier than their counterparts of the same age today. This situation may have been accelerated by drought, but drought has not been the basic cause.

Meanwhile, there is still money in Zambia – plenty of it – but its concentration in few hands has never been greater. A Zambian friend of mine who helps to run a church lay-training centre there tells me that her ex-schoolfriends look down on her for being crazy enough to work for a modest salary instead of leading a life of leisure as they do. The moral bankruptcy of the elite contrasts with its financial affluence. 'The big thing in their lives,' she explained to me, 'is to go shopping in South Africa.' (Yes, *South* Africa.) They come back laden with fancy wardrobes, and 'as long as they can drive around in their big cars they are happy.' Such women live totally isolated from the majority of their country's people – except, of course, for their servants.[10]

In a burst of sincerity the odd international lender may admit that the lenders too are to blame for the mess Africa finds itself in. As an IMF official told *Washington Post* reporter Blaine Harden, 'What happened in Zambia could have been avoided. It has taken special effort to run this country into the ground.'[11]

One feels sure Zambians will appreciate the pains that were taken with their case.

KENYA: TRAVELLING TOWARDS COLLAPSE?

The way to make your fortune in Africa is to get into the state power apparatus – and stay there. Democratic elections at any level are as rare as unicorns on this continent. In late 1986 I attended religious services in Nairobi, where prayers were offered for President Daniel arap Moi, then in his eighth year of power, despite an attempted *coup*. Afterwards one of the pastors of the church confided, 'I thought during that prayer, if we were in the United States, eight years would be the end of anyone's presidential mandate. But here, there's no end in sight. No one should be allowed to rule indefinitely without consulting the people.'

The Kenyan government is trying to silence the Church, which it considers 'subversive' because Church leaders have dared to suggest that public voting – voting by lining up physically behind candidates, so everyone can see who's supporting whom – is perhaps not democracy at its purest.

The West has never been a stickler for democracy so long as the principles of free enterprise are observed, and from that point of view

Kenya has always been seen as the big East African success story.
Kenyans will tell you that the mentality in their country is akin to that in
the US: more or less rugged individualism; you can reach the top if you
really want to; it's a disgrace to be poor; and a Mercedes-Benz is the
ultimate goal of life.

Besides the tribe of the Wa-Benzis (those who've got their Mercedes
by fair means or foul), Nairobi also boasts – if that's the word – the most
extensive slum in Africa, Mathare, which I visited in the dry season.
God only knows what it's like during the rains. Since not everyone can
be rich, and it's rotten to be poor, Kenyans also tend to take out their
frustrations on one another in what has come to be called the 'Mathare
syndrome' – physical violence inflicted by people who are suffering on
other people who are suffering just as much. This is not very African
behaviour.

Be that as it may, the Kenyan government never hesitates to point out
to its citizens how much better off they are than those of neighbouring
countries. Perhaps so. But even the relatively successful nations of
Africa may soon find themselves in deep, or deeper, trouble because of
combined pressures of the debt, doldrums on the commodities markets
and their own policies, creating further polarization between rich and
poor.

I've been lucky to have an exceptionally good informant on Kenya,
someone in, though not entirely of, the power structures there. He shall
be nameless, since, like the rest of us, he has his living to earn. In the
course of a long conversation this competent Kenyan showed me a
passage from a history of the IMF by its official, in-house historian,
Margaret de Vries.[12]

She explains that world markets have a far greater impact on the
economies of the LDCs than do domestic planning and policies, no
matter what policies and plans are adopted. One wonders if the functionaries of the IMF know, or care, that their own historian has published a tacit indictment of their common employer. The Fund has been
one of the greatest single forces obliging countries to participate fully in
capricious world markets, although it is unwilling or unable to contribute
to changing the market conditions that weigh so heavily on its clients.

In my informant's view, for Kenya, as for other Third World countries, 'There *are* no commodity booms.' Apparent gains are not only
short-lived but illusory – Kenya can profit from, say, Brazil's loss, but
this will result at best in temporary money. No long-term planning is
possible. Boomlets help to clear the most pressing debts; sometimes
they allow for a spate of imports; but they never last. One of Kenya's

major exports, tea, in late 1986 was fetching half what it did a year earlier; the price of coffee is lower than it was in 1976 in terms of the goods it can buy from abroad.

By insisting that all countries pursue the same policies and export flat out, the IMF has succeeded in 'atomizing the Third World'. It even refuses to encourage the Preferential Trading Area (PTA) for Eastern and Southern Africa, although each of the countries in the PTA has separately accepted IMF conditions. Therefore even modest efforts at regional integration, which might in the long run create complementary rather than competing economies, are discouraged and downgraded. It's every man for himself.

Kenya has been under IMF surveillance since 1975, and the Fund has a permanent monitoring official, sitting in an office in the Kenyan central bank, who oversees government budgetary decisions. I asked if one could pinpoint the ways in which IMF conditions affected Kenya by examining the budget. This question made my friend laugh. Budget figures as published, he explained, mean very little. Most of the budget for the armed forces, for example, is classified information. Other large expenditures may also be hidden but keep state overheads high. My informant, along with many other Kenyans, estimates that the presidential entourage – press and PR units, security guards, hangers-on, vehicles, etc. – costs in the neighbourhood of 1 million Kenyan shillings *a day*. That's $62,500 at the 1986 exchange rate of about 16 shillings to the dollar, or close to $23 million a year. The joke circulating about President Daniel arap Moi in non-reverential circles is that he suffers from foot-and-mouth disease – he goes around a lot and talks all the time. But the IMF never applies its restrictions to military expenditure or to this sort of costly foot-and-mouth outlay.

The Fund's top priorities in Kenya were spelled out in a 1983 confidential report. According to this document, the IMF wants to improve 'the growth rate in agricultural output in order to maintain adequate food supplies and to allow larger exports of agricultural products. To that end, producer prices for a range of agricultural and livestock commodities were increased in January–February 1983.' Producer prices for sugar-cane were raised by a third, for maize by 35 per cent, for cotton by 13 per cent, and commodities like milk, beef and rice were better paid by 12 to 17 per cent.[13]

Good news for the peasantry, no? Not altogether. The IMF report continues: 'The Government follows a policy of allowing the pass-through to consumers of all production and import costs. Therefore, the adjustment of agricultural prices will be reflected in higher consumer prices.'[14] A classic case of robbing Peter to pay Paul. But perhaps peasants will at least have gained a better share of the national income? Wrong again. The government's 1985 *Economic Survey* shows that the terms of trade for the agricultural sector in 1984 (that is, farmers' outlays for inputs and necessary consumer goods compared with the income they receive) had declined by fourteen points since 1980, including a decline of nearly 6 per cent from 1983 to 1984, *after* the IMF had instituted higher producer prices.[15] In addition, 'The increase in the cost of agricultural extension services . . . has been duly transferred to the service users through a 15 per cent rise in fees in most agricultural areas serviced' (by irrigation in particular), says the IMF. Farmers thus seem *worse* off than they were before the latest adjustment programme, though the IMF report refrains from saying so.

Urban consumers, particularly the poorest ones, are also worse off. The IMF does not, again, admit these adverse effects. It claims, in fact, that the distributional effects of its policies – which is to say, their social impact on various income groups – are neutral, or nearly so. The IMF even contends that *better-off* social groups may be affected most adversely by the austerity measures it imposes. It sees the problem as largely one of public relations, since these better-off groups are going to make more noise protesting, noise commensurate with their initially privileged status. Adjustment programmes can, in reality, be inherently equalizing, or so the IMF claims in a 1985 report.[16]

I am translating. The Fund itself puts the matter thus:

[T]he available evidence provides no basis for concluding that Fund-supported adjustment programs lead to significantly worse income distributions when compared to any practical alternative *[my emphasis]*.

Why, then, are its programmes criticized?

[T]he adjustment . . . often has an effect on particular groups and especially on groups likely to be vocal and cohesive in their opposition (e.g. urban workers, civil servants, the military, owners of protected businesses) . . . Distributional concerns probably require the brunt of adjustment to be borne by such groups . . . The Fund should recognize and anticipate the source of such complaint and be prepared to meet it [by] trying to identify those who really are 'the poor' and remembering that they are not necessarily (or even most likely) to be those protesting.[17]

But if we measure these assertions in the Fund's 1985 internal document against information contained in its 1983 confidential report on Kenya,

Table 1   Cost increases of basic necessities in Nairobi, 1982 (index 1975 = 100)

	Food	Clothing/ shoes	Rent	Fuel/ power
Lower-income	242	308	314	393
Middle-income	229	220	288	364
Upper-income	232	213	259	311

Source: IMF confidential report on Kenya, Table 3.

we learn that, for this country at least, the policies of the past few years *have* resulted in a heavier burden on the poor. Contrary to the Fund's stated belief, it is not the more 'vocal and cohesive', better-off people but those in the lowest income group that have borne the brunt of adjustment.

Table 1 shows details of some cost increases taken from the Fund's own figures. They concern the basic necessities of life: all figures are for 1982 consumer prices in Nairobi (I have rounded them to the nearest decimal), and the base year, with an index of 100, is 1975, when the IMF arrived in the country. The Fund's figures are weighted, which means they take into account the proportion of its income that each group spends on particular items. For example, the poorest group spends 41 per cent of its income on food, middle-income group 35 per cent, the upper-income group (earning above 2,000 shillings per month) 25 per cent. In *every case* these figures show that the poorest were hardest hit. Though all three categories have been struck by higher prices for basic goods and services, the rich have maintained an advantage. The extra load on the lower income as compared with the upper-income group (so you don't have to do the subtracting yourself) is 10 points for food, 95 for clothing and shoes, 55 for rent, and 82 for fuel and power. If this proves that IMF adjustment policy is 'distributionally neutral', pigs can fly.

I anticipate the Fund's defence will be to assert that such an effect may be true in the case of Kenya – it can hardly claim otherwise – but that Kenya is exceptional and in other countries IMF adjustment policies are indeed distributionally neutral or more detrimental to the richer classes than to the poor. If the IMF hopes to be believed on that score, it should make its own studies available to interested members of the public. I did not come by the Kenyan study through normal scholarly channels.

Data on Kenyan wages are also alarming. Nominal (monetary) wages have increased, though not as much as inflation. The average nominal wage has more than doubled since 1975, and the minimum wage has risen by 60 per cent. But their purchasing power (the 'real' wage) is another story. A study carried out by a scholar at the Institute for Development Studies at the University of Nairobi on behalf of the Kenyan Central Organization of Trade Unions shows that the average *real* wage declined by 20 per cent between 1981 and 1983 and is even slightly lower than it was in 1964. When the IMF arrived in 1975, the real *minimum* wage, the best most poor people can count on, was 42 per cent higher than it was in 1984.[18]

In another study the same author shows what the government's priorities are, or have become. During the decade 1964–73 social spending was clearly at the top of the list: 'education, health and welfare services grew annually by about 15 per cent per capita, whereas the rate of growth of total expenditure per capita averaged 7.1 per cent yearly.' Unfortunately, in the following decade, 1974–83, this situation was completely reversed. Defence spending and interest payments on debt increased by 11.7 and 13.7 per cent yearly, while education and health spending registered annual growth of less than 3 per cent, and other welfare spending stopped growing altogether.[19] Clearly, debt service and the military are now eating up the funds that were once available for social progress.

This rather dry information on prices, wages and government spending priorities is directly related to the actual welfare of human beings. Child malnutrition is one of the best indicators of how well a society is progressing towards satisfying basic needs and promoting greater social equality. Kenya has carried out three official Rural Child Nutrition Surveys (in 1977, 1979 and 1982). In 1977 it found 24 per cent of the children under 5 were stunted; in 1982 the figure was up to 28 per cent. The 1982 Survey also found that nearly half the children (46.5 per cent to be precise) had been sick in the preceding two weeks.[20]

Although the IMF confidential document on Kenya declares that it wants the country both to 'maintain adequate food supplies' and to 'allow larger exports of agricultural products', it seems clear that the score is now exports 1, food 0. The problem in proving this conclusively is that government data on agriculture account for *marketed* crops, not total production. Still, if we compare one good agricultural year (1976) with another good year (1982), we find that cash crops have done remarkably well, while marketed maize has barely held steady (in spite of better producer prices), and the amount of rice sold has declined. By contrast, marketed coffee increased by 10 per cent between 1976 and 1982, sisal by 49 per cent, tea and cotton by 54 per cent and sugar by a whopping 88 per cent.[21]

Favouring cash crops has two major, far-reaching effects, neither very helpful for feeding the people. The first is obvious: less food is planted. The second is more pernicious. Smallholders get more cash when they sell their tea or coffee (a lot of cash crops in Kenya are grown by small farmers), so normally they should be able to buy food for their own consumption even if the government has to import it, as it has increasingly done in recent years. The rub is that while families may get a higher cash income, they don't necessarily spend it on food. This is because *men* control the money from cash-crop sales. Generally, women get the money only from marketed maize, and even that causes inter-spouse warfare.

When women have money, they spend it on family welfare – first of all on feeding their offspring. As the United Nations International Children's Emergency Fund (UNICEF) notes, 'Female-controlled income *does* go to nutrition . . . increasing food production and increasing female access to income seem to emerge as the two most effective measures to ensure adequate food consumption for rural smallholders.'[22] One study that UNICEF cites could hardly be more explicit: 'The women complained that family involvement in sugar-cane production was hurting more than it was helping . . . although the family as a whole contributed labour on the sugar plots, the money earnings were controlled and spent, most of it on beer, by the husband.'[23] One might add that the vast quantities of beer consumed require grain as the basic raw material, plus lots of firewood for brewing. But in East Africa much of the beer is locally brewed and sold . . . by women, getting some of their own cash back!

The cash-crop versus food-crop argument is usually presented in terms of land use. Critics also note that scarce resources like fertilizer or water are diverted from food production. These are, of course, important aspects. When debt service requires stepped-up agricultural exports, there does seem to be an immediate, quasi-mathematical effect on planting choices, if the above figures on marketed crops are any guide. But the implications of choosing cash crops go much further than that.

Whereas African women have power over decisions relating to food and food crops, they have precious little say over the disposal of household money. This is the husband's province.[24] Men may further appropriate their wives' *labour* in order to earn more cash. Women then have even less time for producing food, not to mention childcare duties. African women, as nearly everyone now realizes, work longer days than most slaves and simply cannot squeeze in other activities. Something has to give.

UNICEF notes some of the things that do give when 'reallocation of [female] labour towards agricultural production [of cash crops] takes place':

– *Cooking practices change. Quick, easy-to-prepare meals, usually of nutritionally poorer staples, are produced once a day or in bulk, and vitamins are destroyed by food kept simmering in the pot.*
– *Intra-family distribution of food is affected. Women have no time to prepare special infant foods and cannot supervise the distribution of food during the day. Children are asleep before the daily meal is eaten.*
– *Housecleaning, essential in overcrowded and unsanitary conditions, tends to decline.*
– *Fuel and water collection is constrained by time.*
– *Care of children is relegated to other siblings or elderly grandparents.*[25]

What's more, several observers have noted that when older brothers and sisters feed the little ones, the little ones get smaller portions because the older ones are hungry too and may eat more than their share. Mothers who aren't around can't arbitrate these conflicts among siblings. Studies cited by UNICEF show that growth and development may be deeply affected by *who* feeds the children.

Choosing cash crops is thus not just an economic decision. In order to pay back debts, African countries like Kenya must also accept enormous disruption in social patterns, often doing great harm to women and children, always the weaker members of society.

TANZANIA: THE POVERTY PLUNGE

The intensity of the economic decay has demoralized large segments of the population. Public morality and social responsibility have declined. The political enthusiasm of the late 1960s and early 1970s has been replaced by widespread apathy and resignation.

Nguyuru H. I. Lipumba, University of Dar es Salaam[26]

Tanzania, under the visionary leadership of 'Mwalimu' (the Teacher) Julius Nyerere, was the darling of many development theorists and of some donors (for example, Sweden) during the late 1960s and the 1970s – the period of 'political enthusiasm'. The Tanzanian model seemed to guarantee socialism with a human face. Now that the country's economy is a shambles, orthodox free-market types are positively cackling with glee that socialism in Africa doesn't and can't work.

Tanzania, it's true, has a lopsidedly heavy state sector, which has proved both costly and inefficient, but the truth is that, 'socialist' or not, the country was always heavily dependent on the outside world. Its fortunes reached a peak in 1976–7, when the coffee boom brought a sudden windfall, almost entirely the result of freezing weather that wrecked Brazil's harvest. Although Tanzania had maintained a strict policy on imports since independence, the boom conveyed a false sense of security, and the pressure to restrict them was relieved. The result was a 39 per cent increase in imports in 1977 – most of them for current consumption, almost nothing for investment in long-term growth. The drain on hard-currency reserves prompted re-imposition of curbs, but too late; by 1981 reserves were zero.[27]

Meanwhile, like other raw-material-producing countries, Tanzania found its export earnings taking a nosedive. The quantities of export crops that it could market also declined. By 1984 export earnings were 30 per cent below the 1980–81 average, in 1985 fully 40 per cent below what they had been five years earlier. Here is what former President Nyerere told a European audience in October 1986:

This year the rains in Tanzania were quite good. The peasants in our major cotton-growing regions have more than doubled their cotton crop compared with that of last year. We are desperately short of foreign exchange with which to buy essential imports, and cotton is one of our major exports; we were therefore pleased about this big output increase. But the price of cotton on the world market dropped from 68 cents a pound to 34 cents a pound on a single day in July this year. The result for our economy – and the income of the peasants – is similar to that of a natural disaster: half our crop, and therefore of our income, is lost. Our peasants – and our nation – have made the effort, but the country is not earning a single extra cent in foreign exchange. That is theft![28]

Just to complicate Tanzania's plight, it got involved, for the best of reasons, in a costly war against Idi Amin Dada's Uganda in 1978–9. The international community was not, however, about to reward Tanzania for defeating a notorious tyrant. The IMF, when approached in 1980 for a loan to finance oil imports, demanded that Tanzania apply, in exchange, the usual adjustment programme – including renewed liberalization of imports and drastic reductions in the state sector. The government said no, and thus began, in 1981, a protracted *mano a mano* between this poor African country and the IMF.

At last, in 1986, partly because of the cotton débâcle that Nyerere spoke of, the government had to cave in. In exchange, the IMF promised $2.5 billion. President Mwinyi announced, 'The pound of flesh usually demanded by the Shylock [IMF] will be taken without shedding a drop of blood.'[29] Many Tanzanians retort that the blood is already flowing freely, and they resent the fact that the actual provisions of the agreement with the IMF have been neither divulged nor explained to the people. The minister for Finance made no reference to the terms of agreement in his annual budget speech in June 1986. One Member of Parliament complained that even MPs had no knowledge of these terms and demanded that the government announce them and state clearly the 'bitterness of whatever prescriptions' the IMF intended to implement.[30]

A good many things are wrong with the Tanzanian economy, and some of the measures demanded by the IMF may do some good. The scene in this country is not, however, as negative as the Western press often claims. Although it is a one-party state, participation in decision-making is far more democratic than in most African countries. Its record for education and health care is exceptional: nearly all children attend at least primary school, and life expectancy has reached sixty years. Contrary to what many people believe, the economy has also grown quite respectably: the problem is that the bureaucracy has absorbed many of the gains. This provides, of course, some employment but no funds for further investment. The share of the public sector in the Gross Domestic Product (GDP) climbed steadily from 16 per cent in 1970 to double that figure in 1982.

Potential agricultural bounty has been stifled by unrealistic policies. The worst is doubtless to assign all agricultural purchasing and distribution to the monumentally wasteful National Milling Corporation. Most Tanzanians agree on this now. The state sector, once looked on as untouchable, has come in for violent criticism, inside and outside the government. Action is following. For example, twenty-two deficit-running sisal plantations are being sold off to the private sector – some to individual producers or trade-union co-operatives and four to a foreign company. State organizations for foodstuffs, livestock, timber, even bicycles, have been abolished, others trimmed or merged.[31]

IMF insistence on making the bureaucracy less top-heavy is therefore not out of place and will save the state some badly needed money, previously wasted. But it will also contribute to unemployment. By the end of 1986, 50,000 government employees had been sacked, according to reliable estimates. A Tanzanian development organization speculates that most of those fired must have been junior, ill-paid people, whereas the 'group of top officials is the one which accounts for higher spending on the part of government departments, ministries and parastatal organizations. It would be interesting to know how many from this group were swept away with the big broom.'[32]

As usual, the IMF has demanded devaluation, and here again there is no doubt that the Tanzanian shilling was selling at an unrealistic rate. When I was there in late 1983 it cost about as much to eat in Dar es Salaam as in New York. But a brutal change in the value of a given currency with regard to other, stronger, ones is not simply a technical financial measure. Let's see what it can mean for ordinary people.

The US branch of OXFAM reports on a project that it sponsors to help villagers in the Kigoma region of Tanzania, who were eagerly awaiting the day they could use oxen to plough their fields. Animal power instead of traditional hand-hoes would allow them to plant a lot more corn and beans and save them back-breaking toil. OXFAM provided the funds for the purchase of eight oxen and veterinary supplies.

But between the time the farmers received the grant and went to purchase their oxen, the price of the animals – like the price of just about everything else in Tanzania – had risen. Instead of eight animals, they could buy only six . . . Worse, some supplies, such as pumps for spraying the oxen to kill deadly ticks, and medicines for protection against the tsetse fly, were not available at all. The medicines are essential to the animals' survival, but, like most veterinary supplies, they must be imported. To conserve funds needed to pay its foreign debt, the government has had to impose restrictions on these and other desperately needed imports.[33]

The Evangelical Lutheran Church in Tanzania (ELCT) is also involved in a great many activities to improve food security. Some of its projects are necessarily dependent on outside donors (particularly where imports are needed), and donors award grants for fixed amounts in Tanzanian shillings, not dollars. ELCT describes what the devaluation has done to one of its ventures:

ELCT started a dairy-cattle project to help the poorest of the poor in the society . . . [They] were given a pregnant cow with an agreement that the first female calf was to be surrendered back to the project to be given to another poor person. These farmers were given the necessary inputs, such as medicines, on the condition that after they start getting some income from their cow, they will be . . . paying back for those inputs that were given to them on loan . . . Devaluation has made the medicines expensive, for they are imported from abroad, hence unaffordable to our

farmers. We will have to think of some ways of subsidizing these farmers,
otherwise we might lose the whole project.[34]

The project is not having the ripple effect on the whole community that
ELCT hoped for because the price of each initial cow has also doubled
since devaluation. All its other projects funded from outside in shillings
have lost approximately half their purchasing power.

This makes us wonder whether the so-called partnership [with foreign
donors] should not be an agreement for the accomplishment of
programmes rather than [an agreement on] a financial figure.

Average income per capita in Tanzania is estimated at 11,200 shillings
annually or $280 at the post-devaluation rate of 40 shillings to the dollar.
Using these 11,200 shillings a year (or 933 shillings a month) as a
reference point, the same Lutheran organization interviewed a few
urban families in order to get an idea of their monthly outlay for
eighteen basic necessities (foodstuffs, plus soap, kerosene or charcoal,
rent and transport). ELCT stresses that its sample is not large enough to
be truly representative; in particular, the families interviewed had
artificially low expenditures for rent, since they were living in Church
quarters. They ranged in size from one to ten members.

However limited the sample, the figures still show what urban dwellers are up against. For families of four or more, six basic food items –
maize, rice, beans, cooking oil, milk and sugar – accounted for over half
their monthly budget. *Every* household, including single persons, spent
far more on just these six items than the theoretical Tanzanian average
monthly income. One individual spent over twice the average 933
shillings on these basics; families of seven to ten (closer to African
reality) needed four to seven times that amount.

True, these are urban people who earn more than the average
national income. Peasants, who make up the bulk of the population,
have lower incomes but can grow part of their food. Even so, the small
ELCT survey shows that if urban families are to keep on eating (and
cooking) basic staples and to buy fruits, vegetables and eggs, if they are
to take buses and wash themselves and their clothes, if they are to live in
rental housing costing about five times what the Church charges, then
they had better earn *at least four times the average national income.*

Usually they don't, so they employ a variety of strategems. University
professors and civil servants come streaming out of classrooms and
offices at noon in order to go home and milk the cow, feed the chickens
and tend the vegetable garden. Most people have access to a *shamba*

(small farm), and any professional lucky enough to work abroad tries to bring back a small van or truck that will add immeasurably to his income by serving as one of the ubiquitous *matatus*, or taxis-of-all-work. Such stories are common currency all over East Africa.

Tanzania does not suffer from a shortage of goods. My informants tell me that the shops are full – because people can't afford the goods in them. In December 1986 a 2-kilo (4.4-lb) tin of cooking oil cost 500 shillings, a kilo of sugar 80 shillings.

In order to assess food import and food aid needs, Paula Park and Tony Jackson went to Tanzania in 1985 on behalf of OXFAM UK. They discovered that the National Milling Corporation was, through its own misguided policies, spurring farmers to avoid it at all costs and to sell food on the black market. 'At the height of the harvest season,' one farmer explained, 'lorries of food moved day and night into Kenya.' The reason is simple, says the OXFAM team. 'While the government paid £22 sterling [about $33] for a 90-kilo [200-lb] bag of maize, the parallel or illegal market paid £72 [$108].'[35] Aside from the gross inefficiency of such 'parastatal' agencies (which Robert Chambers has aptly christened 'parasitals'), state food-pricing policies are simply unrealistic.

In another region, closer to the Burundi border, farmers told Park and Jackson similar stories. One said:

I wake up in the morning to a knock on the door, and it's a driver from Kenya. He has a bag of salt he wants to trade for a bag of maize. I need salt, so I must exchange. Then, another knock on the door and it's a trader from Burundi with a nice shirt made in Britain. I can't buy that kind of shirt here, so I give him some of my maize.

Farmers who can't make a profit selling to the government take the eminently reasonable view that they should sell to someone else. Although the government has increased prices to farmers, the purchasing power of what they receive has declined. Park and Jackson estimate that in constant 1984 shillings, farmers received 70 per cent less for a kilo of maize in 1984 than in 1976. So it is not surprising that in recent years the National Milling Corporation has been able to purchase only about 25 per cent of total marketed maize. The trouble is that the government is also committed to supplying cheap food for urban residents and has thus resorted to imports on an ever-widening scale.

However, IMF insistence on turning everything, including agriculture, over to the free market over-simplifies Tanzania's plight. *Even assuming* that the government raises prices to farmers to an acceptable – profitable – level, costs (of fertilizer, etc.) to those farmers will increase

too, as a result of devaluation. Tanzania is a big country – four times the
size of Britain or West Germany, about a tenth of the landmass of the
US. A poor country paying some $30 million in interest a year on debt
cannot afford to put money simultaneously into desperately needed
infrastructure like roads and vehicles that would help to get the food
from where it is produced to where it is needed. Concretely, the ELCT
reports:

*Many roads are not passable, especially during the rainy seasons. Lack of
fuel further worsens the problem and sometimes shortage of tires is an
issue of concern . . . [All this] delays transportation of agricultural inputs
or products to their final destinations. For example, this year [1986] the
southern part of Tanzania had a bumper coffee crop. However, coffee
could not be transported to Kilimanjaro for further processing . . . Even
though the Government had volunteered to provide fuel and tires over
and above the transportation costs, private transporters were still reluctant
to help because of the bad roads.*[36]

Tanzania is a classic example of the poverty plunge: the less you have,
the less you can invest, so the less you have. Fuel and spare parts are too
expensive to import, with the result that industries operate at less than
30 per cent of their normal capacity. According to Tanzania's Budget for
Economic Recovery, industrial production declined by 6.4 per cent in
1985 alone. Value added in industry – a measure of a country's capacity
to process its own raw materials – went down by 11 per cent a year in
both 1983 and 1984. Shortages of the most essential goods (like cooking
oil, soap or sugar) ensue, and the black market flourishes, exactly the
phenomenon the IMF says its policies are designed to avoid.

As the IMF must know full well, since responsible economists have
been saying so for years, it doesn't matter *how* much you offer farmers to
produce if they can't find anything to buy with what they earn. A
government can increase prices paid them by 1 zillion per cent and
peasants will continue to buy their shirts from Britain, via Burundi, if
their own national economy has no shirts to offer or can't supply means
to transport them to the villages. A lack of goods in the countryside will
discourage export crops as well as food production. With less to sell, the
government will have even less foreign exchange and thus even less fuel
and fertilizer, fewer spare parts, roads in worse shape . . . You get the
picture. According to Tanzania's minister for finance, the country is now
devoting 60 per cent of all its export earnings to debt service.[37]

As a result of budget cuts, the once exemplary educational system is
suffering. Parents are required, for the first time, to help finance their

children's schooling. This will introduce class differences in a country that used to pride itself on educating everyone, even and especially the children of the poor. Law enforcement is deteriorating 'to the point that residents of Arusha, Shinyanga and Tabora regions have resorted to the traditional civil-defence system commonly known as "sungu sungu"', according to ELCT.

Perhaps the IMF will be pleased with this result. At least the police has now partially reverted to the private sector.

African governments accepted many of the major features of the Western model. Most of them loved prestige projects and military spending; they never really had a serious debate about the benefits of growing food crops versus cash crops but were, rather, content to follow the pattern established in colonial times. The real debate was about *which* Africans would benefit from the export-oriented model. The peasantry, as so often, lost. So did the urban majority.

Now the debt is marginalizing these groups even further and depriving them of the little political clout they may have exercised. As Nigerian economist Claude Ake explains:

Current attempts at debt adjustment by Western banks and multilateral lending agencies make matters worse, especially when interest rates are high and commodity prices low, as they are today. IMF-dictated adjustments mean that subsidies to the poor in the receiving countries must be cut back. Moreover, these outside pressures enable African regimes, already repressive enough, to further justify authoritarianism in the name of fiscal responsibility.[38]

Under pressure of debt, debt service and IMF programmes, political repression is flowering and multiplying in Africa. In Zambia, in December 1986, further food riots broke out after an announcement that the price of cornmeal would yet again increase by 100 per cent. Press reports echoing government statements noted thirty dead; from previous experience one must assume the true number of deaths was higher. In Kenya reports on human-rights violations, including torture, have become a daily occurrence – and the President is digging in. Even from Tanzania, the most egalitarian of the three, I've received requests from colleagues to protest against police attacks on sugar workers claiming higher wages. Claude Ake says that political repression is the 'greatest single obstacle to development', and he is quite right, but behind political repression lies the financial burden. International agencies and their insistence on delivery of pounds of flesh help to provide a convenient alibi for the abuse of power.

7.
ZAÏRE: ABSOLUTE ZERO

Most African leaders are removed by *coups*, not elections. One who has, sadly, escaped overthrow for a period verging on for ever is General Mobutu Sese Soko of Zaïre. His rule has cursed his country for over twenty years, with devastating results for his people. It's hard to imagine a country with greater natural resources – or in worse shape. Zaïre has suffered little or no drought. Its farming land is rich. Vast deposits of cobalt, copper, diamonds and other scarce minerals lie under the surface. It still has immense forests, and its rivers provide a natural transport system as well as a huge potential source of hydro-electric power.

And yet, as we shall see in gruesome detail, life for the average Zaïrian has never been so hard. Real wages are a tenth of what they were at independence; malnutrition is chronic; 80 per cent of the people live in absolute poverty: a familiar litany. Never mind. As Jim Chapin reports in *Food Monitor*, 'Things are bad in Zaïre, but not for everyone.'

The debt of the country is 5 billion dollars, and coincidentally, that is the estimate of how much General Mobutu and his family have stolen from Zaïre. He owns no less than seven châteaux in Belgium and France, as well as palatial estates and residences in Spain, Italy and Switzerland. He owns buildings in the Ivory Coast, Presidential mansions in each of the country's eight provinces, and a palace in his home province. No one knows how much he has in Swiss banks, and he has exclusive use or ownership of numerous ships, jet planes (including a Boeing 747), at least fifty-one Mercedes, and so on. His plantation empire, C E L Z A, is the third largest employer in Zaïre and produces about one-sixth of the country's agricultural exports . . . [He also owns] shares in every major foreign company in the country, in the banks, and [takes commissions of] 5 per cent of the country's minerals paid to his overseas accounts. Thirty per cent of the country's operating budget flows through the Presidential office with no further accounting.[1]

Actually, the latest debt estimate is creeping towards $6 billion, and Belgian researchers have published the addresses of eleven *châteaux* and large properties in Belgium, a building on the exclusive avenue Foch in Paris, a palatial residence in Nice, a thirty-two-bedroom villa in Switzerland (permanently staffed with twenty-six servants), a Costa del Sol beachside villa and a sixteenth-century castle in Spain – but what's a few castles more or less?[2] The same researchers give details on the corporations, banks and agro-industrial companies that have been appropriated by Citizen President Mobutu.

With such a sterling (pun intended) example at the top, it is not surprising that even schoolchildren have been infected with the virus of greed. Two Zaïrian teachers note:

When we ask young pupils what they want to be later on, they invariably answer that they want to become big businessmen, politicians or music and sports stars. When asked the reasons for their choice, they say it's so they can give everyone orders, make a lot of money and do very little work. What strikes us is their exaggerated desire for opulence, coupled with a decided repugnance for any sort of sustained manual or intellectual work . . . If asked, 'Why do you cheat and swindle others?', many reply straightforwardly, 'Because we're Zaïrians.'[3]

Official theft continues unabated and the people are bled, yet Zaïre still receives plenty of new money. The World Bank loaned the Mobutu government over $1 billion, including $375 million between 1984 and 1986 alone.[4] The IMF has instituted its usual measures. Here is some testimony to the brutal living conditions in this unhappy land as it was transmitted from inside Zaïre. For reasons that will become obvious, most sources are not identified.

A year after the devaluation was imposed by the IMF in September

1983, an *average* family in the town of Bukavu (in the eastern part of the country) needed 80 zaïres a day for food alone (without any meat or fish), whereas the salary of a semi-skilled worker or a teacher was 20 zaïres a day. By 1986 salaries had risen, but so had prices, so the proportions remain essentially the same.

Malnutrition has been on the rise since 1983; cases of kwashiorkor (the swollen-belly syndrome) are way up; in some regions 'People say half the children are now dying before they reach the age of five.' One survey shows that in the two biggest cities – Kinshasa, the capital, and Lubumbashi – the average daily calorie rations are 1,450 and 1,425.[5] According to the Food and Agriculture Organization (FAO), the daily calorific intake needed for a reasonably active life is 2,300; levels in Zaïre are thus indicative of slow starvation.

Insecurity is rife. A nun who works in Shaba province wrote in 1984:

People who live in our neighbourhood don't dare go out after six in the afternoon because soldiers are patrolling all over town and are robbing and holding people for ransom. They actually have to live this way, because they're so poorly paid themselves [200 zaïres per month]. But they really exaggerate. In broad daylight, they stole the only goats belonging to a poor widow . . . Since the September 1983 devaluation of 450 per cent, salaries were officially increased by 100 per cent. But in our hospital, twenty-nine people got a 20 per cent rise, and the 120 others got nothing. Where is that money? The teachers are furious. They only earn 300–350 z. a month, yet a sack of manioc flour costs 740 z. A family can live for two weeks on one sack if they only eat once a day.

A Belgian volunteer wrote in 1986:

In Kananga town [in central Zaïre, about half a million inhabitants] life is really getting hard. Yesterday, I saw a little girl eating grass and another one who was eating the waste from the brewery. She was scooping it up to take some home. She told me she hadn't eaten for three days. There was a rumour of a revolt among the non-commissioned officers. But, according to [. . .], Mobutu heard about it through his American informers and he bought them off.

A Roman Catholic missionary from the Kwilu region has written:

For the people here, the so-called 'economic recovery' so highly praised by the I M F and the rich countries (and by the Belgian press) is an absolute

*disaster: salaries continue to stagnate, while inflation goes on as before –
it's even worse now because it touches local produce. Poverty is so
widespread that people are coming back here from Kinshasa! They can't
possibly survive on what they earn – yet one has to pay for everything –
just to cross the bridge over the Kwilu, or to get past a military roadblock,
or to get into school (and for grades once you're in).*

*The sisters at the hospital are doing the best they can, but they now have
to ask the patients to pay, even the poor ones, because the money the
hospital is supposed to receive from the state never turns up. Meanwhile,
the rich and powerful steal – the director of the hospital at Mosango stole
200,000 z. worth of medicines that he got free from the central pharmacy
depot. The administrator responsible for education in this district has
stolen 3 and a half million zaïres from the Catholic schools . . .*

In 1984, in accordance with IMF prescriptions, 46,000 teachers (20
per cent of the total) were fired. A third of the personnel in higher
education was also sacked. For those who remain, as a priest who
teaches in a technical school writes:

*Teachers' salaries are becoming simply ludicrous . . . but the young
people and the intellectuals understand what's going on and are growing
[politically] conscious. We've already had two teachers' strikes, which
start at the base and haven't any visible leaders, so they can't put them in
prison. But the resistance movement is slow to build; most people are still
too bound to tradition, to the chief, the clan and the medicine men.*

These remarks help to explain why there haven't been any IMF riots
in Zaïre – yet. But there have been protest strikes, even though strikers
risk severe repression. School teachers have been in the forefront, but
there have also been strikes among bank and postal workers and in some
of the nationalized industries.

Another description of conditions is supplied by a Belgian woman
who works for a Christian organization. She is still in Zaïre and her
name, like those of other witnesses cited above, cannot be published.
Here is part of her confidential report concerning Kivu province after
she travelled extensively there in November–December 1984:

*'I'm hungry' is what I hear all over. There has been a local drought and
people won't be able to make ends meet before January when the next harvest comes in. Prices are galloping – yesterday a kilo [2.2 lb] of beans was
selling on the local market for 10 z. Today (if you can find any) they cost at*

least 35 z. A lot of families are eating only every other day and at least 20 per cent of the children aren't attending school, 'due to the famine'. This part of Zaïre is supposed to be the country's granary. The drought only underscores in a particularly sharp way the country's ongoing economic, social and political catastrophe.

Around here, a peasant sells a kilo of rice for 3.5 z., but even an egg or a small box of matches costs him 5 z. – a kilo of sugar or a litre [1.8 pints] of oil costs at least 40 z. The roads are going completely to hell and with gasoline selling at 85 z. the litre, the only people on them anyway, what with the potholes, the felled trees, etc., are the occasional missionary and the traders. The peasants are completely dependent on these trader-usurers.

Everything people try to do to cope is thwarted. In this diocese, we already have twenty teams of younger peasants who are tilling crops in common and who have also launched a project for improving housing. Working together, they've now built twenty-seven new houses, really beautiful ones adapted to the climate, but they can't get any tools to finish them. All the tools have to be imported from Bukavu 500 miles [800 kilometres away] or from Kinshasa. There aren't any roads, everything has to come by plane. Between transportation prices and inflation, a crosscut saw which cost 2,900 z. two months ago now costs 4,250 z. A kilo of nails sells for 360 z.

The peasants are still better off than the civil servants – teachers, nurses, soldiers, minor functionaries. Their 'salary', if you can call it that, is 200 z. a month, whereas you need 100 z. a day for even a modest family food ration. Just the charcoal a family needs for cooking here costs 100 z. a week.

Economic repression is so great that among ordinary people, no one can live on his salary, so everyone has to rely on 'Article 15'. [The first Congolese Constitution after independence had fourteen articles – thus 'Article 15' is any activity, legal or illegal, that helps you look out for yourself.]

Teachers and school directors make pupils cultivate gardens for their private use, or make them pay to attend classes; hospitals don't have any medicines, because they are systematically stolen and sold in private pharmacies or on the black market. Soldiers are often delinquents themselves and are sent to their posts without any training at all. They get miserable salaries and they terrorize local people – anyone travelling is likely to be completely stripped of his belongings. The peasants are maltreated, their houses ransacked. People everywhere are terrified.

What's the answer? Zaïre today means 2,500 immensely rich families and 27 million who are desperately poor. There are plenty of people

*around who criticize present policies – even openly. The government
posters in Bukavu and Goma don't fool anyone – they say, 'The whole of
Kivu Province voted 120 per cent [sic] for Mobutu the Peacemaker and
Father of the Zaïrian People.' There have been a few collective actions,
like the teachers' strike, but they've had a limited impact, especially since
the media never talk about them. Some say the only tactic that would be
effective would be to have the Catholic Church declare a general strike of
religious education. But the Church is silent.*

*There are feelings of opposition, but all the most knowledgeable leaders
I've met say that a political opposition movement in this country is
non-existent. There may be some opponents abroad. But they don't
represent much inside the country.*

In spite of impossible conditions, under-nourishment bordering on
starvation and repression, there are stirrings – however ambiguous some
of the signs of change may be. The *leitmotiv* in all the news coming from
Zaïre is the constant struggle for survival – by any means. Sometimes
individual survival is directly opposed to solidarity – i.e., some strikes
have been broken with the help of informers who turn in their fellow
workers for a price. In an increasing number of cases, however, people
are learning that the best way to survive is to act together.

The Lisala region, for instance, is one of Zaïre's richest agricultural
areas, but peasant families have always been at the mercy of a few big
commerçants – traders – who buy their crops at a fraction of their real
value. Now a Zaïrian agronomist is living in one village with them and
has helped them to organize in order to bargain collectively with
the traders. The agronomist has been arrested several times, but the
people are getting three times the price they used to get for their
produce.

In other villages people have chipped in to buy a communal rice mill.
They can sell milled, as opposed to unhusked, rice for twice as much and
use the profits to pay back the cost of borrowing for the mill. The
traders, used to getting their own way, have come to the villages with
soldiers in tow and have tried to take the rice by force. The peasants
have organized a common defence and a system for alerting neighbouring villages to danger. Local government commissioners used to slap
fines on people for any small offence, real or imagined, and grew rich on
the proceeds. Recently one of these commissioners asked to be sent
to another district because the fines he can extort have gone down
dramatically since the people formed a co-operative and now refuse to
pay.

One communal effort is so successful – and thus under such threat – that I'm not even going to identify the region. Jules Devos from the organization NCOS in Brussels, who has country-wide knowledge of Zaïre, thinks it's one of the more hopeful signs going. For one thing, it's exceptional because all ten *animateurs*, or organizers, are Zaïrians. Foreigners have never been involved. Over 5,000 peasant families from several villages have set up co-operatives for all the activities that affect their livelihood – fishing, animal raising, marketing of rice, sorghum, corn and cassava, purchasing basic products, savings and credit. Women's groups manage co-operative milling and water arrangements.

Economic difficulties and scarcities seem to have reinforced solidarity rather than discouraged their work; now that these are on a strong footing, they're branching out. The *animateurs* have made available a legal service (with a volunteer lawyer) to defend the peasants' rights. They are also concerned with discrimination against women and urge women to play an active role in all the co-operatives and planning meetings. The organizers are looking beyond their own region as well: several exploratory missions have visited co-operatives elsewhere with the idea of ultimately creating a province-wide, then a country-wide, peasants' movement. By the end of 1985 they had set up a federation of eighty co-ops throughout their region, with a total membership of some 20,000 peasant families. A major priority remains the training of new leaders.

None of this is easy. The *animateurs* describe some of the problems:

We have to work with poorly trained organizers. We really need training materials and documents about how peasant movements were started and developed in other countries. We want to be financially self-sufficient, not to depend solely on outside partners – because our partners might not agree at some point with what we're doing. We have almost no means of information and communication – no telephones, not even any mail, unless it comes via the Church.

If we're going to work regionally and inter-regionally, we have to have some means of getting around without waiting for a missionary who has a free seat in his car. We're all watched by the police and considered as the opposition. There's a huge demand for information, but we're in danger if we receive bulletins like 'Liso ya Nkolo' ['The Eye of the Ancestors', an information and liaison tool] at the same address regularly – even those who were getting it through a post box in [a neighbouring country] have been indexed by the police. The only safe way is to pass documents to each other when we meet.

Other tactics of solidarity are paying off. People in Zaïre are taxed every time they turn around – but most of them have no idea which taxes are legal and which aren't. Churches and other organizations are drawing up lists of illegal taxes and distributing them at markets, after religious services, etc. People can start making demands once they know what their rights are and know the article of the Penal Code that states that 'Theft committed by an employee of the state while exercising his duties may be punished by imprisonment of up to ten years.'

Thus a group of 400 women villagers simultaneously confronted the two army road blocks on the way to the closest market. The 'taxes' they were obliged to pay the officers were depriving them of any gains they might make from selling their crops. The soldiers weren't prepared to take on such a united group. Their captain accused the local parish of subversion, but the people stuck together and the road blocks were finally removed.

In another case villagers co-operatively dug 800 ponds for fish-farming as a way of improving their diets. As soon as they had finished, the authorities slapped a tax of 800 z. on each pond. The fish raisers' association unanimously decided that no one would pay the tax. The local bigwigs had to give in.

Survival arts are being practised in the towns as well. Some tactics employed may seem fairly timid to Westerners who take basic civil and political rights for granted. In Zaïre bearing witness to a violation of the law (even writing a letter – not to mention more vehement forms of protest like going on strike) can have extremely disagreeable consequences. Merely getting Zaïrian authorities to obey their own laws is a major victory.

Women are beginning to confront the 'big mamas' who control the markets, charging extortionate 'taxes' for the right to sell anything – 'taxes' they share with the local army officer and government official who help to enforce their authority. One local committee set itself the task of documenting each illegal exaction – and getting witnesses to sign their testimony. Then they went up the hierarchical chain until they finally found an official willing to give an order. The big mama disappeared – but several key people on the committee had their houses ransacked and some were physically molested by the soldiers or armed civilians who had lost their cuts.

Such efforts are encouraging, but they will have to be multiplied by several thousand times before the overall situation can change in Zaïre. The only true change will come about when the West stops supporting Citizen President Mobutu, world-class predator, and ceases to demand that poor Zaïrians starve in order to transfer 50 per cent of the value of exports abroad.

Such a course is, alas, unlikely. Zaïre's creditors have known for years exactly what is going on. But they have a mutually profitable arrangement. For one thing, they want to make sure that the country's rich mineral deposits remain under their control, and a comfortable slice for the Zaïrian elite is the price to be paid for such insurance. Cashing in Mobutu's personal fortune would, sure enough, wipe out most of the debt. Organized state banditry is not, however, the only cause of it. Zaïre is another showcase country for ill-conceived, useless, detrimental projects – in which Western interests have always had a substantial stake.

The 'average' Zaïrian has an annual revenue of $140 (1984). The revenues of Mobutu and his cronies figure in this average . . . As a Westerner, I find it morally revolting to list just a few of the items contributing to the debt on which every Zaïrian theoretically owes $200, the debt the Zaïrian people are paying in starvation and dead children, but here goes.

The ONAFITEX (national textile enterprise) in 1973 purchased thirty ultra-modern cotton-treating plants in the USA for $7.5 million. The Zaïrian delegation that made the deal got $450,000 worth of commissions. None of the plants has ever functioned. One was set up at Gandijika, but the high-tech electronic control system was omitted, so nothing worked. The rest of the material has been lost, stolen, dispersed or has deteriorated, so that no complete plant now has a prayer of getting built.

Immediately after the runway at the Kisangani airport had been completely repaired and lengthened, a *second* runway was undertaken (the airport serves five flights a day maximum) at a cost equal to a *year's income* for the region. A worker in Kisangani would need several months' wages just to pay a taxi to the airport, but, once there, he could put his bags on an automatic conveyor belt and enjoy air-conditioned comfort. Total cost: $36 million.

The twenty-two-storey tower of the Kinshasa International Trade Centre is virtually deserted. You wouldn't want to work there either – there are no windows, and the air-conditioning, supplied by a French firm, broke down a month after the supplier's guarantee lapsed.

The TV–communications complex for the 'Voice of Zaïre' (Cité de la Voix du Zaïre), at $110 million, was a really good buy – surely far better than paying 165,000 primary school teachers for five years, which is another thing one could have done with that amount of money. In

December 1980 the system was declared completed. The French manufacturer announced that Zaïre was now 'one of the first countries in the world to posses its own domestic satellite communications network'. As Jonathan Kwitny, a *Wall Street Journal* reporter and author of a remarkable book called *Endless Enemies*, notes, 'The president of that manufacturing concern was Philippe Giscard d'Estaing, the first cousin and lifelong close friend of the (then) president of France. The contracts for the communications system *and* the fancy buildings were awarded during the presidency of Valéry Giscard d'Estaing, who twice sent French troops to Zaïre to protect the Mobutu government.'[6] In any event, the fancy infrastructure for La Voix du Zaïre broke down almost immediately. There is rarely any retransmission towards the interior of the country because the relay stations seldom work. Anyway, most Zaïrians live, as Kwitny points out, 'a day or more's hard travel from the nearest electricity. Most have never seen a telephone. So they don't need the ultrasophisticated communications system.' But foreign enterprises do.

Foreign enterprises, in this case American, are also deeply involved in the Inga-Shaba power project, perhaps the number-one boondoggle in a country that holds championship boondoggling honours. The total cost of the project is over $1 billion, Belgian sources say (Kwitny says $1.5 billion) or about 20 per cent of Zaïre's foreign debt. Zaïrian researchers note that the country could pay 290,000 Zaïrian teachers or nurses for twenty years with that kind of money.[7]

Any serious energy policy for Zaïre would have chosen to exploit the huge local reserves of hydro-electric power and built a series of small dams. Instead, due largely to the influence of the (then) American Ambassador, Sheldon Vance, the government opted for an 1,100-mile power-transmission line over rough terrain, as Jonathan Kwitny shows in detail. A US Embassy official told Kwitny in 1980 not only about the escalating costs but also that 'It's taking so long that a lot of the equipment they're putting in at the two ends is deteriorating.' Whatever the state of the equipment, General Electric and the US contracting firm, Morrison-Knudsen, landed handsome contracts. Morrison-Knudsen's Washington lawyer is none other than Sheldon Vance, now in private practice.[8]

The Inga-Shaba power line is supposed to furnish electricity to a copper refinery and an iron and steel complex. The Maluku steel plant has never operated at more than 10 per cent of its capacity; the 'steel it produces is of poor quality and costs three or four times as much as imported steel. It employs 1,000 people instead of the 10,000 promised.'[9] The copper refinery has not, so far, produced a single pound of copper. What the project is *not* supposed to do is to furnish power for any of the Zaïrian villages along its 1,100-mile stretch. In fact, 'an engineering technique was intentionally employed making it difficult or impossible for any electricity to be siphoned from the line before it gets to Shaba.'[10]

At least two studies done for the Zaïrian government concluded that the mining industry could get more than enough power, and far more cheaply, by damming rivers in Shaba itself without going to 1,100-mile lengths to bring it in. Why, then, were the studies junked and construction of the monstrously expensive project undertaken? Kwitny explains that 'plenty of Zaïrians and Americans, some in the State Department, say [one of the real reasons] the power line is being built [is to] provide a big construction contract for US industry in return for US support of the Mobutu regime.'[11]

This regime is not content to kill its people merely by starving them. According to an April 1985 report in the Belgian newspaper *La Libre Belgique*, an ex-bodyguard of President Mobutu, of the presidential Special Brigade, admitted that he had participated, between 1980 and 1983, in the assassination of approximately 500 opponents of the regime and had personally executed, under order, 'a good many' people. The public prosecutor's office of Bochun, West Germany, placed the Zaïrian under preventive detention after he had asked for political asylum. Amnesty International affirms that the Special Brigade has direct responsibility for a military camp at Mont Ngaliema, near the presidential palace of Kinshasa, where torture and executions are carried out.[12]

One needs *haute couture* blinkers to avoid seeing the Zaïrian regime for what it is – a gang of thieves and murderers – but the international agencies and commercial banks spare no expense in that regard. Propping up Mobutu is a well-entrenched custom: a decade ago, the magazine *Institutional Investor* devoted a cover story to 'Heading off Zaïre's default',[13] in which we are treated to a long saga of how the banks saved the day, as well as a photograph of Mobutu and Walter Wriston enjoying lunch together. We also learn therein how Dr Irving Friedman, senior vice-president of Citibank, engineered on behalf of thirteen leading banks (themselves representing over a hundred lesser banks) '$250 million in new money [which] would not be used to repay old debt, but would be used to help develop the nation's vital mineral resources'. Dr Friedman 'hailed the agreement as a real model' because Zaïre had agreed to go to the IMF for extra funds and to get its financial house in order, thus proving to his satisfaction that 'any country that has lost its creditworthiness has the ability within itself to restore it.' Admittedly, Dr Friedman was particularly well placed to bring off his *coup*: because of his previous positions with the IMF and the World Bank, 'I had a long relationship with Zaïre before coming to Citibank, so I was able to approach [Zaïrian central bank] Governor Sambwa as a friend, on an informal basis.'[14]

In 1976 the Paris Club,* representing Zaïre's Western government creditors, had decided that 85 per cent of Zaïre's repayments due on government debt would be put off for three years, then stretched further over the next seven. This too was a normal reaction, for, as Dr Friedman also observed, Zaïre's rich resources ensured that 'There is all the pressure in the world for capitalist governments to support Zaïre's economy.'[15]

A decade later they were still doing so. In May 1985 the Paris Club completed the *seventh* rescheduling of Zaïre's debt since 1975. According to an EEC publication, Zaïre benefited from more reschedulings than any other country in the world between 1975 and 1985 (except Togo, which also had seven, for seven times less money).[16] The 1985 rescheduling followed hard on the IMF arrangement for new 'stand-by' credits of $160 million to Zaïre; the Fund seemed satisfied with Mobutu, since he devalued the currency by 500 per cent in 1984.

Alas, the creditors were to be disappointed once again. Amazingly enough, Mobutu has not become a model of private probity and public financial management. But he was back in Paris and Brussels with the begging bowl in September 1986 to demand rescheduling of another $900 million. The *Economist* ('confidential') *Foreign Report* commented:

Fraud, black marketing and the illegal export of capital are said to be rampant in Kinshasa, the capital. The prime minister's programme of austerity, privatization and encouragement of foreign investment is getting nowhere. But there is no alternative policy [sic!]. Our sources doubt, however, that Mobutu's position is in danger even though the mess in Zaïre is getting worse.[17]

The 'alternative policy' should be obvious – get rid of Mobutu by turning off the money machine. Mobutu seems not to fear retaliation of any

* Governments involved in the Paris Club agreement are those of the US, West Germany, Japan, Britain, France, Italy, Canada, Austria, Belgium, the Netherlands, Norway, Spain, Sweden and Switzerland.

kind: he casually announced in December 1986 that Zaïre's debt repayments would not amount to more than 10 per cent of its export revenues.

All of us, through our tax dollars, have been made inadvertent accomplices to the loans that have never ceased to uphold this tyranny. Our governments show no signs of discontinuing their support. Never send to know for whom the debt tolls; it tolls for thee.

POST SCRIPTUM

In May 1987 Zaïre got an unprecedented extension of its repayment terms from the Paris Club – fifteen years on the principal and interest on $884 million worth of debt, plus a six-year grace period during which no debt needs to be paid. It also received IMF approval for $370 in new loans. Sources close to the Paris Club were quoted as saying that Zaïre's exceptional treatment did not mean the same terms would be extended to other debtor countries. Zaïre's central-bank governor, a member of the team that negotiated what one source described as a 'historic first', is inaptly named Wa Siakasigbo Pay Pay.

8.
LATIN AMERICA: DEBT AND DECLINE

People often think of Latin America as rich compared with the rest of the Third World, and in many ways it is. Per capita GNP, which mainstream economists view as a reliable indicator of wealth, tops an average $1,700 in Latin America, compared with a woeful $220 for the poorer sub-Saharan African countries. By this measure, several Latin American nations, including Argentina, Mexico and Venezuela, are well endowed and boast per capita GNPs well over the $2,000 mark.[1]

The Latin American region has, furthermore, no population problem: Mexico plus Central and South America plus the Caribbean countries are inhabited by fewer than 400 million people – about half the total population of India but spread over a far greater area (for example, Brazil alone is two and a half times the size of India, with about six times fewer people). The continent is endowed with rich resources, including plenty of oil, valuable metals and abundant, fertile farmland.

This apparently rosy picture is marred, however, by two factors: a marked inequality between *countries*, and an even more pronounced disparity between *social classes*. Stark contrasts exist: Brazil's average GNP per capita is over $1,700, while Bolivia's is only $509; Panama enjoys a comfortable $2,200 but Honduras and Haiti only $721 and $320.[2]

'Filthy rich' and 'dirt-poor' are phrases that could have been invented to describe the citizens of Latin America. The continent is the world's record-breaker for unequal income distribution. Brazilian, Mexican or Venezuelan elites need no lessons from the upper classes of New York, London or Milan in the fine arts of money-flaunting. Latin American upper classes are, if anything, more opulent, more flamboyant, in their conspicuous consumption. They can also draw on a larger pool of miserable and unprotected, unemployed people for servants than can their counterparts in the North. It is these elites that have made capital flight a national sport and a bonanza for the banking industry.

Wealth here is so irretrievably skewed that most countries have simply stopped publishing figures on income distribution. The last available figures for Brazil relate to 1972; they revealed that the bottom 20 per cent of the population received a meagre 2 per cent of all household incomes, while the top 10 per cent got half.[3] Observers agree that things have grown worse since the 1970s, though they may disagree about how much worse. The Brazilian Institute for Social and Economic Analysis (IBASE) claims that the average income of the wealthiest class was 225 times that of the poorest classes in 1978, whereas it was 'only' 178 times greater in 1970. A mere third of the Brazilian population is able to afford the recommended dietary intake; the other two-thirds suffer from greater or lesser degrees of malnutrition, according to reliable estimates.[4]

Not a single Latin American country has disclosed statistics on distribution of wealth since the late 1970s. The last to do so, according to World Bank tables, was Mexico, in 1977. Many have never done so at all – and this is not because they lack competent statisticians!

In such a context one must recognize that the big development-bank economists who rely on per capita figures – which are nothing but *averages* – are not telling us anything much worth knowing about Latin America. If you have your head in the oven and your feet in the freezer, you are not, 'on average', comfortable. An average GNP of $2,000 is cold comfort for the thousand who, figuratively, have 10 cents compared with the lucky one with $1,900.

THE GREAT JOB ROBBERY

The debt crisis has exacerbated this already tough situation by causing massive job losses and plummeting wages for those who remain employed. Whoever said money is the root of all evil must have had a job. Lack of money for the majority is far worse and engenders the multiple

social evils that go hand in glove with the debt burden. Unemployment
may increase for obvious and straightforward reasons. When the IMF
tells a government to cut public spending or else, thousands of civil
servants, usually at the lower levels, are sacked from one day to the next.
All Fund programmes include this standard feature.

Unemployment is not, however, a simple concept when applied to
Latin America, and the figures dealing with it cannot be compared with
similar figures for the US or Europe. Open, registered joblessness that
shows up in official statistics is the mirror image of the number of *jobs
declared*. Such jobs routinely occupy a small minority of the active Latin
American population and the figures concerning them leave out the
vast, undeclared, 'informal' sector as well as a great many jobs, often
irregular, in agriculture. Official statistics on jobs in the 'formal sector'
are useful, though, because they do tell us something about the better
jobs. In other words, if the statistical news is bad on the 'open unemployment' front, it's bound to be terrible for those who were only squeaking
by to begin with in irregular or undeclared jobs.[5]

Francis Blanchard, director general of the International Labour
Organization (ILO), reported in 1986 that *open* urban unemployment
in Latin America rose by 40 per cent between 1980 and 1984. 'Assuming
the urban labour force continued to grow as in the 1970s, the number of
unemployed must have grown by 67 per cent.' Moreover, still according
to Blanchard, 'Structural underemployment, traditionally the main
component of excess manpower supply in Latin America, is no longer
on the wane but is growing rapidly.'

Many observers have noted the deterioration of plant and equipment
in Latin America because of lack of investment; the ILO is even more
concerned about the deterioration of human capital. When people can't
find work, they rapidly lose their skills. The longer they are jobless, the
smaller their chances of ever getting work again. The job crisis is worst in
the South but global in nature. Because adjustment in debtor countries
has meant, above all, reducing individual incomes and consequently
imports from the North, the ILO says that North America and Europe
lost 2 to 3 million jobs between 1981 and 1983.[6]

IMF demands unceremoniously deposit countless people on the job
market. Too many people chasing too few jobs means drastic drops in
wages. The debt crisis also contributes a further twist to declines in pay
scales. French economist Pierre Salama claims that a heavy debt burden
implies that wages *must* be reduced and exploitation of the work force
increased. His argument is a bit hard to follow. I'm simplifying here as
much as possible, so bear with me.[7]

With successive devaluations (a standard component of IMF stabilization plans), the *dollar* rather than the local currency is used unofficially in debtor countries for all the more important transactions. This is akin to what happens openly and officially in Eastern Europe, where the more desirable goods are often sold only in shops reserved for foreign-currency holders. As their economies grow increasingly 'dollarized', the local authorities lose command over their own monetary policy. Whereas local Latin American currencies were doubtless *over*-valued with regard to the dollar some years ago, Salama says they are now seriously *under*-valued in the more heavily indebted countries. Exchange rates no longer reflect the relative productivity of the debtor, and the US, economies.

The largest, most modern local businesses are obliged to borrow in dollars (or in local currency pegged to the dollar, which amounts to the same thing). These companies too become 'dollarized', at least as far as their *liabilities* go (what they owe their suppliers and their bankers). But they are *selling* their goods or services for *local* currency, so their revenues are not 'dollarized'.

The more the local currency is devalued (and the IMF is constantly pushing for further devaluations, supposedly to make the country's exports more competitive), the more these businesses actually come to owe their bankers (or their governments). To meet their obligations they must (1) raise prices, thus necessarily spurring inflation locally, and (2) reduce wages in order to compensate for the higher cost of borrowing in their total costs. In other, more Marxist, words, the rate of exploitation *must* be increased or the company will fail.

Whether or not you buy this argument as an *explanation* of the wage-slash phenomenon, there is no doubt about the phenomenon itself. Let's look at a few concrete cases.

In Brazil the legal minimum wage is a convenient yardstick. Outsiders are sometimes puzzled when they first start reading Brazilian sources because incomes, prices, rents, etc., are so often discussed in *multiples* of the minimum wage. Why? Because a *single* minimum wage is hopelessly inadequate to cover the needs of a single person, much less those of a family, though the Brazilian Constitution says it should. Indeed, the Brazilian Research Institute IBASE, using official figures for 1983–5, shows that the nominal minimum wage was, depending on the rate of inflation, one-fifth to one-seventh the amount needed to cover a family's basic needs. Yet less than 10 per cent of the work force employed earned more than 5 minimum wages.[8] As Brazilian newspapers reported in 1986:

Of the 52.4 million Brazilians counted as 'economically active', 12.9 per cent of all (urban) workers have no salary at all. Thirty per cent earn less than, or up to, one minimum wage, while 11.5 per cent earn from two to three minimum salary units. Among rural workers, these percentages rise to 27.3 per cent with no salary, 42.9 per cent with less than, or up to, one minimum salary, and only 22 per cent earning from one to two minimum salaries. This means that 64.8 per cent of the economically active population are at levels varying from misery to extreme poverty . . . While productivity in Brazil has nearly quadrupled since 1940, the purchasing power of a minimum salary has declined by 50 per cent *[my emphasis].*[9]

If you can't survive on a minimum wage in Brazil, how do Brazilians stay alive, given the above figures? Sometimes they don't. Here is a composite portrait, presented by a researcher at IBASE, of one worker and his family who are, for the moment, surviving. The Portuguese title of the article means 'How do they survive on a minimum salary?'[10]

Durval is a typical poor Brazilian, a man of 40. He will probably live only another eight years, or maybe only two if he lives in the Northeast. He will probably die of pneumonia, without doctors or medicine and, finally, without a grave. If he has sons, they will grow up to be laborers like himself, semi-illiterate, anemic, and with defective vison. They will probably not live even as long as their father. They will travel several hours a day just to get to work, if they find work. If they don't find work, they'll end up as tramps or criminals. His daughter will marry a worker or someone who runs some extra-legal scam or business. Although young, she will look old. She will have skinny, malnourished children whom she will help to support by taking in laundry. If she's lucky, she'll get to work as a maid in an upper- or middle-class home. However, there won't be any day-care centers where she can leave her children. Alone at home and with only a little cold food on the table, they will find ways to escape despite being locked in and run free over the hills and streets, totally unsuper-vised. In the huge city, they can readily turn into sneak thieves, pick-pockets, risking their lives for a few cents.
Durval could be found on any train from the periphery. He might be wearing only a T-shirt because of the suffocating heat and carrying a tin pot wrapped in newspaper under his arm, or he might have on an old, frayed overcoat given him many years ago by a former employer of his wife that no longer gives much protection from the cold. In an old suitcase recovered from a trash can, he might have with him an egg sandwich and a soft-drink bottle containing cold coffee or a small pot full of broken

macaroni flavored with lard. He is sleepy and can hardly keep up with the conversation going on next to him. They are talking about yesterday's soccer game. But Durval's house has been without electricity for months, so he ended up selling the radio.

This might be his first day of work in a furniture factory or his last in a metallurgical plant. It is 5 a.m. and he will be on the train for another hour. If he went by bus, it would be still worse – he would have to pay C R 1,060 each way; forty trips at this rate would consume two-thirds of his minimum salary. His stomach growls and his legs tremble; the hot breeze blowing through the crowded train makes him feel sick. The only thing that stirs him from his torpor is the sound of the factory whistle. If he is five minutes late starting work, he loses the whole day's pay plus that for Sunday! And he still has to find time to go to the bathroom before the section chief starts shouting at him. Illiterate, he doesn't notice the newspaper column being read by his fellow passenger announcing an adjustment of the minimum salary.

Whether or not he knows how much the minimum salary is, the result is the same; it continues to be insufficient to support his wife and five children. Above all, he knows the rent on his shack will go up, meat will go up, milk (he has not seen any for a while) will go up and there will not be enough left to pay the overdue electricity bill; the owner of the shack will not reconnect the electricity and he will continue not knowing who won the soccer games. Also, there will not be enough to pay his bill at the store, so his wife and children will have to go on finding what food they can in the garbage. Still worse, the quality of the garbage is falling even faster. Durval is not certain but senses that the amount of organic material in the garbage dumps of the great cities is decreasing each year. In Rio de Janeiro, for example, in 1970, each cubic metre [1.3 cubic yards] of garbage contained 43.8 per cent of organic material, that is, of 'edible' items for marginal people. In 1980, this proportion declined to 36.7 per cent.

Although Durval considers himself the most miserable of men, he has never thought of suicide. He did think of moving to another city. Little does he know that families like his wander over the city dumps in all the major cities. In all of these, ragged children, women and men patrol the stinking mounds in search of scraps of bluish meat, wormy biscuits, withered fruit, a mixture not fit for pigs that causes diarrhea, sometimes fatal – especially to small children – but which fills the void in their stomachs.

In these places, one can also find useful objects. Pieces of furniture, cushions, old pots, wrappings, paper and cardboard which, if they are not used at home, may be sold by the item or the pound to recycling plants.

Those who survive in this way are beyond feeling shame. In the stage at which they find themselves, the next lower level of activity is the life of crime. Now, at least, they only appropriate what the privileged no longer want.

Checking garbage in trash cans or in the dumps is not the only expedient for survival that a family unsupportable on a minimum salary has. An outstanding day in the lives of such families is the day of the open-air market. What remains at the end to be picked up by the city sanitation workers is the choicest of organic garbage. Everything is slightly fresh – it has not been dumped into a truck nor has it sat for days in the sun and rain. Squashed mixed fruit, bits of meat, and withered vegetables fill bags and boxes left behind by vendors. It is a fiesta. One can try a bit of everything: oranges lacking vitamin C after having remained cut open as samples since seven a.m., dried-up chicken skin contaminated by flies, yellowed cabbage leaves, etc. Nevertheless, market day is a day to celebrate in millions of Brazilian homes scattered among the great cities.

At 11 a.m., the factory siren where Durval works sounds for lunchtime. He now has an hour to eat what he brought in his lunch pot. If the factory is well equipped, there may be a stove where he can heat up his lunch; if not, he may use a small alcohol stove. Or, if not even that, he will eat his lunch cold, crouched next to the outside wall, while those in better condition avail themselves of the time to kick a soccer ball around on the sidewalk or even between passing cars. On the lunch pots of his fellow workers, the menu is fixed: rice and beans or macaroni or a mixture of all three. There exists a myth that Brazilians are hungry because they don't know how to eat. But most nutritionists have concluded that this sparse diet is not so unsuitable if supplemented with some animal protein such as egg or meat. Without the latter, however, he would need to consume one kilo of rice, three of beans, and two of macaroni. No one eats this much, so in southern Brazilian cities, one in two poor persons is malnourished.

Durval gets home from the factory feeling too tired to get water for a sponge bath. He drinks some warmed-over coffee and eats a piece of stale bread. He sits on the porch of his shack smoking the single cigarette he has bought, looking out for his children and wondering what will befall them tomorrow. He looks discouraged. His eldest daughter comes in from the street. She has spent the whole day looking for work and has found nothing. At 16, she has barely completed one year of public schooling and can scarcely read or write her name. She has no occupation; the most she can expect is tiring manual work – and, at that, not even in a factory where they require completion of primary school. Her shoes are of plastic, probably received by way of payment – or found in the trash. Her hair hangs lifelessly and her face lacks the sparkle of youth. She is five kilograms [11.0 lb] underweight, has thin, bowed legs; her defective teeth will not last much longer. Durval is afraid only that she will have to sell her body, as do so many daughters of poor parents. He knows that there are parents who leave their daughters in the red-light zone in the morning and pick them up at the end of the afternoon, just as if they were at school or on a job. This idea worries him.

Tattered, dirty, and smelling sour, one by one, his three youngest boys come home. It is the end of a day spent walking the streets, knocking on doors to beg for food, money or clothing; teaming up with a group selling snacks to motorists stopped at traffic signals; rummaging through garbage dumps; and sometimes making friends among the gangs of boys who rob in order to survive. None of them go to school. They tried, but there were no vacancies in the public schools. Even if they had gotten in, having three children in school means large expenses for school materials, clothing and transportation as well as the loss of what they gain through their daily work on the streets.

With the money he obtained as his share in the selling of snacks, the oldest boy, 13, bought some fresh bread. The smell of it spreads – to Durval, who restrains himself. That food is for the children. The two youngest bring in cardboard boxes to be folded and sold by the kilo on Saturday. They are piled up in the back, inside the shack. To leave them outside would ensure their disappearance, due to the general level of misery in this locality. On the wood stove, in which the children put scraps of wood found in the garbage, Durval's wife is cooking a bone she bought with money from selling things she found in the trash. She was lucky – early in her searchings, she found some pieces of metal she sold to the metal scrap dealer. The bone enriched the broth; she added a handful of broken rice, found at the bottom of a sack she brought home from the fair a week earlier. There is about one kilo left in the sack, which will have to last for several days, cooked a handful at a time.

In Durval's home, no one sits at a table. There are no flowered tablecloths, painted crockery, or cut glasses. Each person dips a conch-shell into the pot, pours a little soup into a mug, and retires into a corner to crouch on a box that serves as furniture. They eat in silence, like cave people, satisfying their strongest natural instinct, the appeasing of hunger.

Why so many Durvals? Brazilian industries producing for the domestic market are now in deep depression because so few people have any money to spend. A World Bank study reveals, for instance, that real wages for unskilled construction workers in São Paulo, one of Brazil's richest districts, fell by over 25 per cent between 1980 and 1985. The number of people able to earn even these depressed wages declined sharply too. For example, the São Paulo construction industry (formal sector) employed less than half as many workers in 1984 as in 1978. Casual labourers in rural Brazil fared even worse during the same period – their real wages dropped by nearly 40 per cent.[11]

The numbers of rural people have been rapidly shrinking in Latin America as a whole for two decades, and the continent's country-to-city migration rates are the highest in the world. During the 1970s over 4 per cent of rural people migrated every year in Brazil, Chile and Colombia, while in Mexico, Peru and Venezuela more than 3 per cent left for cities yearly. Countries like Argentina, Chile, Uruguay and Venezuela are now less than 20 per cent rural.[12]

The countryside is none the less an inexhaustible reservoir of poverty because so few who remain there have access to land. Landlessness is the 'key determinant of poverty in rural Latin America', according to the authors of an ILO study. In spite of years of sustained and massive outmigration, there are still 'too many' people in rural Latin America, given the enormous concentration of land in the hands of a tiny elite. Dependent on wage work, the landless must take what they can get – which is precious little. The ILO team notes:

the phenomenon of absolute impoverishment [of rural people] in a majority of Latin American countries has further worsened in the 1980s. During this period, real agricultural wages have fallen drastically in all countries, with the only exceptions being Colombia, Honduras and Panama. In Mexico, for example, where wages had risen enormously between 1965 and 1980, the dramatic fall in wages in the early 1980s has brought the agricultural wage back to its 1965 level.[13]

Official unemployment figures in Brazil varied from 6 to 8 per cent in 1983, depending on the district, but, as usual, hid more than they revealed. Private-sector economists put the rate closer to 17–20 per cent. After a sustained crisis that placed its interest payments in jeopardy, Brazil signed up with the IMF for its usual austerity package on 27 September 1983. In exchange it received $11 billion worth of new credit from a variety of sources. The next day sixteen supermarkets were pillaged in São Paulo alone. By mid-October over 225 markets, warehouses and shops throughout the country had been stripped of their wares. 'I don't apologize for anything,' said Zelinha Sobrinho, a 19-year-old looter arrested in a poor suburb of Rio. 'I am unemployed and no one is solving my situation. The thing to do is agitate. It is the only way to show the authorities that Brazil could explode.'[14]

Brazil did not, however, explode. The *Banker* seemed pleased to report in July 1984 that although

in the last three years the country's industrial heartland has been shedding jobs by the hundreds of thousands and a slump has wiped out a decade of improved living standards . . . Brazil is not about to erupt in revolution. More than the unemployed riots and supermarket lootings of 1983 (they have since died down) it is the 'parallel economy' of crime, now assuming epidemic proportions, that is the real response. That may oblige shops and business premises to maintain armed guards . . . but it is not the stuff of which social upheaval is made . . .[15]

It is a comfort to know that the rich are fighting unemployment by hiring poor people to defend them against other poor people. Consolations elsewhere – in Venezuela, for example – include some wonderful opportunities to become self-employed: 'With unemployment rising and with no effective welfare net for Venezuela's marginal population, street peddling provides a socially tolerable alternative to begging, robbery or starvation,' writes a particularly sensitive analyst quoted in the *International Herald Tribune*. In 1986 the Venezuelan economy decline for the eighth straight year. The 1987 budget approved by the Venezuelan Congress in December 1986 called for 33.9 per cent to be devoted to foreign debt service. Venezuelan consumers have lost 35 per cent of their purchasing power since the beginning of the 1980s; the *official* unemployment rate is 13 per cent; and the 'socially tolerable', informal economy that allows so many lucky people to sell lottery tickets at the bus station is, according to the president of a market research firm, growing by 'leaps and bounds'.[16]

Argentina, under the military *junta* that seized power in March 1976, was an early and willing I M F pupil. Later that year the I M F granted the country a $290 million loan, the agreed signal for the private banks to follow suit. One Fund condition was drastic cuts in public-sector jobs, and estimates of the number of workers sacked within a year range from 100,000 to 200,000. This was only the beginning. So many companies were privatized – though the word had yet to gain general currency – that even the extreme right wing protested against the sell-off of national interests to foreign capital. The proceeds of these sales were not reinvested in industry or public services, and the Argentine economy was virtually stagnant when President Raul Alfonsín took over from the generals in 1983.[17]

Argentine economist Miguel Teubal points out that debt in his country is even more pernicious than elsewhere in Latin America.

At least Brazil and Mexico got their pharaonic projects – though with tremendous impact on income distribution. But in Argentina, debt was associated with deindustrialization, the destruction of productive capacity, and endemic unemployment. Industrial production is now [1986] lower than it was in 1974 and infrastructure – roads, schools, hospitals, etc. – was not replaced.

The *junta* actually organized financial speculation and capital flight through its exacerbated free-market policies. Private and public enterprises were encouraged to use foreign rather than domestic credit. Teubal has a list of 106 transnational companies that borrowed – in many cases from their own corporate headquarters – $7 billion abroad. People could swap (over-valued) pesos for dollars freely and used them to buy a flood of foreign consumer goods, while the generals stocked up on military hardware. Teubal says, 'The whole country went on a speculative spree . . . using "hot money" that could (and did) flee at any moment.'[18]

Here is how the 'hot money' game worked. Assume you have $1 million. In August 1980 you can exchange it for 1,350 million pesos, which you put in an Argentine bank as a one-month deposit at 7 per cent. At the end of the month, you have 1,444.5 million pesos, which you can convert back into dollars at 1,400 to $1 – a rate that was *guaranteed* you before you made the deposit. You are now the proud owner of $1,031,786 and have made 3.2 per cent on your money in *one month* – which comes to a tidy 46 per cent a year if you want to keep reinvesting in the same game. Argentine and foreign speculators emptied their pockets and stripped their companies of all assets in order to play, and sent the proceeds to Switzerland or the Cayman Islands as they went along.[19]

The result of this wholesale conversion of productive capacity into cash was an equally massive shift of job-losers into so-called *cuenta propia*, or self-employed, activities. Or, in the more cautious parlance of a study commissioned by the World Bank, 'there was a swing from more productive to less productive employment.'[20]

Poor Alfonsín hasn't been able to reverse these trends by reinvesting in production; nor could you if you were devoting up to 67 per cent of your country's export revenues to debt service, as he has had to do since he took office in December 1983. Between October 1983 and October 1985 the rate of unemployment rose by 58 per cent. Figures published in January 1986 showed that for greater Buenos Aires (where about 10 million people, a third of the population, live) *official* unemployment now strikes more than 11 per cent of the work force.[21] And Argentina has the advantage of very low population growth – it doesn't have to deal with job creation for the masses of under-20s one finds in Brazil or Mexico.

The international community had no scruples about loaning billions to fuel speculation in a country run by uniformed thieves and murderers, whose only invention was a new transitive verb: to 'disappear' someone. The international community sat by as they 'disappeared' thousands, and it continued to loan frenetically when any first-year student of economics could see that the money was going up in smoke. If ever there were a case for refusing to pay interest on a huge portion of illegitimate debt, now totalling $54 billion, this is it.

MONETARISM RIDES AGAIN

In Chile, since the right-wing military takeover of 1973, monetarist economic theory has enjoyed a status akin to that of divine revelation. The 'Chicago Boys' are in command (so named because most of them trained at the University of Chicago under Milton Friedman). In Chile, as nowhere else, monetarists were given almost unlimited scope to put their economic theories into practice.

For a while, their policies seemed to work. The Boys were rewarded with high growth rates. Most of the growth was, however, spurious and enjoyed only by the upper and middle classes, rejoicing under a deluge of consumer goods, many of them cheap imports purchased with an over-valued peso. During the five boom years, from 1977 to 1981, private consumption went up by nearly 10 per cent a year. Sales of cars, T V sets, home appliances and other durable goods skyrocketed.

Some of this prosperity did spill over into the poorer classes. Practically everyone, at least in urban areas where 80 per cent of Chileans live, gained access to piped water, and wages – for those who had employment – improved by about a third in real terms. Infant mortality rates declined overall; life expectancy rose as well.[22]

Unfortunately, during the same period the Chilean government's own figures show that over 30 per cent of Chilean families were 'extremely poor', while a further 15 per cent were 'poor' according to a variety of criteria. This situation has, to say the least, not improved since 1981. Several studies on food-consumption levels, carried out between 1982 and 1985 after the boom collapsed, all conclude that 35 to 40 per cent of Chilean families are unable to satisfy their basic food needs.

Just as middle-class prosperity masked deepening poverty for nearly half the population, so rising unemployment was papered over by phoney work programmes. Employment figures for the 1977–81 period look fairly good on paper. The government's National Institute of Statistics (INE) places joblessness at between 7.5 and 9.9 per cent – no better and no worse than unemployment in the United States during the same years. A closer look at job-holders *by social class* is more worrisome. Even during the high-growth period, unskilled workers and those in the poorest 20 per cent of the population – often the same people – suffered unemployment rates of at least 15 per cent.

During the infamous Pinochet decade official job figures rely on a statistical trick. Anyone registered in the PEM or the POJH (acronyms for the government's Minimum Employment Programme and Occupational Programme for Heads of Households) is classed as 'employed'. In a normal country people earning PEM or POJH wages could in no circumstances be thus labelled. If the PEMers and POJHers are included in the unemployment figures – which they never are in official sources – true joblessness is revealed as alarming, even in 'good' years. With an average 175,000 workers in these programmes during the boom years, PEM and POJH participants made up over 5 per cent of Chile's total labour force of 3.2 million people.

After the monetarist bubble burst a great many new workers joined the PEM/POJH ranks – participants in the two programmes averaged 383,000 between 1982 and 1985. Depending on the year, they represented between 7 and 13 per cent of the total work force, and again all were classed as 'employed'. Real, undisguised unemployment is now 20 per cent at the most conservative estimate; most sources place it far higher.[23]

PEM/POJH workers are engaged in what can only be qualified as make-work schemes. Even though participants must labour for a full working day, their wages are miserable, well below the barest subsistence levels. For example, a PEM worker in late 1982 earned an average of $US32.20 a *month*; POJH heads of households took home $55.30. Compare this with the *minimum legal* wage for a worker in Chile, skilled or unskilled, which was $US130.80 a month during the same period, or with the average monthly earnings of an employed unskilled Chilean worker of $US270.80. Clearly, people who earn four times less than the minimum wage and eight and a half times less than the average unskilled worker's take-home pay are 'employed' only in the sense that they must work full hours (and thus have no opportunity to earn extra money elsewhere). Cooking the statistical books does not change this fact.[24]

There are other glaring inequalities under the *junta*. For one thing, poor people are likely to remain poor because they have such a hard time getting an education in spite of 'universal' primary schooling. Among the children whose families ranked among the 40 per cent poorest in 1979 a shocking 53 per cent had to repeat first grade, while 50 per cent repeated second grade. By contrast, only 8 per cent of the children from the best-off 40 per cent of families repeated first grade; a mere 4 per cent of wealthier children repeated second grade. School drop-out rates are also much higher for the children of poor families.[25]

Urban–rural disparities are also marked. Rural people, though they now account for only a fifth of the Chilean population, make up fully half of the 'extremely poor', whatever the criteria one chooses to apply (poor diet, ill health, sub-standard housing, etc.). They enjoy few of the advantages available in urban areas even to those at the bottom of society. For instance, though piped water is now accessible to virtually every town-dwelling family in Chile, including the poorest (98 per cent), only 11 per cent of rural people have access to clean water.[26]

This is the background of destitution and gross inequality upon which the debt crisis has been superimposed. Poverty is not a new story in Chile or, indeed, elsewhere in Latin America, and the debt crisis has not created or caused it in the strict sense. The new phenomenon to which the debt crisis has, however, unquestionably given rise is the unheard-of scope and prevalence of distress. Large segments of the middle class slide inexorably towards indigence, while the already poor sink to the depths of destitution.

Faced with deprivation on an entirely new scale, the state is revealed as either helpless or indifferent. Far from contributing to popular welfare and preventing mass marginalization, the heavily indebted government often becomes a kind of 'illfare' state, preoccupied chiefly with preserving its own power and thus with repressing popular initiatives that might threaten its authority.

THE DEADLY CONNECTION

One could easily go on describing the contraction of job opportunities throughout Latin America, since all the indebted countries suffer similar ills. The point should be clear by now, though, and it's important to show how the *delayed costs* of debt will weigh heavily upon the South for decades. We've seen, for instance, what sort of future awaits Durval's children: debt is likely to make it even shorter and more painful than Durval's.

UN agency statistics are slowly beginning to register increasing infant mortality rates (IMRs).[27] My own (admittedly spotty) evidence indicates that indeed they *are* climbing throughout the Third World. If confirmed, this is a deadly trend whose significance far surpasses the individual grief of the families losing babies. Even in the worst-off and least developed countries IMRs had been declining slowly but steadily for decades. Since the only really new economic fact in these countries over the past ten years has been runaway indebtedness followed by IMF-style austerity programmes, we may conclude that this has more than a little to do with rising IMRs.

IMRs are usually under-reported in Third World countries anyway, especially for the poorer classes of society, which have the most children, so any increases that show up statistically have to be taken seriously. It will be a long time before the full impact of the debt crisis is expressed in numbers, but there are already statistical warning signs.

If the signs prove true, we must also conclude that, in order to extract their money, Western government policy-makers, directorates of international agencies, bankers *et alia* are quite prepared to reverse the hard-won progress of decades, to undo the life's work of generations of development workers from dozens of disciplines who have struggled to enhance the environment for survival.[28] One thinks of Auden's lines: 'Every farthing of the cost/ All the dreaded cards foretell/ Shall be paid . . .'

The available evidence all points in one direction. A draft study by Brazilian researcher Roberto Macedo highlights effects of the debt crisis on the São Paulo area. Among them is increased infant mortality in 1983 and 1984, after a long decline. The 1984 rise was due largely to an epidemic of measles, which struck an infant population weaker than that of earlier years.[29] Anaemia among children under 5 also increased in the decade between 1975 and 1985, and nutritionists know that 'serious nutritional anaemia is never isolated but always associated with other illness, including parasitical diseases.'[30] Macedo also notes deteriorating health among children in São Paulo's industrial suburbs as well as increased school failure and drop-out rates.

Sociologists Ralph Sell and Steven Kunitz carried out a painstaking mathematical study of the relationship between debt and mortality and arrived at some arresting conclusions.[31] They found that the greater a country's participation in world markets – measured by the degree of indebtedness – the slower life expectancy increased. Just as IMRs have been declining for decades, so life expectancy has been increasing in *every* country, rich or poor. Using data from seventy-three African, Asian and Latin American countries that could boast reasonably reliable statistics, Sell and Kunitz established that the higher the debt, the lower the improvement in life expectancy. Since their data go only to the end of the 1970s, Sell and Kunitz did not find *increasing* death rates – this would have been astounding – but they do describe the 'end of an era' in which the downward mortality trend measurably slows.

In Latin America, the most indebted continent, the 'end of an era' is most pronounced. These authors even found it possible to quantify precisely the debt/mortality effect: 'Each additional $10 a year in interest payments [per capita] reflected 0.39 of a year less in life expectancy improvement over the decade [1970–80].' Their formula works out to an average 387 days of life forgone by every inhabitant of the seventy-three countries under study.*

What did you accomplish during the past year? Would you let financial technocrats and banks deprive you, or your parents, or your children of that year? From the best data currently available, this seems to be precisely the outcome of debt in Asia, Latin America and Africa.[32]

YOU ARE WHAT YOU DON'T EAT

Herculean efforts, like those of Sell and Kunitz, to assess the global impact of debt on human life are necessarily rare. We are, however, beginning to have partial studies for a single country, area or social class that bear out their pessimistic conclusions for the world at large.

Nutritional studies carried out in Peru between 1972 and 1983 show a steady increase in malnutrition for children under 6. In the poorest neighbourhoods of Lima and the shanty towns around it the percentage of undernourished children climbed from 24 per cent in 1972 to 28 per cent in 1978 to 36 per cent in 1983.[33] It is not just that these children are

---

* Sell and Kunitz calculate that for their sample of seventy-three countries, per capita interest payments on debts owed to all public and private sources soared from $2.90 to $27.30 between 1970 and 1982. Applying their own formula (which, for reasons that escape me, they don't do themselves), according to which $10 in interest payments per capita equals 0.39 of a year (142 days) lower average life expectancy, $27.30 in interest = 2.73 × 142 = 387 days of life lost.

hungry – which, God knows, is bad enough. They are being impaired for the rest of their lives, as evidence cited by Dr Jocelyn Boyden in a study for UNICEF and OXFAM shows. A Peruvian researcher compared two groups of children in Lima, one from middle-income private schools and the other from state schools in a shanty town, and found

a strong positive correlation between socio-economic status and intellectual functions which could not be explained by genetic factors and was demonstrated both in verbal ability and performance. Children from low-income areas were at a particular disadvantage in terms of the acquisition of knowledge, having a limited vocabulary and ability to concentrate. They also demonstrated a much lower level of visual-motor co-ordination.[34]

Peru supplies some of the most disgusting food stories I've ever heard. One is about the dish on offer at the back doors of some restaurants in Lima. Poor people buy it – when they can afford it. It's called *siete sabores*, or 'seven tastes', and is made up of the leavings and left-over scraps of all the dishes on the menu. Then there's Nicovita, a fish-meal flour used for fattening chickens, manufactured under extremely dubious sanitary conditions. The good news is that (at least in the late 1970s), a lot of Peruvian shanty-town dwellers were subsisting on Nicovita. The bad news is that, as the once finance minister, Silva Ruete, put it, 'They don't even have chicken feed to eat regularly.'[35]

Hardly surprising, then, that the former governor of the Peruvian Central Bank, Manuel Moreyra, had to admit that the 'social costs of this [IMF adjustment] policy are tragic. It means the death of some 500,000 children . . .' World Bank statistics cited by a Swiss author are said to have placed Peruvian IMRs at 70 per 1,000 in the 1970s but over 80 per 1,000 in the 1980s. Still other sources placed the overall IMR in Peru at more than 100, and some said that in the worst shanty towns *half* the new-borns were dying before the age of 1. The chronic hunger of his compatriots did not appear to bother the former president of the Peruvian Senate, Oscar Trelles. He declared publicly in 1981 that it was healthier to eat less, that thin women were far more attractive than fat ones and that Jewish children who had gone hungry in the concentration camps had not become stupider as a result.[36]

President García of Peru faces an uphill struggle to improve the food situation of his people. Their purchasing power has taken a nose-dive: in 1983 a minimum wage bought less than half of what it could have purchased a decade earlier. When you earn less, you eat less. FAO recommends 2,300–400 calories per day for the 'average' adult who, though non-existent, still provides a useful benchmark. Between 1972 and 1979 average lower-middle-class consumption in Peru dropped from 2,150 calories to 1,600. The diet of the worst-off fell from an already inadequate 1,900 to a starvation-level 1,500 calories. Protein intake showed similar declines. A kilo of rice cost 95 sols in Lima in July 1980 but 1,450 sols in February 1984. The cost of a tin of powdered milk rose from 95 to 960 sols during the same period. To eliminate the effect of inflation these huge cost increases can be better expressed in terms of work: in 1980 a Peruvian earning the minimum wage had to work seventeen minutes for a kilo of rice, in 1984 two hours and five minutes – over seven times as long. A tin of milk cost respectively seventeen and eighty-three minutes of a worker's time.[37]

Even Argentina, where malnutrition and other forms of acute social deprivation were traditionally minimal, shows the stamp of decline. Malnutrition is no longer a marginal phenomenon. Miguel Teubal reported in 1986:

According to official sources, there are 685,000 children in greater Buenos Aires alone who don't eat enough to stay alive – a minister said this – plus another 385,000 children in the province of Buenos Aires, or a third of the children under 14 in this province. One of the first acts of the new civilian government was to institute the National Food Program [PAN, or Programa Alimentario Nacional, which also spells 'bread'] to hand out supplementary food rations to families whose basic needs were not being met. In May 1985, 5.6 million people, or 18 per cent of the entire population, were receiving this assistance. We also have to count on foreign Non-governmental Organizations, the Churches and the school lunch program which was launched to try to avoid school drop-outs. In many cases, this lunch is the only food the children receive all day.[38]

The directress of a 'special' school (for handicapped children) 340 miles from Buenos Aires reported in 1984:

Of the 115 children in my school, ninety-eight are mentally retarded because of early childhood malnutrition. The children's deficiencies are usually not noticed until they reach the age for primary school – then they're sent to me, and it's too late.

A doctor in the same small city says that 5 per cent of the children are born with serious deficiencies because the mothers are malnourished.

He attributes 35 infant deaths per thousand to hunger. Official figures show 28 per cent of Buenos Aires inhabitants malnourished, but as many as 40 to 50 per cent suffer from hunger in the poorer provinces of the north. There is even one small province (with a largely Indian population) where fully 59 per cent of the children under 5 are considered *desnutridos*.[39]

Meanwhile, Argentina is exporting more food than ever before in its history in order to reimburse its $54 billion debt. But it must compete against heavily subsidized wheat exports from the US and the EEC, which also happen to be its largest creditors . . . The finance minister notes bitterly that if agricultural prices had been the same in 1986 as in 1984, Argentina could have earned an extra $2 billion.

The Alfonsín government, in spite of electoral promises that 'debt will not be payed with the sacrifices of the people', has fallen into line and behaved, so far, as a model debtor. The umbrella labour confederation, CGT, has called several general strikes, and its posters bear the slogan 'Enough of lies, unemployment, hunger, misery and the IMF'. But the opposition is disunited, and, at this writing, ordinary Argentinians continue to pay the debt with their sacrifices.

CUT TO BRAZIL

The hut is sinking in the mud near the bridge over the River Guaibe in Porto Alegro, Brazil. A woman social worker is welcomed by five children, the oldest about 8 years old. The parents have gone out foraging in the garbage heaps. Noticing how poorly the children look, the social worker asks them whether they have eaten recently. 'Yes, miss, yesterday Mummy made little cakes from wet newspapers.' 'What? Little cakes from what?' asks the woman. 'Mummy takes a sheet of newspaper, makes it into a ball and soaks it in water and when it is nice and soft kneads it into little cakes. We eat them, drink some water and feel nice and full inside.'

This story comes from the 'Information Newsletter' of the Brazilian Evangelical Lutheran Church. It speaks volumes more than official statistics, but the latter are still worth noting. Between 1961 and 1963 the Brazilian Institute of Economics (IBE), with the help of the US Department of Agriculture, carried out a vast household survey and concluded that 27 million Brazilians (then one-third of the population) suffered from malnutrition. In 1985 the Ministry of Planning, on the basis of other surveys, estimated that 86 million Brazilians, or two-thirds of the population, were malnourished. So much for 'development' under the military dictatorship, which lasted from 1964 until 1985. The Brazilian armed forces admitted that 47 per cent of those rejected for military service were failed because of nutritional deficiencies.

Starvation is endemic in the ultra-poor north-east of Brazil, where it is producing what IBASE calls a 'sub-race' and nutritionists call an epidemic of dwarfism. In the *nordeste* children are 16 per cent shorter and 20 per cent lighter than children of the same ages elsewhere in Brazil, who are not exactly well nourished themselves. The population of north-eastern Brazil is about 35 million, slightly larger than that of the six Sahelian African countries recently featuring so prominently in the hunger limelight. Mario Kertesz, mayor of Salvador, Brazil, says, 'When I visit the people in the shanty towns, they talk to me about the children who have died of dysentery for lack of clean water. All I can says is, "Don't lose hope." I don't have a solution.' Kertesz heads a movement of twenty Brazilian mayors who are demanding that the nation postpone debt payments and use the money for local urban needs. He says the new democracy will commit political suicide otherwise.[40]

Cardinal Paulo Evaristo Arns, Archbishop of São Paulo, a diocese of over 15 million people, has fervently championed the cause of the poor. He does not mince words on the subject of debt. In late 1985 he said:

The huge effort of the past two years resulted in a export surplus of a billion dollars a month. Yet this money served only to pay the interest on the debt. It's impossible to go on this way; we have already taken everything the people had to eat, even though two-thirds of them are already going hungry. When we borrowed, interest rates were 4 per cent; they're 8 per cent now and at one point they went as high as 21 per cent. Even worse, these loans were contracted by the military, mostly for military ends – $40 billion were swallowed by six nuclear plants, none of which is working today. The people are now expected to pay off these debts in low salaries and hunger. But we have already reimbursed the debt, once or twice over, considering the interest paid. We must stop giving the blood and the misery of our people to pay the First World.[41]

THE TORTILLA GAP

Brazilians are suffering horribly, but at least their official statistical institutes know it, and with considerable precision. In Mexico each change of government seems to provoke a change in research personnel and in methodology. People get sacked in mid-study; surveys aren't comparable from one year to another; samples turn out to be not really representative. When the Mexican Food System programme (SAM) was functioning in the early 1980s excellent work on food consumption and nutrition was undertaken, but it was dissolved before the results were all in. To cap it all, as a World Bank consultant stated in 1986, 'No health indicators were available for 1983 and the following years. Apparently stored in the Directorate-General of Statistics computers damaged by the September 1985 earthquake, this information has therefore been lost almost in its entirety . . .'[42]

In spite of the statistical shambles, the picture one can piece together is hardly encouraging. The National Nutrition Institute estimates that perhaps 40 per cent of the Mexican population is malnourished. One study in a Federal District county (greater Mexico City) showed that *half of all households* in this county displayed calorie and protein deficiencies.[43] This survey was carried out in 1984. People with deficiencies ate mostly tortillas, bread, beans and rehydrated milk – all of which were, at the time, subsidized. In 1986 these subsidies were eliminated as part of the IMF programme, requiring sharp reductions in Mexico's budget deficit and the 'opening up' of the Mexican economy. When the new Mexican $12 billion loan deal was signed and sealed in September 1986 the price of tortillas shot up from 45 to 80 pesos a kilo (just over 2 lb) in a single day. Prices for other basic food items also increased by 100 per cent within a six-month period in 1986, according to the Bank of Mexico.

Price hikes on this scale not only worsen people's diets but also cause the economy to contract. Maria and Josefina Mendieta and their mother run a small lunch counter in Tlaxcala. The Mendieta sisters could explain to IMF theoreticians what they should already have learned from a cursory reading of Adam Smith. 'Everything is going up, so we have to raise our prices too,' says Maria. 'And that is when people stop coming. The peasants bringing produce to the market used to come a lot. Now they don't show up any more.' Across the alley from Maria's lunch counter Xavier Cortez and half a dozen other small entrepreneurs make the tortillas. They said that since the cost of (previously subsidized) corn nearly tripled, the price of tortillas had to go up as well. Market rumour, according to Xavier, is that the next tortilla price hike will be 100 per cent.[44]

The National Consumer Institute found in 1984 that about 70 per cent of lower-income Mexicans had virtually stopped eating rice, eggs, fruit,

vegetables and milk (never mind meat or fish). All these products –
sometimes including salt – are such luxuries that they are eaten only on
'the second day of the feast' (about five occasions in the religious
calendar), as peasants from Chiapas explained to André Aubry.[45]

No worker earning the minimum salary or less can possibly cover the
cost of the basic market basket of twenty-eight goods and services for a
family of five as defined by the government. This basket does not contain
any expenditure on health, education, clothing, household upkeep or
entertainment. At least 55 per cent of those employed earn just the
minimum salary, while 27 per cent are unemployed or severely under-
employed, according to figures from various official sources published
by *Pueblo*. In 1985–6, Mexico was paying $27 million a day – $18,750
every minute – to its creditors in interest. That comes to 35 cents per
Mexican per day, or $128 per Mexican man, woman and child every
year. With that, you could buy quite a lot of tortillas.[46]

9.
LATIN AMERICA: GOING TO EXTREMES

If the Babylonian farmer who lost his crop had been forced to pay back his creditor anyway, he would soon have sold off his possessions, his animals and his land. Instead of living as a more or less prosperous and independent farmer, he would have joined the ranks of the landless poor, surviving on casual labour from hand to mouth. A wealthy neighbour or merchant would have bought the farmer's property on the cheap and grown richer exploiting it. Without the King's Code, Babylon would have been a more polarized society, like so many in the Third World today, where debt thrusts millions into hunger and a marginal existence.

Because of the debt crisis polarization and marginalization are accelerating, both *within* and *between* countries. Heavily indebted societies quite literally go to extremes: the middle class tends to disappear, while a very few rich people able to escape the pernicious effects of debt dominate millions who can barely survive. Zaïre is a particularly severe case of this phenomenon, as we've seen. At the international level rich countries also grow richer at the expense of poor ones that are obliged to sell off their property (commodities, labour) at 'famine prices'. Marginalization begins to strike whole nations because they must cash in their assets and cannot save or invest anything in the future.

Acts of God aggravate the process of going to extremes. Regrettably, the Code of Hammurabi does not apply at the IMF. Whereas his Code made allowances for the unpredictable storm god, the IMF does not see natural disasters as mitigating circumstances. A few days after the Mexico City earthquake of September 1985, the Fund's flying squads were back in town, demanding their due. A cartoon in Le Monde shows two IMF types knocking on Mexico's door, behind which lies a heap of rubble. 'What excuse do you suppose they'll come up with this time?' asks one bureaucrat of the other. About the same time a Mexican cartoon pictured a vulture labelled IMF perched above the ruins from which signs of life are beginning to emerge. 'Feeling better, Mexico?' asks the predator. 'Just remember we still have some unfinished business to settle.'

Mexico has about as much control over the price of oil as it had over the earthquake or the Babylonian farmer had over the ravages of the storm god. Yet when oil slumps precipitously, wiping out a large proportion of Mexico's (or Ecuador's or Venezuela's) export revenues, that is no excuse for non-payment of debt. The Fund and other 'sado-monetarists' (Dennis Healey's phrase) think that it is still possible to adjust. Their prescription? Devalue, in order to export more.

EXPORTOMANIA AND POLARIZATION

Even those analysts who do not share the Fund's eagerness for deep cuts in social services tend to see eye to eye with the IMF on the issue of exports. For example, a World Bank summary of the studies on the 'social costs of recession' states unequivocally that conditions in Latin America are bound to grow worse because of the 'collapse of investment and the resulting deterioration of the physical condition of hospitals and schools'. This document pleads for preserving basic services for the poor but still claims that 'it is much harder to maintain, let alone improve, the lot of the poor in the absence of economic growth . . . the lesson, then, is that a resumption of growth is by far the most certain way to stabilize and eventually improve the condition of the poor . . . *Resumed growth will depend on export expansion*' (my emphasis).[1]

When 'Expand exports' is incised on the tablets of our present-day Codes, one wonders how the lot of the poor can ever be 'maintained', let alone 'improved.' The lot of the poor can be improved only when the poor have something useful and productive to do, like providing basic necessities, including food and shelter, to others within their own societies. Those who argue for expanding exports as a road to growth put their faith in comparative advantage, and while they focus on what exports may *earn*, they rarely tell us what they *cost*.

When these exports are agricultural products the first thing they cost is land – land that *could* be devoted to food crops, that *could* be devoted to feeding the millions of hungry people in the indebted countries. But, of course, it won't be because that would not be 'economical'. Mexico, for example, has devoted enormous efforts to expanding beef-cattle production, almost exclusively for export, since so few Mexicans can afford to eat beef themselves. Shipments to the United States more than doubled between 1985 and 1986 – from 577,000 to 1.2 million head. Mexico did not, however, double its revenues because each steer was worth $100 *less* in 1986 than in the previous year. Whether or not these animals fetch a decent price on the US market, they take up more and more space in Mexico, as do the forage crops they eat.[2]

One usually thinks of the United States as an agricultural exporter, which it is, but it is also, somewhat surprisingly, the world's largest food importer ($20.8 billion worth in 1986). Mexico is now the premier agricultural supplier to its northern neighbour: over $2 billion worth in 1986, mostly fresh fruits and vegetables, as well as beef. Meanwhile, Mexico *imported* $1.5 billion of agricultural products from the US in 1985, mostly in basic grains and oilseeds. Surely this is comparative advantage in action? Isn't everyone better off concentrating on his strong suit and importing what the other fellow produces more cheaply?

That would be too blissfully simple. For one thing, Mexico has a comparative advantage in fresh fruits and vegetables grown on the huge, irrigated farms of the northern states of Sinaloa and Sonora only because government spending on the agricultural sector has been so heavily concentrated on these farms. Long before the debt crisis, from 1940 to 1970, 60 per cent of all government investment in agriculture went to these northern states, where only 9 per cent of the small peasant holdings (*ejidos*) are located. Today rich farmers in these rich provinces still get water from government irrigation schemes at less than a third of its real cost. If successive governments had decided to invest in other crops – which is to say, in *other social classes* – Mexico could perfectly well have a comparative advantage in corn, beans and oilseeds today.

There is little that is natural in 'natural advantage'. This theory works only if the government can collect on its export revenues, which it needs in order to purchase from foreigners the staple foods that the theoreticians claim it doesn't need to grow. Unfortunately for Mexico, the large farms that benefit from exports also pay very low taxes, and their owners are as sophisticated in exporting capital as cucumbers. So the rich grow richer and the poor hungrier.

A further pernicious consequence of investing in large exporting farms and neglecting small growers is the huge outflux of people from the countryside. If Mexico grew more of its basic foodstuffs, life in rural areas would become more prosperous and attractive to the peasantry and the cities would be less congested. The sprawl of Mexico City has already reached crisis proportions. In the year 2000 the population of this megalopolis will top 30 million at present growth rates. Some of its residents already compare it with Dante's *Inferno*, though there is some argument about exactly which circle they inhabit.

A turnaround would not be impossible. One estimate, cited by the *Economist Development Report*, says that if 'the government redirected the perks which it is giving to farmers with irrigated land, to improving inputs and credit for rain-fed (small) farmers, it could bring 5 million extra hectares under cultivation, eliminate food imports and create 5 million jobs'.[3] But that would not conform to the iron code of the IMF (nor to the interests of the richest and most powerful Mexicans).

WEALTHY WETBACKS

Mexico has registered spectacular success in its exports of one extremely valuable commodity – rich and educated people. They are leaving in droves and settling in the United States.[4] Official statistics on human capital flight are unavailable, but some researchers believe that over 100,000 upper-middle-class, highly skilled Mexican professionals headed north between 1982 and 1985.

Another, smaller, group, which one sociologist calls the 'post-devaluation exiles', may not be especially smart but, man, are they rich! 'We're buying California back from the US,' boasts a member of one of the twenty-eight families interviewed by this sociologist. Each one of these families arrived with $4 million or $5 million. They, and dozens like them, are buying businesses and luxury housing as if there were no tomorrow. So many Mexicans have bought condominiums in high-rise buildings near La Jolla, California, that racist anglos have christened these apartments the 'Taco Towers'.

The exodus of the elite – and of the elite's money – makes the burden for those who must remain behind even greater. Yet which of us, individually, can cast a stone at these Mexicans? I have that sinking feeling I might join them were I in their hand-made crocodile shoes. They describe Mexico as a four-C society – rife with cynicism, corruption, crisis and crime. Kidnapping and murder aimed at the rich have become commonplace. Mexicans who have a choice say they no longer want to bring up their children in their own country.

All of them watched their fortunes (in pesos) melt with each successive devaluation. One manufacturer who moved to Texas explained that for him the last straw was the bribes he had to pay simply to maintain garbage collection and other basic services. As one escapee says, 'Mexico is my home, but now there is no hope there.' Debt, devaluation and human/material capital outflow feed on each other, and rich Mexicans move to the 'North pole' extreme on the polarization scale.[5]

BOP-PING IN BRAZIL

Brazil is too far away from the US to export as many people as Mexico but compensates by exporting more food. Vincent Leclercq, an economist specializing in Brazilian agriculture at the French National Institute of Agronomic Research (INRA) notes some alarming trends, especially since January 1983, when the IMF first applied its standard analysis and structural-adjustment package to Brazil.*[6]

One of the Fund's chief goals was to *reduce* domestic consumption in spite of huge excess manufacturing capacity and already low demand for food compared with the size of the population. In Fund language this is called 'demand management'. 'Demand' applies only to those requirements that can be expressed in terms of money; it has nothing to do with real needs. The Fund's corrective measures were aimed at restoring a positive balance of payments (BOP) to the exclusion of any other goal – which in turn meant relying on export agriculture, Brazil's biggest money-earner. The economy was declared 'adjusted' when Brazil's

---

* The official IMF programme came to an end in 1985, but Brazil continues to apply most of the same measures on its own.

international books returned to the black – thanks also to sharp curtailment of imports.

Brazil's emphasis on export crops to the detriment of food crops cannot be blamed exclusively on the IMF. Successive governments, heavily influenced by the largest landowners, have consistently encouraged exports and showered credit on the farmers who produce them. Brazil now trails only the US in agri-export revenues, with soybeans, orange juice, chicken and coffee heading the list. Land planted to soybeans increased over ninefold in the 1970s. Brazil has also set up the world's largest fuel-alcohol programme to cut down oil imports, with enormous sugar-cane plantations providing the raw material. The 'green plague' of cane has brought misery to thousands of smallholders by forcing them off the land and into a marginal existence.

These deliberate policies have taken their toll on food production and consumption. The vast majority of poor Brazilians depend on six staple food crops: cassava, corn, beans, rice, potatoes, and wheat. In 1977 total production of these six mainstays was just over 60 million tons, with cassava and corn accounting for 26 and 19 million tons respectively. Any country where people count on cassava for 43 per cent of their staple food supply is already in bad nutritional shape unless they get a good amount of protein from beans or other legumes.

Two disastrous years of unfavourable weather in 1978 and 1979 dragged food crops down by 12 per cent. By 1982 production had crept back up to 62 million tons. The IMF programme was implemented in January 1983. That same year production of the mainstay staples dropped by 13 per cent to 54 million tons, the lowest level since the very poor year of 1978. Bean harvests fell 45 per cent and a further 11 per cent in 1984. These declines could not be ascribed to bad weather. Meanwhile the population was growing at 2.5 per cent yearly. The only food crop that actually did better was wheat, a small factor in Brazil with only about 2 million tons grown annually. Wheat, mostly imported, has none the less been a godsend to ordinary urban Brazilians and has helped to keep their diet from being even worse than it is.

Against this fragile backdrop the IMF decided to (1) eliminate wheat consumption subsidies, (2) squeeze rural credit, (3) push agricultural exports harder than ever.

The Fund argues that subsidies cost the state too much and encourage inflation; that imports of subsidized products (like wheat) cancel out export gains; that subsidies distort the market and prevent other staple food products from competing. Fair enough. Brazilian wheat imports cost over $500 million in 1978 and nearly $900 million in 1980 – a startling

64 per cent jump and a lot of money when one is expected to build up a positive BOP. But wiping out the subsidy when the wheat habit was already firmly entrenched (consumption was increasing by 10 per cent yearly) could only worsen an already precarious national diet.

In the first half of the 1980s Brazil averaged half a billion dollars' worth of imported wheat from the United States alone but in 1985–6 slashed its purchases from 450,000 to 48,000 tons! Can people compensate for the loss of wheat by consuming other staple foods? No, because the IMF stabilization programme prevents this too: agricultural credit has been drastically curtailed. Farmers consequently cut back on inputs – better seeds, fertilizer, etc. – so their yields suffer. Staple foods seem to be everyone's lowest priority – except for the poor and hungry who, by definition, don't count.

The only real hope for Brazilian consumers and peasants alike is land reform. As of the end of 1986, promised reforms had been stymied. The Sarney government announced sweeping changes, then backtracked under concerted assault from the land barons, who pretend that any reduction of their privileges is part of the 'international communist conspiracy'. Their hired thugs murdered 500 peasants and their supporters (lawyers, priests, trade unionists) in 1985–6. In Brazil 2 per cent of the farms occupy 58 per cent of all farmland, while 83 per cent of the farms share only 14 per cent of the land. Four hundred mega-farmers between them own an area equivalent to 85 per cent of Great Britain.[7]

BOLIVIA: THE BREAKING POINT

Since everything is so expensive, I don't give my children breakfast any more. For lunch I give them a little rice soup. I don't buy sugar now that it has gone up. To eat, I have to make do any way I can, because the children can't get along without food. Us adults, we manage without when we have to. Sometimes I say to myself, 'I'm going to give away my children to someone.' But then I think of what my parents might do to me – that's what I'm afraid of.

A Bolivian mother, Zona San José Carpinteros, La Paz[8]

In a chapter devoted to extremes and the forces of polarization, despite heavy competition the sweepstakes winner is Bolivia. This unfortunate country personifies, in a kind of paroxysm, the trials of Latin American debtors.

Compared with other Latin American countries, Bolivia's debt isn't large – $5 billion – but then there are only 6 million Bolivians. These unfortunate people are afflicted with the worst conditions of the entire Latin American continent: highest infant mortality rate, lowest life expectancy, lowest GNP per capita, lowest literacy rate, etc. Over half the population is Indian and still lives in the countryside at altitudes between 11,000 and 13,000 feet.

Life for the peasants is particularly brutal: four out of every ten of their children will not see their fifth birthday; half the rural population cannot read or write (not surprisingly, four out of every five of these illiterates are women); and most will live out their short lives (under fifty years on average) without ever seeing a doctor, since there is only one for every 20,000 rural people. Sanitary facilities, permanent housing, pure drinking water supply and so on are poor to non-existent.[9]

As to food security, it would be simpler to give estimates of those who are *not* under-fed in Bolivia. Health Ministry figures published in April 1986 showed that over 50 per cent of rural women are malnourished and that an alarming 70 per cent of pregnant rural women are both under-nourished and anaemic. The Health Commission of the Bolivian Medical Council announced at its annual Congress in 1986 that 47 per cent of Bolivian children were malnourished.[10] 'In our country, eight out of every ten Bolivians live in poverty; of those eight, four live in misery,' says an organization for popular education.[11]

Bolivia's economy is such a mess that it has suspended much of its debt service. Even so, between 1981 and 1986 the country devoted an average 42 per cent of its vanishing export revenues to interest payments. The figure for 1985 was 60 per cent, for 1986 44 per cent.[12] In 1986 the IMF announced $107 million in new credits, and the World Bank started lending to Bolivia again, after a three-year hiatus. The Bank had cut off loans in 1983 when the democratically elected (for once!) President Hernan Siles Suazo failed to reach agreement with the IMF on an austerity programme.

Since its independence in 1825 Bolivia has chalked up over 180 *coups d'état* and become a symbol of chronic instability. From the early 1960s a variety of generals bled the country dry until late 1982, when there was virtually nothing left to steal and they handed it back to civilians. Military governments were responsible for contracting over 80 per cent of the current debt, and, as usual, the people now expected to make sacrifices for its reimbursement never saw the colour of the money.

The generals put borrowed funds into such projects as the autoroute from La Paz to El Alto (location of the airport), known to connoisseurs as the most expensive road per mile in the world. Proper soil-structure studies were not undertaken, and parts of the road are now sliding downhill into oblivion. A huge oil refinery, completely out of proportion to the amount of petroleum extracted in Bolivia, cost $200 million, or $120 million more than the original estimate. It has never operated above 30 per cent of its capacity. At the time of its construction the national petroleum company, YPFB, was managed by General Banzer's son-in-law. Similar waste occurred in the construction of plants for metals or oilseed processing. Loans were also spent on current consumption, sometimes on illegal imports. Needless to say, money was not invested in health, education or peasant agriculture.[13]

The United States has made much of the Bolivian cocaine connection and has even sent troops – supposedly to root out the dastardly drug traffickers, in fact to produce political theatre for domestic consumption. The U S shows no signs of recognizing that marginal individuals will struggle to stay alive even when it means crime or prostitution, and whole nations can become enmeshed in illegality when crime pays handsomely and nothing else does.

Bolivia, dependent on 'legal' exports of tin, gas and a few other metals, has watched its revenues plummet. Tin prices collapsed by over 80 per cent in 1985 and never recovered. Bolivian inflation that same year attained a mind-boggling 25,000 per cent. It is thus not surprising that so many Bolivians have recourse to the drug trade to survive: illegal exports of coca paste and cocaine are estimated at $3.5 billion–$4 billion a year, seven times the value of legal exports.[14] Two Bolivian research organizations estimate that at least a third of the country's economy is illegal and/or underground when one counts smuggling, drug trafficking, speculation, tax evasion and capital flight.[15]

The top end of the drug trade benefits only a few dozen families, including those of the 'cocaine generals', but with the proceeds they can buy the police, the administration, the customs and the politicians. Bolivian peasants have always chewed coca to ease their hunger, and now thousands are growing it as a cash crop, one that brings in far more than anything else they could plant.

A Bolivian expert, Roberto Jordán Pando, reminds us that the United States has never been able to get rid of any social phenomenon merely by passing a law against it (think of Prohibition or of marijuana). Cocaine use is no different: drug crops 'eradicated' in one place will, so to speak, crop up elsewhere. The US cocaine market was 85 tons in 1984, 125 tons in 1985 and 250 tons in 1986. Is this Bolivia's fault? Supply-side economics is all very well, but without rapidly expanding demand, Bolivia could never have increased its production from 6,000 tons of coca leaves in the early 1970s to 152,000 tons in 1986.

About 66,000 hectares (165,000 acres) are planted to coca in Bolivia. One hectare brings in three harvests annually, worth $10,000 to its owner (and up to $50,000 if the cultivator is also a trader). Compare this with the average annual income of a miner ($827), a factory worker ($649) or a non-coca-producing peasant ($160). The United States, through its eradication programme in Bolivia, is offering a premium of $360 per hectare to incite farmers to plant a substitute crop. Are they kidding? As Jordán says, 'If an American farmer accepted that kind of deal, he would be considered either crazy or a philanthropist. It's not Bolivia's doing if US drug eradication and repression programmes are erroneous and ill-conceived.'[16]

One study of family survival strategies describes how quite ordinary Bolivian peasant families evolve towards the lower echelons of the drug trade. They have a bit of land and are used to moving from countryside to city to sell their crops or animals. It's an easy step towards coca production, easier still to use their habitual travel routes to collect or sell the drug crop. All family members, including the children, participate.[17]

Moving people about on a massive scale is also a government strategy for coping with its financial crisis. When Victor Paz Estenssoro replaced President Siles Suazo in August 1985, the new president did not immediately conclude a formal agreement with the IMF, but he did set in motion all the monetarist measures the Fund requires, wage freezes and drastic cuts in government spending among them. Since the tin mines had become financial bottomless pits whose operation could not even be covered by revenues from tin exports, the Bolivian Mining Corporation (COMIBOL) closed several mines and sacked thousands of miners. Fifteen thousand people were supposed to migrate from Potosi to the eastern part of the country to be settled as peasants and foresters.[18]

This was far from a peaceful process. In August 1986, 5,000 miners and their families marched on La Paz to protest against the policy. They never got there. The Army broke up the march and arrested a couple of hundred trade-union leaders, and the government declared a state of siege. The political opposition remains divided, however, so the programme for sloughing off state companies and sacking more workers is likely to succeed. COMIBOL, in particular, will not outlive the tin crisis. The state railways and the petroleum company will also be privatized or closed.[19]

In Paz Estenssoro's first year 30,000 government employees were fired, and official unemployment rose to nearly a third of the work force. Wages for those employed dropped so low that real salaries were the equivalent of $8–9 monthly. A colleague in La Paz told me in mid-1986 of nurses whose salaries did not even cover their transportation expenses from home to health centre or hospital.[20]

Primary public-school teachers went on strike to demand a living wage. One of them, Freddy Camacho, explained the situation:

Under pressure from the IMF, the government has frozen salaries. Depending on the category, a teacher earns between [$10 and $40 at the May 1986 rate]. With $10 you can buy forty one-way bus tickets, 100 loaves of bread and 6 kilos of potatoes – that's all. The minimum family food basket, as calculated by the COB [Central Trade Union Organization] costs [$160]. We knew we'd never get that from the government, so we asked for [$60]. Well, the government won't even negotiate. They just said that any teacher who wasn't in the classroom Monday was fired and his job would be considered vacant. I don't think enough will go back to stop the movement. Teachers all have to do another job anyway to survive. Some drive taxis or deal on the black market.

The real long-term problem is the quality of teaching. Nobody's motivated to teach with salaries like that, or to prepare the lessons. A lot of children are dropping out in the early grades now in order to work trampling the coca leaves. [This is the first stage in cocaine processing – done the same way wine used to be pressed.] The ones that do come to school are malnourished – their parents don't have enough money to feed them – and they arrive with empty stomachs so they can't concentrate or they fall asleep in class.[21]

Between 1980 and 1984 real salaries shrank for all Bolivians, sometimes by as much as 75 per cent. They were obliged to work much longer hours to earn enough to buy basic staple foods. Table 2 illustrates some changes in food prices between 1975 and December 1984. The figures indicate how many hours one needed to work, at the minimum salary, to purchase 1,000 calories in the form of each of the following foods.[22] (As salaries were frozen, these figures have certainly grown worse since the study was carried out.) Foods that used to be cheapest often increased the most; staples doubled or tripled; poor people's sources of protein (peas, beans, occasionally powdered milk) went through the roof. How do they manage?

Two Bolivian researchers, Julio Prudencio and Monica Velasco, examined thoroughly the effects of the economic crisis on family food

Table 2   Some changes in Bolivian food prices, 1975 – December 1984

	Hours worked to purchase 1,000 calories	
	1975	December 1984
Barley	0.07	0.59
Quinua (buckwheat)	0.11	0.40
Sugar	0.16	0.51
Corn (grains)	0.17	0.64
Wheat flour	0.21	0.52
Dried beans	0.22	3.47
Rice	0.22	0.48
Pasta	0.23	0.53
Bananas	0.23	0.80
Milled wheat	0.24	0.61
Bread	0.28	0.51
Oil	0.28	0.59
Dried peas	0.29	1.38
Potatoes	0.76	2.35
Onions	1.02	3.22
Powdered milk	1.05	3.95

consumption and people's survival strategies.[23] They were amazed to discover that, despite tremendous odds, most people who had always lived with relatively few resources managed to keep their food consumption at approximately the same level. This level was, to be sure, disastrous to begin with. The families studied, from four different poor neighbourhoods in La Paz, were eating only 39 to 50 per cent of the recommended number of calories and between 52 and 61 per cent of the necessary proteins. 'More than 60 per cent of the population is likely to show a high degree of malnutrition . . . the situation could hardly be worse, and, should it deteriorate further, survival would be threatened, especially for children,' say Prudencio and Velasco. Their findings thus show simply that people managed not to starve to death. But what an achievement in the circumstances!

In order not to starve, all family members had to work harder and longer, with most of the burden falling upon women, housewives in particular. The state and the formal economy have little or nothing to do with people's survival – everything that contributes to family livelihood in time of crisis is rooted in the 'informal' economy. Families adopt two main types of strategy to maintain consumption. First, they change the composition of their food basket, cutting out fruit, milk and soft drinks (silver lining!); more important, they use ingenuity to obtain food in any

way that does not involve cash outlays. These strategies include barter-
ing, receiving donations, raising one's own food or animals at home,
acquiring food from the countryside through relatives and processing
food at home for sale. A whole network of food relationships comes into
being as food is acquired to be eaten directly, sold or bartered for other
foods. Strategies are almost invariably family enterprises; communal
cooking or soup-kitchen solutions play a very minor role. All the
strategies involve an enormous amount of *time*, of backing-and-forthing
between the country and the town, the house and the places one can
market or barter. Extended families do better than nuclear ones – for
example, in 1979 three members of a family could earn more than five
members of the same family in 1985.[24]

Many analysts fear that measure taken by the Paz Estenssoro
government to conform to I M F and World Bank criteria will worsen the
plight of most *barrio* (poor neighbourhood) dwellers and of the small
peasantry. Resources will go to export agriculture (agribusiness has
always received priority in Bolivia), and imports will be liberalized.[25]
Contrary to what is often reported, the country is still paying part of its
debt service despite a desperate internal situation, and the government
has promised its public creditors that it will do better. Most Bolivians are
already living on the brink; there is every reason to fear they may be
pushed over the edge.

BLOODSHED IN SANTO DOMINGO

The final exhibit in the gallery of Latin American extremes is the
Dominican Republic, a small country that holds a dubious record. Here,
in April 1984, occurred the greatest number of deaths in the hemisphere
stemming directly from an I M F riot.

The country stands out in other ways as well, none of them, unfortunately, beneficial to the inhabitants. The Dominican Republic is the
eastern half of the island of Hispaniola; Haiti is the western half.
Columbus landed there in 1492, making the island the first outpost of
European colonization of Latin America. The original inhabitants, the
Carib Indians, were slaughtered in short order. Black Africans were
then imported to work on the sugar plantations. Life in the countryside
has improved only marginally since. Today 0.07 per cent (7/1000) of the
landowners monopolize 45 per cent of the arable land, and 300,000 rural
families have no land at all – a lot of people for a population of only 6.4
million.

Income is about as well distributed as land. Four hundred families have annual incomes of over 1 million pesos (about $325,000); another 2,000 families make more than $125,000 yearly; the 'middle class' is composed of some 50,000 households with incomes between $5,000 and $15,000. At the bottom are 3.5 million people who try to manage on less than $400–600 a year. A third of the population – over 2 million – lives in the capital, Santo Domingo, at least 70 per cent of them in slums, known as *cordones de miseria*, for obvious reasons. The *official* estimate of unemployment is 30 per cent, the legal minimum salary about $US80 a month. The debt is $3.6 billion, and interest payments amounted to 40 per cent of export earnings in 1984.

This, briefly, is the social and economic background of the government agreement with the IMF, signed in January 1983 and requiring the usual measures: devaluation of the currency, reduction of government expenditure, etc. In April 1984 the Dominican Republic received a loan of $400 million from the IMF. The blood money required in exchange included price increases of up to 200 per cent for basic necessities, including bread – and, a nice touch, the new prices were announced during Easter week.

The protests that began the following Monday, 23 April, were spontaneous, certainly, but also the result of consultation and conscious decision among literally hundreds of popular organizations in the *cordones*. Tens of thousands took to the streets; President Jorge Blanco announced he would take all necessary steps to 'maintain public order'. On the 24th all the official trade unions joined in demanding a change in the government policy and higher salaries. They, along with the slum dwellers, were met with fierce repression.

After three days of the uprising the people were finally put down. Estimates of the number of deaths vary. One Dominican organization counted 186, plus hundreds of wounded and at least 5,000 people arrested. Newspapers published the identities of seventy-one people and listed fifty other unidentified bodies. The dead were mainly young people under 20, and there were at least eighteen women, including a 13-year-old girl and a 70-year-old woman. President Blanco, in his speech of 25 April, declared, 'The armed forces and the National Police have given an example of restraint [*ecuanimidad*] displaying their high degree of professionalism, elevated human feeling and respect for life . . . they have kept their reactions within the limits of reasonable prudence and displayed excellent training.'[26]

Words fail me.

10.
DEBT AND THE ENVIRONMENT: FINANCING ECOCIDE

Indebted countries have not just borrowed money – they have mortgaged the future. Nature puts up the collateral. The environment is a little-noticed victim of the debt crisis in the Third World, yet one day we shall all pay for the damage this crisis does to ecosystems.

Our economies have short-time horizons at best: bottom lines register quarterly or yearly profits; budgets are annual; and, for a banker, three months can be a very long time. Each nation-state has a licence to inflict damage on the planet as a whole, and global mechanisms for costing (much less stopping) this process do not exist. National economies, both socialist and capitalist, proceed, for the most part, as if there were no long-term costs for anything. There is no sense of solidarity with the future. Many neo-classical economists still flatly deny even the theoretical possibility of limits to growth and refuse the notion that pollution and environmental destruction should figure in their equations. Anything difficult to quantify simply gets left out.[1]

Since the IMF and the World Bank are peopled with neo-classical economists of strict observance, it is not surprising that their loans and adjustment programmes pay scant attention to ecological costs. It will be a long time before anyone can fully estimate exactly what those costs are (and by then it may well be too late), but there is already enough evidence to show clearly that the present road is not only wrong but stupid *even in economic terms*. The price of cleaning up the mess now being made in the Third World is going to be horrendous, and it can only be added to the present debt bill. In all too many cases damage will be irreversible.

DEBT AND DESTRUCTION

There are two debt/environment connections. The first is borrowing to finance ecologically destructive projects. The second is paying for them – and all the other elements of debt-financed modernization – by cashing in natural resources. The two are necessarily intertwined. Many of the grandiose projects that helped to put Third World countries on the debt treadmill to begin with are environmental disasters in their own right. Mega-projects are part of the standard development model; they pay no heed to future penalties for present recklessness. Large dams and hydro-projects are typical examples, now admirably documented by Edward Goldsmith and Nicolas Hildyard.[2]

No one is against irrigation or power. Successful societies must find appropriate ways of improving agriculture and providing energy or perish. Unfortunately, huge dams do neither of these nearly as efficiently as a series of smaller, less costly, ones could, and they create a flood of ancillary problems into the bargain. Nor, perhaps, is 'bargain' the *mot juste* in this context – for example, the Tucurui dam in Brazilian Amazonia, begun in 1976, is expected to cost easily $8 billion.[3]

This figure reflects not its true costs, merely those of the cement, steel, labour, etc. Real costs are systematically masked by so-called 'cost–benefit' analyses. They include losses of silt and fertility downstream, flooding of agricultural land and forests, destruction of wildlife, increased salinization of soils. Those are just a few of the physical effects, which have, of course, an immediate impact on people and their livelihoods.

People are hit directly by the diseases (malaria, schistosomiasis, river blindness) that proliferate when water patterns are disturbed. They are also forcibly uprooted from their homes. According to a 1984 World Bank internal document, referred to by Bruce Rich, then senior attorney for the US National Resources Defense Council, now of the Environmental Defense Fund, '[Hydro-electric] projects approved by the World Bank in the period 1979–1983 resulted in the involuntary resettlement of at least 400,000 to 450,000 people on four continents.'[4] One should add that 'resettlement' is often an optimistic term, since many of those uprooted are simply left to fend for themselves, without compensation.

The World Bank has been a major lender to Brazil's electric power programme. By 1974 it had already made twenty-six loans to this sector; in 1985–6 alone Bank energy-related lending to Brazil totalled over $1.3 billion. The Tucurui dam, whose initial stage was inaugurated in late 1984, is one of Brazil's many hydro-projects supported by the Bank. It has flooded 216,000 hectares (540,000 acres) of forest land. Eletronorte, the government company in charge, was in a hurry. Instead of clearing the forest, it simply left 13.4 million cubic metres (17.4 million cubic yards) of hardwood, from some 2.8 million trees, to rot underwater, having previously subcontracted with a private company to spray the forest cover with the infamous agent orange (dioxin) whose devastating effects have been well known since the Vietnam war.

Some forty people allegedly died from the defoliant. The victims' families are unlikely to receive compensation, yet even this is not the end of the story. 'It seems that a number of full drums of agent orange were never removed from the forest, and now nobody knows where they are . . . they could easily burst under the pressure of water in the dam. The dam straddles the major water supply for the state capital of Belém, home to 1.2 million people.'[5]

A World Bank staff member who carried out an environmental assessment on Tucurui does not mention agent orange in a short description of the project published in 1986; he does state, however, that Tucurui 'entails the resettlement of 5,000 non-Amerindian families, up to 30,000 people', while land previously owned by Amerindians has been significantly decreased by flooding, transmission lines and a highway.[6]

People can also be uprooted without dam-building. Indeed, ecological destruction seems wedded to contempt for ethnic minorities and for the basic needs of poor people. The best (or rather worst) contemporary examples are provided by 'internal migration programmes' – i.e., government-decreed resettlement schemes to move substantial numbers of citizens to somewhere that the government deems more suitable. Both Brazil and Indonesia, among the largest debtors in the world, have instituted costly internal migration programmes with the help of bilateral aid programmes, multilateral development banks and the World Bank. The *Ecologist*, the British magazine that consistently offers exhaustively researched articles on environmental questions, devotes an issue to the Indonesian transmigration programme, the 'Transmigrasi'.[7]

In the initial, grandiose, conception the Transmigrasi was intended to move nearly 70 million people from the 'overcrowded' islands of Bali and Java to the so-called outer islands – Sumatra, Sulawesi, Kalimantan (ex-Borneo), Irian Jaya and others – over a twenty-year period. Mercifully, this plan has been dramatically scaled down, for Indonesia simply hasn't enough money to carry it out. Furthermore, the programme was so blatantly unsuitable, with so few sites in the outer islands adapted to permanent farming, that the original scheme had to be adjusted. Even so, by 1984 over 3.6 million Indonesians had been moved, and the government seems to be shooting for between a quarter and a third of its initial goal. Some 20 million people might ultimately be displaced. This figure does not account for the harm done to the tribal people who *already* live in the outer islands, nor for the costs to the environment.

In spite of the humanitarian rhetoric that surrounds it, the real outcome of Transmigrasi has been, more often than not, to reduce the migrators to destitution, to disrupt or ruin the livelihoods of the tribal people and to wreck everyone's environment by decimating forests and traditional tribal lands. Those who resist – and many tribal people have resisted – are crushed by the Indonesian security forces.

The migration programme, as conceived, could have cost the Indonesian government and its funders an astronomical $75 billion, since the cost of moving each family was calculated at $7,000. The government has shifted gears and now leans more towards plantations on the outer islands, which it hopes will attract a sizeable work force and a lot of 'spontaneous migrators' who won't have to be paid for. Transmigrasi's programmed budget for the 1984–9 five-year plan is still $3.5 billion. Indonesia's outstanding debt stood at $32.5 billion in 1984, putting it sixth on the list of the Third World's most indebted nations. Transmigrasi absorbs about 6 per cent of national spending.

In 1985 the World Bank made its largest-ever loan to the programme ($160 million), bringing its commitment since 1974 to over half a billion dollars. As of June 1985, total foreign funding, including substantial contributions from the Asian Development Bank, the US, West Germany and Holland, amounted to nearly $800 million, with a further $750 million in the pipeline.[8] The Bank's rationale for lending is that Transmigrasi will reduce population growth and soil erosion on Java, take advantage of unused or under-used land on the outer islands and create 200,000 jobs a year. Supporters of the programme stress that it gives poor landless families a once-in-a-lifetime chance to own their own plot on an outer island, while improving living standards for the original inhabitants by its spillover effects. The *Ecologist*'s authors demolish these claims and add evidence of gross abuse of both nature and human rights. Theoretically, the settlers are supposed to receive a plot of cleared land, food aid and agricultural inputs. In reality,

because of the lack of uninhabited land suitable for agriculture, most of the locations chosen are tropical rain-forests. The forests have been cleared by private contractors . . . whose only concern is to complete the job as quickly and as profitably as possible. In many cases, only the commercially attractive trees have been felled with large tree stumps being left behind. The transmigrants, who are moved in as soon as possible (often long before site preparation is completed) have not been able to finish the land-clearance operations themselves.[9]

The heavy machinery used for clearing damages the soil; the promised houses are often not built; nor are roads or other infrastructure in place. Reports compiled from Indonesian newspapers and other sources indicate that the land is not suitable for growing most crops – certainly not rice, which is what Javanese settlers know how to grow. What *is* grown may be eaten by rats and wild boar. Some settlers live close to starvation or in constant fear of the elephants and tigers that surround them – themselves disturbed in their natural habitats by the land clearing. The *Jakarta Post* reported in 1985 that on one site, of 1,000 families that had been settled, only twelve remained. They had been promised 2 hectares (5 acres) each but had never received more than a quarter of a hectare, not enough even for bare subsistence.[10] Some families have simply called it quits and returned to Java. Members of the Indonesian Parliament, on a field trip in West Java in 1985, discovered that a number of returned families had been placed in custody 'to prevent them spreading negative reports and reduce the enthusiasm of others to transmigrate'.[11]

Nicholas Guppy, who has been studying tropical rain forests for thirty-five years, explains concisely the ecological havoc wreaked by this programme and what is actually behind it. We learn that Java is indeed 'overcrowded' when one considers the land-tenure system:

A similar enormous forest colonization programme is now under way in Indonesia, where political pressures are even greater than in Brazil . . . In overcrowded Java, 1 per cent of farmers own 35 per cent of agricultural land . . . half of the smallholders have less than a half-hectare of land each, and half of all rural households own no land at all. So millions of land-hungry but politically reliable Javanese are being 'transmigrated' [many to Kalimantan] . . . *Despite the poverty of its soils (less than 2 per cent are believed to be permanently cultivable), Kalimantan's forests are biologically unusually rich in species and economically exceptionally valuable* . . . *[The plan seems to be] to clear these forests completely,* using some of the logging profits to finance the Transmigration Programme. *Roads are laid out so as to penetrate remote areas and improve control over the indigenous inhabitants, lest they be disaffected – as well they may be, for most of the land is already owned under traditional law, largely ignored in the granting of concessions* . . .

Logging has been proceeding at the rate of over 800,000 hectares [2 million acres] a year, while shifting cultivators following behind cut about 200,000 hectares [500,000 acres] of mostly previously logged and damaged or secondary forest. Extrapolating current clearing rates, there will be no trace of these forests left in thirteen years . . . *Visiting such areas it is hard to view without emotion the miles of devastated trees, of felled, broken and burned trunks, of branches, mud, and bark crisscrossed with tractor trails – especially when one realizes that in most cases nothing of comparable value will grow again on the area. Such sights are reminiscent of photographs of Hiroshima* . . . Indonesia might be regarded as waging the equivalent of thermonuclear war upon [its] own territory *[my emphasis]*.[12]

In the course of all this devastation the needs of the inhabitants of the outer islands are swept aside, for the government sees tribal people as obstacles – 'isolated and alien' is the official phrase. An Indonesian law makes quite clear that 'the rights of traditional-law communities may not be allowed to stand in the way of the establishment of Transmigration settlements.'[13] The government also wants to regroup these people, subject them to the central administration they have hitherto largely escaped and use them as labour on cash-crop plantations. Since 1985 the Army has been given a key role in enforcing Transmigrasi. Meanwhile, some of the objectives of the Department of Social Affairs with regard to tribal people are:

Developing a state of monotheistic religion . . . *by eliminating animistic traits*
Developing their awareness and understanding of state and government . . .
Raising their capacity for rational and dynamic thinking . . .
Increasing the ability to produce more in the agricultural and non-agricultural sectors . . .

Developing and nurturing aesthetic concepts and values . . . [so that they may] produce works of art and culture in tune with the values of Indonesian society . . .
Guiding and inducing the members of isolated communities to settle in an area with government administration . . .[14]

Any responsible anthropologist would readily qualify such attitudes and actions towards tribal people as cultural ethnocide.

Is the programme at least contributing to the stated objective of reducing population pressures? Not in the least. The effects on population growth are nil, as was made clear at the March 1985 confidential seminar of the Inter-Governmental Group on Indonesia (IGGI), the creditors' club. The minutes of this meeting were leaked; in them we learn from an Indonesian ministerial aide that 'Demographically, transmigration of people from Java does not mean very much, because the rate of growth on this island is big . . . It is evident that demographically the target of transmigration is not important . . . The documentation which has been distributed to you, Your Excellencies . . . shows that for 150 years the relocation of people from Java has [had] no effective meaning.'[15]

The World Bank has any number of internal directives and guidelines concerning the proper treatment of migrants, ethnic minorities and the environment. Clearly, in the case of Transmigrasi it is systematically flouting all of them. Some Bank officials have expressed serious reservations about the programme in draft reports that are invariably rewritten and watered down in their final versions, partly to satisfy the demands of the Indonesian government, partly to justify the enormous sums already invested by the Bank. The Bank even admits that after three five-year plans (and half of a fourth) 'an overall assessment of the programme is not feasible' because 'detailed evaluations' are unavailable. As Carmel Budiardjo, a long-time campaigner for human rights in Indonesia, says, 'This gives the impression of a juggernaut hurtling towards some unknown destination with no one pausing to consider the consequences.'[16]

The contributions of huge foreign loans to environmental plunder, widespread impoverishment and ethnocide can no longer be denied. This chapter would have been disproportionately long had I attempted a full description of all the Bank-sponsored ecological calamities currently being perpetrated in Brazil – for example, the Polonoreste project, perhaps better described as the Rape of Rondonia (the Brazilian state in Western Amazonia, on the Bolivian border), which, at the present rate of progress, will have deforested an area the size of Great Britain by 1990.

Further east, the Grande Carajas iron-ore project is said to be the world's largest single development scheme (the Tucurui dam is part of it and will provide the power). Conceived by a Japanese team in 1980, Carajas will cost an estimated $62 billion and will entail partial or total deforestation of an area larger than France and Britain put together. The EEC is contributing $600 million to the scheme. Carajas, with its several billion tons of iron and half a dozen other mineral-ore deposits, is described by the Brazilian government as a 'national export project' and an answer to Brazil's crippling debt.[17]

As of 1984, Indonesia owed $23 billion to public sources, plus $413 million to the IMF, while Brazil's publicly held debt was $66 billion and another $4 billion owed to the IMF.[18] Thus over $93 billion in public money has been showered on these two countries alone. If taxpayers and World Bank bondholders in the creditor countries knew that they were indirectly financing ecocide,'would the money flow so freely?

Ecologists in the United States are working to stem this flow and won major victories in 1985 and 1986 when Congress passed legislation aimed at forcing the multilateral development banks (MDBs), including the World Bank, to walk a straight and narrow ecological path. Since the United States is the single largest contributor to these banks, any restrictions it may impose upon them are of the greatest importance. I quote some of the major provisions of the legislation for its usefulness to lobbyists in other countries. It requires: that the US Treasury Department 'regularly raise' the question of MDB progress in 'improving their environmental performance'; that the US Treasury and State departments 'propose formally' that each MDB board 'hold a special meeting within the next twelve months, focused specifically on environmental performance and better implementation of multilateral development policies designed to protect the environment and indigenous peoples'; that Treasury and State departments undertake 'diplomatic and other initiatives' to 'ensure co-operative implementation of the reforms'. Further provisions stipulate inclusion of environmental reviews in the entire 'project cycle' of the banks, regular ecological monitoring, the active involvement of health and environmental ministers of borrowing nations in all phases of planning and execution, 'rehabilitation and management of the ecological resources of borrower nations on a sustained basis'. Most innovative of all, the MDBs are supposed to accept participation of non-governmental environmental and indigenous peoples' organizations 'at all stages of project planning'.[19]

Given the MDB penchant for secrecy, the provision for the participation of non-governmental organizations may be one of the most difficult to implement. The World Bank usually hides behind a real or purported demand for confidentiality on the part of the borrower. When environmentalist Bruce Rich asked the Bank why it was sponsoring 'rampant deforestation, invasion of Indian lands and destruction of natural lands unsuitable for agriculture' in Brazil, the Bank simply replied that it was 'not at liberty to discuss the details of the implementation of the Polonoreste project because they are part of [its] ongoing discussions with the Brazilian government. These discussions are of a confidential nature.'[20]

Money, fortunately, talks and, as US Senator Kasten pointed out in his report that accompanies the 1986 legislation, 'funding for the MDBs has been reduced because of their failure to address the Committee's critiques and proposals for reform.' His colleague in the House made clear in his report that Congress is looking for real, substantial changes in policies and practices, 'not just promises to do better'.[21]

So the MDBs may have to choose between opening their windows and closing their doors to significant funding. The US Congress recognizes, however, that it cannot force the necessary changes on a recalcitrant Bank all by itself. Legislators hope that the requirement for diplomatic initiatives will cause other lending – and borrowing – nations to bring similar pressures to bear on the MDBs and insist that environmental protection become part of their standard operating procedures. The US legislation could serve as a model for 'green' activists in other countries.

NATURE PAYS BACK – WITH INTEREST

Massive deforestation will probably change the whole world's weather for the worse, though climatologists may disagree about exactly how.[22] What we already know for sure is that it carries heavy economic penalties. Aside from harbouring untold numbers of animal and vegetable species, the habitat of native peoples and a source of fuel-wood, forests have a clear economic role to play because they *protect the very projects that drain so much investment*, including dams. A team of World Bank experts explains:

When forests . . . are cleared, reservoirs often become much shallower due to sedimentation. As a result, less electricity can be generated

*(because less water can flow through the turbines) and the useful econ-
omic life of the hydroelectric investment is shortened. For example, the
useful life of the Ambuklao dam in the Philippines has been cut from sixty
to thirty-two years because of deforestation.*

In Colombia too deforestation has caused a major dam to operate at
one-sixth of its normal capacity, so in Bogota there is now rationing of
electricity.

Forests stabilize the soil and prevent erosion. When they disappear,
so does the soil – into rivers, harbours and canals. 'Deforestation is
jeopardizing the continued operation of . . . the Panama Canal, which
suffers from heavy sedimentation and a lack of sufficient water during
the dry season to operate the locks for the larger ships.' Similarly,
because of deforestation upstream, 'It costs Argentina $10 million a year
to dredge silt from the Plata River mouth and keep Buenos Aires open
to shipping . . . In Thailand, important waterways are no longer navi-
gable because of sedimentation resulting mainly from deforestation.'[23]

Deforestation turns storms, floods or droughts – naturally recurring
and expected phenomena – into major disasters. Forests also play a
major role in agriculture by storing up water and releasing it gradually,
so that droughts are less severe. 'All told, some 40 per cent of developing
world farmers live in villages that depend upon the watershed functions
provided by forests. Agricultural export crop production valued at $36
billion per year depends upon the water supply and soil-stabilization
functions of forests.'[24]

Nearly everyone knows now that tropical forest soils aren't suitable
for cropping – nearly everyone, that is, but the settlers who are lured
there by government promises and a lack of anywhere else to go. It is
criminal to send masses of landless peasants to deforested areas, as
Brazil is still doing, with empty assurances that they will be able to grow
food for a living. Why should a country like Brazil continue to pursue
such a headstrong and discredited policy? The answer to this question
lies in a particularly perverse manifestation of the debt crisis. Brazil has
to pay back between $12 billion and $14 billion in interest on loans every
year. The country will have to go even further into debt to develop
mineral projects like Grande Carajas. So cash crops are one obvious
way of earning debt-service money, and soybeans are a major cash crop.
Soybean prices are low these days because of over-production in the US
and . . . in Brazil. So more and more must be grown just to keep
revenues stable.

José Lutzenberger, a Brazilian agronomist and engineer, and one of his country's foremost ecologists, testified before the US Congress in September 1984. He told how thousands of poor peasants from agriculturally rich southern Brazil were pouring into Amazonian Rondonia because they had been dispossessed of their land, either by large landowners or by government plantations covering thousands of hectares, all bent on growing soybeans and other cash crops. INCRA, the government land agency, paid for television ads to entice them to Rondonia, with slogans like 'We are making the largest agricultural reform in the world' or 'Good land, appropriate land . . . these lands offer excellent possibilities for the expansion of agricultural productivity'.*[25]

In reality, as Lutzenberger explained, the Rondonia Rush was needed precisely because the government *refused* to undertake real land reform and confront the plantation owners. The idea was to get the rural poor out of the south and the north-east so they could not make trouble. Thus the Polonoreste project – financed one-third by the World Bank – has become an infertile dumping ground for peasants who will never be able to earn a livelihood from poor land, leached of all nutrients, from which the tree cover has been removed. According to Lutzenberger and many other experts, there is 'in fact no shortage of land . . . except the shortages created by the concentration of land holdings'.

Now that Rondonia is settled, deforestation can only accelerate because the colonizers are stranded there and get title to land only once it is cleared. 'It is quite common to see settlers give up their clearings after their first meagre harvest. They have to make new clearings every year. Then, when the whole plot is cleared, they move on again.' The Amerindians who lived in the forests have been destroyed, culturally if not physically. Lutzenberger lamented:

Their knowledge of the ecology of the forest, their skills in knowing how to use it are lost even before we can register them. The loss of these cultures is just as irreversible as the loss of a species. A species is the result of millions of years of irreversible organic evolution. An indigenous culture is the result of thousands of years of living in harmony with the ecosystem.[26]

On behalf of Brazil's own environmental movement and 'many co-operating citizen groups', Lutzenberger asked the Congressional committee whether the World Bank should be providing a third of the

* These ads were reportedly stopped in 1986.

money for a project that: (1) makes it easier and socially safer for the powerful to maintain huge estates in the north-east and to promote cash-crop monocultures for export in the south; (2) substitutes unsuitable forms of agriculture for the tropical forest; (3) drives out of the forest the only people who have developed a sustainable way of using it.[27] The legislation passed two years after this testimony indicates that Congress heard what Lutzenberger and any number of other witnesses were saying.

Alas, the strain that debt imposes on the environment is not confined to Brazil. Nicholas Guppy has compiled a table of the world's principal tropical forest countries by area. Coincidentally, the top five countries – Brazil, Indonesia, Zaïre, Peru and Colombia – are all among the top debtors as well. These five countries account for 60 per cent of what is left of the planet's tropical forests.[28] The pressures to decimate them are almost irresistible. Yet, once destroyed, Guppy estimates that it would take *400 years* to re-establish the original components of forest (*if* seeds and seedlings are still present, which is far from sure). Some countries argue that they are replanting trees. This is a spurious solution. Commercially useful trees will grow on the cleared land, yes, but *only once*. They too deplete the fragile soils on which no permanent cropping, including tree cropping, is possible. A tropical forest is a seamless web: all its components are necessary, or it will, in time, become as barren as a desert. Nicholas Guppy suggests a weird and depressing, yet compelling, logic connecting debt and deforestation:

increasingly there are fears that the availability of loans [from the World Bank and other sources] may actually encourage deforestation in poor countries; that they can gain in the short term twice over, first by selling their forests, and then by getting loans to reforest and repair the environmental damage – to pay for which they cut more forest; while the banks and lending countries acquire interest payments, export orders and political and economic power. Indeed, everyone gains, except the environment, which is ruined at an accelerating pace.[29]

Why should we care? Isn't all this destruction going on quite far away from our doorsteps in the North? No, because the biosphere is also a seamless web, and a climatic change would affect everyone, everywhere. But on purely economic grounds, which even the Bank and the IMF should be able to appreciate, tropical forests contain at least 80,000 species of edible plants, none of them yet cultivated. Presently, only sixteen plants provide 90 per cent of the world's food, and any one of the

80,000 uncultivated ones might provide much needed substitutes. Furthermore, forests contain untold numbers of medicinal species, species 'with varied industrial uses, . . . in making clothing, cosmetics and for hundreds of other purposes'. Yet they are destroyed merely to extract the fifteen or twenty kinds of commercially valuable tree they contain. 'Frequently, 90–98 per cent of trees are left unused when an area of rain forest is logged.'[30]

If current trends continue, two World Bank professionals note that 'some 15–20 per cent of the world's estimated 3.5 to 10 million plant and animal species may become extinct by the year 2000 . . . [though they have] tremendous future potential as renewable sources of energy, industrial products, medications, genetic inputs to agriculture and applied biological research, if they are not eliminated first.' *All* our sources of genetic diversity for the crops that keep us alive are now located in the tropics. We have absolutely no idea what vital genetic resources tropical forests actually contain and, at the rate we are going, never will.[31]

There are other quite straightforward debt–environment connections. When the IMF imposes government cuts, environmental programmes are among the first to go, and *all* natural resources, not just forests, are cashed in to pay off the interest. Pell-mell, here are a few examples.

Brazil, contrary to appearances, *does* have the equivalent of an environmental protection agency, but its budget has been cut to the point that it can barely pay its employees. Outnumbered firefighters of the Brazilian national park system can no longer cope with blazes. Costa Rica is asking for private donations to maintain its national parks. Mexico is draining irreplaceable groundwater to produce export vegetables for the US market. It will be depleted within a few years. Peru has fished its anchovy banks nearly to the point of extinction. Bolivia (aside from the drug trade) is actively engaged in massive exports of endangered wildlife. Mexico recently eliminated fifteen governmental under-secretariats, four of them environment-linked.[32] In a word, 'environmental issues become totally marginal' when governments face huge debts, as economist Christine Bogdanowicz-Bindert explains. She ought to know. She used to be with the IMF.[33]

POST SCRIPTUM

Friends in the US environmental movement believe there is now a better than even chance that the MDBs, including the World Bank, can be changed and that their loans *could* promote sustainable, ecologically sound development. Under the new leadership of its president, Barber Conable, the World Bank is beginning to acknowledge its long neglect of any policy on the environment and indigenous peoples and is strengthening the staff of its heretofore laughably small environmental department. To reinforce this positive behaviour, even greater pressure from Northern environmental movements (both on their own governments and on the MDBs) is of the highest importance, and support from the South could be crucial. For perhaps the first time, human rights activists, ecologists and members of indigenous peoples' movements are joining forces to create momentum the MDBs can no longer ignore. This is surely the now-or-never moment to join them!

In a further development Conservation International, a private environmental group, bought $650,000 worth of Bolivia's debt for a heavily discounted $100,000 on the secondary market in exchange for the Bolivian government's commitment to set aside 1.5 million hectares of rain forest as a natural reserve for plants, animals and the native peoples who live there. The Weeden Foundation supplied the $100,000 and intends to aid other debt for conservation swaps. This is a splendid idea (see Chapter 14 for some other possibilities) but should not be left to the private sector.

PART III:
NOW WHAT?

So far I've tried to answer two basic questions about debt: why do we find ourselves in crisis, and who is involved? How does the debt crisis affect ordinary human beings and their environment? The most interesting question, perhaps, remains to be answered, namely, what should we do about it? The answer all depends on who 'we' are. Many different interests are represented by those offering solutions, so here I give the floor to nearly everyone who claims to have an answer, including, at the end, myself.

Some questions first. Can the North go on, for years on end, extracting every last drop of blood and treasure from an increasingly exhausted South? Won't there be social explosions, convincing those in power that more humane policies would also be more practical ones? Such a view may be convenient and consoling but not necessarily accurate.

It is unlikely that human suffering will cause, in and of itself, a change of heart. It never has before. Although the hungry and miserable may revolt sporadically, repression technology has also improved immeasurably in recent years. Without allies inside the elites, including the Army and the police, revolts are more difficult to sustain than they used to be. People must now struggle not just against their own elites and governments but also against the latter's capacity to *import* repression. They are up against their own ruling classes, plus ours.

More likely, living standards will continue to slide backwards. People's lives will grow even harder; they will also be shorter. Unless . . . What might alter this pessimistic scenario? First, we have to understand that we are all passengers on the *Titanic*, although some of us are travelling first-class. We have a *stake* in staying afloat, and only popular pressure can avoid a fast-approaching collision.

But pressure for what? Write-downs or write-offs? Moratoria? Clean slates? Baker or Bradley or, for that matter, Castro plans? Off with their heads? Honest disagreement among honest people exists here. The following chapters summarize the main points of the solutions that have been put forward, roughly in ascending order of my personal preference. My own views may strike some as utopian. My answer to this charge is that Third World debt can be (1) a continuing unmitigated disaster or (2) a fantastic opportunity to get history moving in a different direction. We might as well go for the second option.

Chapter 11, 'The IMF Solution: Interference, Mismanagement and Failure in Jamaica', gives the IMF/Bank answer the greatest possible benefit of the doubt by looking at the case of a small country, Jamaica, which has applied their prescriptions to the letter. The results are not encouraging. We know that the IMF has never claimed to be a development institution, but must it be an anti-development institution?

Chapter 12, 'Dealing with Debt: the View from the North', looks at the alternative proposals that have proliferated on the creditor side. A range of actors – from arch-Republicans to liberal Democrats to investment bankers – say they know how to deal with Third World debt, so we listen to them. Meanwhile, the banks, along with the Consortium, are acting upon the matter while others debate it. Some of their practical solutions, especially as regards the ever-recurring Mexican crisis are described.

Chapter 13, 'Coping with Chaos: the View from the South', explains how problems of political unity have hampered the debtors' capacity to propose or impose their own remedies but also notes some suggestions that have emerged from the South, or from those in sympathy with the South's plight. It points also to some strategies that people are inventing in order to cope, without waiting for their governments to act.

Chapter 14, 'The 3-D Solution: Debt, Development, Democracy', is devoted to my own convictions concerning debt. The continuing existence of the debt crisis fits neatly with the strategy of Low-intensity conflict (LIC) which the North, especially the United States, is waging against the South. Ongoing Financial Low-intensity Conflict, or FLIC, is an under-recognized threat to the aspirations of Third World nations and peoples. But there are other forces in play, forces that could fight FLIC and transform the debt crisis into an instrument of liberation.

The book closes with a 'Philosophical Afterword'. In it I attempt to examine the foundations of the model that created the debt crisis – and many other pathological phenomena – to begin with. We might abolish present Third World debt altogether, but it could soon reappear, for the model itself has become self-generating. Powerful actors in the North and South have a professional, political or financial stake in its perpetuation, yet unless we free ourselves from its grip, we shall only prepare tomorrow's crises as we try to manage today's. This Afterword will not speak directly to every reader's concerns, but I hope those who find it relevant to their work and to their lives will pursue this debate, which can only affect them both.

11.

THE IMF SOLUTION: INTERFERENCE, MISMANAGEMENT AND FAILURE IN JAMAICA

Mr Seaga added that his country had done everything that supply-siders or free-enterprisers could desire. It had devalued its currency to make its exports more competitive; it had diverted government programs to the private sector, even including garbage collection and hospitals; it had got rid of burdensome regulations, rebuilt tourism, increased agricultural output and exports, and reached record levels of investment. Yet all this had not solved the nation's debt problems, Mr Seaga admitted.

Leonard Silk, reporting in the New York Times on the speech of Prime Minister Edward Seaga of Jamaica to the IMF/World Bank meeting in Seoul, 12 October 1985

The IMF and the rest of the Consortium say there is only one answer. Countries in debtors' prison can escape only if they practise adjustment. Adjustment may be painful, but not to adjust will be even more so. The Fund is a venerable and powerful institution; hundreds of very smart economists work for it. Perhaps it is right. But there is no reason to accept its pronouncements as Holy Writ without proof.

Does Fund medicine work, even on its own terms? Do economies grow healthier under its aegis? Can people in adjusting countries look forward to a better life even if they must suffer some temporary discomforts? To test the Fund's claims, one ought first to give it every benefit of the doubt and pick a country case that offers its adjustment hypothesis a truly fair trial. Such a country should be small enough to be manageable and responsive to IMF measures and should thus furnish a convincing laboratory for experiment. It should have been swallowing its medicine long enough for the effects to be plain. It should be politically co-operative and in tune with the Consortium's views. Such a country would, in short, look quite a lot like Jamaica.

THE BACKGROUND

To test the efficacy of the IMF prescriptions we will look first at the Jamaican economy as a whole, then at how ordinary Jamaicans are faring. For the first issue I rely heavily on a thorough and scholarly examination provided by Cameron Duncan in his doctoral dissertation in economics for the American University in Washington, DC.[1] As for the welfare of Jamaicans themselves, I've been blessed with excellent first-hand reports.

If long compliance with IMF/World Bank strategies guarantees salvation, this Caribbean island ought to be paradise. As Duncan explains in rich detail, Jamaica is nothing if not outwardly oriented, dutifully following the doctrines of comparative advantage, openness to foreign investment and external trade. The outside world buys its bauxite and sugar (the US and Britain absorb nearly two-thirds of these exports) and supplies it with a steady stream of foreign tourists. In fact, the island is among the top 20 per cent of the world's most trade-dependent economies and imports *ten times* more food per capita than the average Third World country.

Is this good or bad? These strategies appeared to work for a number of years. Economic growth and commerce boomed during the 1950s; Jamaica was a textbook example of rapid development, with growth rates increasing at 5 or 6 per cent a year between 1950 and 1962. Trade expanded eightfold during the same period. Jamaica achieved standards of social well-being virtually unmatched in the developing world – low infant mortality, high life expectancy, as well as enviable records for literacy and health care. Jamaica also tended to maintain the more presentable aspects of British colonialism, such as the traditions of parliamentary democracy, a lively press, free speech and trade unionism.

But the strategy had its costs. Jamaica is now one of the most indebted countries in the hemisphere, and each Jamaican theoretically owes foreign creditors nearly $1,500 – far more than a Brazilian or a Mexican. According to latest estimates, the country must devote over half its export earnings to debt service.

The spectacular growth that Jamaica previously enjoyed was partly illusory too, since this growth was not internally generated. Foreign investors, especially aluminium companies interested in the island's rich bauxite ore, largely fuelled expansion. When they stopped investing in the early 1970s, the rest of the economy shrank, unemployment doubled, national income gravitated increasingly to the richest 10 per cent and absolute poverty grew as wages fell. Jamaica remained dependent on imports, financed by borrowing.

The upshot is a country that has experienced unremitting economic problems since the 1970s. Since 1977 it has lived under IMF surveillance and a series of structural-adjustment agreements. Duncan thinks this is long enough for us to draw some conclusions about these programmes and proceeds to assess them.

During the 1970s Jamaica suffered all the shocks common to Third World countries – quadrupling of oil prices, lower demand for its exports, declining investment in a climate of international recession. The very openness of its economy made it especially vulnerable to this sort of buffeting. A major political change further complicated the country's life when the people, sick and tired of corruption, mismanagement and police brutality, elected a democratic socialist (or social democrat, if you prefer) government in 1972. The People's National Party (PNP), headed by Michael Manley, set out to implement bold policies benefiting the majority – rent control, a minimum wage, improved health services, equal pay for women, free secondary education, a literacy campaign, partial land reform and the like.

To finance these reforms (particularly in the wake of the 1973 oil-price rise) the government tried to gain more control over its own bauxite. It imposed a production tax on the industry and was the leading actor in forming the International Bauxite Association, a producers' organization modelled on OPEC. The transnational aluminium corporations were not amused. They also had more options than did Manley and his PNP. To register disapproval, they simply moved production out of Jamaica and into Australia and Africa. Tourism also fell victim to anti-PNP propaganda. Duncan says, 'Tourist agents reportedly tarnished Jamaica's image as a tourist paradise by advising clients to visit other parts of the Caribbean.'

For a time, extra borrowing slowed the vicious downward spiral induced by falling revenues and rising costs. Jamaica's foreign debt rose from $150 million to $813 million between 1971 and 1976. Meanwhile, capital flowed out in torrents as Jamaican businessmen and wealthy families stashed their assets abroad and transnational corporations disinvested and stepped up remittances to their home offices. The PNP was re-elected in 1976 with a huge majority but could no longer stave off the inevitable hard landing. Foreign-currency reserves were zero. On the heels of the electoral victory, the Bank of Jamaica was forced to suspend all foreign-exchange payments. The stage was set for the IMF.

I will not detail here the constant skirmishes and protracted hostilities that pitted the PNP government against the Fund.* It is, however, important to note that foreign commercial banks did not exactly trip over each other in the rush to refinance old loans or grant new ones to the Manley government: even after the IMF gave its seal of approval the banking community refused to follow suit. Other sources of finance, like USAID or the United States Ex-Im Bank, also discreetly disappeared into the woodwork. Jamaica thus found itself isolated, and, Duncan writes, 'despite evidence that the critical foreign exchange situation was a product primarily of exogenous [external] factors, the Fund's position hardened. It demanded a massive $US300 million expenditure cut in 1980, equivalent to 26 per cent of the previous year's budget. Measures included the layoff of 11,000 public-sector workers.' The Fund also obliged the government to reverse completely its policies of redistribution of wealth, with the predictable (and undoubtedly desired) result that Manley's party lost popular support. The PNP faced huge internal and external pressures; still, the party was not exactly a model of prudent economic management and political acumen.

Duncan's figures show a drop in real incomes of 25 per cent and inflation up by 320 per cent during the PNP's tenure between 1972 and 1980. Helped along by disinvestment and capital flight, joblessness hit a record 31 per cent in 1979, while factories were operating at less than a third of their real capacity. Debt soared to $1.7 billion. It is not altogether surprising that the PNP was crushed in the 1980 elections by Edward Seaga's rightist Jamaica Labour Party.

---

* Interested readers will find a good account of these in Norman Girvan *et al.*, 'The IMF and the Third World: the case of Jamaica', *Development Dialogue*, Dag Hammarskjöld Foundation, Uppsala, Sweden, Vol. 2, 1980. This whole issue of *Development Dialogue* casts a critical eye on the international monetary system; there are several other articles relevant to Jamaica, plus a short message from (then) Prime Minister Manley.

Theorists may split hairs about the PNP's mistakes. It made a good many, but it held few cards against the transnational corporations that controlled such a large portion of the country's economy. The United States was also, as usual, opposed to any experiments smacking of socialism in its back yard. The advent of a conservative government in Jamaica was, in any case, music to the Reagan administration's ears. Prime Minister Seaga was the first foreign politician Reagan received after his own inauguration, and, according to the US General Accounting Office, Washington 'hoped to make Jamaica an example of what could be accomplished when assistance was provided to a government that shared the US belief that private-sector growth could lead to economic development'.[2]

The private sector is all very well, but a boost from the state sector doesn't hurt either: to help 'make Jamaica an example', Washington gave the Seaga government $495 million between 1981 and 1984 – or *double* the total of US aid for the entire preceding twenty-four years. In 1982, for example, every Jamaican theoretically received about $57 from US taxpayers; Jamaica thus ranked second only to Israel in terms of US aid per capita. By the end of 1986 the Reagan administration had pumped a total of $700 million worth of aid into the Jamaican economy, while Reagan's Caribbean Basin Initiative (CBI) gives Jamaican goods the privilege of duty-free access to the US market.

Prime Minister Seaga did not have to wrench any ideological muscles in return for such largesse – he already favoured the measures he would be expected to take. Just as the United States wished, he broke off diplomatic relations with Cuba and became the linchpin of Reagan's CBI. His economic policies were exact replicas of IMF stabilization programmes and orthodox Reaganomics. Despite Uncle Sam's solicitude, not to mention IMF/World Bank credits of more than $900 million, the economy continued to falter.

Further adjustment, or stabilization, or austerity was called for: whichever word one chooses, it meant, among other measures, 6,200 jobs cut from the public sector in 1984 alone, including 1,500 slashed from the Health Ministry's budget. Public investment fell by 30 per cent; food subsidies disappeared; real incomes were slashed by a drastic 48 per cent between 1983 and early 1985 as the minimum wage was held to $US8.95 per *week*. Some may thus have found it a shade Orwellian to hear the World Bank call 1984 'a successful year for Jamaica'. The government itself trumpeted, 'The response of the economy and the society to the challenge of achieving the [IMF] targets can only be described in superlative terms.'[3] Why the rejoicing? Because the *balance of payments* shifted from a negative $289 million to a positive $225 million in 1984.

BOP figures are the only ones that truly interest the IMF/Bank cohorts. But is this hailed shift from red to black really such an occasion for cheers? Using the trade balance as the single criterion to measure a country's progress (the relevant question is, of course, 'Progress towards what?') seems hazardous in the extreme. For one thing, even without assessing the costs for ordinary people of this dubious victory, it is difficult to speak of a healthy economy when debt has doubled under the Seaga government to $3.3 billion, with no end in sight.

ADJUSTMENT IN ACTION

How are consumers, even middle-class ones, supposed to react when water, telephone and electricity rates all increase by more than 100 per cent, as they did in 1984? When the Consumer Price Index (CPI) goes up by a third, as it did between early 1984 and 1985? This overall CPI increase masks a far steeper rise in staple-food prices during the same period – these escalated at double the rate of the CPI. Jamaica is also lagging behind in local food production, which declined by 13 per cent in 1984, while food imports rose by 57 per cent in the early 1980s.

Some human needs can be met by individual action – for example, food for one's own family consumption if one is fortunate enough to have a piece of land. Others, however, especially health and education, are mainly tasks for the state. When public social-service spending is cut, those who are too poor to afford private schools and clinics are quite obviously the first to suffer. In Jamaica, again according to figures compiled by Duncan, real per capita public expenditures dropped by 19 per cent between 1983 and 1985. Jamaica's already good public health service improved markedly under the PNP, which concentrated on providing services in previously neglected rural areas. Government spending on health was 'at least 30 per cent higher in 1980 than in 1970, and total real inputs may have doubled over the period'. In the 1980s these gains have been seriously eroded. The government's per capita health spending dropped 25 per cent between 1980–81 and 1985.

Nutritional status is one of the first indicators to reflect worsening poverty, for the simple reason that poor people spend most of what little money they have on food. Urban residents are likely to be worse off than rural ones, since their entire food basket must be purchased. In August 1984 an urban family of five would have needed $J 110 a week to provide the recommended dietary allowances. Unfortunately, in August 1984 the minimum weekly wage was $J45. Even assuming both parents were receiving the minimum wage – a wildly optimistic assumption, especially since so many households are headed by women alone – weekly expenditures for the proper feeding of five people would have required 122 per cent of total household earnings! Decidedly, 1984 does not seem to have been a banner year for Jamaicans, whatever the IMF/World Bank may have announced. (This situation had not improved in 1986. Though the minimum wage had risen to $J60, the same basket of groceries was worth $J175. A family with two minimum wages would require no longer 122 per cent but 145 per cent of its income for the same recommended diet.) Duncan concludes, 'The shrinkage of the "social wage" which occurred throughout 1981–5 had a further regressive effect on income distribution, dumping most of the welfare costs of adjustment on the doorstep of the worst-off in the society.'

But this is exactly what the IMF *wants*. According to Fund doctrine, 'redistribution of income' (read 'more to the rich, less to the poor') will result in higher profits, which in turn will result in higher investment and thus create jobs so that people can earn more money, etc., etc. That is the theory. In practice, though there certainly has been 'redistribution', the rich have invested their windfall not in job creation but simply in speculation (a lot in real estate) or even more simply in foreign bank accounts. Here, once more, is a classic case of the banks getting their money back *twice* – in payments on the debt made at the expense of the poor and, simultaneously, in the form of cash deposits that they can then reloan *ad infinitum*, or at least until something cracks.

Jamaica is unlikely to struggle back to the levels of 1981, much less find its way to prosperity through IMF measures. It is now tied more firmly than ever to international markets, with prices for its basic exports in permanent slump. The Fund controls its internal economic policy and shows no signs of easing the pressure. The once vigorous trade-union movement has been weakened, particularly since hundreds more workers were sacked after the general strike in 1985. The country would collapse totally without the outside support of the World Bank, the IMF and USAID, but their support is neither ideologically disinterested nor without cost for national independence. Cameron Duncan puts it this way:

Fund and World Bank conditions, and the deregulation and free-market dictates of the local USAID staff, combined with reliance on foreign consultants in all areas of public policy, reduced the Seaga administration

*to the status of a caretaker government which administered the state for
foreign multilateral agencies and international capital. As it assumed the
caretaker role on [their] behalf, the state became less accountable to
domestic interests and came under tight policy direction from the World
Bank, the Fund and other foreign interests intent on dismantling the
democratic gains of the 1970s.*

So now we know what emerges from the perfect 'laboratory' that
Jamaica provides for social experiments carried out by the pin-striped
doctors of the IMF, the Bank and assorted free-market functionaries.
We will now turn to what this means for flesh-and-blood Jamaicans.

IMF: INCREASING MIS-FORTUNES

Belinda Coote works with the Public Affairs Unit of the well-known
British aid agency OXFAM. In January 1985 she was on an OXFAM
mission in Jamaica and was so appalled by the impact of the financial
crisis on the people, especially on women, that she took a lot of notes,
talked to a lot of Jamaicans and turned her observations into a case study
for OXFAM, 'Debt and poverty'.[4]

As is customary in countries undergoing adjustment, Jamaicans have
been bedevilled by price increases, cancelled subsidies, job losses and
other measures that squeeze poor people. On 14 January 1985 the
government announced a 20 per cent increase in prices for gasoline,
diesel fuel, kerosene and cooking gas. This meant higher prices for
public as well as private transportation, plus an unbearable tax on the
poor's only source of energy. A cartoon shows a dilapidated shack at
night, with a darkened window. Issuing from the window: 'Hey, mama,
we can't see the food.' Mama replies, 'Take your choice. Raw food with
the light on or cooked food in the dark.'

For Jamaicans the new energy prices were last straws. They triggered
massive protests, which Belinda Coote witnessed:

*By 7 a.m. the following day, road blocks made of anything from wrecked
cars to household garbage had been constructed all over the island. The
atmosphere was thick with acrid smoke from burning tyres. Men, women
and children thronged the streets, bringing the early-morning traffic to a
halt. Schools, offices and factories closed and all commercial activity
ceased. Violent clashes with the island's security forces led to the death of
at least seven people and many more were injured. The demonstration*

lasted for two days, but it was a week before the roads were cleared and life on the island returned to normal.

Friends in Jamaica sent me newpaper accounts of the demonstrations. Here is one vignette from the *Daily Gleaner*:

At about 10 a.m. Minister of Industry and Commerce the Hon. Douglas Vaz was caught in a road block . . . His driver was hit several times with bottles when he alighted from the car and tried to clear the road to gain passage. While his driver was outside being pummelled by the missiles, the Minister jumped . . . from the back of the car where he was sitting, reversed, and sped away – his chauffeur having to run to reach the speeding car.

(The *Gleaner* is considered a conservative paper.)

Though six people were reported dead in clashes with security forces on the first day of the demonstrations, Jamaicans never quite lose their sense of humour. As the *Gleaner* also reported, 'Crowds of people gathered on Windward Road and danced to the popular calypso "Capitalism Gone Mad".'[5] Prime Minister Seaga disagreed that it had gone mad. He went on radio and TV to say that the sudden price rises were 'inevitable' because of devaluation, which 'has had the effect of increasing prices in both food and fuel, which is the reason for the pain we all feel'.

Some, however, feel the pain more than others. Although World Bank figures say Jamaican GNP per capita was $1,150 in 1984, this means nothing when the top 10 per cent of the population gets 65 per cent of the nation's income. Poverty is not, perhaps, a new story in Jamaica, but people once had better safety nets and a range of social services exceptional in a Third World country. Massive out-migration has also been a traditional Jamaican strategy against destitution. Today there are 4.4 million Jamaicans, but fewer than half of them live on their own island.

Belinda Coote introduces us to some women who are trying to survive at home. One is Erna. She is lucky, in a sense, because she has a job and one-room lodgings which she shares with her two children. Coote met her on the makeshift barricade she and her neighbours built on their street the day of the 'kerosene riots'. Erna told her, 'I've never been a member of any political party and probably never will be, but this government is too much. We've had enough.'

'Enough' means that her electricity has been cut off for a year. When it quadrupled in price, she could no longer pay the bill. She works as a cleaner in a Kingston hospital, but she's afraid of losing her job since the government announced plans to cut a further 1,500 workers from the public-health-sector payroll. 'If somebody leaves, they don't get replaced these days, and yet we are already overworked. The hospital is dirty, crowded and short of basic items such as cleaning materials. I'm just waiting for them to say, "Erna, we don't need you any more," and then I don't know what I'll do.'

Understandably, Erna already has trouble making ends meet on her salary of $US9 a week. She well remembers when rice cost two and a half times less than it does today – yet her wages have not gone up at all. Having some chicken necks or salt fish to put in the rice is a dim memory. Erna worries about the effects of a poor diet on her children. Since she cooks on a kerosene stove, she will now have to cook less, or eat less, in order to afford kerosene.

Erna is rich compared with Sandra, who has two children aged 6 years and 7 months. The father of her children had a job, and they were happy for the first few years; 'then he lost his job and we had to make do on my earnings. I used to sell fish and bammy [cassava cake] in the market, but the fish got too expensive and no one could afford to buy it, so I had to give that up. We had nothing then, but a boy to support and another on the way. It was too much for him. He left and I haven't heard from him since.' Now Sandra keeps herself and her children alive by begging. 'When I have to go out to get food, I leave the baby with the boy. I have to keep him off school, but what else can I do? Sometimes I send him out to find scraps on the street with the other kids. It's the only way.'

Fatherless households are commonplace in Jamaica. Veronica is another woman whose man left her with two small children. She also cares for her blind and housebound grandmother. 'Friends feed the children sometimes. We can't manage on my earnings [of not quite $US4 a week, which she gets for part-time work making bags]. We eat mostly rice and calaloo [local spinach]. I used to buy chicken necks for the children, but we can't afford that any more. Prices just go up and up. It frightens me to think what will happen. Starve to death, I suppose.'[6]

Since it's too easy to be accused of tear-jerking by concentrating on the worst-off, even if they are in the majority, I asked Jamaican colleagues for a couple of interviews with people who would normally be considered 'middle-class' rather than 'poor'. One of these people is Colleen: 31 years old, mother of five children and fairly well off by present Jamaican standards. She attended secondary school and now lives with her parents – her father is a civil servant of thirty-five years' standing. She was employed as a community health aid from 1975 to 1982 but lost her job as a result of cutbacks in the public health budget. Since then she has tried 'higglering', the Jamaican term for outdoor marketing, but has not been very successful.

(For the reader's convenience, and unless otherwise noted, all figures are given here in U S dollars, converted at the late 1986 exchange rate of $5.50 Jamaican to $1 US.) Colleen says, 'I used to be all right. The cost of goods was cheaper, like rice, flour and children's clothes. I used to pay about $5.50 for a pair of school shoes and school uniform cloth was $1.00 a yard. I earned $64 a month, and with that I used to look after myself and the five children. Medical care was much cheaper and, because of my work, I had an opportunity to take the children to see the doctor regular for their check-up. I used to visit the movies every week and dance very often. Every month I put $5.50 in the bank, plus I paid in $7.25 a month as a partner.' (This is a form of collective saving outside the banking system operated by ordinary people in their work place or community.) 'We always ate three times a day. I was a much more independent woman. I didn't have to rely on my father for anything.'

Commenting on her life between the time she lost her job in 1982 and September 1986 when the interview took place, Colleen said, 'Conditions are worse to the extent if I talk about it often, I might get mad. Chicken is the main kind of meat I am eating, on an average two to three times a week. I used to eat beef. School materials – the cost of these is something else.' School shoes now fetch $12; a satchel is $13.50; uniform material is $3.60 a yard; while lunch money and bus fares for the children comes to $1.45 per day per child, or $7.25, since all five of her children – they range in age from 7 to 14 – are in school. 'I am eating less because I can't afford three meals a day. If I find the money to cook a good lunch, I can't cook dinner – I can only cook one time for the day. I am more fortunate than some people, though, because I have an ackee tree in my yard. I have to rely on my father to provide the funds to take the children to see the doctor. I am not taking them as often as I used to, only when they are seriously ill. I can't save no more. If it wasn't for the fathers of the two biggest girls who are in the U S A and my father, I don't know how I would survive.'[7]

Why is a decent diet now beyond the reach of so many Jamaicans? Partly because Jamaica's own farming sector has been allowed to deteriorate. A lot of food that could perfectly well be produced locally is imported from the United States – over $145 million worth in 1984.[8] Because of successive devaluations, imports are far more expensive than

Table 3   Nutritional purchasing power of $J1, August 1984 and November 1985

Item	No. of calories, August 1984	No. of calories, November 1985	Change (%)
Flour	2,232	1,443	−35
Cornmeal	3,669	2,013	−45
Rice	1,649	905	−45
Chicken	220	174	−20
Condensed milk	1,037	508	−51
Oil	1,003	823	−18
Dark sugar	1,727	1,253	−27

in 1982. In accordance with IMF prescriptions, price controls have been removed, even on basic staples.

The Caribbean Food and Nutrition Institute (CFNI) keeps tabs on food prices and regularly publishes the cost of a 'basket of groceries for a five-person household for one week'. The CFNI includes fruits and vegetables, meat and fish in its basket, even though costs for these items have become prohibitive for most Jamaicans. As noted above, food prices rose alarmingly from the end of 1983 to the beginning of 1985; between 1985 and 1986 they continued upwards but at a somewhat slower rate. Price differences for various categories of foods, from December 1983 to March 1986, look like this:[9]

Fruits and vegetables	+67
Cereals	+125
Milk products	+125
Meat and fish	+146
All items	+97

The CFNI list is made up of twenty-six food items, and the only one that *declined* during this period – by a smashing 2 per cent – is calaloo. Even that goes up seasonally.

Kevin Danaher of the Institute for Food and Development Policy checked Kingston supermarket prices in January 1986 and found that a dozen eggs or a small chicken would cost a day's wages (for a minimum wage-earner), while a week's wages could barely cover the purchase of three quarts of cooking oil. One woman told him, 'I don't even go to the supermarket any more. It's too depressing.'[10]

There's another way to look at the contents of the food basket and the daily diet of Jamaicans, which is the *nutritional purchasing power* of a dollar. Table 3 indicates the number of *calories* supplied by a variety of foodstuffs that could be purchased with $J1 in August 1984 and in November 1985.[11]

Unemployment has grown hugely. The official rate is 25 per cent, but even the conservative *Daily Gleaner* puts it at around 40 per cent. Lay-offs continue in both the public and the private sector, while wage-increase ceilings of 12–15 per cent have been imposed for those who have jobs. Some of the latter, like sugar workers, are paid by the day and have no work at all for six months of the year when there is no cane to cut. Belinda Coote notes that while IMF strictures give sugar-company managers a handy excuse when bargaining with trade unions or staff associations,

For the employee, it's a hopeless situation. While the cost of living rises at a projected annual rate of 67 per cent, wages can only increase by a maximum of 15 per cent. A sugar worker at the height of the season, when earnings are at their maximum, only takes home the equivalent of £12 [$US 18] a week, while basic food needs of a family are calculated to cost £24 ($US 36) a week.

Since the Jamaican government is confronted with soaring prices for food imports and growing popular discontent with unaffordable food prices at home, one would expect it to encourage the local smallholder farming sector. It does nothing of the kind, as an interview conducted by Michael Nieta of the Kingston Social Action Centre shows. He talked to farmer Leroy Taylor, who has been working his 7 acres for twenty-one years, since 1965. Now 44 years old, Taylor attended primary school, has a small two-bedroom house and grows cassava, yam, ginger, banana, potato and vegetables. Like Colleen, Leroy is not someone who would be classed among the 'truly needy', as Mr Reagan might say. But he isn't doing well, and I want to leave the flavour of his language as he explains why.

Up to 1980, he says, 'Along with three days workers who I'man [refers to himself] employed at $16–20 [Jamaican] per day and I'man working five days a week, we used to farm the land. Conditions was most wonderful – the cost of seeds, manure, spray, fork, cutlass and file was 100 per cent times cheaper. I'man used to eat regular – for instance, three times per day. Also I'man used to get assistance from government in the form of fertilizer, sometimes up to sixteen bags.' Taylor knows some annual production figures by heart and ticks them off: yam,

2,000 lb; banana, 30–40 bunches; potato, 1,400 lb; vegetables, 2,000 lb.
That was in 1980.

Since then, things have got steadily worse. 'Everything difficult.
I'man can't buy seed, manure or employ workers to help with the
farming.' His costs of production have skyrocketed. The result? 'I'man
can only farm 2 acres now.' Taylor's food output has dropped pro-
portionally. He now grows only a quarter the amount of yams, 40 per
cent of the vegetables and a third of the potatoes he used to. Only
bananas, which require less day-to-day work, remain the same at
between thirty and forty bunches a year. Leroy Taylor says, 'My survival
is very weak, I can't produce what I used to before – what I am eating is
second-class.' Nor can he get any government – or private – assistance.
'I'man check the bank in 1982 to get a loan, but them say NO. Because in
late 1970s government was giving we [money] to plant peas. I received
[$US72] and the crop failed due to bad weather. Them now saying
I'man have to pay back [$US72] first at 6 per cent interest and I can't
find it. I don't see no way to get money to build up the farm because as
how I'man see it, the small farmer has no argument but to kill himself in
the field while the big man is really them can survive and it is becoming
worster and worster every day.'

Has Taylor ever heard of the IMF? Indeed he has: 'As far as the IMF
is concern, it is the most infiltrate system against the poor man because
every day their government is becoming sterner and my labour is worth
less and less.'[12]

It is not just Taylor's labour that is becoming worthless. As his costs
shoot up, he can no longer employ any labourers himself. The smallholder farm sector, which could supply many jobs, contracts inexorably,
while official preference and investment goes to large-scale, mechanized
farming. The government's approach to farming – sanctioned and
encouraged by the IMF – is not concerned with supplying food for local
people but is export-oriented; over a third of Jamaica's land is planted to
cash crops. Unfortunately, Jamaica is not reaping the dividends expected from this policy. The two largest agribusiness enterprises on the
island, which grew vegetables, fruits, and flowers for export on several
thousand acres, have folded for reasons that are not entirely clear but
appear related to unreliable markets, especially in the US.[13]

The Prime Minister admits that the banana industry is in calamitous
shape – the country exported 162,000 tons of bananas in 1970 and a mere
12,000 in 1985 – but he says the banana industry has been 'reorganized
and is poised for significant expansion'; as are sugar and coffee, still
according to Seaga. Michael Manley points, rather, to the 23,000 small

banana farmers who have been forced out of business by policies favouring large agribusiness concerns. Many poultry and animal raisers have also been squeezed out by increasing feed costs.[14]

Since thousands of people have lost their jobs, and new ones are not being created, many try to make do with 'higglering', but this is a bit like trying to create growth by encouraging people take in one another's laundry. There simply aren't enough customers to go around, and no one has much disposable income. Others attempt to get into one of the few lucrative activities still possible in Jamaica – growing or selling drugs. Michael Nieta writes, 'The level of illegality and insecurity has increased. [This is clear from] the daily long line outside the US Embassy of persons seeking entry visas to the USA and the number of persons involved in the drug trade and taking hard drugs.'

The brightest spots in the economy are apparel exports and tourism. About 1 million visitors now go to Jamaica yearly, and tourism is the number-one foreign-exchange earner ($405 million in 1985). Tourists are, however, notoriously fickle and respond to changes in fashion and to political turmoil, real or perceived. Thanks to the Reagan CBI, duty-free exports of clothing to the United States have achieved growth levels higher than those of any other country: up 90 per cent in $US value, or 158 per cent in terms of square yardage, during the first six months of 1986 as compared with the same period in 1985. The apparel is produced in the Kingston Free Zone (seventeen companies, 7,000 workers, mostly women), where 'enforced overtime, lack of proper eating and bathroom facilities, low wages, rapid staff turnover and intimidation by their foreign supervisors are among the complaints of women workers in several companies,' the *Daily Gleaner* reports. A Jamaican women's collective calls the location the 'Slave Zone'.[15]

IMF: INTERNATIONAL MENACE TO FOOD

Jamaica's economic morass shows up first, as we've seen, in the family market basket and on the dinner table. Lack of the proper quality and quantity of food results, in turn, in more illness, disability and premature death. All responsible sources agree that malnutrition is on the rise, though government data may not necessarily seek to highlight this fact.

National Health Ministry statistics indicate, for instance, that only 2.5 per cent more children suffered from first-degree malnutrition in 1985 than in 1978. Increases for second- or third-degree malnutrition were insignificant. A look at more specific, localized situations, however, gives a different and more alarming picture. Although the figures are still small in absolute terms, the number of children admitted to the Bustamante Children's Hospital for the related problems of malnutrition and gastro-enteritis tripled between 1981 and 1985. Surveys covering very large samples of children in Kingston/St Andrew found 21 per cent of 0–3-year-olds malnourished in 1980, 26 per cent in 1984, 29.5 per cent in 1985.

This dangerous upward creep of malnutrition among small children is compounded by the worsening nutritional status of women, who are eating less too and consequently giving birth to underweight babies more vulnerable to disease. Another survey in Kingston/St Andrew showed that 23 per cent of mothers screened in 1981 were anaemic. By 1984 the proportion had shot up to 43 per cent.[16] Women must now pay a fee of $US12.50 for pre-natal care and delivery. This may not sound like much, but remember that it's more than Erna makes in a week and over three weeks' wages for Veronica. Not surprisingly, as a doctor told Belinda Coote, 'Many women can't afford to come to us. There has been a growing number of cases of pregnant women presenting themselves to us for the first time when already in labour, having received no ante-natal care at all.' His own hospital had recorded four maternal deaths for the single month of January 1985 as compared with seven deaths for the entire year of 1984.

The Senior Medical Officer for Kingston/St Andrew, Peter Figueroa, told Kevin Danaher in January 1986, 'There's no question that health care is deteriorating under Seaga . . . Devaluation has hurt the supply of drugs and medical equipment.'[17] Indeed, since most basic drugs are imported, their costs have escalated by between 50 and 300 per cent, so many must be done without. Hospitals and clinics become run down, dirty and germ-laden when they can no longer purchase detergents, soaps and rubber gloves. Equipment rusts for want of spare parts, and, since the utility bills can no longer be paid, many clinics lack electricity, telephones and even water.

Brain drain receives a direct boost from IMF wage containment ('demand-management') policies. A young medical graduate can expect to earn only about $US4,400 net per year and will be expected to put in a lot of unpaid overtime. A qualified nurse will receive only about $US1,850 net annually. Small wonder that professionals seek to take their skills elsewhere. In the Bahamas, for example, Jamaican doctors can command five times the salary they can expect at home.

Naturally, shortages and cutbacks soon begin to exacerbate each other, so that the whole picture is blacker than any of its component parts. Reduced personnel means fewer travelling nurses. Even those who remain can't make the rounds as they used to because of higher gasoline prices. Dr Figueroa explained to Danaher: 'Travelling nurses have had to cut back from roughly 500 miles a month to more like 200 miles.' A public-health officer told Belinda Coote, 'We've had to abandon our mosquito-control programmes due to lack of funds to replace spraying equipment.' Others explained that school immunization programmes have had to be curtailed. In 1982 Jamaica experienced its first polio deaths in thirty years.

Decades of enlightened policies gave Jamaica a life expectancy of seventy-three years – the same as in Cuba or Israel, higher than in Greece or Portugal. Infant mortality rates were among the lowest anywhere in the Third World (between 16 and 20 per 1,000 live births) at least until 1980. Now, Dr Figueroa says simply, 'More people are dying.' He suggests that official infant mortality rates do not reflect reality and that numerous infant deaths go unreported, particularly since fewer women now give birth in hospitals.

The government has recognized decaying health and nutrition to the extent that it has instituted a school feeding programme and a food-stamp system. Critics contend, however, that these programmes reach only a tiny fraction of the intended target population. To begin with, many of the children who most need food supplements aren't in school.

Schools are understaffed and overcrowded; many parents can no longer afford to send their children to school because they can't afford books, bus fares, shoes or clothing. Jamaica is supposed to have free, compulsory primary schooling, and technically it does. Parents make heroic efforts to keep their kids at school, but, as one mother explained, 'It's cheaper to keep my children at home and feed them from the family pot than send them to school.' She can afford to send them only two days a week, and they must walk 3 miles each way. She can't afford bus fares, and 'The little one [aged 6] gets tired, but what can I do? They must get an education. It's their only hope.' Their school, like many others, does not enjoy a school feeding programme.

The sheer stupidity of such IMF-imposed measures ought to be obvious, and doubtless is, to anyone except the blinkered economists who make up the Fund's staff and draw up its adjustment programmes. No mosquito control today will mean malaria tomorrow. Missed vaccinations will translate into epidemics. Dead mothers, birth-damaged, malnourished babies and unschooled children will necessarily weigh heavily upon the community at large tomorrow. People simply do not produce efficiently when they are faint with hunger. The IMF cannot seem to understand that investing in the kind of healthy, well-fed, literate population that Jamaica once had is the most intelligent economic choice a country can make. For the Fund it's creditors first, and Jamaica owes $3.2 billion.

People have not been quiescent. Besides the 'kerosene riots', there have been a week-long general strike (June 1985), student protests in response to increases in university and technical-school tuition and teachers' walkouts. Trade unionists and small farmers' leaders have called on the government to resign. Most significant of all, in the July 1986 municipal elections Seaga's party was trounced by Manley's PNP.

But whatever the party in charge, so long as the IMF actually runs the show on behalf of the Consortium and barring a major social uprising, little change is possible. The tragic irony is that all the hunger, misery and deaths *will not even help the country to pay back its debts* – ostensibly the reason why so many sacrifices are being demanded. Without high, guaranteed prices on world markets for bauxite and sugar, the country's major exports, and an unending flow of rich tourists, Jamaica doesn't stand a chance. Neither, alas, do Jamaicans.

12.
DEALING WITH DEBT: THE VIEW FROM THE NORTH

Of all the proposals for dealing with debt that have come out of the North, the best-known (and in my view the least interesting) is the Baker Plan, named after the then Secretary of the US Treasury, James Baker, who launched it at the annual World Bank/IMF jamboree conference in October 1985 in Seoul, Korea.

HALF-BAKED

The plan wasn't especially well thought out and, even if fully applied, couldn't possibly solve the debt crisis, but it was important in one respect. Baker's speech revealed that the Reagan administration was finally abandoning the ostrich position and admitting that a crisis existed.

This awakening may have been prompted by the 2 million-plus US jobs wiped out as a direct result of Third World debt, the inability of American farmers to sell their produce to the southern hemisphere or an uneasy recognition of growing social unrest in any number of indebted countries. If Reagan's people were smart enough, or Machiavellian enough (which is far from certain), they may even have seen the Baker Plan as a way to extend the economic doctrines fashionable in the United States to the world at large, at no cost to themselves.

Whatever its motives, the Baker initiative signalled Washington's concern for renewing world growth and its willingness to co-operate with, or coerce, other members of the Consortium to achieve it. Whatever its failings, the plan was a cut above previous US policy, which had been limited to sermons exhorting the Third World to pull up its socks, tighten its belt and solve the debt crisis by itself through double doses of self-discipline and austerity.

The components of the Baker Plan are straightforward:

* commercial banks should loan another $20 billion over a three-year period (1986–8) to the fifteen largest debtors;
* official multilateral financial institutions should increase their lending by 50 per cent above 1985 levels to $9 billion during the same period, with the World Bank making the biggest effort; this makes a total of $29 billion, or under $10 billion a year;
* the $2.7 billion IMF Trust Fund should be used as a new borrowing facility for the poorest (mostly African) countries with annual per capita income below $550.[1]

In exchange for being helped to grow, as Baker claims they would be, debtor countries would adhere to a strict set of conditions. The media did not always report Point One of Baker's Three-Point Program. It concerned the increased efforts that *debtors* were expected to make, in line with standard monetarist economic principles. They were required to liberalize trade; remove controls that hampered foreign private investment; reduce government involvement in the economy in order to unleash entrepreneurial energies; focus on 'supply-side' growth; and improve export capacity.

The Baker Plan thus served to reinforce and legitimize IMF conditionality and guaranteed Reaganomics for the millions without the US having to provide any additional cash itself. It called on the World Bank to work with the IMF as 'joint enforcer'. More important still, it served notice on recalcitrant countries like Peru. Baker's Seoul speech included this warning:

Countries which are not prepared to undertake basic adjustments and work within the framework of the case-by-case debt strategy, cooperating with the international financial institutions, cannot expect to benefit from this three-point program. Additional lending will not occur. Efforts by any country to 'go it alone' are likely to seriously damage its prospects for future growth.[2]

Need he say more?

Who liked Baker's plan, aside from the US administration itself? The private banks expected their money to be safer when lent in tandem with the World Bank. Bank tutelage would accompany and intensify IMF conditions. The Bank's own loans would help finance the kinds of economic structural-adjustment policy reforms the US/IMF want – called, aptly enough, structural adjustment loans or SALs. Initiated in 1980, SALs now represent roughly 10 per cent of all Bank lending (about $3.5 billion).

If the Baker Plan is applied, the IMF/Bank will become *de facto* protectors of the private banks, since they will co-ordinate both the lending and the conditions for receiving loans. The commercial banks need not get their feet wet or fork out any money until the country in question has complied with the senior partners' directives and signed on for its own official IMF adjustment programme. This is called the 'in-together, out-together' formula.[3] Some major private banks now even participate on an equal footing in the debt-rescheduling nego-tiations that used to take place exclusively between Third World governments and official multilateral lenders. The Consortium appears to be functioning more smoothly than ever before.

The IMF and the Bank like the Baker approach too, though there were turf-defending reactions at the outset. Federal Reserve chairman Paul Volcker had been heard to remark it might be time to 'phase out' the IMF, and the Fund did not want to lose pride of place to the Bank, which it saw as assuming too much importance under Baker auspices.[4] The Bank, on the other hand, was wary, perhaps resentful, of a US-sponsored plan that called for it to come up with quite a lot of extra money, none of it necessarily to be put up by the US itself. It feared that governments would simply deposit bad bank debts on its doorstep, and it didn't care much for Baker's public criticism (in the event, justified) of its past lending performance.[5]

In early December 1985, however, the heads of the Bank and the Fund took the unprecedented step of issuing a joint communiqué, endorsed by their boards, to express their 'strong support' for the Baker initiative. And in March 1986 the two institutions got together to put their money on the line and approved a new joint fund of $3.1 billion to help the poorest debtors.

The Bank/IMF are equal-opportunity structural adjusters – they believe no country should be left unreformed just because it's poor or black. The new jointly managed fund, called the Structural Adjustment Facility, is intended for sixty poor countries and 'marks the first time that the IMF and the World Bank have co-operated formally in helping debt-ridden countries'. The Facility even throws $400 million more into the pot than Baker asked for in Seoul ($3.1 billion as opposed to $2.7). Eighty per cent of the money is supposed to go to sub-Saharan Africa.[6]

This new Facility will lend at 0.5 per cent interest, or virtually nothing, but only after the Bank/IMF tandem has worked out a 'policy framework' with the recipient government for restructuring its economy. The *Wall Street Journal* reports:

They will use these frameworks as a guide in approving and administering loans . . . the frameworks will establish broad 'benchmarks' that borrowing countries must meet each year in restructuring their economies . . . countries that fail to meet the goals won't be eligible for the second stage of their loans . . . Adoption of the plan was viewed as a major success for the Reagan administration, which had been pushing quietly for the new program since the Treasury Department proposed it in October.[7]

The Facility is, however, the smallest component of the Baker Plan. What about the proposed $29 billion from commercial banks and the multilateral lenders? What has actually become of this idea since October 1985? To tell the truth, not much. Many observers see the Baker initiative as a flagrant case of too little, too late. Latin American response has ranged from lukewarm to hostile. Indeed, after Baker's rather ill-prepared launch in Seoul, the US had to scurry around trying to find a customer. Argentina, offered the signal honour of going first, courteously declined. Mexico was considered too big and unwieldy to make a convincing example of 'growth with adjustment', which is what the Plan is intended to produce. Finally, after much casting about, little Ecuador, with 8 million people and a (relatively) modest $8 billion debt, was seized upon as the first Baker beneficiary. In fact, as its finance minister made clear, 'Ecuador hadn't waited for the Baker proposal to undertake a reformist policy to restore the economy to health. But we're lucky that we'd already made progress in that direction when Mr Baker began to call for new loans to Latin American countries that had successfully applied austerity programmes.'[8]

It is hardly surprising that debtors are not beating down Baker's door. First of all, his plan does not provide for much extra money to be shared out – only $9.3 billion a year, if the $29 billion is apportioned in equal slices. For the largest debtors this borders on the ridiculous. Consider the needs of Mexico, which in 1986 alone amounted to $12 billion, or 129 per cent of that sum. Why should fifteen countries, perhaps even more,[9] fight over crumbs when conditions for access are even more stringent than the ones to which they must already submit?

The Debt Crisis Network, a group of scholars and activists in the US working to change the terms of the present debt debate, points out that Baker billed his plan as a 'programme for sustained growth', leading the public and the press to believe that 'growth and the World Bank' were about to replace 'austerity and the IMF'. This just isn't so – no country will get a Baker loan *unless it has already agreed* to IMF conditions.[10] On top of them, it will get plenty of World Bank (and doubtless private) advice.

There is, furthermore, no reason for debtors to be enthusiastic about a plan that completely disregards their real concerns. As *Business Latin America* notes, 'No mention is made of cutting interest costs or restructuring debt, for example. Moreover, by relying heavily on variable-rate bank loans as the source of new funds, the Baker Plan may only exacerbate an already precarious situation.'[11]

THE BRADLEY INITIATIVE: BREAKING BAKER'S MONOPOLY

Senator Bill Bradley holds precisely this view. Baker kept the floor, and the media, to himself for eight months after he proclaimed his plan. Bradley changed the debate at a stroke by stating point-blank:

Since the Baker Plan calls for new loans instead of interest-rate and debt relief, it creates more debt, not less. This will increase the already precarious exposure of banks to a possible default. And adding to the debt burden of these countries will discourage new investment and increase capital flight. In other words, the plan prolongs the policies that created the debt crisis in the first place.[12]

Indeed, as Bradley sees it, the Baker Plan is nothing but a disguised transfer to the banks, since the level of lending that it proposes corresponds to a mere 20 per cent of annual Latin American debt service. Under Baker auspices 'new loans will simply return to creditors in the form of interest payments or capital flight. No cash will change hands. Only the books will look better,' says Bradley. He proposes to grant relief, not just new loans, by offering countries each year for three years:

• three percentage points of interest-rate relief on all outstanding debt owed to banks and governments;
• 3 per cent write-down and forgiveness of principal on all outstanding loans;

• $3 billion worth of project and/or structural-adjustment loans from multilateral lending institutions, particularly the World Bank.[13]

This is an improvement, no doubt. But Bradley and Baker are united on the free-market approach to the debt problem. Because his aim is to promote world-wide growth, Bradley proposes a strong trade component as well. He wants the US President to convene a 'trade-relief summit' for three years running to coincide with the proposed debt-relief talks, using the new GATT round of multilateral trade talks as a forum. Third World countries would have an incentive to participate because 'any concessions they made in trade negotiations would simultaneously increase their prospects for receiving debt relief.'

Bradley clearly wants the Third World to stop exporting so much and clawing its way into US markets in order to earn vital debt-servicing dollars. 'Relief' is not limited to foreign debt but applies as well to American industries. This is a major concern of the Democratic Party, which has been introducing protectionist legislation fast and furiously. As Bradley points out, 'Since 1981, Argentina's soybean drive has claimed 80 per cent of the world-wide markets lost by US growers. Between 1980 and 1984, Brazil expanded textile and apparel exports by a factor of 11.'[14] Presumably, such countries would see reason and bow out gracefully if they were offered debt relief as an incentive.

To make sure that new money really contributes to growth and doesn't simply fly northwards, the value of each year's trade/debt-relief package 'should depend on the uses that each debtor has made of the previous year's package'. The debtors would be expected to adhere to six guideline instructions: liberalize trade, reverse capital flight, encourage internal investment, promote economic growth, choose policies 'with broad internal support', and keep debt management 'free from scandal'. A vast programme, as General de Gaulle said when he overheard a subordinate calling for 'death to imbeciles'.

Bradley compares the choices presented by this moment in history with the opportunity lost at Versailles after the First World War or seized after the Second World War with the Marshall Plan. We can either burden Latin America with impossible debts and watch it, like Germany, repudiate them and possibly revert to Fascist regimes, or act boldly to strengthen the international financial system and Western economies that have been sorely tried by Third World debt.[15]

Faced with a choice, for me it would be Bradley over Baker, hands down. His arguments are sound; he sees clearly the damage done to the North by debt-induced stagnation, yet he is also sensitive to the drop in living standards and the hardships suffered by ordinary people in the South.

The banks, however, do not warm to his plan for obvious reasons – they would have to forgo some earnings from interest and principal. Paul Volcker and the president of the World Bank, Barber Conable, have both criticized the Bradley Plan. As of December 1986, there was no legislation pending in the US Congress that embodied his main points, but this could change under the Democratic majority.

Bradley's great virtue is to pose a high-level challenge to the Baker/ IMF scenario. Because it comes from him, it has to be taken seriously. He has legitimized an approach that does not simply pile debt upon debt and has made it OK to talk aloud about relief. It is slowly dawning on official Washington that when new money merely serves to finance old and is not invested in anything productive, the prospect of ultimate pay-off grows ever more remote. The problem is that, in order to work, Bradley's plan must be accepted simultaneously world-wide. Otherwise governments and banks that made no concessions would gain an advantage over those that did. Bradley is aware of this:

Suppose Japanese and British banks provide debt relief to an indebted developing country, but Canadian and German banks do not provide it to the same country. Then the Canadian and German banks benefit from having more creditworthy debtors at the expense of Japan and Britain. The Japanese and British banks would take a loss and operate at a competitive disadvantage to the banks that did not provide debt relief. A workable debt proposal must be country-specific, related to debtor efforts to restore investor confidence, and co-ordinated among all creditors.[16]

Getting 'all creditors' to act together – particularly private banks ever ready to knife a rival – sounds like a daunting proposition unless a higher authority could be invoked.

A NEW DEAL AT THE IMF?

What chance is there that 'higher authority' might get behind a more innovative plan than Baker's? In December 1986 Jacques de Larosière's successor as managing director of the IMF was finally chosen after long and unseemly intra-European haggling. The Frenchman won: he is Michel Camdessus, whose previous job was governor of the French central bank, a position to which he was appointed by socialist President

Mitterrand. Though Larosière and Camdessus resemble each other superficially – same prestigious school, same top civil service jobs in the French Finance Ministry – Camdessus has certainly the more interesting, creative mind.

Few people are yet likely to know much about him and his views. Since he will be a key figure until at least 1992, it's useful to summarize an article on Third World debt that he wrote for a French journal well before anyone thought Larosière would retire (at 57, his decision was unexpected) or that he, Camdessus, could be tapped for the top Fund job.[17]

Writing after the annual IMF/Bank conclave in September 1984, Camdessus cautions against the 'cowardly sense of relief' felt in several quarters and the belief that the debt crisis is a thing of the past. In spite of the Fund's 'decisive role in preserving the world financial order' by getting the private banks to reschedule all of the principal and half the interest for the major debtors, in spite of averted defaults, lower interest rates and higher growth, there is no reason for euphoria. Although adjustment programmes have been accepted by nearly everyone, they have brought about a drop in living standards of 10 per cent or more in the debtor countries. Furthermore, every debt crisis in history since Solon of Athens has ended in inflation, bankruptcy or war, and there is no cause to believe we've solved this one, even if it has been postponed.

Camdessus then reminds us that the IMF lists no fewer than *ten* conditions that will have to be met in order to defuse the crisis: (1) adjustment policies must be pursued until at least 1990; (2) GNP in the industrialized countries must grow by 3.25 per cent minimum annually; (3) floating interest rates must move downwards and banks must charge lower fees; (4) prices of manufactured goods must not increase by more than 4 per cent a year; (5) oil prices must hold stable; (6) terms of trade for the debtors must improve; (7) protectionism must be eliminated; (8) commercial banks must maintain their present exposure until at least 1990; (9) official aid must remain at 1984 levels in real terms; (10) higher direct private investment must take place in the Third World. Wow.

Assume that all ten of these conditions are actually met – that the poor maintain austerity and the rich growth, that debt service owed by the twenty-five largest debtors does get paid, though it will have soared from $35 billion in 1984 to $85 billion in 1987. Even if we accept this unlikely hypothesis, the *best* we can hope for is that economic conditions will grow only slightly *worse* in 1987. By 1990 they may return to levels of the early 1980s. There will be *no improvement in present (depressed) living standards* and *no reduction of indebtedness*. Developing countries will have to maintain austerity with high human costs; their only reward will be debts every bit as high in 1990 as they were in 1981. This grim scenario strikes Camdessus as clearly unacceptable: we cannot wait until the 1990s to improve the lot of people in the indebted countries.

His own solution is threefold: (1) the costs of austerity must be better shared; (2) we need to make better use of existing financial instruments; (3) North–South dialogue on debt must become standard policy, and it must be a political dialogue.

(1) The heart of the crisis (as well as its origins) should be sought in two sets of figures: growth rates and interest rates. In the mid- and late 1970s the average annual growth rate of non-oil developing countries ranged between 4 per cent and 6 per cent, while real long-term interest rates were frequently negative and never went as high as 2 per cent. So there was a terrific incentive to borrow. Since the beginning of the 1980s these vital statistics have been exactly reversed – growth for these same developing countries is down to 1 or 2 per cent, while real interest rates are up to 5 per cent. The difference between growth rates and interest rates is what Camdessus calls the 'critical gap'; the way this figure evolves gives a capsule view of debtors' hardships.*

By themselves the debtors cannot bridge the critical gap. A return to economic stability requires that the *industrialized* countries accept the same kind of discipline that the I M F imposes on the poor. In particular, the United States absolutely must reduce its deficits, while Europe should modernize and improve its growth rates in order to be able to purchase more from the developing countries.

(2) A good many 'miracle solutions' to the debt crisis have been suggested. They generally want bad debts transferred to some new, publicly financed body, or they call for global refinancing of loans, which would be sure to create inflation in the long run. These brilliant plans, however, make no use of existing financial instruments like Special

* Growth rates for non-oil developing countries (China excluded) and real interest rates on borrowings, 1973–83, in Camdessus:

	1973	1974	1975	1976	1977	1978	1979	1980	1981	1982	1983
Growth rate	6.1	5.4	3.3	6.0	5.2	5.4	4.6	4.3	2.5	0.8	1.2
Real interest rate	1.2	−3.5	−0.9	1.6	1.0	1.1	−0.2	0.6	4.3	6.3	6.2
Critical gap	4.9	8.9	4.2	4.4	4.2	4.3	4.8	3.7	−1.8	−5.5	−5.0

Drawing Rights (the IMF's own currency), which could provide the world with badly needed liquidity. If countries with an excess balance of payments (like Japan or West Germany) put their money at the IMF's disposal, the latter could recycle it in the poor countries. Conditions would be applied in order to avoid the wasteful use of these fresh funds.[18] Some $30 billion or $40 billion could be recycled in this way; this is far less than we allowed the private banks to handle in the 1970s, with no guarantees whatsoever.

We should also encourage public financing for growth in the poor countries through an increase in the capital of the World Bank and through the Bank's long-term, low-cost loan window, the International Development Association (IDA). The meagre capital replenishment of the IDA ($9 billion in 1984) is 'deplorable'. Individual industrialized countries should also invest directly in developing countries: the private sector can't take on this job and, indeed, will invest only if the public sector has already pledged itself. Such investments would, again, take place under adjustment programmes so as to guarantee the efficient use of funds and would create jobs, giving hope to young people in the debtor countries.

(3) Dialogue between debtors and creditors must start right away, and it must be a *political* dialogue. This means that the industrialized countries have to accept discussion of their own national policies. Leaders of the developed countries should not make their financial contributions dependent on one another. Note the extremely important, if unspoken, point made here: Michel Camdessus seems prepared to abandon the sacrosanct case-by-case approach, which has traditionally amounted to all the creditors ganging up on a single debtor.

Camdessus ends his piece with a 'utopian' list of preconditions for an end to the debt crisis: Europe gets rid of all its internal barriers and doubles its growth rate; the US reduces its deficit and contributes heavily to multilateral institutions; Japan opens its markets and reduces and recycles its trade surplus; OPEC invests *directly* in the Third World without transiting via the banks; the more advanced countries of the South start contributing to development aid; and everybody eliminates protectionism.

We could do far worse than have Camdessus as top man at the IMF! But we should remember that the top man does not, by himself, make policy. He can influence, colour, stress, persuade; he cannot supersede the will of the Group of Five or Ten, and, whatever the name of the managing director, the United States retains veto power over the most important decisions.

BRILLIANT IDEAS

Camdessus refers with mild sarcasm to several 'miracle solutions' and 'brilliant ideas' that have been launched as panaceas for dealing with the debt crisis. We will mention only the major ones here and give them less space than the Baker–Bradley–Camdessus trio. The trio have political backing and occupy positions of power; the bright-ideas men don't, at least not today, though they may be financial wizards and appallingly rich in private life.

One drawback of some of the brilliant ideas is their failure to recognize that the debt crisis, for Third World governments, is not one but *two* huge problems: how to pay back what they owe, of course, but also, even more tragically urgent, how to ensure continued access to new money. They cannot afford to sign on for any 'solutions' that might solve the immediate repayments issue but offer no hope of finding fresh funds.

Even an ideal plan that ensured both smooth repayment and painless replenishments (there is no such animal) would still be open to the fatal flaws of the Baker and Bradley plans. The politicians, bankers and financial specialists have nothing to say about the mal-development models that got the debt snowball rolling. Their unspoken premise is that once the debt crisis is brought under control, countries should pursue the same model but manage it better. Even worse, they are concerned only with major actors – Consortium members such as governments, the Bank and the banks, the IMF, etc. The needs of ordinary citizens in the debtor – and (why not?) creditor – countries are rarely, if ever, addressed.

Many Western ideas men offering quick fixes for the debt crisis look only at the Third World itself and ignore the huge and deleterious influence of the United States' deficit on poor countries. Camdessus is an exception here; so is the brilliant Felix Rohatyn, whose own plan has spawned a good many variants. He was the inventor of the Big MAC, the Municipal Assistance Corporation, which refinanced New York City and brought it back from the brink of the abyss. What he did for New York Rohatyn would now like to repeat for the entire world.

First, he wants real discipline to replace present financial non-chalance in the United States. The US should institute an energy tax, cut the military budget, freeze government spending and coax the dollar downwards in order to reduce the dangerous trade and budget deficits that drain so much capital from the rest of the world. Rohatyn also wants the US government formally to guarantee the debts owed to major US banks by Latin American debtors.

Having put the credit of the US behind its commercial banks,

We should use the leverage conferred by this commitment to defuse a situation that could . . . cause havoc not only to the banks but to all of Latin America. The current formula for dealing with this problem is to impose austerity on Latin America in order to maintain the myth that our bank loans are worth 100 cents on the dollar. I believe this policy, if it continues, will create more communists during the next decade than Fidel Castro and the Sandinistas could during the next fifty years.[19]

Since several debtors have already defaulted in all but name, banks have become their hostages. They must keep on providing money or watch their loans become non-performing and risk a crisis of confidence. Rohatyn would apply his Big M A C formula: some institution, either an I M F/Bank subsidiary or a new one, should buy up the creditor banks' debts at a discount (of at least 10 per cent) in exchange for long-term, low-interest bonds, which this institution would issue itself.

The banks would thus no longer receive any payments from the debtors, but they would be free of their most troublesome borrowers once and for all. The debtors would continue to reimburse the new institution now holding their debt but at the much lower interest rates, and over the much longer periods, that such a government-guaranteed entity could provide. The banks would be happy because they too would have government-guaranteed assets on their books (the bonds) instead of dubious Third World loans under constant threat of default. This would be a small price to pay for the losses they would incur by selling off these loans at less than face value.[20]

Various other financial experts, notably New York investment banker Richard Weinert, have proposed similar schemes in Rohatyn's wake. Weinert would basically ask the World Bank to take on the truly rotten debt and leave the relatively healthy loans in the hands of the banks. His refinement is that commercial banks wouldn't be allowed out entirely – they would have to keep a stake in the L D Cs' economies and hang on to, say, 20 per cent of their loans. But they could trade in their 'weaker credits' and keep any debt they wanted to on commercial terms.[21] The only alternative to such a scheme, Weinert says, is a drastic reduction of interest rates so that the debtor countries could pay. Some European banks seem disposed towards this solution; so far US banks are adamantly opposed.

Lord Lever, no financial slouch himself, is polite about it, but essentially he finds these proposals hare-brained. If you try to use a central institution to buy up bad debt in exchange for bonds, the scheme is likely to 'provoke the very crisis it is designed to cure'. His language is neutral, but what he means is that this would be a perilously shaky exchange because based on the junkiest of junk bonds. 'In the real world . . . any secondary market which effectively made bank debt into traded bonds would rapidly show such large discounts on the debt of some of the big borrowers as to call into question the solvency of debtors and banks.'[22]

Demands for a 'debt-discount' agency, existing or proposed, neglect the 'new money' problem facing Third World governments. 'Which of the banks selling present Third World debt to such an agency, at a forced discount and a substantial loss, is going to be willing to extend further funds to the indebted countries?' asks Lever, reasonably enough. Without new flows of capital the existing debt, no matter who holds it, is likely to become worthless.

Lever's own approach would put a stop to 'reverse transfers' (poor countries paying back more in interest than they receive in aid and new loans) and would insist on rich-country government guarantees for new lending. In exchange for these guarantees, the banks would each year write down part of the debt and reschedule it over much longer periods. The idea is to stretch out the process over a period long enough to ensure that the banks' 'profitability, capital position or ability to lend' do not suffer unduly.

As a corollary Lord Lever also suggests extending to the banks the kinds of guarantee that industrial firms get from their home governments. The US or UK widget manufacturer is sure to get his money – in the US from the Export–Import Bank, in Britain from the Export Credit Guarantee Department – even if Peru or Nigeria fails to pay for its imported widgets. Why not insure currency just as one insures products, through the same existing agencies? Conditionality would continue in order to prevent foolish use of the new money, but it would be more growth-oriented than it is at present.

Lever argues that bankers today are terrified and unlikely to resume voluntary lending to the Third World. 'Recovery' based on austerity and export surpluses alone is illusory and leaves both the debtors and the bankers chronically fragile and vulnerable. The higher the net transfers from poor to rich, the greater the temptation to default. The debtors must be allowed to grow; the 'details of a new reform are less important than the mustering of political will in the advanced countries to change a perilous and unsustainable situation'.[23]

Note that all the ideas, brilliant or not, proposed by Northern politicians or bankers for containing the debt crisis involve greater co-operation and co-ordination between public and private institutions. In some cases they would, indeed, become functionally indistinguishable. Most proposals put the maintenance of bank profits at the top of their list, even if they recommend temporary sacrifices. All, however, bend over backwards to explain that they are not really suggesting we 'bail out the banks'.

Depending on one's temperament and consequent choice of vocabulary, this claim can be labelled disingenuous or a bare-faced lie. Whatever the rhetoric in which these schemes are couched, the banks *would be* saved from the consequences of their own recklessness. Through the channel of the IMF, taxpayers are *already* expected to foot the bill without getting anything concrete in return. One can argue that, for the said taxpayers, paying even more to bail out the banks is preferable to universal financial collapse and loss of their personal savings, but the debate ought at least to be framed in clear terms.

The only proposal I have seen with the courage of its private-enterprise convictions comes from a vice-president of Chemical Bank who also worked on debt-restructuring negotiations as a special adviser to the State Department from 1980 to 1982.[24] Charles Meissner thinks that the whole debt problem hinges on interest rates that, in turn, depend on huge US government borrowing to finance its deficit. Anyone who pretends the deficit makes no difference is practising 'ostrich economics'. Meissner agrees with Lever that a debt-discount agency is a non-starter. Industrialized countries and their commercial banks won't – and the World Bank and the IMF can't – provide the necessary new funds.

The only way to solve the 'new money' problem is to start a global reserve bank funded by *the private banks*, not public agencies. It would do part of the work now done by the IMF, which could sit on its board and provide its usual conditionality, but an International Reserve Bank (IRB) would make its own credit decisions. Meissner reminds us that state central banks (the Federal Reserve, the Bank of England, etc.) were originally created by the private banks to suit their own needs. 'They financed these organizations and eventually governments found it in their interest to control these institutions. Financed by a group of fifty international banks, the International Reserve Bank could eventually be purchased by creditor governments.' This IRB would work towards common regulatory and accounting standards for all its members. We live in an age of global banking, and we need a global regulatory system. An international bank would obviate the need for any single member to become dangerously over-exposed in a single country. Meissner concludes: 'The banks can either help create a new structure that will overcome the problems of the past or take their chances while others fumble with alternatives. The first option gives them an opportunity to influence their future. The second option may provide them with hardly any future at all.'

GETTING OUT UNSCATHED: THE SEARCH FOR AN EXIT

What are the banks actually doing, as opposed to what politicians and assorted financial wizards think they should do? They are still very much present on the Third World debt scene, albeit against their will. 'Involuntary lending', at the behest of the IMF and other powerful members of the Consortium, has become a feature of international finance since the 1982 Mexican rescue. Though still forced to lend, the banks' true idea of a 'solution' to the debt problem is to reduce their overall exposure in high-risk countries as quickly as possible and to let these nations fend for themselves, using someone else's money.

Since they can't get out in one fell swoop, banks are now also trying to secure something more tangible than government promises and doubtful paper. Thus they are beginning to swap part of their loans for capital in a variety of enterprises. Whatever their strategies, the banks are not standing still, and they are not waiting for governments and international bodies to 'solve' the debt crisis for them.

TOP OF THE SWAPS

If you were a banker, which prospect would you find more attractive: a touch-and-go loan to a foreign government at 8–10 per cent interest that might or might not be paid on time (if at all), or participation in the capital and management of a firm that could well appreciate by 25 per cent a year? This rosy description, of course, makes the answer too easy but shows how attractive equity, as opposed to debt, can be for a bank. The chance of reaping handsome profits is both alluring and plausible – between 1976 and 1983 average annual returns on eleven Third World stock markets (including those of Brazil, Argentina, Mexico and Chile) were indeed a shade over 25 per cent in dollar terms. In contrast, returns on all US stock markets averaged 13.5 per cent yearly during the same period.[25]

A good many banks are now quietly proceeding with debt-for-equity swaps. So far, only about $6 billion worth of debt has been eliminated in this way, but it's a trend worth watching and is probably the wave, or at least the wavelet, of the future, though it won't help the Third World. Banks can do these deals in one of two ways: via governments – the bank swaps its debt directly to a developing country government (at a discount) in exchange for equity in a firm; via transnational corporations (TNCs) – the bank sells its debt at a discount to a TNC, which sells it back to the government, at a profit, and is paid in *local currency*, which it then uses to set up a new subsidiary.[26]

In the summer of 1986 the Philippines announced a blanket plan to encourage swaps and limit the hard-currency outflows of debt service. Private banks hold $14 billion of the Philippines' total $26 billion debt; Cory Aquino's plan calls for the banks to sell their loans to the government at a 30–40 per cent discount. They would be paid in pesos, which they could then use to buy Filipino corporations. The plan, however, includes rules about repatriating profits, which may be enough to dissuade the banks from participating.[27]

In late 1986 about five dozen foreign banks exchanged a chunk of debt for a controlling stake in Mexico's biggest private manufacturing conglomerate, Grupo Alfa, which is strangled with debt and in deep financial water. The banks are to receive company stock, government bonds and $25 million in cash; in exchange they will wipe out Grupo Alfa's $920 million worth of debt. This sum is less than 1 per cent of the country's total debt, so Mexico itself is unlikely to feel much relief. The difference in interest on $97 billion rather than $98 billion worth of debt comes to about $10 million at most – a drop in the ocean, given the $10 billion annual interest that Mexico owes in debt service. Sloughing off one thousandth of the interest leaves a huge balance still to be paid – three-quarters of Mexico's foreign-currency earnings. The banks, on the other hand, will be taking over a huge network of synthetic fibre, chemical, paper and other manufacturing companies.[28]

Many bankers and Mexican government officials believe that about $4 billion to $5 billion of Mexican debt can ultimately be swapped for corporate equity; some put the figure as high as $10 billion. The Alfa deal is the largest so far, but it is not unique. The debt-swap programme was officially inaugurated in April 1986; by the end of the year fifty-five other operations, retiring $650 million in debt, had already been authorized, with a further thirty deals (against $300 million in debts) in the pipeline. Chile has paid off $280 million of debt in twenty-six deals and was aiming to get rid of at least another $900 million in 1987.[29]

The transnationals are effectively getting their Mexican pesos at about a 30 per cent discount. Among the companies investing in Mexico through this swap-and-shop programme are Shell Oil, Gillette, Polaroid and a veritable bevy of automotive industries, including Volkswagen, Ford, Chrysler, Nissan, Honda and Daimler-Benz. In Chile Banker's Trust has acquired 51 per cent of a pension-fund managing company and 97 per cent of an insurance company. Banks that help orchestrate swaps for others are not exactly making sacrifices either. 'Banking analysts say the fees can be handsome indeed – as much as $1 million for every $100 million swapped. To many analysts, the fees explain the banks' fascination with swaps.' In any event, Walter Wriston's successor as chairman of Citicorp, John Reed, has thrown his weight behind swaps – a significant development, since Citicorp is the acknowledged leader in all debtor/bank negotiations.[30]

It will not have escaped the reader's notice that where national economic sovereignty is concerned, a heavily indebted country can't win. Its economy will be increasingly controlled from outside, either directly through the subordination of all productive investment to debt-servicing demands or indirectly through growing foreign investment in key sectors. Whichever way you slice it, the debt crisis turns out to be the best opportunity for neo-colonialist pursuits ever invented. Debt–equity swaps will give a great push forward to transnational migration of capital and industry but will reduce debt and debt service only marginally. Third World countries lose on both counts, and their governments will become progressively irrelevant to the determination of economic policy.

TIPTOEING TOWARDS THE DOOR

Ever since the hot summer when the Mexican near-default gave the banks cold feet, they have taken every opportunity to remove their money quietly from debtor countries. They now have less cause to worry about their over-exposure: US banks somehow managed to reduce their overall LDC loans by nearly 10 per cent in 1984, while the four largest British banks reduced theirs by about £3 billion between 1984 and 1985. (Japanese banks have taken up much of the slack: do they know something the rest of us don't?)[31]

Banks dilute their risks by increasing their capital on one hand and reducing lending drastically on the other. By early 1985 the American big nine had already forced their LDC loan-to-capital ratios down to 1978 levels.[32] Do they do it with mirrors? How could US banks engineer a drop of over $17 billion, and British ones accomplish a similar feat, despite forced lending?

Doubtless some debt has simply been written off as uncollectable; some has gone into swaps; and some has been sold on 'secondary markets', where lurk speculators prepared to take debt off the banks' hands in the hope of making a profit. One might, for instance, buy up Peruvian debt at 25 cents per dollar of face value, betting that Peru might actually pay back the equivalent of 30 or 35 cents. The banks use all these tactics to water down their Third World exposure until shaky loans can no longer endanger their balance sheets.

Meanwhile, they are feeling little pain. I wish I could tell you that Citicorp's profits reached $1 billion in 1985, making it the first American bank to scale such heights. Alas, I cannot do so without stretching the truth: Citicorp's 1985 earnings were only $998 million. Chairman John Reed says 1985 was 'an OK year, but not great; 1986 will be better . . .'[33]

And it was! In 1986 Citicorp's profits crossed the magic billion-dollar threshold. With that sort of cushion, chairman Reed could well afford to make a bold move. On 19 May 1987 he took the financial community by surprise, announcing that Citicorp was adding $3 billion to its loan-loss reserves, thereby admitting that his bank no longer expected all its Third World loans to be paid back. The *New York Times* headlined, 'Citicorp accepts a big loss linked to foreign loans: gloomy world outlook', but that was not exactly the whole story. Reed's announcement did *not* mean that the bank was writing down, or forgiving, any Third World loans. Adding to loss reserves does not even mean one is dealing with *current* unpaid debts, just that a provision is being set against a future day when some debts may not be paid. A technical loss shows up in the bank's 1987 accounts, but in reality it has simply put the money in a different pocket. The money still belongs to the bank, and the Third World debtors are no better off.

They may, indeed, be far worse off. Reed has been the toughest customer among bankers the Third World has had to face, constantly urging his colleagues, the US Treasury Department and the Federal Reserve to take a harder line. His move has enhanced Citicorp's position as pace-setter among banks. All the majors had to follow suit, and, as of July 1987, the fourteen largest banks had added a total of $14 billion to their reserves against bad debts, in essence taking their lumps earlier rather than later.

But these are short-term lumps. The debtors are not going to be let off the hook. Reed's strategy is to get rid of as much debt as possible through debt-for-equity swaps and sales on the growing secondary markets, while strengthening his bargaining position on the rest. The financial markets clearly admired what one analyst called Reed's 'gutsy move', and Citicorp's stock went up 6 per cent the day after he made it. He served notice on the US government that the levels of bank lending that Baker and the Fed hoped for were not to be, thus driving another spike through the Baker Plan's heart. Even though the banks, by adding to their reserves, have made it plain that Third World debt is not worth 100 cents on the dollar, the debtors still owe the 100 cents. Terms for new money will still be case by case, and tougher for the debtors, now that the banks are on a less shaky footing. As of mid-1987 we were further away than ever from a global solution to the debt crisis.

A ROLLING LOAN GATHERS NO LOSS?

If the banks and the rest of the Consortium wanted to lighten the Third World's burden, there are all kinds of technical ways they could do so. The Institute for International Economics, a Washington think-tank, has invented twenty-four different debt-relief measures. The trouble is that most meet with cold stares from bankers, who are, in particular, scared rigid of anything smacking of lower, fixed, interest rates.

Consequently, the line of least resistance has consisted in rescheduling, or rolling over, loans into the disappearing horizon of the twenty-first century. Loan maturities (how long the debtor has to pay, and when he must start doing so), interest rates and rescheduling fees – themselves a lucrative source of income for banks – are all subject to protracted, case-by-case negotiations. More sophisticated, co-ordinated roll-overs are increasingly frequent and are the essence of the Baker Plan. They illustrate how the Consortium functions and acts to keep the situation under control.

Whenever keeping up with the details of debt starts to grow a little boring, I always thank God for Mexico, which regularly provides suspense and excitement. My fattest current clippings file is always Mexico's because this country has the knack of precipitating panic in financial circles, then lurching through a series of cliff-hanger negotiations towards an ultimate multi-billion dollar roll-over settlement, whereupon everyone congratulates everyone else and the process recommences two years later.

Mexico has funded its public enterprises on a truly heroic scale and is fast overtaking front-runner Brazil for total debt owed. What with earthquakes and collapsing oil prices, it has had more than its share of hard luck. Since Mexicans also hold the world's record for capital flight, there's an unquenchable thirst for flows of new money. But hope springs eternal, and with each roll-over rescue Mexico again becomes teacher's pet – for a while. No less an authority than Jacques de Larosière thus showered praise on Mexico in 1984 for showing a trade surplus due to 'adjustment policies implemented with determination':

With the progress already realized and the policies now being implemented . . . the country is in a strong position to achieve a resumption of growth and an increase in imports and, as evidenced by the agreement just reached with its creditors, is now in a better position to obtain external financing on much more favorable conditions than last year.[34]

Similarly, the Mexicans who bring off these deals are heroes at home – until the bubble bursts again. Thus the dapper, Yale-educated (now ex-) finance minister, Jesus Silva Herzog, practically ran the country from 1982 to mid-1986, leaving President Miguel de la Madrid in the shade. A joke about Silva ran: 'Why won't Jesus Silva Herzog be the next President of Mexico?' Answer: 'Because in Mexico re-election is against the law.'[35]

The 1986 version of the biennial Mexican drama can be recaptured through the headlines. First come ominous threats of insolvency: 'Oil prices push Mexico near financial collapse,' 'Mexico calls for help.' Indeed, the country counts on oil for 70 per cent of its export revenues, and the President announces that the country will have to limit its debt service to its 'capacity to pay'. Bankers whip out their pocket calculators: if Mexico limits debt service to, say, 30 per cent of exports, that will make $3 billion less for them yearly.

Silva goes to Washington in February to plead for an extra $6 billion, fast. US authorities respond with a list of the economic measures that Mexico must take to show how serious it is about pursuing austerity and free enterprise. The Reagan administration refuses to nudge US banks without proof of 'substantive structural reforms' and the conclusion of a new pact with the IMF.

Talks with the IMF are ponderously slow and hinge on the level of further spending cuts in the Mexican budget. In June Silva hints that Mexico may have to suspend payments, especially since the peso has just suffered a further 30 per cent decline in relation to the dollar. The US begins to worry, since Mexico is one of its largest trading partners; the Reagan administration makes more positive noises about a loan package involving fresh credits from the IMF, the World Bank, the Paris Club countries and the private banks. In other words, the Baker Plan is wheeled out.

In the fine old tradition of killing the messenger or changing horses in the middle of a dangerous stream, Silva is suddenly sacked in June and replaced by civil servant Gustavo Petricioli, little-known outside Mexico. Petricioli is a friend of the President of Mexico; Silva is perhaps too close for his own good to Fed chairman Paul Volcker, with whom he is wont to take bone-fishing holidays off the Yucatan coast.

Petricioli gets the job of announcing to the beleaguered Mexican people further cuts in subsidies for food and transportation. But within a month of taking office he concludes the general terms of a $6 billion deal with the US government, the IMF and the World Bank, reportedly by putting a knife to the Consortium's throat. Mexico has let it be known that if it gets no fresh money, it will deposit interest owed to foreign banks in a special account in the Mexican central bank – but the funds won't leave Mexico until its foreign-currency reserves have substantially increased.

If the Mexicans follow through on this threat, it will be tantamount to default and will involve far more money than the $74 billion Mexico owes to private banks ($24 billion to US banks, the rest to banks in Europe and Japan). 'Bankers knew that within a week every other Latin American debtor would be announcing something similar,' says one international financial official. 'The threat to suspend payments was the key to the negotiations' success.'[36]

The big innovation in the 1986 Mexican deal is that the lending institutions must provide extra funds if the price of oil falls below $9 a barrel, but they also get to reduce the $6 billion package if oil rises above $14. Mexico gets slightly lower interest rates but must, in exchange, promise to practise strict Reaganomics as stipulated in the Baker Plan. 'Structural change' is the new buzzword. For a country where the state has been substantially involved in the economy – and has protected internal markets – since the Mexican Revolutionary Party was founded in 1929, this is a revolution in itself.

In his annual State of the Nation speech in early September 1986, President de la Madrid underlines his acquiescence. He tells the people, 'The economic austerity [of] the past four years must become a permanent feature.' He further pledges that Mexico will avoid confrontation with international lending agencies and foreign banks.

The bankers, however, still need cajoling. As one of them, refusing that his name be used, puts it, 'The Mexicans are going to get the . . .

new loans they want from us this year because the United States government will make us loan them the money. But if Uncle Sam didn't have a gun at our backs, there would be very few banks that would loan Mexico another nickel right now.' The IMF tells the banks they have until 29 September (when its big annual joint meeting with the World Bank and the entire international financial community starts) to cough up. After that, they are warned, the whole intricate financial negotiation could come unstuck.

The fourteen Western governments that belong to the Paris Club hold an emergency marathon meeting and push quite a lot of Mexican debt forward. There will be no payments of interest or principal on what is owed them until 1992. This agreement is reached just in time for the IMF/Bank meeting.

As the IMF/Bank meeting is already under way, the big banks, kicking and screaming, at last reach an agreement with the Mexicans. Significantly, those who blearily emerge from the final session at 2 a.m. with a promise to contribute $6 billion to the overall package are not the banks' usual committee of negotiators. Although the majors have top executives whose permanent job it is to deal with debt rescheduling, this time it is the big bosses – the banks' chairmen, plus Volcker, Larosière and Barber Conable, new head of the World Bank – who have been around the table.

All of them know that failure to conclude would be a signal to the Latins to default. Secretary Baker calls the agreement – which now comes to $12 billion – a 'milestone' and takes quite a lot of the credit for it in his speech to the IMF/Bank meeting.[37] A month and a half later 90 per cent of the 500 banks expected to join in the forced lending have more or less willingly signed on.

What actually happened during this exercise in Mexican brink-manship? Though the news was drowned out by the din of bankers throwing tantrums, the banks got an unbelievably good deal. Remember that over three-quarters of Mexico's debt is owed to private banks. The $12 billion in new funds, even if it is labelled as money to 'promote growth', will serve first of all to keep Mexico current on interest payments. *Yet half that money will be put up by public entities* – the IMF, the World Bank, the Inter-American Development Bank and Western governments – which is to say by taxpayers. Citizens are already, like it or not, 'bailing out the banks', and nearly all of them are blissfully unaware they are doing so.

The World Bank's commitment of close to $2 billion for Mexico is another new development. The Bank was never supposed to be a financial crisis-management institution. That has historically been the role of its sister, the IMF. One report says, 'To entice commercial banks to lend as much money as the IMF says they should, the World Bank agreed to guarantee repayment of at least $500 million of the bank loans and perhaps as much as $750 million.' This is precisely what the Bank said it would *not* do when the Baker Plan was initially launched.[38] Barber Conable quickly announced that the Mexican deal was not a precedent, that the Bank would not give such guarantees 'routinely'. This may depend upon the likes of Mr Baker as much as it does upon Mr Conable.

This huge package is, however, unlikely to change anything fundamental in Mexico. The country may be getting $12 billion but stood to lose about $16 billion in oil revenues in 1986–7 as compared with the period of pre-crash oil prices. Mexico *may*, if all goes well, rack up a trade surplus of between $2 billion and $3 billion but will still have to pay $8 billion in interest, even with the improved terms it got during the laborious talks. The Mexican economy also has a flaming case of stagflation: in late 1986 inflation was running at 100 per cent, internal interest rates hit 150 per cent, and a full-scale recession was in progress with a 4 per cent drop in GNP during the year. Capital flight is rolling merrily along. Mexican newspapers, reviewing the hard-won debt package, speak in terms of 'quick fixes' and 'temporary relief'.

I can hardly wait for the next thrilling instalment.

13.
COPING WITH CHAOS: THE VIEW FROM THE SOUTH

The problem of the debt is fundamentally political, more than financial, and should be confronted as such. What is at stake is not the accounts of the international creditors, but the lives of millions of people who cannot endure the permanent threat of repressive measures and unemployment that bring poverty and death.

Cardinal Paulo Evaristo Arns, Metropolitan Archbishop of São Paulo, Brazil,
in a message to the Havana Conference on Debt, 30 July 1985

The poor populations cannot pay intolerable social costs, sacrificing the right of development, which for them remains elusive, while other populations enjoy opulence.

Pope John Paul II to Colombian leaders, Bogota, 1 July 1986

Such statements from the most highly respected religious leaders have yet to provoke serious action on the part of their political counterparts. The Organization of African Unity serves upon occasion as a forum for complaints, seldom for undertaking concerted action. Latin Americans docilely reiterate 'our will to do all we can to fulfil the foreign credit obligation of our countries in a complete and timely manner', as one of their leaders put it in Cartagena, Colombia, in June 1984.[1] The South so far has been disconcertingly timid and unwilling to move collectively.

The eleven big Latin American debtors that make up the so-called 'Cartagena Group' have avoided a confrontational stance, but they did take a few hesitant steps towards unity at their Montevideo meeting in December 1985. Although the Argentinian finance minister made clear on their behalf that no 'debtors' cartel' was contemplated and insisted, 'We are not threatening anyone. We are proposing a constructive dialogue,' the *Wall Street Journal* still detected a whiff of revolt in the air.

The debtors had good reason to toughen their rhetoric. Ever since the Mexican crisis of the summer of 1982, the North had not adopted a single one of their suggestions. (The 1985 Baker Plan cannot be termed a response to Latin needs, since its ultimate effect has been to increase their total debt burden.) At Montevideo they made a four-point proposal:

- a sharp reduction of real interest rates;
- separation of new loans from old, and easy terms for old debt, against a promise to pay the going commercial rate for all new loans;
- an increase in commercial bank lending to keep pace with international inflation;
- linkage between interest payments and each country's internal economic growth.[2]

For the first time the debtors hinted that if they weren't listened to, they might be forced to withhold interest payments to the banks. As usual, the North simply let things ride. No general talks were convened; rescheduling proceeded as usual on a country-by-country basis; and the Latins again grew meek and mild.

A Chilean exile with good connections among the Latin American leadership told me a story that I cannot document but sounds plausible. In early 1986 Latin debtor governments had hammered out a more aggressive, unified position. A press conference was called for the next morning to announce unilaterally determined measures, including restriction of debt service to a certain percentage of exports and repayment at reduced interest rates. During the night the Mexican representative received pressing telephone calls from Washington; he was informed that Mexico should expect no new loans from any US bank, Northern government or multilateral agency if it persisted in joining in this declaration. Next morning Mexico's representative was nowhere to be found, support for the measures crumbled and the press conference was called off.

Apocryphal or not, the story shows how the North's case-by-case strategy can continue unchallenged. Debtor countries are like patients hooked up to life-support systems. They fear that any interruption in the supply of vital fluids will result in their instant demise. Only a saint will gamble his own life in the hope of a better future for all. Governments not being noted for saintliness, the solidarity and unity necessary for any *political* solution to the debt crisis are exceedingly hard to achieve.

Without a political approach, Southern 'proposals' will make not the slightest dent; polite requests for relief will fall on deaf ears. The debtors seem to have learned little from the marathon New International Economic Order talks of the 1970s. The North made no concessions then because its interests were not under direct and credible threat. It makes no concessions now for the same reasons. In the late 1980s loans to particular countries will be rescheduled when and if it suits the creditors – and on their terms – so long as debtors refrain from using the very real power that unity could convey.

Latin American repayments continue to bring in astronomical sums (as already noted, $130 billion in net financial transfers between 1982 and 1986) with no end in sight. This figure includes neither the deterioration in the terms of trade suffered by Latin American exports nor untold billions in capital flight. So they pay and pay. Was it frustration with weak knees and pliant spines that brought Fidel Castro to the forefront of the debt debate in 1985? Did he perhaps see an opportunity to act as a Latin American elder statesman and reduce his isolation? Whatever his motives, revolutionary Fidel sounds almost like an ally of free enterprise and a supporter of public order, whether or not free enterprise is prepared to believe it. A sample of his opinions:

I've been asked, 'What do you want – for there to be an explosion in Latin America?' And I've answered, 'No, we want these problems to be solved; an explosion alone won't solve the difficulties.' . . . Right now there is something more important than social change, and that is our countries' independence . . . The [Northern] banks should be rescued. The debts that the Third World no longer can pay will be taken over by the governments, after parliamentary approval. There will be a budgetary transfusion in easy annual payments and a small portion of defense spending will go instead to the banks . . . We do not recommend breaking the banks; we suggest a roundabout way of saving them. With 10–12 per cent cuts in military spending, we would see a miracle – without endangering national defense and without tax increase . . . For the industrialized nations [debt forgiveness] would mean renewal of the structure that

*supplies them with raw materials; more trade with the developing nations
and more business for the multinationals. Latin America could import
twice as much from the US as now . . .'*[3]

Still, Fidel's blueprint for saving capitalism is unlikely to appeal much
to capitalists. His bottom line is that the debt is unpayable and uncollectable. For him, this is a mathematical and economic fact as well as a moral
and political position. Castro doesn't much care what we decide to call
relief – 'I realize that cancellation is a strong term . . . One could use the
term moratorium' – but debt still has to be cancelled, purely and simply.
Banks can be compensated by creditor governments out of current
military expenditures. His 'plan' is no more complex than that: wipe-
out, the North pays off its own banks, Latin America has a clean slate
and is then, presumably, free to follow the same development models as
before. Fidel does not say where they would find the new money to do
so.

Cuba did not especially seek, and is always prepared to relinquish,
leadership on this issue: 'We'll be glad to drop it altogether if another
Latin American government or governments, other leaders, take it up –
just so they do what needs to be done and never betray it. Why have we
taken it up? Because nobody else did,' says Castro. And nobody else has
yet. In an attempt to forge unity on the debt issue, Fidel hosted a series
of conferences in 1985, culminating in a monster meeting of Latin
American and Caribbean representatives for five days in early August.
This affair, barely mentioned in the Western press, brought together
over 1,200 delegates from thirty-seven Latin American and Caribbean
countries. Former Presidents, Prime Ministers and ministers turned up;
heads of state sent personal envoys; the Church, both Catholic and
Protestant, was out in force, and so, surprisingly, was the business
community, along with the trade unionists, economists and intellectuals
one would expect. If Fidel is 'isolated', it certainly didn't show at the
Havana meeting, but this does not mean that his proposals were
universally endorsed.

Speaking in Havana, former Prime Minister Michael Manley of
Jamaica summed up what he called the 'central problem', to wit:

*the political isolation of each country, which is overwhelmed by crisis at a
particular moment in time . . . the first task of this conference is how to
make the political process of the Third World acknowledge that the
isolation we all endure, the isolation that paralyses us in the face of crisis,
is a self-imposed isolation and our first duty is to break this isolation.*[4]

Indeed, everyone present at the Cuba conference recognized that, all by itself, even a very large debtor could not get away with cancellation. Beyond brave rhetoric, however, concrete efforts to break the 'self-imposed isolation' were lacking. Aside from some verbal tributes, no particular outpourings of solidarity for newly elected President Alan García Pérez of Peru were detectable even though García had just kicked off his mandate with a sharp challenge to the IMF and the creditors. Showing more courage than any other Latin American states-man before or since, he announced in his inaugural speech, just two days before the start of the Havana conference, that Peru would hence-forward limit its debt payments to 10 per cent of its export revenues.

Peru's outstanding debt is about $14 billion (including $4 billion owed to private banks), while its annual exports amount to a little over $3 billion. Since García first made his pledge, he has sugared his offer slightly: Peru's payments from July 1985 to July 1986 probably came closer to $370 million than to the $310–20 million expected. The country is, furthermore, careful to pay punctually short-term debt owed to commercial suppliers. But this is a far cry from $1.5 billion or so worth of interest Peru should have remitted in 'normal' circumstances. García refused in particular to pay back his total arrears to the IMF, declaring that he intended to 'treat the Fund like any other creditor'.

Those were fighting words, and the Fund retaliated. In August 1986 Peru was put on the pariah list or, in IMF parlance, declared 'ineligible'. It thus joined Vietnam, Guyana, Liberia and Sudan on the shortlist of countries denied all access to Fund resources (and thus, theoretically, to any others). The practical effects of this decision remain to be seen. The World Bank and the Inter-American Development Bank may well follow suit and stop all loans to Peru.* On the other hand, the IMF hadn't loaned Peru any money for two years anyway, and the private banks had long since closed their windows. García is thus making political virtue out of necessity, and his role as David to the IMF's Goliath plays very well indeed in Lima.

What will happen to him in the longer run? The *Economist* says the country will soon come to ruin, and sounds as though it rather hopes so, in the name of orthodox economics.[5] The country's currency reserves are, however, rising monthly, and the young President (not yet 36 when elected) has never been more popular. A poll taken in October 1986

---

* The World Bank halted all disbursements to Peru in May 1987, but in July the new Peruvian finance minister declared his intention to re-establish 'good relations' with the Bank. How? 'There is only one way to do so: pay,' replied the minister.

gave him a 78 per cent approval rate. *South* magazine reported in
November, 'the economy is booming, inflation has been halved, and
output is set to rise by 5.3% [in 1986] – its best performance since 1974.'[6]

Even more important for Peruvians, García is using the money saved
on interest payments to good account. If any Latin American head of
state merits the 'food first' medal, it is Alan García Pérez. He described
vividly the deadly debt–hunger connection in his lecture to mark the
fortieth anniversary of the FAO of the United Nations and went on to
explain how he was trying to eliminate hunger in his own country:[7]

*In my country, the conditions imposed by the IMF forced us to apply
mistaken economic policies [bringing] about . . . a deterioration in
nutrition, which hit the poor hardest of all . . . We have decided to adopt a
different approach. We have abandoned the prescriptions of the IMF and
are now resolutely following the path marked out for us by the FAO –
rescuing the rural world as a source of well-being and nutrition.*

García praised his host, the FAO, as befits a guest, but he went much
farther than this UN agency usually dares to do. He referred to the
political issues that feed the roots of hunger and explained 'how democracy can be understood through food and how it can be built with food
as its objective'.

First he described the pernicious effects of the dominant model and
told how Peru, under the pretence of modernization, began to consume
food that couldn't be grown on native soils, forgetting its mountains and
its own crops in favour of wheat from foreign plains. National food
dependency is also alienation: 'Food imports are not just a foreign-
exchange problem; they also make a country lose touch with its sense of
its own history and geography.' Peruvians 'have come to accept scarcity
and poverty as an inevitable fact of life, and the peasants without moving
from their land are exiled from their own history'. The Incas once
provided food for an empire with a population larger than today's,
because they applied the right technology, especially terracing, to
master their geography. Social organization and nature are indissoluble.

As the terraces were progressively abandoned, peasant society
disintegrated. And yet, as Alan García noted:

*Societies are born from food, live on food and build up their awareness of
time and space through the food they consume . . . For this reason, the
democracy we want in Peru is not an urban democracy, not a bureaucratic
and administrative democracy. Peru wants a historic re-encounter with*

the land, through national affirmation of our food and our geography . . .
We want to achieve a much more far-reaching transformation, inspired
by the indigenous food model, because only in this way there will
be a revolution on all fronts: national autonomy, justice and social
redemption.

García is not prepared to pay off an unjust debt at the expense of his
people's food security – nor should others:

At this moment when hundreds of millions of people in Africa, Asia and
Latin America are waiting in vain for food, when poverty and violence
loom over our societies, the banks can wait. The poor have waited long
enough for reason and justice . . . We are not going to sacrifice Peru's
historical development and its people's food to the appetites and pro-
posals of the International Bank . . . It will take a long time, but we are
going to replace the food products we consume today by those that Peru's
land can produce.

García must battle with the IMF and the banks on his right and, on his
left, the latter-day Maoist Sendero Luminoso (Shining Path) guerrillas
who have been responsible for 8,000 deaths and countless acts of
economic sabotage since 1980. Other hard-line Peruvian Marxist parties
find García too reformist for their taste, and, in spite of his great
popularity, he must tread a fine political line.

García's policies, in line with his rhetoric, are calculated to improve
conditions for the peasants and thus to dissuade them from joining the
guerrillas. Under his leadership Peru is investing in the food security of
Andean Indian populations for the first time in roughly 400 years. The
Indians are working for themselves and their villages, building terraces
and digging irrigation canals and reservoirs, much as their Inca ancestors
did centuries ago – but today, the government is paying them the legal
minimum wage for their labour.

The Andean plan is eventually intended to cover 110,000 square miles
and reach over 3 million people who live in the barren southern
highlands. Its budget for 1986 was $410 million, devoted to the health,
education and farming needs of the population rather than to large-
scale, distant dams or highways. Resources are going to self-help
projects and providing low-cost or no-cost credit to farmers for purchase
of fertilizers and seeds.[8]

This undertaking shows how a determined government can divert
money directly from debt payments to local food security and human

welfare. Unfortunately, most governments reject the political risks involved in such redirection of resources, while their people's living standards disintegrate. Since the people cannot wait for the spine-stiffening surgical transplants that ought to be performed forcibly on dozens of Latin American leaders, they must somehow fend for themselves.

CREATIVE SURVIVAL

The *New Yorker* regularly reprints small squibs of disastrous news from which some journalist has wrenched an upbeat conclusion; the magazine calls this feature the 'Silver Lining Department'. This is precisely what this section is *not* intended to be. Where the debt crisis is concerned, no chorus of Pollyannas and Little Mary Sunshines can or should outshout the bad news that people are suffering mightily because of the financial obligations their governments have incurred and insist on honouring. Looking mindlessly on the bright side is not, however, to be confused with celebrating human ingenuity and the capacity to survive against heavy odds.

Perhaps, without the debt crisis, lots of exciting and original ways of organizing wouldn't have been tried. If the crisis disappears, so may the new forms of social creativity. At present people have no choice – they must co-operate. It's as simple as the old saw about hanging together or hanging separately. Perhaps tomorrow richer and more authentic democratic practice and more self-reliant, decentralized government will emerge from the hundreds of experiments that Third World communities are undertaking today. One must hope so. One must also deplore the circumstances that have brought them into being. Better natural childbirth than forceps delivery.

As we've seen, Chile has one of the highest debts per capita in Latin America. It is also a country where some of the most original and longest-lived social experiments are taking place. This may be because poor Chileans have had to thread their way between survival and extinction longer than many others and because theirs is one of the few countries still in thrall to dictatorship at a time when Latin America as a whole is moving towards more democratic regimes.

The battle lines between the people and the state in Chile are clearer than in many other countries. Chile has a long tradition of co-operative movements and self-managed enterprises. Popular organizations in both rural and urban areas were particularly encouraged during the pre-*junta* Allende years. They concentrated mainly, however, on acting as pressure groups for particular segments of the population – trade unions, neighbourhoods, women, etc. – and on providing help and solidarity in areas not seen as the business of the state. People got used to working together during those years, so they did not have to start from scratch when confronted with the present crisis. Now, if you visit the poor districts of Santiago, you'll see, as one observer puts it, 'hitherto unknown kinds of organizations: production workshops, labour exchanges for the out-of-work, unions of independent workers, people's canteens, communal "cooking pots", "buying together" groups, committees for the homeless, health groups, women's collectives, etc.'.

'Creative survival' can take many forms. Some people may try to solve their problems individually by begging or hawking in the streets. The better-educated may emigrate or stay home and engage in overt or clandestine political action. But, more and more, people are turning to new kinds of economic, as opposed to political, ventures for self-help and mutual assistance. They may or may not have a simultaneous political agenda; they may or may not receive aid from local or foreign development agencies. Most of these groups are fairly small, and they tackle the pressing problems of daily life. In Chile they are called People's Economic Organizations, or PEOs.[9]

The *raison d'être* of the PEO is to link production and consumption directly, using the national market economy as little as possible – ideally, not at all. PEO members with the most political consciousness see their movement as an embryonic alternative to the competitive nature of capitalism, which has always left out and marginalized significant numbers of citizens. These organizations have grown markedly since the debt-recession crisis began in 1981. A survey made in Greater Santiago in March 1984 identified about 700 PEOs directly benefiting some 80,000 people.

A Chilean observer describes the main types of organization.

● Production workshops. These are small units of between three and fifteen workers – bakers, tailors, carpenters, weavers, launderers, hairdressers, repairmen, bricklayers, painters, locksmiths – producing and marketing their own products.

● Organizations for the unemployed. These are groups through which people help each other to find work, even if only part-time or sporadic. There are several types. *Bolsas de cesantes*, or labour exchanges, are co-operatives of the jobless dismissed for political reasons. Community service centres act as real employment agencies with lists and referrals.

Committees of discharged workers seek work in their own neighbourhoods or nearby and have been helped by international agencies such as
Caritas and its 'Work for a Brother' campaign.
• Consumer organizations. Their goal is to improve people's access to
food. They began with children's canteens, later transformed into
people's canteens. These are not just soup kitchens, though they do
provide a basic ration. They also denounce hunger politically, and their
members collect and prepare food and raise funds to buy it. Community
'cooking pots' distribute food to poor families, while 'supply committees' channel food aid from local or foreign non-governmental
organization sources. 'Buying together' groups make wholesale purchases and store non-perishables in community warehouses; they also help
with family nutrition planning. Recently they have branched out to city
gardens and mini-farms for vegetable growing and animal raising to
supplement community consumption. These food-related P E Os are the
most numerous and benefit the greatest number of people.
• Housing committees and committees for the homeless. Such groups'
activities range from negotiating with landlords and/or utilities suppliers
to communal house-building, land occupation and squatter organizing.
They are generally vocal, political and directly critical of government
policies (or lack of same).

P E Os dealing with education, culture, communications have also
sprouted; others may focus on the overall needs of particular groups like
women, children, pensioners, etc. Nearly all engage in some economic
activity.

THE FORM OF THE 'INFORMAL' ECONOMY

Alan García may be the one Latin American leader who has hit on the
best way of extricating his country from debt bondage, but Peru is also
living proof that nature, and neighbourhoods, abhor a vacuum. At first
glance less organized than the P E Os of its southern neighbour Chile,
Peruvian improvisation against the consequences of financial crisis still
scales hitherto unheard-of heights in the art of self-management.

A bit of background. Peru started early racking up staggering debts in
order to follow the industrialization model. It already owed $1 billion in
1968; a decade later its *public* debt reached $4.8 billion (with a further
$3.4 billion owed to banks). Between 1968 and 1978 Peru paid back
nearly $4.5 billion in interest and amortization *on its public debt alone*:
an enormous drain on its resources. By the late 1970s this impoverished

country was expected to scrape together over $1 billion annually to service its debt (i.e. 55 per cent of all export revenues). Not surprisingly, Peru failed to do so.[10]

So it came under IMF supervision earlier than most other Latin American countries. Many Peruvians claim that their government of the period was only too happy to have the IMF as whipping boy for policies that it wanted to implement anyway. In any event, whether initiator or scapegoat, the Fund had already forced a strong dose of medicine on Peru by 1977, when price rises provoked the first general strike the country had known since 1919. Purchasing power dropped drastically but not drastically enough: in 1978 the Fund prescribed a further one-third cut in the government's budget, which entailed a sharp reduction in jobs in an economy where official unemployment and chronic under-employment already affected *half the population*. In May 1978 prices of fuel, public transport and basic foodstuffs doubled as all government subsidies were outlawed. Predictably, riots broke out, over a dozen people were killed, Peru was placed under martial law and hundreds of labour leaders were jailed – none of which prevented another general strike.[11]

When an entire society comes this close to the brink, it must either invent survival strategies or perish. The official economy was clearly incapable of providing a livelihood for the vast majority of Peruvians. In 1984 the Instituto Libertad y Democracia in Lima completed a four-year study of the *villas de miseria*, or shanty towns, where well over half Lima's population lives. It discovered an underground economy of enormous proportions, entirely escaping government notice or regulation. At least *65 per cent of the entire work force of Peru is engaged full-time* in this alternative economy, covering nearly all sectors, according to the institute. For example, alternative garment production provides about 80 per cent of all the clothing that Peruvians buy. Underground shoe and furniture production accounts for three-quarters of the entire national output in these areas, while 300,000 unregistered people in Lima alone make a living as vendors of underground economy products – including smuggled foreign goods.

It may seem unremarkable that shirts and shoes are manufactured in thousands of informal shops. More surprising is the finding that 85 per cent of Lima's bus lines are controlled by underground operators who succeed in an area where the state has traditionally failed. The 'underground' (which is to say, surface) transport network makes it possible to get from any point to any other point in Lima with a maximum of two transfers for less than 10 US cents. The informal operators watch where people actually go and then serve these spontaneously created routes.

Much of this activity is prompted by bureaucratic requirements. The Instituto Libertad y Democracia research project decided, as an experiment, to set up a small apparel company according to the official rules. It took the institute seven months of five-day weeks and eight-hour days to fulfil all the bureaucratic requirements. Even though it had sworn not to pay any bribes, it still had to pay seven just to keep its experiment going. Had it really depended economically on setting up a business, the institute's calculations showed that some thirty bribes would have been required.[12]

The underground economy is not, however, particularly associated with criminality, though many people must pay protection money to keep their vending sites unmolested. And it is anything but anarchic. Because it is outside the official legal sphere, this parallel economy has had to generate its own rules and regulations to guarantee property rights, commercial transactions, vendors' locations, transport routes, etc. Without this highly organized and sophisticated system, for which 'informal' is an ill-chosen adjective, millions of Peruvians would starve.

All is not rosy, of course. Many of the small enterprises can be qualified only as sweatshops. There are about 200,000 children at work on the streets of Lima – paid, if at all, a fraction of adult wages, which are themselves woefully inadequate. Thousands of children have no adult to whom they can turn. One study found that there are 11,000 'households' headed by children between 6 and 11 years old and at least 6,000 totally abandoned children who live and work permanently in the streets. Children may also be 'adopted' specifically in order to make them work long hours, in appalling conditions, for free.[13]

But there are also efforts to improve children's welfare in Lima. The city-wide 'glass of milk' campaign began in 1984 as part of the response to the economic and food crises. Six days a week over 1.1 million children under 13, as well as pregnant and nursing mothers, benefit from free milk distribution. The government supplies the powdered milk (a gift from the Dutch government), and 7,000 local committees see to its preparation and distribution. One hundred thousand mothers donate volunteer labour, often up to three hours a day, to the programme.[14]

By mid-1985 there were 850 communal kitchens in Lima, serving hundreds of thousands of meals daily. These kitchens may range from neighbourhood associations of eight to twelve families to far larger enterprises. In their simplest form, neighbours pool resources to buy food wholesale, with each family contributing according to the number of family members receiving rations. The kitchen is based in one family's home, and the women take turns cooking. Larger kitchens are more formally organized and have their own premises; their work force is usually paid in the form of free meals, and they sell hundreds of rations in their neighbourhood. A lot of them receive subsidies or aid from non-governmental organizations, especially food aid; some have started their own vegetable gardens to add variety to the cooking pot.

These kitchens are obviously beneficial to the community from the nutritional standpoint, but just as important for many families are the savings in time and the practical experience of co-operation. The effect on women's lives has been especially dramatic. As one observer notes, 'It's the first opportunity they have ever had to emerge from their isolation, to talk together, study and act co-operatively. Women participate in shanty-town management as equals with their husbands and are trying to convince the men that they should help with child care. Many are building their own houses, even participating in the night security patrols' (important in a country where people place scant trust in the police).[15]

In the slums on the outskirts of Lima people are building their own schools and day-care centres. They have carted away tons of accumulated rubbish and built 'more houses than the state and the private sector combined', as the College of Architects admitted in 1984. One particularly well-organized group in the Villa el Salvador black-topped several miles of dirt track into the slum and then demanded that the municipal authorities provide them with a bus service. In the past few years the inhabitants of the *villas* south of Lima have planted over half a million trees. They are painting their houses, and flowers are appearing in window boxes.

Between them, Alan García and the Peruvian people may well win, in spite of the banks and the IMF.

'WE SHALL NOT BE MOVED'

Gustavo Esteva tells how the Mexican earthquake of September 1985 reinforced solidarity and creativity in the Tepito neighbourhood, a poor quarter in the middle of Mexico City.[16] The city planners, after the initial shock, tended to see the earthquake as a blessing in disguise: they could finally remove 'the rubbish-people along with the rubble' and make a garden-like government centre out of the remains of Tepito, an ideal location. The foreigners who poured into Mexico saw the earthquake rightly as a disaster and wrongly as a case for indiscriminate aid. Though Mexico lacked neither, half a ton of food and a hundred bottles of medicine arrived for each victim, according to one estimate cited by Esteva. Distribution of this aid squandered precious time and resources that could have been better employed elsewhere.

The people of Tepito wanted neither aid nor rehabilitation. They refused food aid – 'We don't want to eat foreign *escamocha*' (roughly, 'slop') was how they put it. There was no malnutrition to speak of in Tepito; even worse, free food would compete with one of the major sources of the Tepitans' own livelihoods – the production and sale of food.

Tepito refused to be cowed by the tragedy. On the day of the earthquake improvised shelters sprouted all over the neighbourhood. There were few deaths, since most of the houses were only one or two storeys, but there was a lot of homelessness. The people rose to the occasion and began organizing not only against the consequences of the earthquake itself but also against a threat they saw as even more ominous – their possible eviction.

For years the modernizers and the developers had coveted Tepito as prime real estate. Now it seemed that God was on their side, having sent His own bulldozers. In Mexico it is against the law to evict a tenant from a rent-frozen building, the category of most of the sub-standard dwellings in Tepito. But what legal claim had an ex-tenant of a collapsed building? The landlords followed hard on God's heels, demanding that their ex-tenants go elsewhere.

In a sense, the earthquake provided an opportunity to push through some development solutions that had been resisted by officials for years. Esteva explains that one of the worst, least hygienic and most disgusting things about being a poor person in Mexico City is 'the omnipresence of faeces'. There are 20 million people in this vast urban sprawl, and the water supply has to be piped from 180 miles away, up an incline of about 7,450 feet. Under such conditions it's impossible for everyone to have access to conventional flush toilets and water-based sewage systems, but this is still the goal pursued by the modernizers. They are, according to Esteva, afflicted with an 'obsession for water-closets', and, since only the privileged can actually have these, amoebae and salmonella proliferate.

When the earthquake occurred groups like Esteva's, which had tried for years to introduce 'alternative latrines', simply set them up without permits. They immediately provided sanitary facilities for 80,000 quake victims, far more than the government could possibly manage. Because the water pipes that had previously supplied sanitation for several million people were broken, the authorities had to give up their obsession: now, says Esteva, 'We are working without resistance for the 4 million that were condemned to live among their own faeces by the cultural prison of the W C.'

Tepitans are restoring their lives and livelihoods and bringing back the 'convivial spaces' where people like to congregate but which planners never seem able to build. They are fairly typical of other 'tent people' in Mexico City, who fear that if they go to government earthquake shelters they will never be allowed to rebuild their homes or continue their lives in the neighbourhoods where they were born. The leader of one group, Ricardo Téller, told a *New York Times* reporter that 426 people, including 193 children under 5, lived in his section, about two city blocks of temporary housing. 'Most of us were born here . . . This is our home and we are not going to leave. We have rights to a place, to live here. If we leave, we may lose that right.'[17] A member of another tent community said he would not go to a shelter where the government administrators were despotic. 'Even if we are cold and they have cut off our food, we prefer our life here because we have freedom. The shelters are far away and life there is too rigid.' The government has issued certificates guaranteeing housing, but people say they do not trust the certificates, the government's promises or the landlords whose buildings were destroyed.

CAN THE FUND ADJUST TO A HUMAN FACE?

Should the South seek to replace or abolish the IMF? Even if such a Herculean feat were possible, this strikes me as the wrong goal, precisely because the Fund is supra-national and because it is an instrument. If enough pressure and political skill were applied, it could become an instrument for governments more enlightened than that of the United States under Reagan.

Some valuable alternatives to present Fund policy have been put forward, often by Northerners, but Northerners who have a Southern exposure. They may not question the need for adjustment in the Third World and see it as an inevitable fact of life. They are none the less deeply troubled – as well they may be – by the Fund's present intervention and its conditionality. They call for 'basic-needs conditionality' or 'adjustment with a human face'.[18] These demands for reform of IMF policy should become the basis for a *minimum* programme to gain time while we work to end the debt crisis and transform it into a powerful tool for development and democracy, as I argue in the next chapter. 'Human-face' adjustment could save the lives of a lot of people who cannot wait for a definitive solution.

Richard Gerster cites ample evidence that, *even on its own terms*, the Fund's programmes are largely ineffective. They don't contribute to economic growth; they don't slow rates of inflation (indeed, many experts believe they accelerate them substantially); and they rarely improve even the balance of payments. Writing in a law journal, Gerster provides useful insights into the legal mechanics required to institute a 'basic-needs conditionality' approach by Fund member governments. Activists who want to start pushing for better national IMF-related legislation could begin by consulting Gerster's piece. His goal is to help developed-country legislators and IMF staff alike recognize that

Basic goods and services have to be defined so that they may be treated differently in economic analysis and policy. That set of goods and services must be adapted to local conditions. The access of the population below the level of absolute poverty to these basic items must not be obstructed any further by inappropriate stabilization policies. The entire cost of adjustment, therefore, should be borne by the production and consumption of non-basic goods and facilities.[19]

Richard Jolly, deputy director of UNICEF, takes a similar, though less legal–practical, line. He finds the present thrust of 'adjustment' not only harmful but economically stupid:

To miss out on the human dimension of adjustment is not only a human tragedy. It is an economic error of the most fundamental sort. Much evidence already exists of the economic returns to investment in human resources. To fail to protect young children at the critical stages of their growth and development is to wreak lasting damage on a whole generation, the results of which will have their effects on economic development and welfare for decades ahead.[20]

Adjustment programmes should concentrate on placing floors under nutrition, health and education; countries undergoing adjustment should get outside support in the form of more flexible financing and longer pay-back periods, says Jolly. He wants a 'shift to much greater self-reliance, decentralization, small-scale production and community action, empowerment of people and households' – don't we all? He also believes that 'human-face' adjustment would be cost-effective and need not incur the wrath of the IMF. Jolly argues, for example, that UNICEF's Oral Rehydration Salts method for treating diarrhoea costs 6 cents a dose as compared with $50 for intranvenous feeding. Many other health and nutrition programmes could be carried out on a similar low-cost basis. 'It is possible to combine adjustment to cost and foreign-exchange restrictions *and to expand coverage and impact*,' he concludes (emphasis in the original).

Canadian economist Gerald Helleiner has considerable experience in counselling Third World countries negotiating with the IMF and advises them to have their own alternative set of goals ready before the Fund team turns up. Helleiner, like Jolly, contends that alternative approaches to adjustment are economically as well as humanly justified and that it is the job of economists to work out the costs in terms the Fund's people can deal with. 'My impression,' he says, 'is that a good many people in the Fund would be only too happy to have new ways of having the sums come out right, and of getting new resources developed. They are probably right in saying that their staff is unaccustomed to dealing with poverty issues!'[21]

Indeed, no one (least of all me) wants to condemn *individual* employees of the IMF. They depend on the orders and the orientation they receive from on high and could perfectly well put their considerable professional skills to work for more humane goals. A united and determined South, with some help from allies in the North, could concentrate their minds wonderfully.

14.
THE 3-D SOLUTION: DEBT, DEVELOPMENT, DEMOCRACY

At this point I go out on a limb. Having laid out what practically everyone else thinks we should do about debt, I feel I've earned the right to say what I myself think. Here I propose a personal interpretation of the political and strategic meaning of the debt crisis before suggesting how it might be turned inside out and used not as an instrument of oppression but as a tool to promote both development and democracy.

However uncomfortable one may feel with broad-brush geopolitical analysis, I fear one must struggle with it in order to understand what is going on behind the scenes and beneath the surface, while the more straightforward aspects of the debt crisis occupy the front page and centre stage. Such an approach is all the more necessary as an avenue towards solution, since faulty analysis always leads to faulty action. We must try to understand what debt means and of what underlying forces it is an indicator. So here goes.*

* No one is better at geopolitical explanations than my friend and TNI colleague Fred Halliday, who has influenced both me and the lines that follow. See his 'Beyond Irangate: the Reagan Doctrine and the Third World', a *Transnational Issues* paper available from TNI, Paulus Potterstraat 20, 1071 D A Amsterdam.

After the Second World War, the hegemony of the United States was an accepted fact. Until, say, the end of the Vietnam War, or at least until the end of the 1960s, it was the unquestioned superpower. However necessary the Soviet Union may have been as foil or as adversary to fuel the arms race, it had nothing like the wealth, productive capacity, influence or even military power of the US, and still hasn't. US supremacy was political, military, economic, financial, cultural – even agricultural: I spent much of the decade between 1975 and 1985 trying to dissect, describe and discredit the dominance of the Great American Food System as it spread its grip over the rest of the planet. In each of these areas, US power is still an important factor, but it is no longer paramount in all of them. Naturally, Rome wasn't built in a day and empires don't crumble in a week. The cracks in this one's foundations are, however, growing threateningly visible. Depending on your politics and your place in the world system, you may find this state of affairs cause for rejoicing or for despair. As for the people who run the United States, they are well aware of the cracks and are feverishly trying to cement them, or at least paper them over.

Vietnam was the first major trauma. Subsequently, the leadership of a great many other Third World states changed hands, and regimes friendly to the United States toppled in their turn. Some of these changes resulted quite clearly from national liberation struggles (Nicaragua, the ex-Portuguese colonies of Africa); others were more ambiguous or bloodthirsty (Khomeini's overthrow of the Shah in Iran); all appeared to the American establishment as failures of US power and control.

This erosion of US power has engendered new thinking and new strategies. Although the United States can no longer run the world completely according to its interests or whims, it can still effectively prevent others from doing so, paralyse progress towards a different, more humane global system, and attempt to put the clock back to the time when the US enjoyed uncontested world supremacy.

The advent of Ronald Reagan and his neo-conservative entourage was, I believe, about putting back the clock. Those who baptised him the 'Teflon President' missed an essential point, for Teflon is a substance of fairly recent invention. More accurately he was the Bakelite or Celluloid President, shaped in the pre-Second World War period, in his prime in the 1950s. 'Reagan', of course, serves here only as a convenient metaphor for all those who hope to make the world safe for their own profitable pursuits, and who will be around long after the movie actor has been replaced by a butcher, a baker or a fundamentalist preacher (even if he – it won't be she – is a Democrat).*

A return to the halcyon fifties requires an activist policy to wipe out the many gains made by popular forces over past decades. In the US itself, it means breaking the back of the peace movement, the civil rights movement, the women's movement, workers and others who reject the brave new world in store vigorously enough to protest. Towards the end of the 1980s these goals were largely – though one must hope only temporarily – realized.

In spite of all the peace overtures of the Soviet Union, levels of confrontation as evidenced by the US military budget remain alarmingly high. The 'debate' is reduced to hair-splitting over the rate of increase of defence spending, or the number of billions to be devoted to Star Wars. Only marginal voices, excluded by respectable thinkers in the mainstream, continue to display the bad taste inherent in asking fundamental questions about war, peace and the continued existence of civilization.

Jobs are massively destroyed in the US; often they are the well-paid, unionized ones that used to go to white males as a matter of course. Black people (especially black women) and other minorities suffer disproportionately from unemployment. Jobs created, on the other hand, are in poverty-line service employment, epitomized by the McDonald hamburger-flipper. 'Runaway shops' relocate abroad where wages are lower; industries that stay on make it clear to their workers

* This President turns out to be George Bush, who was Director of the CIA in 1976 when Orlando Letelier and Ronni Karpen Moffitt were assassinated in Washington by agents of DINA, the Chilean Secret Police with which the CIA maintained routine and friendly relations. Orlando was a former Chilean ambassador and government minister under Allende; after the coup and his release from Dawson Island he had become Washington Director of the Transnational Institute. Along with the rest of the TNI community I had met with him in Amsterdam only three weeks before he was murdered. Ronni was twenty-five. She had just been named fund-raiser at the Institute for Policy Studies, TNI's sister institute, and was the new bride of Michael Moffitt, then an IPS/TNI Fellow. Michael, riding in the back seat, escaped with minor injuries when the car was blown up by a remote-control bomb. DINA's guilt has been proved in court; at TNI we do not believe these murders could have been carried out in the United States capital without government knowledge and at least tacit consent. For details on the Letelier–Moffitt murders and the CIA connection, see John Dinges and Saul Landau, *Assassination on Embassy Row*, Pantheon Books, New York, 1980.

that they, too, can move if and when it suits them. Capital is mobile, workers much less so. Social polarization increases, part of the middle class slides into poverty, homelessness grows (accurate numbers are not available; 2–3 million is a conservative guess). In 1985 the Physicians' Task Force, led by a professor at the Harvard School of Public Health, reported 20 million Americans going hungry.

Farmers' protests are silenced by the simple expedient of their ceasing to be farmers at all. The traditional ethical backbone of the United States, the family farm, is rapidly vanishing. Studies published in 1986 said that the southern and western regions of the US both suffered a huge 16 per cent drop in their farm populations in the single year 1984–5. The number of farms with sales of $20,000 or less fell by 60 per cent during the 1975–85 decade; nearly a third of the farms that remain are owned by people over sixty-five. The number of black farm residents was halved between 1980 and 1985 (from 240,000 to 120,000 people).[1] Rural America has fallen into deep decline and deeper debt: American farm debt is greater than that of Brazil or Mexico. In such a demoralizing climate it's almost impossible to muster enough energy to fight back.

Abroad, turning the clock back means rivalry with one's allies, keeping them off balance and as divided as possible (for example, trade wars against Europe and Japan, attempts to dictate Europe's relations with the USSR, tensions within NATO). The West–West conflict is as virulent as the East–West one, though more muted in its expression. As for the Third World, which concerns us more in the context of this book, one must prevent 'emerging' nations from emerging too far. Above all, liberation struggles and broadly based popular movements, invariably viewed as threatening to US interests, must be kept in check.

These various themes of American policy may merge, as they do when the US claims that movements and governments of which it disapproves are dominated and controlled by the Soviet Union. The defence budget thus finds further justification. The most notorious example is that of Nicaragua, decreed a threat to US national security although its population is five or six times smaller than that of greater New York. Other candidates for putative Soviet satellization have included Southern African movements or governments. Though doubtless flattering for the USSR, this analysis is altogether wide of the mark. Autonomous movements with independent motivations are legion; the USSR does not control them, however much it might like to or try to, however convenient it may be for the United States to reduce North–South issues to East–West confrontations.

Strategists have known since Sun Tzu (*The Art of War*, 500 BC) that winners win because they adapt to the terrain and to changing circumstances. The US has learned from its failure in Vietnam. Highly visible, debilitating and exhaustively reported interventions have given way to Low Intensity Conflict (LIC). LIC has become the officially sanctioned and widely practised strategy against movements popular in the Third World and governments unpopular in Washington.

LIC is also LCC, or Low Cost Conflict – for the perpetrator. It costs little in money and in manpower; above all, it costs little in political opposition and turmoil at home, because it is so hard to focus on. Real, overt wars have to be based on consensus, or they eventually come to grief, as the Pentagon has learned to its cost. LIC allows the intervenor to bypass this need for approval, or at least acquiescence at home. Branding 'the enemy' part of 'the global communist conspiracy' usually suffices for successful manipulation of Congress and public opinion. For the victim, on the other hand, LIC is high-cost conflict. Defence spending requires, for example, nearly 60 per cent of Nicaragua's national budget.

Unlike conventional warfare, LIC does not seek to eliminate an enemy physically. It seeks instead to isolate him internally and externally, to exclude him from the international community (and from its aid), to delegitimize his government (or his political influence in the case of a popular movement). Support for *contras* in various parts of the world is one part of LIC. Making economies 'scream' or 'cry uncle', to use Reagan administration terminology, is another – realized through blockades, sabotage and other forms of economic intimidation.

LIC thus redefines the very nature of war. Military history focuses on objectives, battles in support of them and conclusions – from treaties to unconditional surrenders – but an outcome which can be labelled as 'victory' by one or both sides. LIC entirely alters this view because it is not after 'victory'. Much has been made of the fact that the *contras* have been unable to establish any bases or popular following within Nicaragua. This is true, but misses the point. The meaning of LIC is well expressed by Sara Miles in a letter to the North American Congress on Latin America's *Report on the Americas*:

The frightening thing about LIC is that winning, as we normally think of it, might not matter so much any more – at least not as much as does the creation of a system for waging permanent war in the Third World. LIC is not 'won' in the sense that conventional wars are won. Most of us still assume that war-makers conceive of war as a linear activity, with a beginning, an escalation and an outcome. But US low-intensity strategists

*have, if you will, discovered dialectics; they understand it as a permanent
global struggle. LIC is not just a fad, or a fluke or a flare-up in trouble
spots; it is the new norm for relations between the United States and the
nations of the Third World.*[2]

FINANCIAL LOW INTENSITY CONFLICT

*Conquered states . . . can be held by the conqueror in three different
ways. The first is to ruin them, the second for the conqueror to go and
reside there in person and the third is to allow them to continue to live
under their own laws, subject to a regular tribute, and to create in them a
government of a few who will keep the country friendly to the conqueror.*

Niccolò Machiavelli, *The Prince*, 1513

Now let me take the LIC concept a step further. I'll call it FLIC, or
Financial Low Intensity Conflict. FLIC is, aptly enough, the French
slang word for 'police', the equivalent of 'cop'. Third World debt is now,
perhaps, less a 'crisis' – though I have followed convention and called it
that – than an ongoing, dialectical FLIC waged against the South; a
permanent global struggle exactly like LIC, but played out on another
terrain. As with LIC, FLIC does not seek to 'win', because total victory
– complete payback – would also mean total bankruptcy for the debtors.
The war would be over, and everyone would have lost.

FLIC does, however, help to prevent the Third World from posing a
threat, from dictating its terms, from changing the political balance of
forces in the world. When creditor nations and institutions wage FLIC,
they are not engaged in a 'linear activity' comparable to traditional war
in which debts are contracted, mature and are paid off. Rather, they are
carrying out a process without any foreseeable end, a process which
allows the North to keep a check upon any pretensions to real independence on the part of the South and to ensure privileged access to the
South's resources.

The impoverished become the financiers of the affluent. As the
nineteenth-century French humorist Alphonse Allais perceptively
noted, 'If you're after money, look for it where it is most abundant, that
is to say among the poor.' FLIC is a variant of neo-colonialism with
neither an ugly nor a human face: the colonizer need not show his face at
all in order to achieve his aims.

Is this analogy overdrawn? Not if one takes seriously the great
nineteenth-century theoretician of war Karl von Clausewitz and his
classic *Vom Kriege* ('On War'). Debt allows 'the continuation of politics

by other means'; it also conforms to Clausewitz's less famous axiom which states that 'War is an act of violence whose goal is to force the adversary to do our will'.

True, the debt weapon cannot accomplish some goals of classical warfare, territorial expansion for one. But what rich country with a stable or declining population wants that? Attempts to exert political control through occupying armies are also outmoded. They drain the treasury, attract bad publicity world-wide and don't work, as the US in Vietnam, the USSR in Afghanistan and the Israelis in the occupied territories have all discovered.

For achieving the other goals of classical warfare, however, and for 'forcing the adversary to do our will', debt is an efficient tool. It ensures access to other peoples' raw materials and infrastructure on the cheapest possible terms. Dozens of countries must compete for shrinking export markets and can export only a limited range of products because of Northern protectionism and their lack of cash to invest in diversification. Market saturation ensues, reducing exporters' incomes to a bare minimum while the North enjoys huge savings. Likewise, debt-for-equity swaps and massive privatization facilitate foreign takeovers – sometimes in partnership with local businessmen – of indebted countries' national manufacturing and servicing capacity. Whatever looks like being profitable is fair game; the debtors are welcome to the rest.

In an altogether logical development, the first debt-for-people swap occurred in November 1988. The Dutch transnational corporation Philips cashed in $4 million worth of Brazilian debt for 1.5 billion Brazilian cruzados with which it then purchased Mr Romario Farias, a 22-year-old soccer star, for PSV Eindhoven, the Dutch club sponsored by Philips in its home town. Mr Farias might be described as the first prisoner taken in the debt war, although he will be handsomely compensated.

In traditional warfare, a clever strategist will also make the adversary pay for his own oppression. When the Germans occupied France, the French paid. Since the beginning of the debt 'crisis' in 1982, the poor have financed the rich on an unprecedented scale. The OECD 1987 *Debt Survey* contains valuable information on this point.[3]

The first set of OECD figures concerns all the net resource flows from North to South: this category includes official multilateral and bilateral development aid; total short- and long-term export credits; total private financial flows, including direct investment from OECD countries, international private bank short- and long-term lending and grants by non-governmental organizations (*In*).

The second set of figures concerns debt service payments from South to North: this category includes long-term debt service, both interest and amortization payments; interest payments on short-term loans (mostly to banks); plus reimbursement of IMF credits (*Out*).

Combining these two sets of figures, we get the following:

Table 4   Net resource flows and debt service payments (current $ billion, rounded)

	1980	1981	1982	1983	1984	1985	1986	1987	*Total*
In	128	138	116	97	88	84	82	85	*818*
Out	84	102	132	131	132	152	144	147	*1.024*
Difference	+44	+36	−16	−34	−44	−68	−62	−62	*−206*

This table shows that 1981 was the last year in which inflows of aid, loans and investment exceeded outflows of debt service. In 1982, commonly accepted as the first year of the debt crisis, resources transferred from the poor countries to the rich ones for the first time exceeded resources received. Ever since 1982 the gap has continued to grow. Total transfers since the beginning of the decade show over $200 billion in the North's favour. But if we eliminate the pre-debt crisis years of 1980 and 1981, the contrast is even more stark: $552 billion inflow, $838 outflow, a net gain to the industrialized countries of $286 billion. This is the equivalent of approximately four Marshall Plans financed by the developing for the developed countries.

Naturally, these figures need refining, since some Asian NICs, or Newly Industrializing Countries, like Korea and Taiwan, and large and populous countries like China and India, account for part of the outflow. These countries are on the whole servicing their debt without great difficulties, although their people are undoubtedly paying in extra hardships. The *In/Out* situation for other groups of countries varies. For the six calendar years 1982–7, twenty-six 'lower-middle-income countries' with per capita GNP between $800 and $1,400 suffered a drain of $48 billion. The highest transfers of all were incurred by fifty-three 'upper-middle-income countries' with per capita GNP above $1,400. This category includes most of the biggest debtors: they sent $339 billion to the North, net.

These huge South-to-North outflows can be ascribed partly to the precipitous drop in public and private financing. As we've seen, private banks are moving out of the Third World as fast as they can: bank loans fell from $52 billion in the last boom year of 1981 to a mere $5 billion in 1986 and $8 billion in 1987 and 1988. Also alarming is the decline in official development finance. Compounding the bankers' withdrawal, public funding also fell by 28 per cent in 1987 compared to 1985 (the peak year for the decade) and was 10 per cent below the level of 1986. The World Bank contributed in no small measure to this downward trend, lending 10 per cent less in 1987 than in 1986 despite embarrassingly large capital surpluses.

Debt service has been a boon to Northern treasuries as well as to bankers. Each year between 1982 and 1987 developing countries as a group paid back an average 14 per cent of total debt outstanding. The sum they collectively remitted to the North between 1982 and 1987 was equal to almost 100 per cent of the total debt they owed in 1982 and to 70 per cent of that outstanding in 1987.* In spite of these massive payments, their debt burden has grown by fully one third since 1982. This is the reality of FLIC: the more they pay, the more they owe.

A further goal of classical warfare is to prevent the adversary from challenging the dominant system, in the present case the one organized by the North. Debt effectively discourages such challenges. For example, when Oscar Arias announced his peace plan for Central America, the United States immediately placed unusually strict bans and restrictions on Costa Rican exports; it further refused, for the first time, to intervene with US commercial banks on Costa Rica's behalf. With $4.5 billion of debt to service – a huge sum for a small country – Costa Rica found itself ineligible for further bank loans and the US move also held up agreements with public sources of credit. Other leaders will doubtless think twice before taking political initiatives unwelcome to a major creditor.

Debt also leads to direct and unmistakable violence when people riot against sudden and unsustainable increases in the cost of survival. Peruvian economist Denis Sulmont provides a valuable résumé of the major anti-austerity uprisings in twenty-two countries. His figures (probably underestimates, since he takes them from Western press tallies) add up to some 3,000 dead, 7,000 wounded and 15,000 arrested.[4] Since these victims are dealt with by the army and police forces of their own governments, they seldom appear on television screens in the North. Their near-invisibility is a crucial element of FLIC because it

---

* For the period 1982–7, amortization of long-term debt (i.e. repayment of principal) owed to all sources amounted to $363 billion; interest payments on both long- and short-term debt were $430 billion, and reimbursement of IMF credits $41 billion. Of total outflows from the South, OECD governments received 30 per cent, banks 54 per cent, official multilateral lenders 8 per cent, the IMF 5 per cent and non-OECD countries (OPEC and the Eastern bloc) 3 per cent.

forestalls protest and dissent in the creditor countries themselves, where few people show signs of taking to the streets in protest.*

The debt war is also fought against most citizens of the North. Remittance of debt service to banks exhausts available resources and nothing is left to purchase farm products, manufactures or services from other sectors of Northern economies. Jobs are lost and farms fail.

The Brazilian labour leader Luis Ignacio Silva, better known as 'Lula', sensed this new reality of FLIC and expressed it vigorously at the Havana Debt Conference in August 1985:

Without being radical or overly bold, I will tell you that the Third World War has already started – a silent war, not for that reason any the less sinister. This war is tearing down Brazil, Latin America and practically all the Third World. Instead of soldiers dying there are children, instead of millions of wounded there are millions of unemployed; instead of destruction of bridges there is the tearing down of factories, schools, hospitals, and entire economies . . . It is a war by the United States against the Latin American continent and the Third World. It is a war over the foreign debt, one which has as its main weapon interest, a weapon more deadly than the atom bomb, more shattering than a laser beam . . .

FIGHTING FLIC: THE CANCELLATION TRAP

If FLIC is the reality, how does one fight back? Many good people demand cancellation of all debt as the only way to go: I fear this solution would be a trap. First, let's clarify the vocabulary. Creditors cancel, debtors repudiate. In either case, what you get is called default. If Southern debtors can unite to declare partial or total repudiation (i.e. default), I will applaud, but I fear such action is unlikely. And without a united stand, the prospects are grim.

Peru tried to limit debt service to 10 per cent of export revenues and has been effectively isolated by the 'international community'; by late 1988 its economy was in shreds. Peruvian defiance of the banks received no support from anyone, but the harsh reaction of the creditors shows that the strategy was feared and could have been successful had it been adopted by several debtors at once. Brazil declared a moratorium on payments for nineteen months in 1987–8, then backed down under

---

* In a startling and welcome development, some 50,000 people did take to the streets in Berlin in September 1988 to protest against IMF/World Bank debt policies as these two organizations held their annual meeting.

internal and external pressures, promising its creditors 'Never again' in order to qualify for fresh money. In the absence of solidarity and the safety of numbers, going it alone has worsened the economic and social situation of countries that have tried it, and this fact has not been lost on those that haven't.

Joint repudiation by the South seems an unlikely prospect because Southern elites and governments have so little to gain from it. They rarely suffer and sometimes profit from the debt crisis. When public services deteriorate, they can afford private ones. They go on eating, however much hunger and malnutrition grow around them. They have larger, more miserably paid labour forces to draw upon as a result of IMF measures. They want to be first-string players in the international financial system, and have more in common with their counterparts in New York or London than with their fellow-citizens. Most of their money is abroad anyway, safe and sound.

In August 1988 I spoke at length with Luiz Carlos Bresser Perreira, former finance minister of Brazil. I asked why he hadn't tried joint action with other debtors. He had tried, he said; he had had a plan with Argentina ready to go. For it to work, he needed more resources internally, and begged President Sarney not to increase military salaries and to impose progressive taxation on the rich. Sarney refused, Bresser Perreira resigned and no joint action was taken. 'Our own elites,' he told me, 'are the biggest single obstacle to solving the debt crisis.'

If joint action from the South is not forthcoming, should we then organize campaigns in the North calling for unilateral debt cancellation by our own governments? This idea has enjoyed growing popularity ever since Fidel Castro first broached it in 1985 (though Castro's call was more for repudiation by the debtors than for cancellation by the creditors). Cuba, by the way, is servicing its own debts faithfully . . .

The Castro position can be expressed on a banner or a ten-second television spot, a singular advantage for any campaign. It also reflects the plain truth that much debt won't be paid and is clearly illegitimate as well. To show just how illegitimate it is, we should demand that banks disclose how much money they loaned, to whom they loaned it and for what purposes. They should also be obliged to reveal to government regulators and thus to the public the deposits they hold from foreign nationals, particularly past or present officials of heavily indebted countries. No interest should be paid, for example, on flight capital, or on debt incurred for arms purchases by military regimes. Researchers in North and South should dig for more detailed information and we should not allow bankers to profit twice over from loans or to hide the proof of their own poor financial judgement. They owe at least that much to taxpayers who are now helping to bail them out.

Debt cancellation could, however, work to the advantage of the very system now spreading unprecedented hunger and poverty throughout the Third World. How?

First, it risks rewarding the worst and most profligate governments – for example, African tyrant Mobutu, who holds the world record for public debt reschedulings (eleven at the last count). When France announced partial debt cancellation, one African dictator was heard to remark, 'I should have borrowed more.' Cancellation would simultaneously penalize governments that have made heroic efforts to pay back on time.

Second, cancellation would turn recipient countries into financial pariahs for the foreseeable future. A default is a default whoever declares it, and the debt crisis presents debtor countries with not one but two dilemmas. The first is to pay back what is already owed; the second, to maintain access to fresh funds. Except, perhaps, for very large debtors like Brazil, these countries will not be able to rely entirely on local resources, though they should rely on them far more than they do now. Cancellation would make forgiven debtor countries somewhat more flush at the beginning. Soon afterwards, however, in the absence of massive new aid, they would be pushed into autarchy – especially the poorest and the most politically expendable among them – unable to import basic necessities, their credit-worthiness at zero. To avoid this, they should honour their debts to suppliers in particular. Greater self-reliance is a worthy goal; forcible cut-off from the rest of the world is not. The last time we had that was in Cambodia.

Third, cancellation, if less than 100 per cent, would be a mirage or downright damaging to Third World majorities. Costa Rican economist Franz Hinkelammert demonstrates that, despite immense sacrifices demanded from their populations, Latin American governments are still paying back only about 50 per cent of the financial charges theoretically owed. These countries cannot remit any more, because their peoples cannot be squeezed any drier. This is the main reason why the debt mountain rises ever higher, as interest arrears are added to the principal.

Assume that private banks and public creditors pretend to accept demands for cancellation; that they forgive, say, 50 per cent or less of the debt, but insist that debtors then remit with no further discussion both interest and principal on the remainder. Either the situation for Latin America would become worse, or would be unchanged, since the

continent is now servicing only 50 per cent of its loan charges. True, the debt pile-up would stop growing or grow more slowly, but this would be a comparatively minor benefit. As Javier Iguíñiz, chief economist for the Peruvian United Left Party, says, 'Don't cancel what we're not paying!'
Hinkelammert explains:

. . . partial cancellation of the debt [has] obvious advantages for the banks. By cancelling up to half the debt, they can make a show of generosity . . . without renouncing a single effective repayment. Moreover, they can make their claim for repayment of the remaining debt appear legitimate. And yet the maximum transferable surplus to the major creditor nations continues. These creditors go on collecting as before while being able to give the appearance that they have provided as much aid as can be expected of them . . . any debt cancellation which does not substantially exceed 50 per cent of the nominal value is more in the interest of the banks than of the Latin American countries . . . (the same arguments hold if interest rates are reduced by half or less).[5]

UNCTAD has called for 30 per cent cancellation. Either this UN agency has not grasped the financial realities of Third World debt or it is on the side of the creditors. Other advocates of cancellation may retort that they want not 30 per cent or 50 per cent, but 100 per cent. No doubt. Alas, one rarely obtains 100 per cent of any political demand. In the present case, getting half a loaf or less would be a disaster. To date, I had refrained from stating this argument in public for fear the banks might have missed it, and might suddenly see what a fantastic coup cancellation of up to 50 per cent of Third World debt could be for them. Attacks on my own position force me to abandon this prudent stance. Already the head of the Deutsche Bank, Alfred Herrhausen, has proposed just such a 'solution', though other bankers are slow to follow.

While in no way improving – and quite probably worsening – the situation of people now straining under the debt burden, cancellation advocates who think of themselves as progressive would forfeit the high ground to Northern banks and governments who would reap a public relations bonanza while still making as much or more money. Most ordinary citizens in the North would see cancellation of a third to a half of Third World debt as magnanimous, perhaps unwarranted, and certainly a better deal than the said citizens could hope to obtain on their own mortgages or consumer loans!

Fourth, cancellation should be examined as part of total resource flows. At the Toronto Summit in June 1988, President Mitterrand announced that France would cancel a third of poor African countries' debt, but only the part of it coming up for rescheduling. His declaration was hailed as a breakthrough. The money involved, however, according to Treasury figures cited after his announcement, is equivalent to just 10 per cent of annual French aid to Sub-Saharan Africa. If the promised debt relief is deducted from the normal aid budget, the Africans are on square one; if it is added to it, the additional sum involved amounts to about $2.50 or £1.50 per French person – hardly an intolerable burden.

The French proposal was put on the post-Toronto 'menu' from which creditor governments were supposed to choose a solution for African debtor governments. In late October 1988 the *Financial Times* carried the headline 'Debt-relief package is agreed for Mali', the first African recipient of Paris Club attention. The amount of debt affected by this 'relief' is $70 million. According to the OECD, Mali's total debt is $1,790 million. The Paris Club elephant has thus given birth to a mouse. Furthermore, whether the relief comes from an individual creditor government like France or from the whole Club, no debtor gets anything without strict observance of an IMF adjustment programme.

Creditors may well be tempted to create an illusion of largesse while actually reducing their overall aid contributions. But even if they don't, the relevant questions remain 'Aid to whom?' and 'Cancellation for whom?'. Unconditional cancellation means writing a blank cheque for debtor governments. If one trusts Third World governments and elites to share the benefits of cancellation with their peoples, fair enough. My own confidence in them is admittedly limited.

In particular, I fear that cancellation would not enhance popular control over the elites, who would be the chief beneficiaries of debt relief and who would, in the absence of other changes, remain in power. Even if we assume the most unlikely scenario – 100 per cent cancellation *and* fresh money in the form of aid or new loans – this could simply provide governments with a licence to go right back to the disastrous and discredited development models that got them into trouble to begin with. Those practising these models are not generally noted for their sensitivity to the needs of poor people.

People who believe cancellation would automatically work to the benefit of Third World majorities must have faith in the 'trickle-down' process. Precious little has trickled down for the past thirty years: why should it begin to do so today? A single example: eight Sahelian states received $14 billion in aid during the decade ending in 1984. This comes to about $44 per head per year. Only 4.5 per cent of total aid received went to rain-fed, as opposed to irrigated, agriculture – even though rain-fed agriculture accounts for 95 per cent of Sahelian cereals production. Less than 5 per cent also went to the livestock sector. These eight governments thus invested less than 10 per cent of all aid money in the activities upon which over 90 per cent of their populations depend.[6]

Income distribution is already heavily skewed in most debtor countries and there is little incentive for those who have spent decades preventing 'trickle-down' to help their poorer compatriots benefit from debt cancellation. Let us remember too the toll of anti-IMF riots. The thousands of people killed, wounded or detained were victims of their own governments.

WHAT ARE THE CHOICES?

As I see it, the Third World has three options. The first is the one still accepted as of the end of 1988: acquiescence to FLIC. Under the FLIC scenario, the South remains divided, accepts the dominant, export-oriented, outward-looking model; goes on playing the game on the North's terms, and sees its lifeblood gradually drained – though never quite emptied – through reimbursement. The time-scale and the intensity of financial pressure will be dictated by the creditors case by case; one may assume they will string out the process for as long as it suits them. If this course is chosen, the North remains in control of the world's major resources and keeps a near-monopoly over the management of the international system. It also continues to set interest rates, the ideal strategic tool for modulating the political costs and economic impact of FLIC.

Southern acquiescence and its payments *ad vitam aeternam* will keep the North awash with capital and help the United States to go on running up huge deficits, financing in particular the military budget, without causing runaway inflation. Debtors will thus contribute to maintaining America's capacity to intervene world-wide at a much lower cost than the US would otherwise have to pay. They will, in a word, ensure their own continued subservience to interests altogether contrary to their own.

The second option is total or partial repudiation, but this works only when undertaken jointly, as shown in the cases of Brazil and Peru. If debtors were to take unilateral action, they should keep in mind Franz Hinkelammert's arguments and refuse to pay more than half the debt, or cut interest rates by more than half.

The third option is a negotiated settlement recognizing that debt is not an economic but a political problem, and that it can be in everyone's interest to resolve it. My own basis for such a settlement is called 'creative reimbursement', or the '3-D solution', standing for Debt, Development, Democracy.

Creditors, too, have options. One is refusal to budge. They fear that a more creative approach towards African debt, for example, would set a 'bad example' for Latin America. From inertia or design, they may simply continue to lurch along from crisis to crisis. In a context of prostrate raw material prices, creeping international protectionism and collapsing economies, especially in Africa, continued insistence on payment is not just sadistic but almost certainly doomed.

A second option is once-and-for-all write-off – unlikely, and a pseudo-solution anyway in my view.

The third, again, is to accept creative reimbursement, ensuring a more politically stable and prosperous world for all. The basic idea of the 3-D solution is that countries are allowed to pay back interest and principal over a long period of time in local currency, calculated so as not to create inflation. Their payments are credited to national development funds whose uses are determined by authentic representatives of the people working with those of the state. For the creditors, 3-D would come to the same thing as cancellation, since the local currency would be used internally.

Because governments contracting for a 3-D solution would have to accept greater popular control over the development process, a kind of conditionality would still apply; but the conditions, unlike those of the IMF, would promote real development and encourage real democracy. Politically speaking, the chief advantage of 3-D – and, to be honest, a huge obstacle to its acceptance – is that it would get money and the power that goes with money down to the grass-roots majorities which have never enjoyed either before.

Utopia? Maybe. Still, like past political utopias such as ridding the world of slavery or the divine right of kings, creative reimbursement is plausible. Because virtually everyone, in both North and South, is losing from present debt management strategies, exceptional opportunities exist for coalition-building to push for the use of debt as an instrument of development and democracy. In the North, environmentalists, peace activists, women's movements, trade unions, farmers and export-oriented industries, as well as Third World support groups and Non-Governmental Organizations (NGOs), all have an interest in the changes that 3-D would encourage. Together, they might oblige Western governments to put their money where their mouths are in defending democratic values.

In the South, the vast majority of the population would benefit because such a programme would require that debtor governments direct economic activity away from international markets and towards the satisfaction of their own people's real needs. A more inner-directed economy would mean (for the least developed countries of Africa in particular) a strong agricultural sector as the basis for growth, providing both food crops and renewable sources of energy. The cornerstones of social policy would become primary health care, literacy, education and the promotion of women; all investments in the future. Available foreign exchange would be used to acquire capital goods and basic equipment – not to pay for debt service, arms or prestige items.

Creative reimbursement needs the full participation of Northern and Southern NGOs. They have a proven record of project management and innovative development thinking. While not perfect, NGOs are almost always less corrupt than entrenched bureaucracies and more disinterested than local elites. Wherever independent local NGOs do not exist, or have been stifled, their creation and development should be part of the conditionality package. Freedom of association is basic to success.

Is 3-D affordable for the creditors? Absolutely: the international financial system would not collapse even if Third World debt went entirely unpaid. Because the plan is political, it would have to start with public money, but even the banks could afford to join. Since 1982 they have drastically reduced their exposure; by 1988 their Third World loans accounted for only 6 per cent of their total loan portfolios. Furthermore, only about half the total $1.2 trillion owed by the South is 'problem' debt, of which the banks hold about $325 billion.[7] The debt crisis is now a crisis for at most two or three large US banks. Their minority interests should not be allowed to prevent a viable political solution.

Nor can creditor governments argue that 3-D would set a dangerous precedent – what bankers call a 'perverse incentive' or 'moral hazard'. Historically, debt, including that of the United States, has often gone unpaid. The precedent of twentieth-century debt forgiveness under certain conditions was in any case set long ago, by the United States itself. British economist Mike Faber reminds us that in 1946 the terms of a large US loan to war-torn Britain stipulated that interest payments would be waived – not reduced, but forgiven entirely – should that interest exceed 2 per cent of British export revenues in any given year. British parliamentarians and the press bitterly denounced these 'harsh' terms, and Lord Keynes, who had led his country's negotiating team, was hard pressed to defend them.[8] In other words, we no longer have any excuses for allowing the debt crisis to fester. Why not use it creatively?

CREATIVE REIMBURSEMENT, THE 3-D FORMULA AND AFRICAN DEBT

Creative reimbursement and the 3-D formula would be easiest to apply in Sub-Saharan Africa (SSA). African debt is internationally insignificant, a paltry sum for the creditors, however crushing a burden it places on the continent. Africans do not benefit from exaggerating the amount they owe. Some of them seem to believe that the higher the figure they cite, the more the 'international community' will take pity on them. This is not a wise tactic – bankers and governments are not noted for their soft hearts. The figure of $200 billion or more, for example, mentioned on various occasions by former Tanzanian President Julius Nyerere or the Organization of African Unity, is far too high. One suspects the OAU threw in North African heavies like Egypt and Morocco, and perhaps even South Africa for good measure!

According to the OECD, SSA debt at the end of 1987 was $129 billion. Subtract Nigeria, the Ivory Coast and Sudan and it's down to $85 billion, a paltry 7 per cent of total Third World debt.[9] Only 10–15 per cent of Africa's debts is owed to banks; most of these private creditor loans are concentrated in a handful of countries like the Ivory Coast with $6 billion, followed by Nigeria, Ghana, Sudan and Zaïre.

Africans should highlight, not hide, these low figures, which are their trump cards. Because their debt is overwhelmingly owed to public creditors, there is more room for negotiating political solutions than in cases where commercial debt predominates. Indeed, the smaller the figures, the greater the political advantage: Africa cannot upset, or even tip, the international financial applecart in any threatening way – which is what the creditors are worried about. For this reason, the latter could afford to experiment, innovate and take modest risks in managing the reimbursement process to the ultimate benefit of everyone involved. Africa could thus become the scene of a feasible utopia.

Unless creditors want Africa to slide off the world map, they should adopt creative reimbursement and the 3-D scenario. Although they would receive no more debt service payments *per se*, much of the hard currency freed would come back to their economies in the form of purchases. This scenario would also offer the debtors an honourable path, keep them relatively credit-worthy and ensure their continued participation in the world economy, but on much better terms. Everyone would gain as, little by little, they became more prosperous and paying customers.

My proposals have been criticized on the grounds that they violate the principle of national sovereignty. What, then, have the IMF and the World Bank been doing all these years? True, governments opting for 3-D plans would be expected to share responsibility for development with their own people and to allow genuine democratic participation; but frankly, I see nothing wrong with that. Naturally, the most repressive among them would be the least amenable to 3-D programmes. The worst – especially the military regimes – would be the first to protest 'intolerable interference in the internal affairs of X', since they would be most threatened by heightened democracy and popular participation. Governments would, however, have a choice. Those refusing democratic development could continue to service their debt in hard currency – this might concentrate their minds wonderfully.*

Another objection is that Western governments are not exactly shining examples of democracy themselves and have no business preaching to others or imposing any conditionality at all. Creditor governments too should be accountable to their own people on whose behalf they have made innumerable problem loans. If creditors forgo hard currency payments, they have a duty to prove to their own citizens that the money is being wisely spent in the debtor countries. The 3-D plan could also be a step towards making the World Bank and the IMF publicly accountable. Democratic conditionality does not necessarily imply Western-style parliamentary institutions; it does concern citizen access to, and accountability of, the institutions making decisions that harm untold numbers of people. The Universal Declaration of Human Rights, whose fortieth anniversary is observed as I write, is the best basis for determining the guiding principles of creative reimbursement.

Some governments opting for a 3-D plan would try to get around the conditions and I don't propose we try to start with, say, Zaïre! Others, however, have already recognized that the state can't do everything; they admit the need for decentralization and for sharing development tasks with popular organizations. As the UN has said in innumerable documents, it's a question of 'political will'; the will of Northern and Southern institutions to set up adequate machinery for the 3-D process.

---

* In proposing any principle, one is ethically bound to accept its universality; thus I would be delighted if foreign creditors of the United States renounced debt payments on condition that the US use the savings for the hungry, the homeless and the illiterate in America.

This is not the place to draw up blueprints for the machinery, which could be readily assembled if the political will were present. The task for activists is to push for this political will.

Creative reimbursement would involve two aspects: reimbursement in cash and reimbursement in kind.

REIMBURSEMENT IN CASH

The time-scale of reimbursement (twenty to twenty-five years seems adequate in most cases) and the size of local currency payments would be based on a mutually determined proportion of internal GNP, averaged over, say, the previous five years so as not to constitute a licence to print kwachas, shillings, etc. After negotiating the amounts and the calendar with creditors (through a single spokesman like the IMF or the Paris Club), each government would make regular payments into a national development fund.

The creditors would require in exchange that these funds be co-managed with authentic representatives of the civil society. Rural people should enjoy representation proportional to their real numbers in the country. Special precautions should be taken in order to ensure fair representation for women and, in some cases, ethnic minorities. Where necessary, the creditors would help with, and if need be oversee, the initial process of information, consultation and choice of the representatives in order to avoid to the fullest extent possible corruption and governmental deck-stacking. NGOs from both the creditor and the debtor countries should be fully involved in this process.

Once chosen, this broadly based development fund management body could not be overruled by the state, although the government would naturally participate fully in decision-making and supply its own technical expertise. The fund would finance projects and programmes determined by consultation and consensus, focusing primarily on rural areas. Various groups (village councils, associations of young people, women, artisans, peasants, etc.) could apply to the fund for seed money to undertake their own self-managed projects.

The fund would also provide money for revolving credit schemes to make modest loans directly to farmers and other small-scale rural entrepreneurs (with priority here given to the landless and to women). Loans granted to small groups of people seem to fare extremely well, with reimbursement rates running at close to 100 per cent. The Grameen Bank in Bangladesh is one successful model which could be adapted to specific conditions elsewhere. The International Fund for Agricultural

Development (IFAD) has broad experience in developing rural credit institutions and administering small farm loans; its advice and assistance would be invaluable and should be actively sought by creditor and debtor governments at an early stage.

Each payment made by a government into its own development fund would trigger a corresponding reduction (or, on the matching grant principle, doubled or tripled reduction) of its external debt in hard currency on the part of the IMF, the multilateral development banks and the official bilateral creditors. Foreign exchange saved by eliminating most debt service would be freed for purchases of essential goods, particularly 'pump-priming' goods for establishing small-scale local enterprise serving agriculture and environmental preservation – seeds, tools, basic means of transportation and communication, food-processing equipment and the like. Fresh aid money could be added to 'top up' the development funds.

Rigid, IMF-type conditionality would give way to a more flexible system. Whereas adjustment has always meant increasing agricultural exports, no matter how dire the internal food situation, and drastic curtailment of basic services in health, education or food subsidies, democratic conditionality would take the form of contracts. Continuing dialogue between creditor and debtor governments would assess progress and problems, both assisted and seconded by their own NGOs.

The negotiated contracts would concern equitable management of the development funds and the terms for matching, in hard currency, each step towards improved performance. A similar contract formula was launched by Edgard Pisani during his tenure as Development Commissioner of the EEC in the framework of its 'food strategies' policy. This model, properly applied, need not smack of neo-colonialism. In any event, compliance with present IMF demands is far more painful than the requirements of such contracts would be.

French agronomist René Dumont tells of a conversation with Senegalese President Abdou Diouf. Diouf said Dumont was right to insist on a peasant-based development strategy, but that he, Diouf, would need outside help to overcome the opposition of urban classes in order to help his own peasantry. 'Creative reimbursement' might be just the right catalyst for much-needed changes in many African countries. Favourably disposed governments within disgruntled urban constituencies could, if they needed a convenient scapegoat, place the blame for a new rural bias on their creditors.

In some cases it might be preferable to envisage payments into a regional rather than a national fund when this might reduce the risks of corruption and counterbalance the power of certain particularly non-representative governments. Regional funds would, however, have the disadvantage of being farther away, administratively speaking, from many of the people (especially peasants) who should be able to call on them and benefit from the money.

REIMBURSEMENT IN KIND

The second component of the 'creative reimbursement' formula is reimbursement in kind. Even so-called 'poor' Africa is home to natural, material and cultural treasures which are part of humankind's heritage. Under pressure from present 'development' strategies, these treasures are being squandered, eroded or irrevocably destroyed.

Allowing African states to pay off a part of their debt by preserving their own national heritage would benefit everyone. African elites who are often anxious to imitate Western culture and lifestyles might take a new pride in their own surroundings and traditions once these were seen to be valued (and, what's more, in hard currency!) by outsiders. Mobilization of local people's energies for reimbursement-in-kind projects would accomplish a great deal more useful work, and more cheaply, than could international aid and outside experts. Again, foreign assistance should fulfil only a 'pump-priming' function.

Here are some examples of possible payments in kind:
- collection, conservation and reproduction of genetic species and varieties (both animal and vegetable);
- soil conservation/anti-erosion measures;
- reforestation with local varieties of trees and shrubs, or, if imported, tested by and for the peasantry and pastoralists;
- development and improvement of wells and small-scale irrigation techniques;
- collection, recording and, where appropriate, improvement of building techniques, particularly for traditional earthen architecture; new construction, particularly of public buildings, employing these techniques;
- development of new bio-mass sources for energy purposes as an alternative to wood and charcoal (deforestation) and as an alternative source of income for poor people;
- collection and recording of traditional agricultural, medical, nutritional and pharmaceutical knowledge; establishment of scientific institutes to examine (and in some cases upgrade) this knowledge in the light of Western science and technology, generally and often

erroneously assumed to be 'modern'; a particular effort to collect female knowledge should be made;
• improvement of local and village-level food- and water-storage facilities;
• establishment of mobile services for pastoralists, particularly in health and education;
• compilation of dictionaries and grammars of local languages;
• revalorization and dissemination of these alternative stocks of knowledge through the schools; new texts, teacher training, literacy campaigns for men *and* women based on rural, life-enhancing themes.

One could easily add to this list; the main thing is, however, to get across the idea of recognition and remuneration for past and future contributions of African peoples to our common heritage. These contributions would be assigned a monetary value in negotiations between debtors and creditors; the debt would be progressively written down by equivalent amounts as headway was made on the various programmes and works projects chosen as part of the reimbursement-in-kind programmes. People should be paid a democratically determined minimum wage out of the development fund for participating. Ecological renewal simply will not happen unless people are paid to do it, because they cannot take the time from vital short-term survival activities to plant trees, dig irrigation ditches, etc.

The ultimate goal of repayment in kind and in (local) cash is to strengthen particularly the peasantry, the pastoralists and the agricultural sector, and thus work towards the elimination of hunger and the poverty on which hunger thrives, to rehabilitate the environment and provide income-generating activities for people who live in it. In a word, 3-D seeks greater equality and social justice.

Why should the creditors accept a 3-D plan – i.e., what's in it for them? They should welcome such a solution, first because it is the only feasible way to keep African countries in particular as players in the world system. Otherwise, the logic now set in motion will lead to their greater and greater marginalization and decline. Writing off this huge continent and leaving it to its fate would be extremely shortsighted – but this is the direction we are taking today.

Second, Western creditors should choose this option as the ultimate weapon in the conflict between democracy and totalitarianism in which they profess to have such a deep stake. Once they have experienced democracy and basic freedoms, has any people ever willingly given them up? Debt has been, to date, one symptom of a profoundly undemocratic system. In nine cases out of ten, it was first racked up by non-elected leaders. When it became unmanageable, the adjustment process was administered on behalf of official creditors or banks by non-elected bureaucrats from the IMF or the World Bank. Who gave them their mandate? Anti-democratic practices which would not be tolerated inside a single one of the Western creditor countries are imposed without a second thought on the 'subject peoples'. It's time the West proved it's commitment to democracy – on pain of losing it even at home.

AND LATIN AMERICAN DEBT?

Would 3-D proposals for Africa be valid for Latin America as well? Up to a point, yes. Both continents are overburdened, but their problems are not identical. One difference is the sheer magnitude of the debt; another is its provenance.

Let us again make the destinction between public and private debt, and a further distinction in each of these categories. In the public category are bilateral and multilateral creditors, who together hold by far the greater share of African debt. In the private category is money owed to banks and to suppliers. (Just to confuse the issue, financing of such purchases is often arranged through public entities like the US Ex-Im Bank. They should receive priority for payment just as suppliers should.) Solutions for Latin America thus imply strategies *vis-à-vis* (1) bilateral and multilateral public creditors and (2) private banks.

First, the publicly held debt. Assume, for the sake of argument, that the North accepts a 3-D relief programme for Latin America and that official (bilateral and multilateral) creditors announce they are willing to forgo the money owed them on the condition it is invested in authentic development. Could Latin America actually absorb the money thus freed for a 3-D programme?

The question is not as odd as it may seem. The mal-development model that got these nations into debt in the first place is fabulously expensive. Spending untold billions to finance it is no problem and, on the whole, Latin American elites are still wedded to this costly model – they want grandiose, 'pharaonic' projects involving copious imports of foreign capital and technology, as well as Western consumer goods, the more the better.

This model is, however, precisely the one a 3-D solution would have to junk in favour of programmes and projects relying much more on local resources, catering much more to local markets, with far greater popular control over the development process. The hitch is that a more humane, more efficient and more autonomous development model would also be far less expensive than the one pursued to date. This could be a drawback. If we stick with the principle outlined above – debt is marked 'paid' when equivalent sums in local currency or in kind are channelled into democratically managed development activities – the 3-D model might not cost enough, because Latin America's debt is so huge!

Sub-Saharan Africa, with half a billion poverty-stricken people, minimum infrastructure and enormous needs, should be able to absorb, over a couple of decades, up to $100 billion – approximately what it owes public creditors – for 3-D schemes. In contrast, at the end of 1987 Latin America owed approximately $450 billion, roughly two-thirds (about $310 billion) to private creditors.[10]

Even if Latin America reimbursed only the official debt in local currency or in kind, $140 billion would still be a lot of money to get rid of. This continent has fewer people and its needs are also different from Africa's – it has more existing infrastructure, though much of it is in bad shape precisely because of the debt-servicing burden. It would be no laughing matter to spend all those billions, unless one indulged again in nuclear plants, sophisticated arsenals, ecologically disastrous mega-dams and the like. Nor should one forget the 'Hinkelammert factor': for real relief, Latin America's burden must be reduced by half or more; otherwise the development promoted by 3-D schemes would be wiped out by interest payments on private debt.

Thus part of Latin American debt could be paid back in a cash-and-kind 3-D package, but a comprehensive proposal for this continent would require other components. In particular, banks will refuse to participate in politically innovative solutions unless forced. Proposals that ignore the banks are non-starters, since the need for fresh capital, much of it from commercial money markets, will be a fact of life for as long as any of us can foresee. No Latin American government wants to be cut off from these markets; this is one reason they have been so timorous in dealing with their debt.

Indeed, the first issue to confront in an overall approach to Latin American debt is the unequal balance of forces. The creditors are united: this is the whole point of what I have called the Consortium. They speak with a single voice (with the IMF or the London or the Paris Clubs as mouthpiece) and thus obtain what they want; certainly they have kept the political initiative. The debtors, in contrast, are in disarray, straggling, often suspicious and jealous of each other, forever looking out for number one, in spite of regular 'debtors club' meetings.

Given Southern willingness to play the game according to Northern rules, it seems unrealistic to call for debtor unity to match that of the creditors. The debtor countries are largely run by people whose political clientele benefits from present arrangements. Only popular movements inside Latin America can push their own governments towards greater unity. Alas, escalating violence may be the only way to convince them – but whatever the methods, the North's role here is peripheral.

Be that as it may, the first thing this particular Northerner wants to say to the debtors is: 'For pity's sake, get your act together.' Failing that, an outcome that deviates from the basic economic and political agenda of the North is an illusion. With unity, however, anything is possible. Assuming that the sheer pain of reimbursement causes agonizing reappraisals, or that political pressures result in a sudden conversion, what might 'anything' be?

In the first edition of this book, I came out strongly for Alan García. I still think his stance was a courageous one (limit debt service to 10 per cent of export earnings), but Peru at the end of 1988 was in worse shape than any other Latin American country, with the possible exception of Bolivia. This is not the place to detail García's many failings; here are excerpts from a letter I received from Peru in December 1988 that says more than I can:

Development in the Andes is costly – it has just cost the lives of two young (French) 'coopérants', full of dreams and illusions. Shining Path couldn't tolerate that. It's easy to lose hope here. The spiral of violence is frightening, but I fear even more the political vacuum. No electricity, so no water. No water, so diarrhoea and dehydration, but no hospitals either (because no electricity, no water . . .) 630 murders in November, 1,000 per cent inflation for 1988 and Christmas is coming – but the vast majority of the people can't hope for even a small celebration to break the monotony of just trying to survive. Even our women's associations are shaken . . . No one in authority seems capable or reacting, and I'm not just speaking of those who 'hold' the reins of government . . . My work is losing all meaning . . .

García and his APRA party undeniably bear a heavy responsibility for this shambles, but as of the end of 1988 Shining Path had murdered about 15,000 people: anyone who cooperates in any way with the government is a target – doctors, agronomists, engineers, mayors and town councillors and peasants. Several peasants had their throats slit for good measure when Sendero Luminoso murdered its first foreigners –

the French agronomists, a young man and young woman – to frighten off NGO cooperation with Peru. The country has been financially isolated by the North; the friend whose letter is cited above calls the people's organizations 'the last rampart against barbarism'.

García said at the beginning of his term of office:

The debt has been used for irresponsible expenditures, for non-productive investment, and, almost exclusively, to benefit the 30 per cent of our population at the top of the social pyramid . . . Let the world hear that President Alan García knows that Peru has one great and primary creditor, her own people, to whom this government will allocate the resources necessary for the reconstruction of our lives.

In the spring of 1987, when he still enjoyed 75 per cent popularity among Peruvians, I wrote:

García's achievement is remarkable not only because he has dared to stand up, alone, to his creditors, but also because he has seized the occasion to break significantly from the dominant development model. Peru is beginning to prove that what matters is not just the money you save on debt service but how you use it. For this reason the country is a logical target for retaliation and García's own future a shaky one.

I would not now suggest that any debtor try to tread such a path unless all do. The Peruvian example is meant to convince others not to step out of line, and I was naïve to believe a payment-reduction strategy had any chance at all, even if García had been a better and a stronger president. *Mea culpa.*

The other strategies one can recommend also depend on the degree of unity and of solidarity that can be achieved. Here are some suggestions.

(1) SPREAD THE MONEY

Indebted countries should make clear to their creditors that the latter are jeopardizing their own economies by allowing their banks to cream off all the incoming revenues from the South. Debtors should exploit the existing contradictions between the interests of transnational banks and all the other sectors of Northern economies. As the banks cash in on the crisis, industries and farmers see their sales slumping disastrously, since the Third World cannot afford imported food or new equipment.

Recognizing this, unified and determined debtors could negotiate a 'trade-off' approach linking their debt service to the purchase of foreign goods vital to their development. Each debtor government would draw up a list of basic imports it could not produce (or not produce yet, or not in sufficient quantities) at home. Such items might include fertilizer, foodstuffs, pharmaceuticals, machine tools, spare parts, transportation and communications equipment, etc.

Each debtor country would then contract to import these products from each creditor country in proportion to the debt held by the latter. For example, if the US held 20 per cent of Venezuela's debt, Venezuela would contract to buy 20 per cent of its list of products from US firms and farms. (If one wanted to include debt owed to multilateral creditors in such a scheme, one could allocate extra purchases among creditor countries according to the proportional contributions of each of those countries to the multilateral agencies concerned, but this would tend to benefit the United States disproportionately).

The total current cost of such a list of products, from which luxury goods should be specifically excluded, would be deducted from annual debt service. Creditor economies would thus receive the total amount 'due' to them, but the money would be much better spread between their industrial suppliers, their farmers and their banks. Such a repayment plan would help to maintain jobs in the industrial countries as well as free a lot of the debtors' hard currency for useful, development-oriented purchases. If the creditor countries deemed it necessary, they would have to compensate their own banks. Normally they should be able to do this simply out of increased tax revenues on increased business.

These purchases by the debtors should not, in so far as possible, create new dependency. They should be directed towards improving capital equipment and enhancing job creation. Self-sufficiency in basic foods, in particular, remains a desirable goal for indebted countries, and purchases from outside should be seen as transitional, while the country invests some of the money saved on debt service in its own food producers.

(2) THE GARCÍA FORMULA – WITH A TWIST

As a corollary (or as an alternative) to the Peruvian strategy, one could link debt service not to export earnings as García tried to do, but to export volume. There would be a certain poetic justice to such an action, especially when applied to the multilateral agencies (the IMF and World Bank). This point needs elaboration.

The debtor would agree to pay back creditors, but in 1979–80 commodity dollars (or marks, pounds, francs, etc.). To wit: commodity prices in those years were decent if not spectacular (one could choose another good year during the past decade or so for some commodities). As we know, since the beginning of the 1980s, commodity prices have gone steadily downhill. This tailspin is partly due to IMF/World Bank export-led strategies and adjustment plans indiscriminately imposed on a great many countries at once. These agencies share responsibility for the price-depressing surfeit of goods on the market, because they insist that everyone exports a limited range of raw materials and semi-finished or finished products. They also encouraged countries on the road of 'export-led growth', helping to create their debt burdens. Thus these official creditors should be singled out for payment in pre-1980 commodity dollars. They should not be allowed to impose their policies with impunity, and should have to take the consequences of a depression they helped to create. Some examples of plummeting prices are shown in Table 5.

Table 5   Prices of certain commodities (per lb), 1979 and 1986

	1979	1986 (end)
Coffee	$2.70	$1.26
Copper	$1.00	$0.58
Sugar	$0.29	$0.06

Each country would list its present exports, calculate what they fetched in 1979 (or another good year) and discount debt service by an equivalent amount. For example: Peru exports copper. Peru would refuse to sell more than 1,000 lb of copper to pay $1,000 in debt service (copper sold for $1.00/lb in 1979). Peru would not deplete its resources by exporting the 1,725 lb needed to earn $1,000 in hard currency when copper brings 58 cents/lb.

In the same way, sugar producers would limit sales to 3,450 lb in order to remit to the IMF and the World Bank $1,000 worth of debt service (at 29 cents/lb in 1979), rather than the 16,666 lb required if sugar sells for only 0.06 cents/lb; coffee producers would remit the proceeds of 370 lb, not the 793 lb needed in 1986 to earn $1,000 with coffee at $1.26/lb. Such an export-volume formula could be easily combined with a percentage-of-earnings formula and it could apply just as well to semi-finished or finished exports (based, for example, on the number of yards of cotton or of transistors and T-shirts needed to earn $1,000 in a peak year during the past decade as compared to the present).

Copper exporters do not control world copper prices and should not be the only ones who suffer when they decline. Nor should debtors be obliged to exhaust their raw materials reserves and deplete their environments simply because a market in London or New York decrees that copper is 'worth' only so much. The 'laws' of supply and demand would function quite differently if the World Bank and the IMF were not constantly intervening in dozens of producer economies. The World Bank's cash reserves were huge in 1985 and 1986, so it could well absorb the shock of loans paid back in discounted commodity dollars. Bilateral creditors should share this burden too: they cannot expect both a fantastic discount on raw materials and full debt service.

(3) BRINGING HOME PRODIGAL CAPITAL

Unified debtor governments could also exercise enough clout to force banks to give back, or to loan back at greatly reduced interest, the flight capital deposited by their own nationals. Although these governments may choose not to recognize or to use their strength, they could simply go on an interest-paying strike until the banks capitulated. The banks know perfectly well where the fly-away capital landed, and who squirrelled it away; they could simply draw down (or threaten to draw down) the account of every non-resident Mexican or Argentinian by a fixed percentage in order to provide fresh funds to Mexico or Argentina. Alternatively, the banks could keep the flight capital but reduce the country's debt by a fixed percentage each year. The point is to keep them from having and eating their cake.

Such measures would put a stop to the endless haggling and foot-dragging that now occur at semi-annual, or shorter, intervals, as banks resist pressure to cough up new money. The banks claim that 'involuntary lending' is scandalous. The really juicy, and wholly underreported, scandal is the double pay-off which banks receive on a hefty proportion of their Third World loans. Unfortunately, most debtor governments are unlikely to demand that the banks turn over these ill-gotten gains when their own ministers or their boon companions may themselves be suitcase-carrying members of the capital flight mafia.

These proposals could complement or replace the more frequently cited calls for unilateral interest-rate reduction or glorified Baker or Bradley plans. These suggestions do have, in my view, one big advantage. They attempt to make the punishment fit the crime. They underscore some of the major causes of the present crisis – capital flight, dismal commodity prices, costly development models and the privileged and unjustified position of the banks. Thus they help to point fingers at those responsible for the mess as well as towards solutions to it.

WHAT ABOUT THE BANKS?

Good question, if I say so myself. Plenty of technical proposals have been floated; none has met with acceptance. Lengthening that list is not my purpose here. However, one good idea proposed in 1985 has not received the attention it deserves. Economist Alfred Watkins and Congressman Charles Schumer believe that

Banks should be forbidden to report profits on any foreign loans on which the banks are lending borrowers the money to pay interest. This will not only reduce the rewards for loaning money to pay back loans; it will also give banks an incentive to lower their interest rates to levels that debtor nations can pay without taking out new loans. [4]

We should be concerned with equity issues not only for the Third World but for the people and, yes, even the banks of the rich countries. Not all the banks are rich by a long chalk: recall the 428 US failures between 1982 and 1986; remember also the staggering farm debt that afflicts so many families in the US.

First, governments and international institutions like the IMF/World Bank are already lavishing rescue funds on the majors through a variety of stratagems described earlier. These ought decently to be coupled with help to the minis in difficulty, especially those in the troubled farm states. Help to *any* banks, large or small, ought to be accompanied by an equivalent popular control over the profits. Such help could, for example, be tied to better terms for farmers, small businesses, etc.

An initiative along these lines that already exists in several US cities is the Community Reinvestment Campaign. From large conurbations like Chicago and Philadelphia to smaller towns like Harrisburg and Gary, the campaign is trying to make banks more accountable to the public. Popular control of profits in this context calls for local banks to lend for local needs at reduced rates. In Chicago, for example, the local campaign obtained a commitment from Continental Illinois for $20 million in home-improvement loans. In Baltimore a coalition of civil rights, student, community and labour groups got Maryland National to guarantee $50 million in low-rate loans to low-income Baltimore neighbourhoods over a five-year period. Reinvestment campaigns are also making the connections between Third World debt and the working people of America who are hard-hit by the banks' present policies. The Baltimore coalition's platform states:

Banks should reevaluate the impact of their international lending on standards of living in the Third World and on the health of manufacturing and agricultural sectors in the U S; banks should address the needs of the poor and working people in both the First and Third worlds for relief from the international debt crisis.

The Community Reinvestment Campaign is on the lookout for community groups in sister-city locations in Latin America for future alliances. 'If such a relationship can be established, it may result in banks making low-interest loans or grants to progressive Third World development groups as well as large loan commitments in U S cities,' says the Debt Crisis Network *Newsletter*.[5] There is no reason why such campaigns could not be adapted to the particular circumstances of other countries in the North.

Here endeth my 'what to do' and 'how to do it' chapter, and it's nearly the end of the book as well. In a sense, it *is* the end, which is why I've called the pages that follow an 'Afterword'. Here, in any case, is the place to speak personally. Some readers, some critics (I can hear them now) will ask, 'But why must you be so confrontational, so polemical, so, well, *strident*? How can you talk about the International Monetary Fund as if it were practically Murder Incorporated? Poor taste, my dear, and, what's more, it won't get you anywhere. The very people you want to change will be turned off.'

The very people I want to change will not be changed by a book – mine or anyone else's. From the time I published *How the Other Half Dies* in 1976 – and others published similar books in a similar vein around the same time – it took the World Bank ten years to admit that poverty lies behind hunger.[6] We can't afford to wait another ten before it admits that oppression and injustice lie behind poverty.

Those in the South whose lives are devastated by Consortium policies are in a greater hurry than the Bank. So am I, and so are thousands of others in the North. Those in positions of authority who disparagingly call our work or our activities 'polemical' might recall that the word comes from the Greek *polemos*, meaning 'war', and that it is they, not we, who have declared it on poor people.

If I thought 'moderation' and muffled language would do more good for these people, I would employ them, but I am not encouraged in this regard by what I see around me. A team of eminently qualified economists who benefited from the IMF's full co-operation to carry out their studies have shown as irrefutably as one could wish that present Fund conditionality doesn't work and should be scrapped. I am all for people burrowing from within, especially people whose credentials cannot be seriously challenged.[7] But the sad fact is that these scholars are not, as far as one can judge, taken seriously. They are polite and respectable; they write without stridency; they carry on the debate in the proper journals – and still they are brushed aside. Nothing of substance changes.

Why not? Because we are talking not economics but politics. Politics is not about who has the best arguments but about who has the most money, and power, to achieve unfailingly unaltruistic aims. My future and my self-esteem do not, thank God, depend upon those who have money and power. A convergence of chance and historical circumstances too long and too boring to recount has resulted in my enjoying greater freedom than most of my contemporaries.

Freedom unused is nothing. This is why I affirm, stridency and all, that Third World debt is decidedly not a problem for the financial journals or for competent economists alone. It is a mechanism by which the poor in the poor countries can be forced to finance the rich in the rich countries. Because debt allows the rich to maintain and reinforce their control over the poor, it will not be readily relinquished. Yet we must try to get debt off the financial pages and on to the political agenda.

Many people in the North will champion freedom-from-debt struggles in the South because of a simple and straightforward sense of justice and moral or religious outrage. They are the spiritual children of those who have always brought about desirable change; without their vision we would have perished long ago. But such people are the salt and the leaven, not the bread itself. If we are to develop a broad-based debt-crisis *movement*, we must convince large numbers of industrialized-country citizens that we too are being seriously harmed by the *status quo*. Financial Low Intensity Conflict – FLIC – is being waged against us as well. We are losing our jobs and our farms. Our national economies are contracting; our wages are being driven down; our living standards are deteriorating; we might well lose our savings; our children's opportunities are dwindling. We live in an ever more dangerous world.

It is not always easy to see these connections, and those who profit from the debt crisis count on our structural blindness. Americans and

Europeans would, for example, be immediately better off if 'basic-needs conditionality' were applied in the Third World and even more if substantial 3-D programmes were instituted. Southern economies would become more inner-directed, satisfying first the needs of their own people; fewer export goods would compete with those of the North. Eventually, the kind of prosperity that alone can keep all our economies humming would emerge as millions of people hitherto forced to the margins of existence achieved a life of dignity.

A world in which everyone must live by the same outer-directed model is a contradiction, a snare and a delusion. So long as the Consortium can impose its will, North and South will be pitted against each other in a fruitless and mutually destructive struggle. The interests and the needs of the vast majorities in both North and South are one. Only by greater democracy, here and there, can they be satisfied. We must learn to see Third World people as our allies, not our enemies, and to forge the alliances that alone can create for us all a future worth having.

A PHILOSOPHICAL AFTERWORD

A new scientific truth does not triumph by convincing its opponents and making them see the light, but rather because its opponents eventually die, and a new generation grows up that is familiar with it.

Max Planck, Scientific Autobiography, *New York, 1949, pp. 33–4, cited in Thomas Kuhn,*
The Structure of Scientific Revolutions, *2nd edn, University of Chicago Press, 1970, p. 151*

In the foregoing pages I've tried to show that Third World countries have fallen deep into debt because they have accepted, internalized and followed the development model promoted by the World Bank, the IMF and similar institutions. The debt crisis is a particularly ugly, acute manifestation of a chronic condition, the predictable outcome of economic strategies concerned far more with the world market than with local needs. Like an outbreak of carbuncles, it is spectacular on the surface but also a sure sign of underlying infection.

By any normal standards we ought to be able to affirm confidently that this model has failed, since it has plunged countries adopting it into a quagmire from which they show few signs of escaping and has caused immeasurable suffering for their people. Yet these same countries are now told, by those in a position to enforce their advice, that they must apply the same policies, only more so, in order to qualify for further loans and continuing membership in the international community. It is like prescribing cyanide as an antidote to arsenic.

As I've worked on this book, I've grown increasingly intrigued and troubled by the sheer illogic of much of what passes for sober thought, by the nearly seamless, consensus position of those who matter on the 'development' scene. One has to put that word in quotes now – it has become too embarrassing to use otherwise. One must also wonder why such a high-visibility débâcle, of which the debt crisis is a part, has not yet provoked general dismay and a serious search for theories that could lead to a way out. I am not sure how one can induce changes in dogma and mindsets. I am, however, certain that millions of poor people will continue to pay for the absence of a theoretical revolution.

In the physical and natural sciences world views change because science has criteria, on which everyone can usually agree, for validating and substantiating its claims. Frameworks within which scientists look at nature – often called paradigms – are not immutable, but they last as long as they can accommodate a greater number of observed phenomena than any rival paradigm. Scientific truth may not be eternal, but, for a time at least, it works or it doesn't; observations fit or they don't. Every science must develop ways of recognizing error and correcting it, otherwise it will not remain a science and will become more of an amusement, like astrology, or will be discarded entirely, like alchemy.

Max Planck, quoted at the beginning of this Afterword, is pessimistic about the timescale, but he still affirms that new scientific paradigms will triumph, if only after the demise of the stone-wallers. Young scientists with brilliant, unorthodox and often unwelcome insights surely find it trying to wait – if, indeed, they must – for the last diehards to die, but if their hypotheses stand up to experimental scrutiny and explain more phenomena than previous ones, they will eventually prevail.

Since the pursuit of 'development' is, presumably, a rational activity, can we hope for – even count on – a similar revolution in our understanding of, and solutions for, hunger and mass poverty? I would like to believe so. I fear, however, that mainstream development theorists and practioners, unlike scientists, have so far been *unable or unwilling to establish criteria for recognizing, correcting and avoiding error*. For this reason, development theory hews closer to astrology than to astronomy.

Scientists are trained to mistrust their models and to rely on them only when they are borne out by rigorous observation. Normally development theorists should be trained to test their models by observing *what they do to people*, since human welfare is theoretically the goal of development. 'People' in this context means not well-off, well-fed elites but poor and hungry majorities whose fundamental needs are presently not being met. When the reigning development model, or paradigm, has been applied for decades and has failed to alleviate human suffering and oppression – or, worse still, has intensified them – it should be ripe for revolution.

Why, then, does this revolution not occur? Part of the answer to this question lies in the history of the dominant development model. It has always been, for the most part, the handiwork of economists. Sociologists, historians, anthropologists, ecologists, etc., have contributed little to its elaboration. Largely funded and employed by major Western-controlled political institutions, most development economists must accept, consciously or not, some subservience to the goals of those who now dominate the world economy and derive the most benefit from it. Although in no sense the result of a conspiracy, the reigning paradigm does reflect a convergence of world views, a shared vision of the desirable society and a keen, common perception of economic and political self-interest. In sum, it is riddled with ideology.

For the past thirty years the dominant escape-from-poverty paradigm has been bounded on the north by 'growth', on the east by 'trickle-down', on the south by 'comparative advantage' in trade and on the west by 'modernization' or 'transfer of technology'. The total size of the economic pie must be increased (growth) without worrying about who receives the largest slices, since the benefits will eventually percolate from the topmost levels of society to those beneath (trickle-down). Each national economy must forge the strongest possible links with world markets, selling those goods that it can supposedly produce better and more cheaply than other countries and buying those that are better and more cheaply produced elsewhere (comparative advantage). Agriculture, industry and economic life in general must be transformed using techniques and technology originating in the now industrialized countries, generally through sales or investments of transnational corporations, supervised by expatriate experts or nationals trained in their methods (modernization).

Sub-models help to buttress the dominant theory, and here economists may call upon other disciplines to help shore up their arguments and practices. Demographers have helped to establish the 'truth' that overpopulation is a major cause of hunger. When basic scientific research is called upon, the dominant model sets its goals, not vice versa. The Green Revolution is an obvious case. Plant geneticists specifically sought seeds that would grow best with a maximum of purchased inputs, whereas it would have been perfectly feasible, scientifically speaking, to breed risk-reducing, drought- and disease-resistant plants for poor peasants who could not afford such inputs.

Applied sciences like agronomy, hydrology, engineering, etc., also function in the context of the technological fix and serve to link recipients more tightly with the international economy. The underlying philosophy, in so far as there is one, is that nature is there to be harnessed or mastered, not to say plundered and polluted. Economists give such notions as renewable resources and ecology short shrift because the value of the environment, and the costs of destroying it, are hard to quantify.

Nor can mainstream development theorists readily cope with problems posed by gender. A worker is a worker, but the huge loads and low rewards of women are of scant interest precisely because so much of their work is unpaid. Workers' welfare and exploitation are not their concern either: if an 'efficient labour process' in Third World production demands the sacrifice of human rights, so be it. The mainstream is also ill-equipped to deal with politics and power structures – indeed, the ideology of the model itself denies conflict and thus prevents their incorporation.

This ideology assumes that harmony reigns at the international level (all nations will profit equally from trade according to comparative advantage; technology transferred will modernize the recipient society without social costs). Harmony rules also at the national level (growth benefits all, since elites will share their gains with the less fortunate through the trickle-down process). In this dominant world view greed and the power to oppress (heaven forbid) have little to do with the wealth of nations and the condition of the individuals who compose them. In short, almost none of the real forces that actually shape people's lives can be taken into account by the model. This description may be brief; I regret that it is not a caricature.

Most 'emerging nations' have accepted and implemented the model with greater or lesser diligence and efficiency. They receive aid proportionate to their willingness to comply, since the World Bank, the IMF and the aid agencies of the United States and most other industrialized countries insist that they follow this scenario. Countries adopting a Soviet development model (one hesitates to call it 'socialist') also want growth, modernization and foreign technology but are less inclined to trade for trade's sake or to seek global integration. They tend to stay within their own commercial and financial zone – and, while they may receive a lot of advice, with few exceptions they get far less aid.

The dominant model has not gone unchallenged for the perfectly valid reason that it doesn't work. Its deep and accumulated flaws can no longer be hidden. Three decades have passed during which its magic should have operated but has all too visibly failed to do so. We witness, rather, a fiasco: unmanageable debts, stagnant trade, a permanent slump in commodity prices, tragic hunger and poverty on a hitherto unheard-of scale. Even the terminally myopic can see that the emperor has no clothes.

The food crisis in Africa was doubtless the clinching event in this regard. Lesser-known phenomena, however, such as the net transfer of $140 billion from Latin American nations to Western banks in only five years, should cause respectable development thinkers to blush at the very mention of the word and to take to the streets in search of a better theory. This is a course they have almost universally managed to avoid.

What can be done, besides waiting for them to die off? And, even if they do, what are the chances of their replacement by people holding other views? Are there challenges that might stick and force real change? These are vital questions because development is unlike science in one crucial respect – the success or failure of its ruling dogma is measured in marginalization, misery and death.

A first group of challengers of the dominant model holds that while the emperor may indeed have no clothes, he is still wearing his underwear. This group is occupied in taking his ceremonial robes to the cleaners, and we can expect him back any day, in full and resplendent regalia. These paradigm-cleaners, who often have a lifetime investment in the dominant model, are a small minority of high-level national and international bureaucrats mixed with a smattering of enlightened financial and commercial types. They fear that the diehards in their own old-boy networks (they mostly *are* men) will wreck the system through sheer pig-headedness and refusal to admit failure.

Thus they attempt to convince their mulish colleagues that concessions are necessary – the better to save the present system as a whole. A structure that is too rigid is also brittle and creates a bad climate for business, high finance and other pursuits of happiness. Changes made in time, however, preserve the major advantages of the *status quo*. They may, in fact, sometimes be the *only* way to do this (as soon-to-be-beheaded kings and countries engaged in disastrous colonial wars have always failed to see).

Many of them have lately climbed on the privatization bandwagon. Let the market do it, and the less state the better. While the market should be allowed to do what it does well, we should harbour no illusions that it can ever provide food, shelter and clothing – much less education, health and culture – for everyone. These lessons too are part of the history of the past thirty years.

The paradigm-cleaners are challengers of surface rather than substance. They have produced warnings like the Brandt Report, a document elaborated at the behest of the World Bank, under the chairmanship of Willy Brandt. Eminent representatives of the elites of the First World and the Third gathered to demand large transfers of wealth from elites of the First World to those of the Third; their report concerned plausible ways to revamp growth, trickle-down, comparative advantage and modernization.

Brandt Commissioners failed to note that huge transfers of wealth from Northern to Southern elites had already taken place. Because these transfers served largely to buttress the dominant model and created little wealth in their turn, they have come to be called 'debt'. In sum, the paradigm-cleaners asked for a face-lift rather than a revolution, offered no evidence that trickle-down would benefit the poor more next time around and continued to call for integration into world markets but on somewhat better terms. So far, however, the dominant paradigm is holding firm and the Brandtish types have got none of the concessions they demanded (unless one counts the Baker Plan), so we may perhaps move on.

A second group of challengers are more genuine. They are honest and humane economists and other development professionals who are valiantly trying to incorporate richer variables – the environment, women's special problems, human rights, political constraints, etc. – into the dominant models. They may find niches in the halls (or the broom closets) of power-houses like USAID, the World Bank or the IMF, where they are rarely given an opportunity to affect policy more than marginally. It is not sure, however, that they could do more good if they were outside. Large and faceless institutions need resident consciences, even if they rarely listen to them.

A third and final group may be called radical challengers, since they reject the basic premises of the dominant model and try to attack it at its roots. Radical intellectual workers have done their best to undermine the reigning model by speaking, writing and encouraging others to follow a different development path, one diversely labelled 'autonomous', 'self-reliant', 'sustainable' and the like. In the present case I have tried to show how even the debt crisis, creatively managed, could help trace a path towards democratic development.

Can we convince? Make enough converts? Expect that in time a new generation weaned on our ideas will take over and practise under a new dominant model, open to challenge from younger, smarter, more radical people?

Would it were so! Radicals should rejoice in the defiance of the younger, the smarter – and the more radical. If nothing else, it would at least prove us worthy of notice as occupiers of the intellectual high ground. We are, however, in little danger because, I fear, we have failed. Such changes as have occurred have been brought about more by force of circumstance than by the power of new ideas. This failure raises serious questions, the kind I necessarily ask myself.

The high ground is still occupied by the dominant paradigm, and the challengers are still hammering on closed doors and closed minds. When it comes to imposing policies, spending vast sums of development money or protecting the interests of the powerful, the old guard is firmly in command. The dominant development model differs from a scientific world view in a crucial respect, and for this reason it does not appear open to revolution. It escapes confrontation with validation criteria because it is fundamentally ideological.

Put more simply, it doesn't matter how many 'mistakes' they make. Because mainstream development theorists are protected and nurtured by those whose political objectives they support, package and condone, they have a licence to go on making them, whatever the consequences.

This is true not only for economists but also, in more subtle ways, for other disciplines – even, and especially, the apparently technical ones. Development practitioners working within the confines of sub-paradigms may also serve, wittingly or not, the aims of those who profit most from present arrangements. Agronomists, nutritionists and other competent professionals may believe that the reigning development model is simply not their concern, that *their* models are not ideological but scientifically testable. Snug – indeed, sometimes smug – within the havens of their own disciplines, they may live out their working lives unaware that the dominant paradigm encompasses and shapes their own, prevents them from asking *for whom* they are ultimately practising their arts and shields them from the need to consider such intrusive moral issues as equity and justice.

Although more radical thinkers can and must continue to chip away, the relevant question is not so much 'Can we convince?' as 'Can we help to make sure the paradigm-pushers are finally called to account?' They go on getting their comfortable salaries no matter how much human suffering their policies demonstrably cause. They are not subject to ostracism by their peers. They continue to dominate the 'respectable' publications and the institutions where those who will follow in their footsteps are trained. They are not accountable.

And yet validation criteria for development models are tragically obvious: how many are losing their land, having to leave their villages, watching their children waste away, working fourteen-hour days for next to nothing or not working at all, drinking polluted water, suffering from hunger and avoidable disease, being imprisoned or tortured or murdered if they speak out and try to change their lot? In short, how many people have to die before the ruling paradigm is beaten back and we are rid of it once and for all?

These are the simple, and embarrassing, questions that nearly everyone, except for those immediately concerned, would rather evade. Honest answers to them, had we really been dealing with a science, would have brought the dominant model crashing to earth long ago as worse than useless – murderous. The honest answer to 'How many must die?' is 'We don't know.' Untold numbers. More than 15 or 20 million yearly, at any rate. More than the equivalent of a Hiroshima every two days. I believe in my profession and in its value. I can, I hope, help to prepare the ground for genuine theoretical and practical change. But those who will ultimately effect change are the known and unknown heroes and heroines, from North and South, working to show that democratic development is possible.

One radical wit says, 'Development results from what people do against the official developers.' In the North many are already working outside the model, often as members of innumerable popular movements for change, called too negatively non-governmental organizations, or in their churches, trade unions, civic groups, etc. In the South people are inventing the means of their own survival, placed, as they are, in further jeopardy by the official paradigm-pushers, against tremendous odds.

It is perhaps an illusion to see one's own moment in history as uniquely one when crucial choices will be made, as a 'now-or-never' time. It is perhaps, further, a cliché to point out, in rather solemn tones, that the direction we choose today will decide the fate of millions in the Third World and in the First for a period longer than any of our individual lives. Cliché or not, we must all take a stand; declining to take one out of ignorance, indifference or cowardice can only reinforce the *status quo*. We can allow the guardians of the ruling model free rein and consent to their command over us all, or we can refuse. We can submit to the present global disorder or reject it. We can acquiesce to power, and to the ideology that undergirds it, or fight back. One way or the other.

The debt crisis is a symptom – one among many – of an increasingly polarized world organized for the benefit of a minority that will stop at nothing to maintain and strengthen its control and its privilege. The way in which this crisis is resolved will be one sign of the success or failure of that minority. No one who cares about freedom can afford to be absent from the battle, for we are all on the field. Whether we live in the North or in the South, it is the shape of our own lives and those of our children that is at stake, like it or not. The old paradigm may entrench its control and win. But we are also present at the birth of a new one, and millions have chosen to protect, nurture and sustain it. For such a revolution many have already given their lives. My own choice is clear: the only honour is to make common cause with them.

NOTES AND REFERENCES

INTRODUCTION

1. The Debt Crisis Network, *From Debt to Development*, Institute for Policy Studies, 1601 Connecticut Avenue, NW, Washington, DC, 20009, 1985.

2. Arthur MacEwan, 'Latin America: why not default?', *Monthly Review*, Vol. 38, No. 4, September 1986.

PART I: THE PLAYERS AND THE PROBLEM

1   HOW MUCH IS $1 TRILLION?

1. Lord Lever, *et al.*, *The Debt Crisis and the World Economy*, the Commonwealth Secretariat, London, 1984, p. 10, paragraph 23.

2. Frederick F. Clairmonte and John H. Cavanagh, 'Transnational corporations and services: the final frontier', *Trade and Development: An UNCTAD Review*, No. 5, 1984.

3. Cited in Benjamin J. Cohen, 'Banking gone bad', *Worldview*, October 1983.

4. André de Lattre, Director of the Institute of International Finance, personal interview, Washington, DC, 3 February 1986.

5. 'Le Monde déchiffré', *Rapport Annuel Mondial sur le Système Economique et les Stratégies (RAMSES) 1985–86*, under the direction of Thierry de Montbrial,

Paris, Editions Atlas Economica, p. 126; and Rudiger Dornbusch, *External Debt, Budget Deficits and Disequilibrium Exchange Rates*, Working Paper No. 1336, National Bureau of Economic Research, Cambridge, Mass., April 1984.

6. See *Procurement of Goods, Sample Bidding Documents*, compiled by the Asian Development Bank, the Inter-American Development Bank and the World Bank, September 1983. (N.B. The African Development Bank is conspicuously absent from those who signed on to use these model documents.)

7. Simon Watt and Conrad Taylor, 'Playing with fire', *Inside Asia*, June–August 1985; and *Philippine Report*, Philippine Resource Center, Berkeley, Vol. 2, No. 8, August 1985, cited in *Philippines Information*, Bulletin No. 37, December 1985, Paris.

8. Fox Butterfield, 'Marcos linked to $80 million; Westinghouse paid "commission" for nuclear plant in 76', *International Herald Tribune, New York Times* service, 8/9 March 1986; and 'Westinghouse denies charge', *IHT*, 10 March 1986.

9. James S. Henry, 'Where the money went', *New Republic*, 14 April 1986.

10. 'Teller's window', *South*, August 1984, citing Alexander Lamfalussy of the BIS.

11. Cited in 'Economic and financial indicators', *Economist*, 14 March 1986.

12. Henry, op. cit.

13. Karen Lissakers, 'Money in flight: bankers drive the getaway cars', *International Herald Tribune, New York Times* service, 7 March 1986.

14. Rita Tullberg, 'Military related debt in non-oil developing countries', *SIPRI Yearbook 1985*, Taylor & Francis, London and Philadelphia, pp. 445–55, and 'World military expenditure and arms production', pp. 277–8.

15. International Monetary Fund officials in both Washington and Paris used this 'interference in sovereign affairs' argument. Fund ground rules for interviews preclude citing particular officials' names. The role of the IMF is more fully explored in Chapter 4.

16. GNP figures from World Bank, *World Development Report 1985*; military figures from Ruth Leger Sivard, *World Military and Social Expenditures 1985*, Table 3, pp. 42–3.

17. *Defense & Technology* magazine, cited by Richard House, 'Taking on the big guns', *South*, November 1985.

18. Calculated from Tullberg, in *SIPRI*, Table 12.3.

19. Tullberg, in *SIPRI*, citing the US Arms Control and Disarmament Agency.

20. *RAMSES 1985–86*, op. cit., p. 29.

21. Daniel Patrick Moynihan, Senator from New York, 'The "vig" gets too big: a formula for trouble', *International Herald Tribune*, 24 September 1984.

22. I borrow here from the definition of 'Interest' in Rupert Pennant-Rea and Bill Emmott, *The Pocket Economist*, Basil Blackwell and *The Economist*, London, 1983.

23. William R. Cline, *International Debt and the Stability of the World Economy*,

274 NOTES AND REFERENCES

Institute for International Economics, Washington, DC, September 1983, pp. 20–21; see also a shorter version in Cline's 'The issue is illiquidity, not insolvency', *Challenge*, July–August 1984.

24. Joseph Kraft, *The Mexican Rescue*, Group of Thirty, 725 Park Avenue, New York, NY 10021, 1984, p. 27.

2 THE MONEY-MONGERS

1. S. C. Gwynne, 'Adventures in the loan trade', *Harper's Magazine*, September 1983, pp. 22–6.

2. All passages in quotes from Gwynne, ibid. (his emphasis).

3. Richard W. Lombardi, *Debt Trap*, Praeger, New York, 1985.

4. Richard W. Lombardi, 'Multinational banking and the Third World', Special Supplement on International Investment, *International Herald Tribune*, 18 March 1981.

5. Lombardi, *Debt Trap*, p. 85.

6. ibid., p. 87.

7. Lombardi, 'Multinational banking and the Third World'.

8. Harold Lever and Christopher Huhne, *Debt and Danger: The World Financial Crisis*, Penguin, Harmondsworth, 1985, Table 2, p. 28.

9. X, 'Bad business for almost all concerned', *International Herald Tribune*, 16 October 1985.

10. ibid.

11. Salomon Brothers, Inc., *A Review of Bank Performance: 1986 Edition*, cited in *The Impact of the Latin American Debt Crisis on the US Economy*, a Staff Study prepared for the Joint Economic Committee, US Congress, 10 May 1986, calculated from Table 6. For British banks, War on Want, 'Profits out of poverty? British banks and Latin America's debt crisis', n.d. [1986], p. 11.

12. Lombardi, *Debt Trap*, pp. 100–103.

13. *The Impact of the Latin American Debt Crisis on the US Economy*, Table 5; also War on Want, 'Profits out of poverty?'; Lever and Huhne, *Debt and Danger*.

14. Erik Ipsen, 'After Mexico the regionals are in retreat', *Euromoney*, January 1983.

15. ibid.

16. Rudiger Dornbusch, 'Dealing with debt in the 1980s', *Third World Quarterly*, Vol. 7, No. 3, July 1985.

17. Ipsen, 'After Mexico the regionals are in retreat'.

18. See, for example, his letter to the chairman of the Interim Committee of the IMF/World Bank, 26 March 1985.

19. *The Impact of the Latin American Debt Crisis on the US Economy*, Table 4.

20. Calculated from ibid., Table 6, 'Net income at nine money center banks

1982–1985'; Table 7, 'Total dividends declared 1982–1985'; Table 8, 'Market price per share of common stock, 1982–1986'.

21. ibid., Table 4, plus press reports concerning 139 US bank failures in 1986.

22. Joseph Kraft, *The Mexican Rescue*, Group of Thirty, 725 Park Avenue, New York, NY 10021, 1984.

23. Angel Gurria, cited by Kraft, ibid., p. 3.

24. Lopez Portillo, *Informe* before the Mexican Parliament, 1 September 1982, cited in Kraft, ibid., p. 39.

25. Walter Wriston, cited by Kraft, ibid., p. 40.

26. Paul Volcker, 'Sustainable recovery: setting the stage', speech before the 58th Annual Meeting of the New England Council, Boston, 16 November 1982.

27. Kraft, *The Mexican Rescue*, p. 65.

28. Lombardi, *Debt Trap*, Chapter 9.

29. ibid., note 11 to Chapter 9.

30. On OPEC borrowing see André de Lattre, director of the International Institute of Finance, 'International equilibrium – some longer-term issues', speech to the World Trade Conference, Amsterdam, 5 September 1985 (roneo).

31. Cited in Benjamin J. Cohen, 'Banking gone bad', *Worldview*, October 1983.

32. ibid.

3 THE INTERNATIONAL MONETARY FUND: LET THEM EAT SPECIAL DRAWING RIGHTS

1. 'Why the LDCs bear a grudge against the IMF', *World Business Weekly*, 23 June 1980.

2. Three pamphlets, all available from the IMF, give basic information on the Fund's origins, evolution and functions: *The International Monetary Fund: An Introduction*, 1984; *The International Monetary Fund: Its Evolution, Organization and Activities*, IMF Pamphlet Series No. 37, 1984; *Bretton Woods at Forty* (containing articles reprinted from *Finance and Development*, various issues, 1984). Fund Headquarters is 700 19th Street NW, Washington, DC, 20431; the Geneva office is 58 rue de Moillebeau, 1209 Genève.

3. David Ricardo, 'On the principles of political economy and taxation', in Piero Sraffa, ed., *Works and Correspondence of David Ricardo*, Cambridge, 1962, Vol. 1, p. 132.

4. Joseph Gold, *Conditionality*, IMF Pamphlet Series No. 31, Washington, DC, 1979.

5. IMF, *The IMF: An Introduction*, brochure, August 1984, p. 21.

6. Manuel Guitian, *Fund Conditionality: Evolution of Principles and Practices*, IMF Pamphlet Series No. 38, Washington, DC, 1981, p. 4. In Fund language, debtors must 'restore a sustainable balance between the aggregate demand for, and the aggregate supply of, resources in an economy'.

7. See Jacques de Larosière, then managing director of the the the IMF, *Adjustment*

Programs Supported by the Fund: Their Logic, Objectives and Results in the Light of Recent Experience (remarks before the Centre d'Etudes Financières, Brussels, 6 February 1984), IMF, 1984; and, for an altogether different approach, Cheryl Payer, 'The IMF in the 1980s: what has it learned; what have we learned about it?', *Third World Affairs 1985*, Third World Foundation for Social and Economic Studies, London, 1985.

8. *The Nonpolitical Character of the International Monetary Fund* is, pointedly enough, the title of an IMF brochure by Joseph Gold, Washington DC, September 1983.

9. Jacques de Larosière, *Does the Fund Impose Austerity?*, IMF, brochure Washington, DC, June 1984.

10. Susan George, *How the Other Half Dies*, Penguin, Harmondsworth, 1976, Chapter 10, especially pp. 258–62.

11. IMF *Survey*, 22 May 1978, cited in Richard Gerster, 'The IMF and basic needs conditionality', *Journal of World Trade Law*, Vol. 16, No. 6, Nov.–Dec. 1982, p. 511.

12. Tony Killick, *IMF Stabilization Programmes*, Overseas Development Institute, Working Paper No. 6, London, 1981.

13. Tony Killick, *The Quest for Economic Stabilization*, St Martin's Press, New York, 1984, p. 246.

14. IMF, 'Fund supported programs, fiscal policy and the distribution of income', prepared by Fiscal Affairs Department, SM/85/113, 25 April 1985, p. 7 (document marked 'Not for public use').

15. ibid. p. 67.

16. Regan's testimony in *Hearings* before the Subcommittee of the International Finance and Monetary Policy of the Committee on Banking, Housing and Urban Affairs, United States Senate, 98th Congress, 14 February 1983; cited in Richard Gerster, '40e anniversaire de Bretton Woods: le fonds monétaire international face à l'évolution de l'économie mondiale', *Information Tiers Monde*, Dossier n°15, Lausanne, 1984. (Thanks to R.G. for supplying the original quote in English.)

17. 'Background notes on the International Monetary Fund', in *Development Dialogue*, special issue on the IMF and the New International Order, Dag Hammarskjöld Foundation, Uppsala, 1980, Vol. 2, paragraphs 18–20. This entire volume is highly recommended.

18. Jorge Sol, formerly of the Inter-American Development Bank, personal communication, 29 January 1985.

19. Felix Rohatyn, 'The debtor economy: a proposal', *New York Review of Books*, 8 November 1984.

20. Inter-American Development Bank, *Annual Report 1985*, p. 1.

21. Interview at IMF, Washington, DC, 29 January 1985. Ground rules are that nothing is attributable to particular officials since they 'do not make but only

interpret Fund policy as made by the Board'. Citing names is therefore irrelevant. Subsequent passages in quotes also from this interview.

22. The Brandt Commission, *Common Crisis*, Pan Books, London, 1983, p. 62.

23. 'The US feels the backlash', *South*, August 1984, p. 16.

4 CONDEMNED TO DEBT?: THE TRADE TRAP AND THE DANGERS OF DEFAULT

1. See Susan George, Part I of *Feeding the Few: Corporate Control of Food*, Institute for Policy Studies, Washington, DC, 1978, for a fuller discussion of the substitution phenomenon.

2. 'Poor man's gift', *Economist*, 30 November 1985, p. 13.

3. Alan Spence, 'End of the road for international commodity agreements?', *Banker*, March 1985, p. 63.

4. See graph and text, 'Poor outlook for poor nations', *Economist*, 9 November 1985, p. 73.

5. David Tinnin quoting *International Trade 1984–5* in 'World trade lags this year, GATT reports', *International Herald Tribune*, 27 September 1985.

6. Brij Khindaria reporting on what 'United Nations analysts' in Geneva had to say about the future for commodity prices in 'Commodity prices appear to stabilize after a small boom', *International Herald Tribune*, 19 January 1984.

7. CEPAL, preliminary overview of the Latin American Economy 1985, *CEPAL Newsletter*, December 1985, Table 14.

8. Jacques de Larosière, 'Interrelationships between protectionism and the debt crisis', speech before a symposium organized by the Federation of Swedish Industries, Stockholm, 6 February 1985.

9. William E. Brock, 'Trade and debt: the vital linkage', *Foreign Affairs*, Vol. 62, No. 5, Summer 1984.

10. Calculated from data in *Outlook for US Agricultural Exports*, USDA, 3 February 1986.

11. Calculated from *FATUS (Foreign Agricultural Trade of the United States)*, various years, 1981–7. N.B. Only commercial imports are considered – PL480 programmed food aid is left out.

12. *The Impact of the Latin American Debt Crisis on the US Economy*, a Staff Study prepared for the Joint Economic Committee, US Congress, 10 May 1986.

13. Silvia Nasar, 'America's war on imports', *Fortune*, 19 August 1985.

14. M. Winkler, *Foreign Bonds: An Autopsy*, R. Swain & Co., 1933, cited in Rudiger Dornbusch, 'Dealing with debt in the 1980s', *Third World Quarterly*, Vol. 7, No. 3, July 1985, p. 532.

15. R. T. MacNamar, 'Treasury News', US Department of the Treasury, copy of speech delivered to the International Forum of the US Chamber of Commerce on 12 October 1983 (mimeo).

16. Paul Fabra, 'La dette du tiers monde et l'insuline', *Le Monde*, 16 April 1985.

17. Gary Hector, 'Third World debt: the bomb is defused', *Fortune*, 18 February 1985.

18. Fabra, 'La dette du tiers monde et l'insuline'.

19. Anatole Kaletsky, *The Costs of Default*, written for the Twentieth Century Fund, Priority Press Publications, New York, 1985.

20. The Comptroller made this declaration in 1984. Kaletsky, *The Costs of Default*, p. 42 and note 10 to Chapter 6, p. 91, citing 'US won't let biggest banks in nation fail', *Wall Street Journal*, 20 September 1984.

21. Kaletsky, *The Costs of Default*, p. 44.

22. ibid. p. 45.

23. ibid. p. 72.

24. 'Contentieux américano-brésilien dans l'informatique', *Le Monde*, 21 May 1986, and Charles Vanhecke, 'Les Etats-Unis accentuent leurs pressions contre la politique brésilienne d'informatisation', *Le Monde*, 30 May 1986.

25. Stuart Auerbach, 'US tightening import access for third world', *International Herald Tribune*, 3 April 1986.

PART II: THE PEOPLE AND THE PLANET

5 MOROCCO: A MEDDLESOME MODEL AND A BITTER HARVEST

1. Laurence Tubiana, 'La CEE et les pays méditerranéens', paper presented at the Working Conference of the Stratégies Alimentaires, Stratégies Paysannes Network, Paris, 10–11 June 1985.

2. Najib Akesbi, 'Les illusions d'une politique de vérité des prix au Maroc', *Le Monde*, 20 March 1984.

3. Zakya Daoud, 'La situation explosive de Casablanca', *Lamalif*, July–August 1981.

4. All figures calculated from official price and wage data kindly supplied by Najib Akesbi.

5. Cited by Daoud, 'La situation explosive de Casablanca', p. 22. The companion of the Prophet was Abou Dar el Ghifari.

6. David Sedden, 'A winter of discontent: economic policy and social unrest in Tunisia and Morocco', paper presented at the Conference on the World Recession and the Crisis in Africa, University of Keele, England, 29–30 September 1984.

7. Najib Akesbi, 'Dépendance alimentaire et "vérité des prix": mythes et réalités', contribution to the International Colloquium of the Association of Moroccan Economists on International Financial Organisations and Development Problems in the Third World, 21–4 April 1986. This paper is copiously documented, but I will not cite here Akesbi's sources, usually official, that

support his points. Interested readers are asked to get in touch with him directly for details or a copy of the paper: Najib Akesbi, c/o Direction du Développement Rural, Institut Agronomique et Vétérinaire Hassan II, B P 6202, Rabat-Instituts, Maroc.

6 DEBT IN AFRICA: THE BLACK MAN'S BURDEN

1. UNCTAD, *World Trade Supplement 1984*, figures for 1982.
2. *World Commodity Outlook 1987*, Economist Intelligence Unit, London, 1986.
3. The following information draws on Bill Rau, 'Conditions for disaster: the IMF and Zambia', unpublished paper prepared for the Interreligious Taskforce on Food Policy, Washington, DC, December 1983; and Edward Zuckerman, 'A study in red: Zambia succumbs to its debts', *Harper's Magazine*, April 1986.
4. Zuckerman, 'A study in red', p. 50.
5. ibid.
6. Rau, 'Conditions for disaster', p. 4.
7. Blaine Harden, 'As Zambia's debt rises, output and quality of life plunge', *International Herald Tribune*, 26 September 1985.
8. Zuckerman, 'A study in red', p. 52.
9. ibid.
10. Omega Bula, personal communication, October 1986.
11. Harden, 'As Zambia's debt rises, output and quality of life plunge'.
12. Margaret de Vries, *The IMF, 1972–78: Cooperation on Trial*, IMF, Washington, DC, 1985, pp. 370–73.
13. IMF, Kenya, 'Staff report for the 1982 Article IV consultation, supplementary information', prepared by the IMF African Department and the Exchange and Trade Relations Department, 18 March 1983, pp. 1–4 (mimeo).
14. ibid., p. 4.
15. Government of Kenya, *Economic Survey 1985*, p. 109, using 1982 as the base year with an index of 100.
16. IMF, 'Fund supported programs, fiscal policy and the distribution of income', prepared by Fiscal Affairs Department, SM/85/113, 25 April 1985 (marked 'Not for public use').
17. ibid. pp. 6, 2 and 68 (my emphasis).
18. Jan Vandermoortele, 'The wage policy in Kenya: past, present and future', Institute of Development Studies, University of Nairobi, June 1984, Appendix: 'The 1964–1984 Data Base'.
19. Jan Vandermoortele, 'Causes of economic instability in Kenya: theory and evidence', *East Africa Economic Review*, December 1985, Table 5, p. 94.
20. Republic of Kenya, *Third Rural Child Nutrition Survey 1982*, Central Bureau

of Statistics, Nairobi, December 1983, Tables 5.1 and 6.1. Comparable data on illness for 1977 not available.

21. UNICEF and Kenyan Central Bureau of Statistics, *Situation Analysis of Children and Women in Kenya*, August 1984, Section 2, calculated from table on p. 21.

22. ibid., p. 24.

23. P. Muzaale and D. Leonard, 'Women's groups and extension in Kenya: their impact on food production and malnutrition in Baringo, Busia and Taita Taveta', report to the Ministry of Agriculture, 1982, cited in UNICEF and Central Bureau, *Situation Analysis of Children and Women in Kenya*, Section 3, p. 23.

24. J. Hanger and J. Morris, 'Women and the household economy', in R. Chambers and J. Morris, eds, *Mwea: An Irrigated Rice Settlement in Kenya*, Afrika-Studien No. 83, IFO, Munich, cited in UNICEF and Central Bureau, *Situation Analysis of Children and Women in Kenya*, Section 3, p. 24.

25. ibid., Section 3, p. 26.

26. Nguyuru H. I. Lipumba, 'The economic crisis in Tanzania', in N. H. I. Lipumba, ed., *Economic Stabilisation Policies in Tanzania*, Economics Department and Economic Research Bureau, University of Dar es Salaam, 1984, p. 19.

27. W. Biermann and J. H. Wagao, 'Response to crisis: the IMF and Tanzania', paper presented at the Conference on the World Recession and the Crisis in Africa, University of Keele, England, 29–30 September 1984.

28. Julius K. Nyerere, address to the twentieth-anniversary celebration of the National Centre for Co-operation in Development, Brussels, 17 October 1986.

29. As reported in the *Daily News*, Dar es Salaam, 29 June 1986.

30. MP Stephen Wassira, as reported in the *Daily News*, 24 June 1986. Both quotes cited in the Evangelical Lutheran Church in Tanzania (ELCT, Arusha) report 'The economic crisis in Tanzania: can the IMF loan be a cure?', September 1986 (mimeo).

31. Omar Maiga, 'Tanzania rethinks its state sector', *AFRICASIA*, June 1986.

32. ELCT, 'The economic crisis in Tanzania'.

33. Kathy MacAfee, 'Third world debt: payable in hunger', OXFAM America, *Facts for Action*, No. 16, May 1986.

34. Communication from ELCT, Arusha, September 1986.

35. Paula Park and Tony Jackson, *Lands of Plenty, Lands of Scarcity: Agricultural Policy and Peasant Farmers in Zimbabwe and Tanzania*, OXFAM, May 1985, p. 14.

36. Communication from ELCT.

37. Budget speech delivered to the National Assembly, 19 June 1986.

38. Claude Ake, Dean of the Faculty of Social Sciences, University of Harcourt, Nigeria, speaking at a seminar held at the Woodrow Wilson International Center for Scholars, quoted in *World Development Forum*, Vol. 3, No. 12, 30 June 1985.

7 ZAÏRE: ABSOLUTE ZERO

1. Jim Chapin, 'Zaire: Mobutu's kleptocracy rules while the people starve', *Food Monitor* (World Hunger Year), No. 37, Summer 1986.

2. *Liso ya Nkolo*, No. 4, 1984, from Belgian publications.

3. Mutombo Mpinda and Thsiamala Mupangi, cited in 'Demain le monde', (Brussels), supplement to the magazine *Afrique*, No. 4, 9 March 1986.

4. World Bank, *Annual Reports*, 1984, 1985, 1986, Tables 5–1 and 5–6.

5. Marc Pain and Jean Flouriot, 'L'approvisionnement des centres miniers du Sud-Shaba', presented at the colloquium 'Nourrir les villes en Afrique Sud-Saharienne', Paris, 15 November 1984.

6. Jonathan Kwitny, *Endless Enemies*, Congdon & Weed, New York, 1984, p. 19. Kwitney notes that 'details may be found in a page-one article in the *Wall Street Journal*, April 23, 1981'.

7. *Liso ya Nkolo*, No. 3, 1984.

8. Kwitny, *Endless Enemies*, pp. 21–4.

9. *Liso ya Nkolo*, No. 3, 1984.

10. Kwitny, *Endless Enemies*, p. 21.

11. ibid.

12. Centre de Recherche et d'Information, Brussels, *Fiche Technique d'Information du CRI*, No. 3, 1985, citing *La Libre Belgique* and other Belgian newspapers of 12 April 1985.

13. Nancy Belliveau, 'Heading off Zaire's default', cover story, *Institutional Investor*, March 1977.

14. ibid., pp. 24–5.

15. ibid., pp. 23, 28.

16. European Community, *Le Courrier*, No. 97, May–June 1986, special dossier on debt, table on reschedulings, p. 88.

17. *Economist Foreign Report*, No. 1938, 2 October 1986.

8 LATIN AMERICA: DEBT AND DECLINE

1. Inter-American Development Bank, *Annual Report*, 1985, Table 1; World Bank, *World Development Report*, 1985, Table 1.

2. Inter-American Development Bank, *Annual Report*, 1985, Table 1.

3. World Bank, *World Development Report*, 1985, Table 28.

4. Suzanne Williams, *et al.*, 'Survey of socioeconomic conditions and the nutritional status of children 0–5 years in three communities in Ceara, Northeast Brazil', a report for OXFAM, January 1984 (mimeo).

5. See the World Bank, *Poverty in Latin America: The Impact of Depression*, ('Gray Cover', i.e. restricted) Report No. 6369, 6 August 1986. This report has now become publicly available.

6. Francis Blanchard, *Report of the Director General* to the 12th Conference of American States Members of the International Labour Organization, Montreal, March 1986, I LO, Geneva, 1986.

7. Pierre Salama, 'Endettement et appauvrissement en Amérique Latine', *Amérique Latine*, CETRAL, Paris, No. 18, April–June 1984, and id. 'Endettement et accentuation de la misère', in 'La dette du tiers monde', *Revue Tiers Monde*, Paris, Presses Universitaires de France, Vol. XXV, No. 99, July–September 1984, pp. 491–507.

8. Instituto Brasileiro de Analises Sociais e Economicas (IBASE), 'The IMF and the impoverishment of Brazil', São Paulo, 9 August 1985, pp. 14–15 and Table 2.

9. *O Globo*, 13 April 1986, and *Folha de São Paulo*, 5 April 1986, in Project Abraço Newsletter 'Who owns whom?', Summer–Fall 1986 (c/o Resource Center for Non-Violence, P O Box 2324, Santa Cruz, C A, 95063).

10. Excerpted from Ana Lagoa, *Como se Faz para Sobreviver com um Salario Minimo*, Vozes, IBASE, São Paulo, 1985. The translation is by Keith Elliott, in the Project Abraço Newsletter 'Who owns whom?'.

11. G. Pfeffermann, 'The social cost of recession in Brazil 1986' (one of the contributing studies to the World Bank, *Poverty in Latin America*, data from Tables 6, 8, and 11.

12. Alain de Janvry, Elisabeth Sadoulet, Linda Wilcox, *Rural Labour in Latin America*, World Employment Programme Research Working Paper, WEP 10–6/WP79, I LO, Geneva, June 1986, Figure 1, Table 4 and accompanying text.

13. ibid., p. 51, 'key determinant' quote, p. 81.

14. Jackson Diehl, 'Lootings in Brazil: a reflection of a growing crisis', *International Herald Tribune*, *Washington Post* service, 13 October 1983; also Jean Pierre Clerc, 'Brésil: le FMI, ennemi public numéro un', *Le Monde*, 30 September 1983.

15. Basil Caplan, 'Will Brazil make it?', *Banker*, July 1984.

16. The unnamed 'analyst' is quoted in Tyler Bridges, 'Venezuela's "informal" economy', *International Herald Tribune, Washington Post* service, 25 July 1986; other information on Venezuelan economy in Latin America Data Base ('Latin American Debt Chronicle'), 8 January 1987, printout.

17. The beginning of the process of disinvestment in Argentina is described in Julian Martel, 'Domination by debt: finance capital in Argentina', *NACLA*, Vol. XII, No. 4, July–August 1978: the consequences of it in Hector L. Dieguez, 'Social consequences of the economic crisis: Argentina', contributing study to the World Bank, *Poverty in Latin America*, note 5.

18. Miguel Teubal, economist with the Centro de Estudios y Promocion Agraria, Buenos Aires, personal communications and unpublished (as of 1986) manuscript, 'Economia y politica de la deuda externa'.

19. I've borrowed the hot-money example from Pablo Glikman and Oscar Cismondi, 'La dette extérieure: l'exemple Argentin', Rome, 23

March 1985 (mimeo). (It is not clear from their paper on what occasion it was presented.)

20. Dieguez, 'Social consequences of the economic crisis', p. 7.

21. 'Fuerte aumento del desempleo' (report on figures issued by the National Institute of Statistics and Census–INDEC), *Clarin*, Buenos Aires, 18 January 1986. Figures on debt service vary: the ECLAC (or CEPAL – the UN Economic Commission for Latin America and the Caribbean) shows 55–58 per cent for 1983–5, whereas the Central Bank of Argentina figures are 67–9 per cent for the same period. Unless sources specify, which they generally do not, whether interest *plus* principal reimbursement or interest only is calculated, it is impossible to quantify and to compare debt service to exports ratios accurately.

22. 'The social cost of recession in Chile,' study commissioned by the World Bank, June 1986 (mimeo). The figures that follow on economic conditions in Chile are also drawn from this study. The conclusions of this and other studies in the series are summarized in *Poverty in Latin America: The Impact of Depression*, World Bank, Report No. 6369 (a 'Gray Cover', i.e. restricted report, since published). In this report it is noted that Aristedes Torche is the author of the Chile study.

23. 'The social cost of recession in Chile', Tables 11 and 12.

24. ibid.; earnings, p. 6, and Table 19.

25. ibid., Chilean Ministry of Health figures, Table 7.

26. ibid., Table 5.

27. Giovanni Andrea Cornia, Richard Jolly and Frances Stewart, eds, *Adjustment with a Human Face: Protecting the Vulnerable and Promoting Growth*, UNICEF and (probably, I'm told) Oxford University Press, forthcoming.

28. The best comprehensive volume on this struggle will be found in Jacques Vallin and Alan Lopez, eds, *La Lutte contre la mort* ('The struggle against death'), proceedings of a colloquium on factors affecting life expectancy and mortality, Paris, 28 February–4 March 1983, published by Presses Universitaires de France as Cahier No. 108 in the 'Travaux et Documents' series.

29. This study may be one that Macedo did for UNICEF, *Adjustment with a Human Face*, since he contributed a chapter on a similar subject to an earlier UNICEF volume. His conclusions are cited in Pfeffermann, 'The social cost of recession in Brazil 1986', unpublished contributing study on Brazil for the World Bank, *Poverty in Latin America*, note 5. They are also in the final paper, p. 12.

30. See Ivan Beghin and Marc Vanderveken, 'Les programmes nutritionnels', *in* Vallin and Lopez, eds, *La Lutte contre la mort*.

31. Ralph R. Sell and Steven J. Kunitz, 'Debt, dependency and death in the 1970s: the political economy of mortality in the capitalist world system', paper presented at the annual meeting of the International Sociological Association, New Delhi, August 1986, reprinted as 'The debt crisis and the end of an era in mortality decline' in *Studies in Comparative International Development*, 1987.

32. ibid., pp. 14–17, Table 3, and calculations from data in Table 5.

33. Data compiled by Hilary Creed in 1985 and cited in Dr Jocelyn Boyden, *Children in Development: Policy and Programming for Especially Disadvantaged Children in Lima, Peru*, a report for UNICEF and OXFAM, 1986.

34. Work by Martha Llanos, cited in ibid., p. 30.

35. The *siete sabores* in Boyden, *Children in Development*, p. 84; Nicovita in the statement by Richard Gerster, co-ordinator of Communauté de Travail Swissaid, at a press conference given by four Swiss development NGOs in Berne, 9 September 1983. Silva Ruete, cited by Gerster, was quoted in the *Los Angeles Times*, 9 December 1979.

36. Moreyra's declaration was in an interview in the *New York Times*, 24 August 1979, cited by Gerster (see note 35). The other items, including the quote from Oscar Trelles, are from Bruno Gurtner, 'Pérou: "Le FMI, Hérode du 20e siècle"', *Le Fonds Monétaire International et le Tiers Monde: Les 40 Ans de Bretton Woods*, dossier No. 15 of the Swiss organization Service Information Tiers Monde, July 1984.

37. From Gurtner, 'Pérou', who does not give his sources for the nutritional data. If he's wrong, I'm wrong.

38. Miguel Teubal, personal communication. The numbers of children malnourished by province come from a statement by the Minister for Social Action of the Province of Buenos Aires, reported in *La Nacion*, 13 May 1985. This quote and much other useful information on unemployment and the social impact of the crisis in Nicolas Inigo Carrera and Jorge Podestà, *Analisis de una relacion de fuerzas sociales objetiva: Caracterizacion de los grupos sociales fundamentales en la Argentina Actual*, CICSO, Buenos Aires, Serie Estudios No. 46, 1985.

39. Norberto Baruch, 'Desnutricion: la impunidad del Hambre', *El Porteno*, Vol. 3, No. 28, April 1984.

40. Juan de Onis, 'Third world and its creditors deadlocked', *International Herald Tribune*, 22 September 1986.

41. Cardinal Paulo Evaristo Arns, interview in Switzerland in *La Liberté*, 9 October 1985, reprinted in Déclaration de Berne, *Pour un développement solidaire*, November 1985, No. 81.

42. Hector L. Dieguez, note 24 to 'Social consequences of the economic crisis: Mexico', study commissioned by the World Bank as a contribution to *Poverty in Latin America*.

43. A. Espéndola Yanez and E. Ortiz Villasenor, *El consumo de alimentos en la ciudad de México: el impacto de la crisis*, Colegio de México, Estudios Sociologicos, No. 8, 1985.

44. Edward Cody, 'In Mexico, repayment squeeze spreads into the hinterland', *International Herald Tribune, Washington Post* service, 5 September 1986.

45. André Aubry, 'Mexique: manger, un acte politique', *La Lettre de SOLAGRAL*, No. 51, September 1986.

46. The calculation of interest per capita is based on $10 billion a year and a population of 77 million Mexicans.

9 LATIN AMERICA: GOING TO EXTREMES

1. World Bank, *Poverty in Latin America: The Impact of Depression*, Report No. 6369, 6 August 1986, paragraphs 48 and 49.

2. 'Country life', *Economist Development Report*, September 1984, and *FATUS* (Foreign Agricultural Trade of the United States), USDA, November–December 1986, various tables. The export figures given are for fiscal years (i.e., 1 October to 30 September).

3. ibid., both sources in note 2.

4. See 'Nation in jeopardy: Mexico's crisis grows as money and the rich both seek safer places', *Wall Street Journal*, 11 October 1985; and Larry Rohter, 'Exit of the skilled dims Mexico's future', *International Herald Tribune*, New York Times service, 28 October 1986.

5. Quoted in Rohter, 'Exit of the skilled dims Mexico's future'.

6. Vincent Leclercq, 'Politique d'ajustement structurel et politique agricole au Brésil 1980–1985', paper presented at the Journées d'Etude, Réseau Stratégies Alimentaires, Paris, 10 June 1985.

7. Patrick Postal, 'L'Enlisement de la réforme agraire', *Le Monde Diplomatique*, November 1986.

8. Julio Prudencio and Monica Velasco, 'Crisis de abastecimiento y estrategias de resistencia en Bolivia: el caso de La Paz', March 1986 (mimeo).

9. Figures from CERES and UNICEF, Bolivia, *Datos Basicos*, 1985.

10. Articles in *Presencia*, La Paz, 11 and 23 April, 14 May 1986.

11. SENALEP and CERES, *La Crisis*, Cuadernos Populares (Serie Abastecimiento y Participacion), No. 5/1, La Paz, 1985.

12. Foro Economico, *Propuesta para la Reactivacion Economica*, No. 9, La Paz, February 1986, table p. 10; and *Presencia*, 3 May 1986.

13. Pablo Ramos Sanchez, *Siete Anos de Economia Boliviana*, Universidad Mayor de San Andres, La Paz, 1980, p. 121; and Freddy Peña, CERES, personal communications.

14. 'Boodle for Bolivia', *Economist Development Report*, March 1986.

15. SENALEP and CERES, *La Crisis*, note 11, pp. 20–21.

16. Roberto Jordán Pando, 'Coca, cocaina y narcotrafico', *Presencia*, La Paz, 14 and 15 March 1986.

17. Case studies in Jorge Dandler and Carmen Medeiros, eds., *La Migracion Temporal Internacional y su Impacto en los Lugares de Origen (Bolivia)*, Chapter VI, 'Esposas de migrantes y mujeres migrantes', CIM–CIPRA Proyecto de Migracion Hemisferica, 1985.

18. Press reports in *Presencia* of 25 April and 24 May 1986.

19. 'Ghost towns of the Andes', *South*, November 1986; and *Economist Development Report*, March 1986.

20. Minimum salary figures (from 1982 to end 1985) in Jeroen Strengers, *La Pesada Carga de la Deuda*, CEDOIN, La Paz, 1986, table p. 39, and communication from Freddy Peña, CERES, May 1986.

21. Interview with Freddy Camacho, primary-school teacher, by Carmen Medeiros of CERES, La Paz, May 1986.

22. Joseph Laure, *Evolucion de salarios y precios de los alimentos en la ciudad de La Paz (1975–1984)*, Instituto Nacional de Alimentacion y Nutricion & ORSTOM (France), Table 34, p. 135.

23. Prudencio and Velasco, 'Crisis de abastecimiento y estrategias de resistencia en Bolivia', note 8.

24. SENALEP and CERES, *Los Barrios Populares*, Cuadernos Populares No. 2/6, La Paz, 1985, p. 16.

25. See the debate on the new laws, especially Decreto Supremo 21060, which contains no incentives for local food production, in *Presencia*, from November 1985, various authors including Miguel Urioste F. de C. and Jorge A. Muñoz Garcia.

26. This account is compiled from Christian Rudel, 'Bidonvilles en Amérique Latine', *CCFD Dossiers*, No. 86–11, Paris, November 1986; Ramon Quinones, 'IMF plunges Dominican Republic into acute economic, social crisis', IDOC Internazionale, 85/3, dossier on Third World indebtedness; Françoise Barthelémy, 'République Dominicaine: la porte à droite', *Le Monde Diplomatique*, July 1986; and information compiled by Dra. Josefina Padilla of CIAC (Centro de Investigacion y Apoyo Cultural), Santo Domingo, especially for the events of April 1984. The translation of Blanco's speech is mine. The relevant passages of the original run: 'las Fuerzas Armadas y la Policia Nacional han dado un ejemplo de ecuanimidad revelando su grado de professionalizacion con alto sentimiento humano de respeto a la vida . . . asi como que mantuvieron sus reacciones dentro de una prudencia razonable y con una preparacion excelente.'

10   DEBT AND THE ENVIRONMENT: FINANCING ECOCIDE

1. Robert Goodland and George Ledec, 'Neoclassical economics and principles of sustainable development', Environmental and Scientific Affairs, Projects Policy Department, World Bank, April 1986, para. 46ff. (draft). 'The views expressed are those of the authors and should not be attributed to the World Bank . . .' Also W. C. Baum and S. Tolbert, 'Development projects', Draft chapter for the World Bank on 'The role of environmental management in sustainable economic development', World Bank, Office of Environmental Affairs, Projects Advisory Staff, September 1983, pp. 40–43, on 'inadequate time horizon of cost-benefit analysis'.

2. Edward Goldsmith and Nicolas Hildyard, *The Social and Environmental Effects of Large Dams*, 3 vols, Wadebridge Ecological Centre (Worthyvale Manor, Camelford, Cornwall PL32 9TT, UK), 1984–7.

3. Robert Goodland, 'Environmental aspects of Amazonian development projects in Brazil', *Interciencia*, Vol. 11, No. 1, January–February 1986.

4. Bruce M. Rich, 'Multi-lateral development banks; their role in destroying the global environment', *Ecologist*, Vol. 15, No. 1/2, 1985. Rich himself cites World Bank, 'Social issues associated with involuntary resettlement in Bank-financed projects', 1, 1984 (internal document), and quotes various other sources on particular Bank-funded dam projects.

5. *Economist Development Report*, London, November 1984, p. 3.

6. Goodland, 'Environmental aspects of Amazonian development projects in Brazil', note 3.

7. Various authors, *Ecologist*, Vol. 16, No. 2/3, 1986 (available from same address as in note 2).

8. Marcus Colchester, 'Banking on disaster: international support for transmigration', in ibid.

9. Mariel Otten, '"Transmigrasi": from poverty to bare subsistence', in ibid.

10. Carmel Budiardjo, 'A catalogue of failures' in ibid.

11. ibid.

12. Nicholas Guppy, 'Tropical deforestation: a global view', *Foreign Affairs*, Vol. 62, No. 4, Spring 1984, pp. 942–3.

13. J. M. Hardjono, *Transmigration in Indonesia*, Oxford University Press, Kuala Lumpur, 1977, p. 40, cited in Marcus Colchester, 'The struggle for land: tribal peoples in the face of the transmigration program', in *Ecologist*, Vol. 16, No. 2/3, p. 105.

14. Policy paper of the PKMT, the special office for dealing with tribal people in the Department of Social Affairs, 1981, cited by Colchester, 'The struggle for land'.

15. Proceedings of the Meeting between the Department of Transmigration and the IGGI, Jakarta, 20 March 1985, cited in Colchester, 'Banking on disaster', note 6, p. 62.

16. Budiardjo, 'A catalogue of failures'.

17. See in particular Bruce Rich, 'Multi-lateral development banks', and 'Development beyond the law', *Economist Development Report*, London, November 1983, pp. 2–3.

18. World Bank, *World Development Report 1986*, Table 15.

19. James N. Barnes, Threshold International Center for Environmental Renewal, memo on the new US legislation on environmental reforms for the World Bank and other MDBs (Section 539 of Continuing Resolution on Appropriations), passed on 17 October 1986. Further details from Threshold, 1845 Calvert Street NW, Washington, DC, 20036, USA.

20. Quoted in 'The jungle bank', *Economist Development Report*, London, December 1984, p. 5.

21. ibid. The 'Committee' is the Subcommittee on International Development Institutions and Finance of the Committee on Banking, Finance and Urban Affairs. The full text of the legislation appears in *The Congressional Record* of 15 October 1986.

22. See Peter Bunyard, 'World climate and tropical forest destruction', *Ecologist*, Vol. 15, No. 3, 1985.

23. Examples of silting from J. W. Kirchner, *et al.*, 'Carrying capacity, population growth and sustainable development', World Bank *World Development Report VII*, background paper, Office of Environmental and Scientific Affairs, November 1983, pp. 26–7.

24. ibid., p. 25.

25. José Lutzenberger, testimony before the Subcommittee on Natural Resources, Agricultural Research and Environment, House Committee on Science and Technology, 19 September 1984; reprinted in *Ecologist*, Vol. 15, No. 1/2 1985, pp. 69–72.

26. ibid., p. 70.

27. ibid., p. 71.

28. Guppy, 'Tropical deforestation', note 13, Table 1, p. 930.

29. ibid., p. 956.

30. ibid. pp. 948–9.

31. Baum and Tolbert, 'Development projects', p. 8. See also Dennis Coules, 'Fragile forests', *Environmental Action*, November–December 1985, p. 17.

32. These examples are drawn from Thomas Lovejoy, 'The debt crisis can pay an ecological dividend', *International Herald Tribune*, 8 October 1984; Barbara Bramble and Tom Plant, 'Third World debt and natural resources conservation', an undated (approximately March 1986) paper of the US National Wildlife Federation; and Andy Feeney, 'Sacrificing the earth', *Environmental Action*, November–December 1985.

33. Quoted in Feeney, 'Sacrificing the earth'.

PART III: NOW WHAT?

11 THE IMF SOLUTION: INTERFERENCE, MISMANAGEMENT AND FAILURE IN JAMAICA

1. Cameron Duncan, unpublished Ph.D. Thesis, Department of Economics, American University, 4400 Massachusetts Avenue NW, Washington, DC, 20016). See also Winston James, 'The IMF and democratic socialism in Jamaica', in *The Poverty Brokers*, Latin America Bureau, London 1983.

2. Duncan, citing US General Accounting Office, 'AID's Assistance to Jamaica', GAO/ID 83–45 Washington, April 1983, p. 1.

3. Duncan, citing Planning Institute of Jamaica, *Economic and Social Survey 1984*, 1985, p. 1.

4. Belinda Coote, 'Debt and poverty: a case study of Jamaica', OXFAM Public Affairs Unit, May 1985 (mimeo).

5. 'Transport halted, reds patrol roadblocks', *Daily Gleaner*, 16 January 1985.

6. Coote, 'Debt and poverty'.

7. Michael Nieta of the Social Action Centre in Kingston spoke to Colleen (last name omitted here) on 14 September 1986.

8. US Department of Agriculture, *Foreign Agricultural Trade of the United States (FATUS)*, Calendar Year 1985, Table 13.

9. Calculated from Caribbean Food and Nutrition Institute data. Market-basket estimates are based on a household of five, composed of female 35 years, male 40 years, girl 15 years, 2 boys 10 and 6 years.

10. Kevin Danaher, 'Jamaica: free market fiasco', *Food First News* (IFDP, San Francisco), No. 24, Winter 1986.

11. Data from CFNI supplied by Michael Nieta. Source: Jamaican Ministry of Health.

12. Interview conducted by Michael Nieta in Kellits, North East Clarendon, Jamaica, on 14 September 1986.

13. 'Spring Plain owners said in receivership', *Daily Gleaner*, 3 September 1986; and Wilberne H. Persaud, 'Are winter vegetables viable in Jamaica?' *Sunday Gleaner*, 7 September 1986.

14. Ed McCullough, '"I'm not going to hand over power," says Seaga', *Daily Gleaner*, 19 September 1986.

15. 'Free zone girls tell of "abuses"', *Daily Gleaner*, 19 September 1986; and *Sistren*, Vol. 8, Issue 2, August–September 1986.

16. I am grateful to Michael Nieta for collecting the national health, or local survey, data on malnutrition, hospital admissions, maternal anaemia. Some of the facts cited in this section are from Coote, 'Debt and poverty', or Duncan's unpublished thesis.

17. Thanks to Kevin Danaher, who kindly communicated his interview notes.

12 DEALING WITH DEBT: THE VIEW FROM THE NORTH

1. Statement of the Honorable James A. Baker III, Secretary of the Treasury of the United States, before the Joint Annual Meeting of the International Monetary Fund and the World Bank, 8 October 1985, Seoul, Korea, in 'Treasury News' (mimeo), same date, hereafter 'Baker Plan'. Details of use of the IMF Trust Fund are more fully explored in 'Statement by Secretary of the Treasury James A. Baker III at the IMF Interim Committee Meeting on use of Trust Fund Reflows', 6 October 1985, in 'Treasury News'.

2. Baker Plan, p. 4.

3. For further explanation, see (on 'in-together, out-together') 'Baking Baker', *Economist Development Report*, January 1986, and 'Baker's hot gospel in Seoul',

South, November 1985. An example of commercial bank participation in official loan negotiations is given for the case of a $300 million loan to Colombia by A. W. Clausen, then president of the World Bank, in his address to the Society for International Development North–South Roundtable, SID World Conference, Rome, 3 July 1985, p. 10.

4. Quoted in *South*, November 1985.

5. In his statement before the Development Committee of the IMF and the World Bank (Seoul, 7 October 1985, in 'Treasury news') Baker noted pointedly, 'As we are all aware, current Bank resources are sufficient to sustain lending of $13.5 to $14 billion per year, compared to the 1985 lending of $11.4 billion . . .' Art Pine, in the *Wall Street Journal* ('World bank is under pressure from US to expand its role in global debt crisis'), 1 October 1985, writes that not only was Bank fiscal 1985 lending below its own goal, but 'much to its embarrassment, the Bank made a $1.14 billion profit on its own financial transactions last year. The performance has raised questions about the leadership of A. W. (Tom) Clausen . . .' These questions were resolved with the appointment of Barber Conable to replace Clausen a few months later.

6. Art Pine, 'IMF approves loan program to help debtor countries revamp economies', *Wall Street Journal*, 27 March 1986.

7. ibid.

8. Francisco Swett, Finance Minister of Ecuador, quoted in Françoise Crouigneau, 'Les Etats-Unis ont choisi l'Equateur pour tester le plan Baker,' *Le Monde*, 4 February 1986.

9. Fifteen *or more* countries, because, as a Treasury spokesman said, 'The fifteen [were] named simply for illustrative purposes, as they are the countries with the largest debt . . . Mr Baker never meant that lending expansion should be limited to those countries but intended that it should cover all countries with problem debts . . .' In Carl Gewirtz, 'Haziness of detail clouds US plan on world debt', *International Herald Tribune*, 9 December 1985.

10. Debt Crisis Network (Cavanagh, *et al.*), *From Debt to Development*, Institute for Policy Studies, Washington, DC, Appendix II, appended to the second printing in October 1986.

11. *Business Latin America*, 11 December 1985, cited in Debt Crisis Network, *From Debt to Development*.

12. Senator Bill Bradley (Democrat, New Jersey), 'A proposal for Third World debt management', Zurich, 29 June 1986.

13. Copies of Bradley's Zurich debt speech are available from his office, United States Senate, 731 Hart Building, Washington, DC, 20510. See also Carl Gewirtz, 'US Senator seeks annual debt summit', *International Herald Tribune*, 30 June 1986.

14. Bill Bradley, 'The debt challenge is an opportunity', *International Herald Tribune*, 8 October 1986.

15. ibid.

16. Bradley, 'A proposal for Third World debt management'.

17. Quotes that follow are from Michel Camdessus, 'Dette: sortie de crise?', *Politique Internationale*, Vol. 26, Winter 1984–5.

18. In late December 1986 Japan announced special loans totalling $6.2 billion to the IMF and the World Bank.

19. Felix Rohatyn, 'The debtor economy: a proposal', *New York Review of Books*, 8 November 1984, p. 16.

20. Details in Felix Rohatyn, 'The state of the banks', *New York Review of Books*, 4 November 1982, and 'A plan for stretching out global debt', *Business Week*, 28 February 1983.

21. Richard Weinert, 'Banks and bankruptcy', *Foreign Policy*, Spring 1983, No. 50, and in *Journal of International Affairs*, Columbia University, Special issue on 'Perspectives on global debt', Vol. 38/1, Summer 1984. N.B.: It is not clear how a public institution could take the 'bad', and leave banks with the 'good' debt of country *x* or *y*, since bank regulators would presumably have to value the entire portfolio for a given country at the same price.

22. Harold Lever and Christopher Huhne, *Debt and Danger: The World Financial Crisis*, Penguin, Harmondsworth, 1985, pp. 138–9.

23. ibid, p. 143.

24. Charles F. Meissner, 'Debt: reform without governments', *Foreign Policy*, No. 56, Fall 1984, pp. 81–93.

25. Donald Lessard and John Williamson, *Financial Intermediation Beyond the Debt Crisis*, Institute for International Economics, Washington, DC, 1985.

26. The two variants on swaps are succinctly described in the Debt Crisis Network *Newsletter*, Vol. 1/3, Washington, DC, October 1986 (mimeo).

27. 'Les Philippines prêtes à convertir partiellement leur dette en prises de participation', *Le Monde*, 13 August 1986.

28. 'Foreign banks to take control of Mexico's Alfa', *International Herald Tribune*, New York Times service, 12 December 1986.

29. Eric N. Berg, 'Latin countries turning to debt-for-equity swaps', *International Herald Tribune*, New York Times service, 12 September 1986; and William A. Orme, Jr, 'Swaps said to have little impact on Mexico debt', *International Herald Tribune*, Washington Post service, 26 December 1986.

30. Berg, 'Latin countries turning to debt-for-equity swaps'.

31. Morgan Guaranty Trust Co., 'International banks lending trends', *World Financial Markets*, July 1985; for British big four banks, Nick Powell, researcher at War on Want, London, personal communication.

32. Carl Gewirtz, 'BIS says banks cut exposure', *International Herald Tribune*, 27 October 1986.

33. Robert A. Bennett, 'He calms bank while pushing Wriston's goals', business profile of John S. Reed, Citicorp's chairman, *International Herald Tribune*, New York Times service, 8–9 February 1986.

34. Jacques de Larosière, 'Adjustment programs supported by the Fund: their logic, objectives and results in the light of recent experience', remarks before the Centre d'Etudes Financières, Brussels, Belgium, 6 February 1984 (issued as a pamphlet by the IMF).

35. Mary Williams Walsh, 'Mexico's finance minister, a hero two years ago, comes under fire as economic malaise intensifies', *Wall Street Journal*, 12 December 1985.

36. William A. Orme, 'Threat reportedly got US to back Mexico loans', *International Herald Tribune*, *Washington Post* service, 5 August 1986.

37. This account is compiled from several dozen clippings that appeared in the *International Herald Tribune, Le Monde, Wall Street Journal* and *Economist*. It would be pedantic to cite chapter and verse.

38. James L. Rowe, Jr, 'Mexico rescue thrusts World Bank in to a debt-crisis role', *International Herald Tribune*, *Washington Post* service, 6 October 1986.

13 COPING WITH CHAOS: THE VIEW FROM THE SOUTH

1. 'The Cartagena Proposal', address by the President of Colombia, Belisario Betancur, at the inauguration of the conference of ministers of Foreign Affairs and Treasury, Cartagena, Colombia, 21 June 1984. The Cartagena countries are Argentina, Bolivia, Brazil, Chile, Colombia, Dominican Republic, Ecuador, Mexico, Peru, Uruguay, Venezuela.

2. Alan Riding, 'Latin debtors ask for lower interest rates', *International Herald Tribune*, *New York Times* service, 19 December 1985; and S. K. Witcher, 'Latin American debtors display an unusual degree of agreement', *Wall Street Journal*, 23 December 1985.

3. Fidel Castro's statements on several occasions: interview with the Mexican daily *Excelsior*, 2 March 1985; interview with US Congressman Mervyn Dymally and Professor Jeffrey Elliot, 29 March 1985; interview with the Mexican daily *El Dia*, 8 June 1985; address to the 4th Congress of the Latin-American Federation of Journalists, 7 July 1985; interview with the Brazilian paper *Folha de Sao Paulo*, as reported in the *New Internationalist*, November 1985. All but the last of these have been published by Editora Politica, Havana.

4. Manley at the Havana conference, quoted in *Cuba Update*, Center for Cuban Studies, New York, Vol. VI, No. 3, Fall 1985.

5. 'Pariah' and 'The IMF's rogues' gallery', *Economist*, 23 August 1986.

6. Michael Reid, 'García rides high', *South*, November 1986.

7. Alan García's speech 'Peru: food and democracy', from which the following quotes are drawn, was the 14th McDougall Memorial Lecture, delivered to the FAO Conference in November 1985 and reprinted in the FAO Bulletin *Ideas and Action*, No. 166, 1986.

8. Alan Riding, 'In Peru, priority in aiding Andeans', *International Herald Tribune*, *New York Times* service, 19 November 1986.

9. José Antonio Viera Gallo, 'The people's economic organizations in Chile', *Ideas and Action*, FAO, FFHC/AD No. 167, 1986.

10. Barbara Stallings, 'Privatization and the public debt: US banks in Peru', *NACLA Report on the Americas*, Vol. XII, No. 4, July–August 1978, debt service calculated from table on Peruvian debt and debt service 1968–78, p. 16.

11. ibid.

12. Enrique Ghersi reports on the 'Economia de las "villas de miseria" en Peru' in the *CCPD Network Letter* (Commission on the Churches' Participation in Development), World Council of Churches, No. 21, September 1984.

13. These studies are cited in Dr Jocelyn Boyden, *Children in Development: Policy and Programming for Especially Disadvantaged Children in Lima, Peru*, a report for UNICEF and OXFAM (c/o Children in Development, 94 Kingston Road, Oxford OX2 6RL), 1986.

14. Described in ibid., pp. 92–3; and Jean-Michel Rodrigo, 'Pérou: renaissance d'un peuple andin', *Faim Développement* magazine, No. 36, CCFD, Paris.

15. Rodrigo, 'Pérou'. Boyden also describes communal kitchen arrangements.

16. Gustavo Esteva, chairman of the Center for Rural Development Research (COPIDER), Mexico City, 'From earthquake to social-quake', October 1985 (mimeo).

17. William Stockton, 'In Mexico, 12,000 homeless scorn quake shelters', *International Herald Tribune*, *New York Times* service, 27 December 1985.

18. For example, Richard Gerster, 'The IMF and basic needs conditionality', *Journal of World Trade Law*, Vol. 16, No. 6, November–December 1982; Richard Jolly (deputy director of UNICEF, 'Adjustment with a human face', the Barbara Ward Lecture, delivered at the 18th World Conference of the Society for International Development, Rome, 1–4 July 1985.

19. Gerster, 'The IMF and basic needs conditionality', p. 512.

20. Jolly, 'Adjustment with a human face', p. 5.

21. Gerald K. Helleiner, personal communication and unpublished papers. See his 'The IMF and Africa in the 1980s', *Essays in International Finance*, No. 152, International Financial Section, Princeton University, July 1983. Helleiner's economic work on the IMF is varied and extremely useful. He is at the nexus of much activity around this topic and generous about supplying information. Other economists would certainly be welcome to help in the task of demonstrating that 'human-face', anti-poverty adjustment is not only possible but long overdue on *economic* grounds. Helleiner can be contacted at the Department of Economics, University of Toronto, 150 St George Street, Toronto M5S 1A1, Canada.

14 THE 3-D SOLUTION: DEBT, DEVELOPMENT, DEMOCRACY

1. Keith Schneider, citing a USDA/USDC study, *Farm Population of the United States 1985*, 'US farm population falls sharply', *International Herald Tribune* (*New York Times* service), 12 August 1986; also Andrew H. Malcolm, 'On US farms, a depression of the soul', *IHT* (*NYT*), 12 January 1987.

2. Sara Miles, a letter to NACLA in NACLA's *Report on the Americas*, Vol. XX, no. 4, July–August 1986.

3. Inflows and outflows from OECD, *Financing and External Debt of Developing Countries, 1987 Survey*, Paris, July 1988, Tables III.1 and V.2. In the table, reimbursements to the IMF are not included for 1980 and 1981, so outflows for those years are underestimated.

4. Denis Sulmont, *Deuda y Trabajadores: Un Reto para la Solidaridad*, ADEC-ATC, Lima, 1988, pp. 64–73.

5. Franz Hinkelammert, 'La deuda externa de América Central en el contexto de la deuda de América Latina', paper presented at the NGO International Conference on *External Debt, Development and International Cooperation*, Lima, Peru, 25–29 January 1988. The proceedings have been published in English under the same title by L'Harmattan, 5–7 rue de l'Ecole Polytechnique, 75005 Paris. Hinkelammert's paper, pp. 93–119; the quoted passage from pp. 112–13.

6. Independent Commission on International Humanitarian Issues (ICIHI), *Famine: A Man-made Disaster?* A report for ICIHI, Pan Books, London, 1985, pp. 87–8.

7. Roy Culpeper, *The Debt Matrix*, The North–South Institute, Ottawa, Canada, April 1988.

8. Mike Faber, 'Conciliatory Debt Reduction: Why it must come and how it could come', the Fifth Dudley Seers Memorial Lecture delivered at the Free University of Berlin, 25 September 1988, text available from the Institute of Development Studies, University of Sussex.

9. OECD, op. cit., Table V.11.

10. ibid., Table V.15.

11. Charles Schumer and Alfred Watkins, 'Faustian Finance', *New Republic*, 11 March 1985, cited in Debt Crisis Network, *From Debt to Development*, Institute for Policy Studies, Washington, DC, 1985, p. 51.

12. The Debt Crisis Network *Newsletter*, December 1986. More information on Community Reinvestment Campaigns from Patrick Bond, Institute for Policy Studies, 1601 Connecticut Avenue NW, Washington, DC, 20009.

13. Shlomo Reutlinger, Jack van Holst Pellekaan, *et al.*, *Poverty and Hunger*, a World Bank Policy Study, Washington, DC, 1986.

14. Tony Killick *et al.*, *The Quest for Economic Stabilization: The IMF and the Third World* and *The IMF and Stabilization: Developing Country Experience* (2 vols.), Heinemann Educational Books, London, and St Martin's Press, New

York, in association with the Overseas Development Institute, 1984. Also Tony Killick, ed., *Adjustment and Financing in the Developing World: The Role of the International Monetary Fund*, IMF and ODC, 1982. These volumes are part of the standard bibliography for anyone seriously pursuing the debate, but the general reader is directed to Killick *et al.*, 'IMF policies in developing countries: the case for change', in *Banker*, April 1984, which provides a short, useful summary of their theses: balance-of-payments focus is too limited; the Fund is not flexible enough; it pays no attention to income distribution; it doesn't mobilize all that much capital from other sources; it should change the criteria of conditionality and work with countries for much longer periods.

INDEX

Selected Titles from Grove Weidenfeld
Food First and Latin American Studies

___ EVITA	0-8021-5124-8	Barnes, John EVITA—FIRST LADY: A Biography of Eva Peron	$5.95
___ CENTR	0-8021-1185-8	Barry, Tom THE CENTRAL AMERICA FACT BOOK (Revised)	$19.95 (cl)
___ CENTRP	0-8021-3038-0	Barry, Tom (ed.) THE CENTRAL AMERICA FACT BOOK	$14.95
___ OTHSID	0-8021-5125-6	Barry, Tom OTHER SIDE OF PARADISE: Foreign Control in the Caribbean	$11.95
___ CUBA	0-8021-3043-7	Brenner, Philip THE CUBA READER	$14.00
___ CUBAC	0-8021-1010-X	Brenner, Philip THE CUBA READER	$24.95 (cl)
___ OUTLAC	0-8021-5094-2	Cockcroft, James D. OUTLAWS IN THE PROMISED LAND	$14.95
___ OUTLA	0-8021-1206-4	Cockcroft, James D. OUTLAWS IN.THE PROMISED LAND	$19.95 (cl)
___ NICAR	0-8021-3067-4	Collins, Joseph NICARAGUA: What Difference Could a Revolution Make?	$11.95
___ NICARC	0-8021-1207-2	Collins, Joseph NICARAGUA: What Difference Could a Revolution Make?	$22.50 (cl)
___ COSTA	0-8021-3124-7	Edelman, Mark THE COSTA RICA READER	$14.95
___ COSTAC	0-8021-0181-9	Edelman, Mark THE COSTA RICA READER	$24.95 (cl)
___ FREED	0-8021-5156-6	FREEDOM FIGHTER'S MANUAL	$2.00
___ GUATE	0-394-62455-6	Fried, Jonathan (ed.) GUATEMALA IN REBELLION	$12.50
___ FATE	0-8021-3121-2	George, Susan A FATE WORSE THAN DEBT	$8.95
___ FATEC	0-8021-1015-0	George, Susan A FATE WORSE THAN DEBT	$17.95 (cl)
___ ELSAL	0-394-62345-2	Gettleman, Marvin E. EL SALVADOR	$12.95
___ BETR	0-8021-3027-5	Lappe, Frances Moore BETRAYING THE NATIONAL INTEREST	$8.95
___ BETRC	0-8021-0012-0	Lappe, Frances Moore BETRAYING THE NATIONAL INTEREST	$18.95 (cl)
___ HUNGER	0-8021-5041-1	Lappe, Frances Moore WORLD HUNGER: Twelve Myths	$9.95
___ NICUN	0-8021-3106-9	Rosset, Peter NICARAGUA: Unfinished Revolution	$15.95
___ PEDRO	0-8021-3119-0	Rulfo, Juan PEDRO PARAMO	$4.95

TO ORDER DIRECTLY FROM GROVE WEIDENFELD:

YES! Please send me the books selected above.

Telephone orders—credit card only: 1-800-937-5557.
Mail orders: Please include $1.50 postage and handling, plus $.50 for each additional book, or credit card information requested below.
Send to: Grove Weidenfeld
     IPS
     1113 Heil Quaker Boulevard
     P.O. Box 7001
     La Vergne, TN 37086-7001

☐ I have enclosed $_____ (check or money order only)

☐ Please charge my Visa/MasterCard card account (circle one).

    Card Number_____

    Expiration Date_____

    Signature_____

Name_____

Address_____ Apt._____

City_____ State_____ Zip_____

Please allow 4–6 weeks for delivery.
Please note that prices are subject to change without notice.
For additional information, catalogues or bulk sales inquiries, please call 1-800-937-5557.   ADCD